"*Triathlon for the Every Woman* is a hilarious, heartfelt memoir of one woman's amazing journey from being an overweight working mom to a fully-fledged triathlon finisher. Together with sharing her own inspirational story, Meredith Atwood (a/k/a 'Swim Bike Mom') and her contributors also provide a comprehensive practical guide to get YOU from the couch to the finish line… So that you too can become a triathlete: no matter what your age, your background or your ability…This book will help you change 'I CAN'T' into 'I CAN' and give you the tools, advice and inspiration for how to do it. With this book, you will realize that your life truly has NO LIMITS!"

–CHRISSIE WELLINGTON
IRONMAN WORLD CHAMPION
AND AUTHOR OF A LIFE WITHOUT LIMITS

TRIATHLON FOR
THE EVERY WOMAN

TRIATHLON FOR THE EVERY WOMAN

You Can Be a Triathlete. Yes. You.

MEREDITH ATWOOD

www.SwimBikeMom.com

COVER PHOTO BY: SPORTS IN MOTION PHOTOGRAPHY
SWIM BIKE MOM LOGO AND COVER DESIGN: BECCA PARO, JUMPING JAX DESIGNS
REAR COVER PHOTO: BIRD'S EYE VIEW, INC. | TRICYCLE STUDIOS
AUTHOR PHOTO BY: MEG DAVIDSON PHOTOGRAPHY

For Mombow.

If **Every Woman** had a grandmother like you…
the world would be a better place.
I love you.

Triathlon

Tri·ath·lon - One of the best and most addicting forms of competition consisting of swimming, cycling, and running all at varying degrees of distances. Triathlon is not for the weak, for it puts the athlete in an indescribable amount of pain, but when the race is over, you want to do it again. **Anyone who downplays the difficulty of a triathlon or the classification of it as a sport should be beaten**.

— FROM URBAN DICTIONARY[i]

Since 2000 female USA Triathlon membership has grown from 27 percent of the total of the annual members to more than 38 percent at the end of 2011. Factors leading to this growth are society's acceptance of "active" women, women feeling more comfortable living an active lifestyle, the growth of women's-only events …and races focusing on charity involvement and fundraising.

— FROM USA TRIATHLON[ii]

The Transitions

Part I I

Foreward

Reading *Triathlon for the EveryWoman* is like sitting down for coffee with a friend. Your friend in this scenario is Meredith Atwood (better known as "Swim Bike Mom") …and she is trying to convince you to do a triathlon.

"No, no, no, I can't do a triathlon," you say.

Then, over her latte, Meredith gets a strange fire in her eyes. She says (way too loudly for the coffee shop), "But of course you can! You can become a triathlete!"

(Now she's almost squealing)

"You just have to believe in yourself! Look at me and how far I've come!"

(She's waving her hands and flailing about).

"We just have to get you ready. You can do this, lady! You'll be a triathlete before you know it!"

Then, like a good friend convincing you that you need to buy those leopard-print high heels, Meredith convinces you to buy into the EveryWoman triathlon dream. But unlike the shoes, you really *do* need the triathlon dream. Just by reading, you will somehow know that she believes in you when others don't.

In this book, Meredith does an amazing job conveying heart, honesty and information about swimming, biking and running—in addition to the juggling act that is family, work and training. She has gathered an incredible team of expert contributors, including Gerry Halphen (a/k/a Coach Monster), an experienced coach and Ironman, to talk you through the logistics of the swim, bike and the run, as well as nutrition, mental toughness and more.

Meredith's everyday experiences—hiding in her closet with jars of peanut butter, facing her body in the mirror, motherhood, marriage, and of course, the leap into triathlon—are so relatable. Her words will hit home with anyone who has set out to take on anything new.

Triathlon for the Every Woman is an informative and hilarious read if you are looking for encouragement to get off the couch and find out what you're made of. The couch is precisely where Meredith began her triathlon journey. She had absolutely no prior knowledge of triathlon. In fact, when she started tri-ing, Meredith was so far flung from any athletic goals that she proves that *you* have no excuses—because she had used them all. The book is full of training ideas, tips and inspiring race reports for those looking for answers on how to make a change…for once and for all.

For the experienced triathlete—you will relate to so many of the book's anecdotes, *and* pick up some amazing tips from the experts. For the triathlon newbie—even if you don't know that the swim comes first in a race (it does)—this book is *the* answer. The best part is that *Triathlon for the Every Woman* will address all your questions and concerns about diving into the sport—without you having to ask. Meredith covers topics from what to wear under your triathlon suit to taking care of the Queen on long rides. (Who is the Queen? You'll find out!) The message is loud and clear: create your dreams and just keep moving forward. I like that.

Enjoy the *Triathlon for the Every Woman* ride, because you'll be signing up for your first race before you have even finished the book.

— Bree Wee

Ironman Louisville Champion, 2012

Bree Wee is a mom, professional triathlete and Ironman champion. In her rookie season as a pro, she earned podium finishes in both Ironman and Ironman 70.3 events. She also claimed her first half Ironman win at Hawaii 70.3 in 2010. Bree most recently took 1st place at Ironman Louisville 2012. Bree is proof that you can be a mom, be a triathlete and be awesome. She blogs at <u>www. HiBreeWee.com</u>

Introduction

I woke up one morning and decided I would become a triathlete.

My Decision was not particularly interesting, aside from the fact that I was super fat. And slow. And tired. And angry.

And out of three of the sports that make up triathlon (swimming, biking and running), I had never done any real swimming, biking or running. Well, I would sometimes run to Dairy Queen. *Does that count?*

To add insult to fat injury, I was busy. Really busy. A mom of two kids under two years of age. Married. I worked full-time as a lawyer. I commuted twelve hours a week. But I was mostly busy being tired, fat, isolated and angry.

In light of the stuff I had going on in my life, my Decision to become a triathlete seemed fairly insane. I mean, where would I actually find the time? Even worse, the Decision was riddled with all sorts of odds against me, sizing concerns, and lots of fat jiggling this way and that. For years, I sat and wreaked havoc on myself by eating crap and drinking more crap. But one day—with my Decision—I decided that I would not continue to destroy myself.

Little by little, I started moving forward. I walked. I ran. I biked. I wore a bathing suit (*horror!*). I set goals. I chiseled away at workouts. I did some small races. I met people who believed in me. I met people who did *not* believe in me. But I started believing in myself, and I kept going.

And one year later, I crossed the finish line at a half Ironman triathlon. A race made up of 1.2 miles of swimming, followed by 56 miles of cycling, and topped off with a half marathon run of 13.1 miles. A total of 70.3 miles by sea, bike and foot. The race took me seven hours and fifteen minutes to complete. Arguably the best and worst seven hours of my life. I crossed the finish line wearing a size 10 running shoe and a 2XL triathlon suit. I was probably the biggest girl within a ten-mile radius that day. I may have been big in size, but I was huge in heart.

Since my Decision, I have finished over twenty triathlons and races ranging from sprint triathlons to half marathons. I recently finished my second half Ironman in September 2012, taking almost forty minutes off my first half Ironman time.

And why stop there? I plan to finish my first full Ironman in June 2013. That's right—the big dog. *Whew. I need a nap...*

So. How in the world does someone like me go from a serious couch dweller to a *bona fide* triathlete...while juggling a life, a job and a family? That's why I wrote this book! So I can tell you!

This giant book is divided into two parts:

In Part One, some serious experts and I will give you the tools to get you to your first triathlon. If you are already a seasoned triathlete, there's good stuff for you too—especially on nutrition and mental toughness. Part One will convey tons of information about swimming, biking, running, nutrition, mental strength, gear, and race day preparation. Not only that, but I've included some tips and humor about how to balance it all (life, kids, relationships) while keeping yourself happy and sane. If you are teetering on the triathlon edge—not knowing if you really *want* to tri—I swear this book will push you right on over! Follow Part One, and you *will* finish a triathlon. It's simple math, really.

Part Two is the story of my one-year triathlon extravaganza—from slug to first-time half Ironman finisher. And while I'm not a fancy coach, trained nutritionist or skilled expert in any athletic field, I *am* someone who has experienced an authentic triathlon journey. This is more like the fuzzy math portion of the book, but I think you'll enjoy the tale.

This book is for the Every Woman. Who is the Every Woman? Well. She is me. She is you. She is young, middle-aged, old, tall, short, fat, thin, average, single, married, partnered, divorced, widowed, with or without kids, with or without job, with or without animals, with or without money, with or without sanity.

I wrote this book because I do not want any woman to feel the way I felt two years ago.

Isolated. Fat. Sad. Angry.

I am the Every Woman who is over-worked, over-tired and under-appreciated. I am chunky, covered in stretch marks and hoarding a closet full of fancy jeans that I can't pull up past my thighs. I am the Every Woman who happens to also have a husband, kids, bills and crayons coming out of her ears. I am the Every Woman trying to be everything to everyone. I am trying to keep all the plates spinning without losing my ever-loving mind.

And really, I am pretty sure I have just described *every* woman I know. Well, I'm sure some of you aren't chunky or don't have stretch marks. (*You dirty wenches.*)

With so much going on…how does triathlon fit into your life? It *does*. Promise. I have experienced triathlon as a tired Every Woman, not as a super-fit, well-rested hottie mom. Not only that, but triathlon has made me unbelievably peaceful, happy and (semi)sane. I have not stopped life or taken time off from work or the daily grind to make triathlon part of my reality. I also have not taken time off work to write this book. I just tried to squeeze it in the rest of the chaos. (I'm sure you'll find thousands of typos, but I was probably changing diapers at some point and forgot where I was.)

I wrote this book for three reasons. First, no matter *who* you are or *where* you are in life, I believe you can experience the joy of becoming a triathlete. However, it's tough to know where to start! When I jumped into triathlon, I quickly realized that not a single resource available spoke to someone like me (the soon-to-be-locked-up-in-the-loony-bin Every Woman). No book or magazine could be purchased that told a real story of an Every Woman's journey from a stressed Mommy Dearest to a grounded Zen-master triathlete. (Unfortunately, I am not a grounded Zen-master, so we are still looking for *that* book). But I have lived the Every Woman experience of debt, struggles with weight, stress, marriage, kids, terrible bosses and an unfulfilling career… which I combined with a less-than-graceful swan dive into triathlon. So I wrote *the* book I wish *I* had found two years ago.

Secondly, so many people in my life have given me hope and inspiration while standing behind me, foot up my rear-end, screaming "Yes you can!" as loud and as long as I could tolerate. I owe these individuals so much. I owe them a thank you, yes. But I owe them the duty of paying it forward, of sharing their life-changing core messages in the context of how they changed *me*. If this book can change just one person in the way that these folks have changed me—then my mission will be accomplished.

Thirdly, I would really like to get out of the legal profession. Although I am unqualified to do anything else on this planet except wash briefs and read briefs, I thought I'd try my hand at: *author*.

Ah-hem.

No matter how tired, chubby, lazy or indifferent you may be right in this moment, today is a new day, full of new opportunities...and things can be better for you. And I think the sport of triathlon is the path to *better*.

Your road to becoming a triathlete starts out with a basic Decision. So what is the Decision? It's simple. You just *decide* to become a triathlete. Sounds stupid? Sounds embarrassing? Sounds impossible? Perfect. You are right where you need to be. But it truly *is* simple:

You can float/doggie paddle/swim.

You can ride a tricycle/bicycle/tandem/hand-cycle.

You can walk/jog/run/wheel.

You can do all three back-to-back in a little race called a triathlon. Even if you can't do any of it right now. Even if you have disabilities and hurdles and major obstacles to overcome. You can do this.

You will do this.

And that's all you need to decide. Make the Decision that you will. You *will* move forward. You *will* create your goals, and you *will* achieve. Slowly but surely, you *will* do it. As my coach says, *Trust the process. Create your goals. Believe. And you will.*

To that, I say...Amen.

-Meredith Atwood

"Swim Bike Mom"
December 2012

PART ONE

Becoming a Triathlete
The Every Woman's Guide

ONE

Making the Decision

Making a decision to change is always the first step to actually changing. As such, the first step in my long list of brilliant advice about becoming a triathlete is to:

> ### Decide to Become a Triathlete.
>
> *(No matter how you look on the outside.*
> *No matter how badly you hurt on the inside.)*

First, you might want to know more about triathlon in order to make an informed decision about whether you want to join the sporty cult of Spandex-covered weirdos. You might have a few questions before you put on a hideous wetsuit and jump into a cold lake on a Sunday morning with a bunch of Neoprene-clad freakazoids. You might want to know exactly how difficult those early morning wake-up calls actually are—especially on days that feel more suitable for Bloody Marys than bloody foot blisters.

Alas, I am telling you too much already! I should not scare you away at this early juncture!

So I am asking that you trust me. Trust me and believe that triathlon is something you *need* in your life, much like a washing machine. However, triathlon is also something that you *want* in your life. Like a spouse who actually knows how to use the washing machine.

How the Decision Happened to Me

I am not exactly certain how the Decision to become a triathlete came to me. Maybe it was an organic process that began in my first Spinning class, which I will tell you about later. Maybe that class made just the impression I needed to continue showing up to workouts week after week. Maybe I liked being surrounded by fit people. (No, that's not true. Super fit people freaked me out then and honestly, continue to freak me out now.) Maybe my crazy vegan runner colleague, Mountain Goat, crept inside my psyche a little. She was always running and eating beans and I thought, *I want to run, and eat beans too!*

Finally, I considered a certain someone's comments about my ability to do a triathlon. This person looked me dead in the eyes and nonchalantly said, "You could do a triathlon right now, if you really wanted to."

Regardless of the *how* the Decision happened, all I know is that in August of 2010, I made a simple, one-sentence Decision: *I have decided to become a triathlete.*

Notice that I did *not* say: I have decided to *do* a triathlon. Deciding to become a *triathlete* is different than completing a triathlon. Wait? What? You might argue, *Well, if I do a triathlon, then I am obviously a triathlete.*

Yes and no. Mostly, no.

Deciding to *do* a triathlon is making a goal to complete a single event, to succeed in a solitary moment. You cross the finish line and you are done, and you can head for the Waffle House to celebrate.

Deciding to *become* a triathlete is a new game entirely. My Decision to become a triathlete indicated several things:

1. I intended to do more than just *one* triathlon;
2. I would identify myself with a group of people who were serious athletes;
3. I would learn about triathlon, including rules and safety, and the proper way to compete in a race; and
4. I would *become* someone very strange to the outside, non-triathlon "real" world.

And I wrote it on the very first post of a blog: *I have decided to become a triathlete.* Then I held my breath. And I felt a little sick at first. But interestingly, once I made that incredibly crazy, yet simple Decision—things began to change.

THE FAT STRANGER

During this time of my life, each day was the same for me. My life was freaking *Groundhog Day.* Every day: wake up, get ready for work, tend to two babies and talk to (or argue with) the spouse. Each day, I would walk to the bathroom and look in the mirror. And every single day, there she was.

The Fat Stranger.

The Fat Stranger? Yes, the Fat Stranger was staring back at me. A twenty-nine year-old Fat Stranger. I had kinda gotten to know the Fat Stranger over the recent years. I would sometimes look in the mirror and ask the Fat Stranger questions like, *How did this happen to you?* Sometimes, I would ask, *How did you let yourself get like this?* The Fat Stranger would just stare back, blankly, with absolutely no answers. She was a snobby fat bitch, that Fat Stranger.

I did not like her.

I did not appreciate the Fat Stranger's post-baby boobs or the jiggly butt that looked like it had been hit with ping pong balls. I could find no beauty in the bags under the bloodshot green eyes. I saw no love in the flappy arms. I especially did not like the Fat Stranger's droopy belly. That belly, a saggy-skin house that had cultivated two babies, fourteen months apart. Didn't matter that she had actually grown *people* inside of her...that Fat Stranger was hideous.

I did not like *any part* of her.

So really, I think the Fat Stranger may have had a bigger impact on my Decision than anything or anyone else. The Fat Stranger was not a bad person. She was just someone I did not want to know (or see).

At the time of my Decision, I knew absolutely nothing about triathlon. Nothing. I had no idea about swimming and biking and running. I was pretty sure that triathlon meant doing all three of those things in a row, but I was not sure in which order or how far.

The Order of Sports in a Triathlon:
Swim first.
Bike next.
Finish with the run.

Knowing absolutely nothing about triathlon, I still decided I would go for it. I started a little blog that no one read. Really, I was scared that someone besides my mom *might* read it. After all, making public comments about my physicality (or lack thereof) was pretty much salt on an open fat wound.

But I needed to put it out there.

I was very tender to the fact that I was completely out of shape, teetering on depressed and repulsive in my own eyes. Even when I told my parents about the blog and my Decision, they gave me a three-second-too-long pause before saying, "That's great, honey!" Now, they were absolutely supportive. I probably have the two most cheerleader-y parents in the world. But their "that's great" did not have enough *oooomph* behind it. So it hurt me. I looked for negativity from every place. I was overly sensitive. My insides literally hurt from so many different angles.

But I had *decided*.

And for once, I was going to stand by my decision.

THE DECISION: THE TURNING POINT

You may already think I am crazy, and therefore a declaration like "I have decided to become a triathlete" can be dismissed as the words of a crazy woman. You may think that this declaration is horrifically embarrassing and logistically impossible for *you* to make. Fine. I will admit to being a tad nuts. But regardless, I am still a woman, a human being and a member of the real world. So my Decision was also *very* embarrassing for me. So I understand your fear.

"I have decided to become a triathlete" is a daring statement and a scary thought. But I want you to forget about all the negative feelings associated with such a bold move for a bit.

6

If you are *anything* like I was a few year ago, then you feel stressed, exhausted, and may have your own Fat Stranger staring you in the face. Or maybe she's a Sad Stranger. Or a Mad Mom. Doesn't matter *who*. But you may be staring back at someone you just don't like. I understand that.

To add a preposterous statement like "I will become a triathlete" to your hectic mix may feel irresponsible and comical. (Lord knows as women we cannot be irresponsible!) Yes, the words are scary. But I am also convinced that those few words were the turning point of my life. Maybe I should repeat that. *Those few words were the turning point of my life.*

The. Turning. Point. Of. My. Life.

Turning.

Point.

Of.

My.

Life.

Yes, I suppose I could have said, *I'll do a triathlon.* I suppose that would have been fine. But to become an actual *triathlete* required more than just gutting and getting through a single race and heading out for pancakes afterwards. Also, I think simply *getting through* a race is a bad attitude which causes racers to ill-prepare, discourages life change *and* can be very dangerous during a race.

To become a triathlete means to become a different person. Becoming a triathlete required an epic shift in my entire being. I wanted more than just a solo finisher's medal for finishing some random race. And only a few months into training, I realized that I wanted many more things—not just in triathlon—but also in my life.

You can become a triathlete both inside and out. This book is not about casually training for triathlon in order to have a fun race with your girlfriends. Do not set out to merely finish the popular sprint distance race, Iron Girl, *one* time. Set out to finish Iron Girl every year…for the next twenty years! I like girl power as much as the next girl. But I do not like *lazy* girl power. I like power! And powerful women! And women doing the seemingly impossible! And kicking butt and taking names! And yeah! See? Yeah! By default, a fun race day is part of the triathlon deal. However, becoming a triathlete is an amazing way to change your life and find *your* power.

The Every Woman triathlon transformation is about more than simply looking better—triathlon will transform your entire life. From your relationships to your job and your dreams. Will you look better? Yes. A friendly side-effect of triathlon is a better looking body. But we are not talking about "Swim Bike Mom's 30 Days to a Rocking Bikini Body." In case you haven't noticed, this Swim Bike Mom has no bikini body. What a poor selling book *that* would be. But do I look better from triathlon? Oh, hell yes. However, I still will not wear a bikini within three miles of a beach.

Triathlon is not a fitness program or a diet. Triathlon is not a gimmick. Triathlon is a *bona fide* sport. Having tighter buns is a nice bonus, but your buns are not the *focus* of triathlon. It took me well over two years of triathlon training to beat the "look better" ideal out of my subconscious. I do not think there is anything wrong with wanting to look better. But to beat myself up for my body, when it can swim, bike and run for miles and miles? *That* is not only unhealthy—it's absurd.

Triathlon is a sport that works for working women with kids and significant others. It works for single women. It works for older women, smart women, funny women, silly women. It works for *women*. Triathlon works for women because there is so much spirit, love and scheduling involved in swimming, biking and running.

> Becoming a triathlete is an amazing way to
> change your life and find your power.

How? How will you find the time? You will. And you will be surprised how triathlon becomes a part of your life. Just make your Decision to become a triathlete. The Decision does not have to be well-informed. We women tend to make calculated, responsible and well-informed decisions all the time. The Decision is not about making a well-thought-out-super-smart decision. Seriously. Do not start researching time management. Do not look into if you can afford it. Just make a completely blind leap with me. Make the Decision that you want to be a *triathlete*. Decide to become a triathlete. The rest will follow. One step at a time, you will find a way. Cross my little Swim Bike Mom heart.

> "Tell me, what is it you plan to do
> with your one wild and precious life?"
>
> — MARY OLIVER

WHO AM I TO TELL YOU ...ANYTHING?

So I made the Decision and I was instantly a triathlete! Ha. Okay. *No.* After making the Decision, I was a complete *flounder*. Fish-like, floundering, flopping all over the place, completely lost. I had made a bold statement, but I had no idea what to do next.

Because I had no idea what to do, I ran a little. I flailed in the pool for a bit. I went to some indoor cycling classes. But after a few weeks, I was nowhere close to triathlon nirvana. Really, I was just plain confused.

Actually, I had been confused for some time. About a lot of things. Actually my whole life...

A SWIM BIKE MOM HISTORY LESSON

1979

I was born a healthy baby tipping the scales at a nice eight pounds. My mom was a hero, popping me out 100% naturally and drug-free, and acting like it was no big deal.

1980-1987

I was a semi-fat kid. But I was one of those husky, strong specimens. "Give the bat to Meredith, she'll hit a home run," my dad would tell the softball coach. I would put down my doughnut on the bench and proceed to bat.

"She's strong!" everyone would say. But rarely did I hit the ball. However, I could punch the catcher in the face and then hit McDonald's for a tasty Filet-o-Fish if the situation called for it.

The truth of the matter: I really *was* strong. I was big and strong and I hated it. I picked on other kids because I felt like crap about myself. I was miserable and that misery caused me to eat more. I was lonely, so I ate. Then I was fat, so I was mean. Food was my friend, my enemy.

1989

At age ten I started the Weight Watchers plan. I was getting fatter by the second and back in the 1980's no one knew that kids did not belong on diets. My parents were faced with a miserable little portly kid, so they did the best they knew to do. And I can thank Weight Watchers for my love of drinking water.

So with the diet, I entered the world of carrot sticks, cottage cheese and water (*Mmmmm....*) for lunch. When I got home in the afternoon, I followed up lunch with secret handfuls of butter crackers. I stuffed those delicious round crackers in my cheeks so tight and so fast that my mouth would burst open and I would "poof" crumbs everywhere. I was just so hungry, especially on the diet. My parents would go to sleep and I would creep to the kitchen for chips and cookies. My ten-year old self would eat, eat, eat and then cry, cry, cry.

1990

I lost ten pounds. I entered middle school weighing 125 pounds.

1991

By the time Aunt Flow arrived, I had shot up to 5'7" and 155 pounds. Looking at pictures from that era, I was not obese. I played sports and was pretty healthy. But I believed I was fat, because I had *always* been fat.

Fat was what I *knew*.

Body Image Innocence

Now, in my thirties, I am blown away by the intensity of fatness I felt at a young age. Like the fatness was a part of who I was. Where did it come from? Why was "fat" even a word I knew? What kind of kid, at age ten, is even worrying about weight and looking good?

Of course, the body image epidemic is even worse now. Our daughter is almost four. Any reference towards "piggy" or "chunky" in our house and I lose it. I am trying to shield her from any reference to her body image whether good, bad or otherwise for as long as I can.

I am not sure when I lost my body image innocence. But one thing I know is that when the body image innocence vanished, it disappeared for good.

1997

I was a healthy teenager. I had a teenager pot belly, but overall I was fit and I worked hard at my sport of the time, Olympic weightlifting. ("She's strong!" *Ugh*.)

But like any stupid seventeen-year old girl, I spent entirely too much energy and time bemoaning my fatness, when hindsight shows me that I was actually kind of cute. Stupid, but cute. Wasted cuteness. Wasted years and years of absolutely perfectly good cuteness.

In my wasted cuteness, I was still strong. I could hoist 220 pounds over my head and squat 300 pounds for sets. That had to count for something. *Right?* It should have. But really, all I could think about was my pot belly.

1998

I graduated from high school.

I wore a pretty white dress to graduation. At the time, I thought I looked fat wearing it. Looking back, I was a babe. More wasted cuteness headed straight into college.

New Year's Eve, 1998

I began dating the Expert. Our first date was at Denny's. A cup of coffee and romance at its finest.

Who is the Expert? Oh, he's the dude who is now my husband. I lovingly refer to him as "The Expert" for reasons that will need little explanation in this book. Simply put, the Expert knows *everything*. He's also a rockstar of a husband and a father and I love him dearly. You probably have one of these so-called experts in your life. Just saying.

1999

I hung up the Olympic weightlifting belt and shoes.

Then I started my second year of college, determined to be a journalist. But then I learned that journalists made about ten dollars a year and attempted to live in New York City—which meant most ended up back home, living with their parents. I love my parents. They are the best parents in the world. But I could not imagine returning home as an adult.

I treasured my new-found freedom more than anything. And my new found freedom required some cash. Hence, my dreams of writing for the *New York Times* gave way to an even stupider pursuit: an English degree.

I sailed through college in pursuit of my "lucrative" English career. Whatever that meant. I look back on it, and I think I chose English as a degree because I loved to read and write. As a result, I could finish reading the assigned novel by five in the afternoon, spit out a five-page paper by seven-thirty and land in the bar with a drink in hand by nine o'clock.

College was like college should be. I ate three pizzas a week, drank too much beer and had more fun that you could shake a stick at. I also learned Latin and managed to squeak out a college degree from a Top 25 university, so I consider the college years a bloody smashing success. (From what I remember of them.)

August 2001

I graduated. Time to make millions!

October 2001

The Expert put a ring on it and we were married. Because we had been dating for "so long" we decided that the next logical step to dating was to weld ourselves together for all eternity with the fiscal chains of marital bliss.

The Expert was handsome and smart and everything I wanted. I was a chubby, reasonably happy, twenty-one-year-old newlywed college graduate. *Hot dog.* I knew absolutely nothing about the real world, but I knew I was free to make my own decisions from that point forward. I liked that. Freedom was my new drink of choice. Freedom and bourbon.

2002

Newlywed-dom was the best. With my lucrative English degree, I made six dollars an hour selling discount eyeglasses. At night, the Expert and I drank beer and partied with our friends.

I have no idea what people complain about regarding the newlywed years. The Expert and I had awesome weekends without worrying about expectations, grades or other foolishness. We had no real money, but we rented and ate on the cheap. We continued to live in a college town where beer was fifty cents a Solo® cup and an entire pizza would set us back a few bucks (and up a few pounds).

2002-2003

I decided that I could not bear to touch another moldy pair of eyeglasses and really, I *should* be doing *something* with my degree. Stupidly, I chose to go back to school to get yet another stupid degree.

I chose law.

I got serious. Well, sort of serious. I watched entirely too much of "The Practice" on ABC. I thought Dylan McDermott was a standard perk of any reasonable law firm. Henceforth and *ipso facto* and *res judicata*, law school seemed like a brilliant idea.

Unfortunately, three additional years of being glued to books by day and drinking beer by night did not do much for my figure. In my mind, I had absolutely no time for anything healthy. I had to *study*. All the time.

While other ladies in law school were picking out their fancy size-two suits for interviews and running five miles before class, I was busting down the door of Cinnabon for a snack…and then hitting August Max Woman, begging the 22W relaxed pant to fit me so I could find a job, any job, any place.

During my third year of law school the workload slowed, and I had a job lined up for my smashing future career as Ally "Only Fatter" McBeal. Because third year did not require the same intensity as the first two years, I was bored and had nothing to do but surf the internet.

2004

In my loving new relationship with the World Wide Web, I found a nice mail order prescription for Phentermine, a weight-loss drug. Apparently, you could just ask China to send you some and they would. I lost fifty pounds and entered Size Ten Land.

Along with my special pill, I had a specific meal plan to remain a resident of Size Ten Land. For breakfast, I ate an over-processed Western Bagel with ultra-processed but low-fat cream cheese.

For lunch, I had Dog Food Soup. (Okay, so it was not actually dog food, but that's what the Expert called the pot roast soup I ate by the case. I can concede that it looked and smelled a tad like dog food. But it was two hundred calories for the whole can…*hot tamale!*)

I ate absolutely no snacks. I did not need snacks. I was not hungry, thanks to my Phentermine addiction.

For dinner, I would eat a baked potato covered in fat-free shredded cheese, ketchup and fat-free Ranch dressing. (I understand if you think I am too gross to continue reading. Trust me, my grossness gets worse, so just put on your big girl girdle and hang on for the disgusting ride.)

I was stoked. I had found the miracle plan for skinny! I was finally skinny! It was so *simple*. Take speed pills, avoid alcohol and eat severely limited quantities of foods, only white or brown in color. Genius!

Wait, I forgot one other thing. You must smoke! Smoke! I was smoking cigarettes at the time. *What?* I must not forget to mention the added benefit of speed pills combined with nicotine. (*Legal disclaimer: I am kidding. Do not do this*.) You have been previously warned of my ever-loving grossness. I shall not apologize going forward.

I can now appreciate the fact that I was lucky to be *alive*, albeit in fabulous Size Ten Land, considering the havoc I was causing my body. I was very impressed with myself around this point in my life. I was "skinny." I was close to being a lawyer. (So young and so dumb.)

To me, skinny was obviously "healthy," so the next logical thing to do was *run*.

A few weeks after hitting Size Ten Land, I started running and entered my first 5k (3.1 mile) race. I was regularly running miles on the treadmill, twice a week, at a 14.5-minute mile pace. In case you are wondering how fast that is—you can walk faster than that *right* now. Yes. Yes you can.

I was captivated with myself because I was running on nothing but cigarettes and Dog Food Soup. Eventually, I decided that smoking was not helping my cardio fitness, so I quit.

The Expert, who miraculously managed to avoid the fat plague until much later in our marriage, ran my first 5k race along with me. He was running and cycling regularly and could easily put down 3.1 miles in twenty-five minutes. Even though the Expert could have blown me out of the water that day, he held back and ran with me to encourage me. So we ran, and completed the 5k in forty minutes.

I can now run a 5k in under thirty minutes. And I'm not even close to living in Size Ten Land.

Size really isn't everything. (*That's what she said*. Yes, yes I did.)

2005

Two months after my first 5k, my father was involved in a near-fatal motorcycle accident, which sent our family into a tailspin. I spent the remaining time in law school pulling together papers and presentations at the hospital or beside my father at home, sharing shift rotations with my mom.

I was tired.

I was stressed.

I started smoking again and eating super-bad brown food like pizza and hamburgers. I no longer cared about portion control. I also had no more money for my skinny pills. I was running on little to no sleep, driving back and forth to Savannah from Athens, Georgia.

My dad made it through and to my law school graduation. He was still in bad shape, but managed to make a fabulous hopped-up-on-Oxycodone toast at my post-graduation party. Really, it was a great toast. And even if it wasn't... Dad doesn't remember anyway. (I kid, I kid.)

2005, Post-Graduation

The Expert and I moved to a tiny little town. I took and passed the bar exam. We went to and hosted fabulous little parties. Gone were the "skinny" days. We spent weekends grilling out, partying with our neighbors and laying like slugs.

Size Ten Land became a vision in my rear-view mirror, and my rear-view grew wider. I flew right through Size Twelve Town, Size Fourteen City and took up a seemingly permanent residence in the booming metropolis of Size Sixteen on a Good Day.

2006

I was living the life of a small-town lawyer (making the money of a New York journalist, mind you). I loved our country house on two acres. I loved the quiet, the homemade guacamole, Sunday back-porch-sitting and twelve packs of Coronas. The slow life. The turning-once-again ultra-fat life.

I adored that town, but I hated practicing law there. (Turns out, I do not like practicing law anywhere, but that's neither here nor there.) When the stress with my boss grew, I ate more and drank more. Luckily, I had enough sense to give up the cancer sticks by that time. I had loads of free time, but I learned to bake gourmet cookies instead of exercising.

2007

Of course, the perfect time to have a baby is when stress levels are high and you have absolutely no clue who *you* really are. I got pregnant in January and things started to unravel at work. Actually, I probably would have been fine except that my boss believed that two weeks of maternity leave was sufficient to have a baby. We then negotiated three weeks.

Obviously, I started looking for another job.

But by the grace of God, a firm in Atlanta hired me *five months pregnant*. So, five months pregnant and with three weeks' notice, we put our country house on the market, packed up and hauled our stuff to an over-priced apartment in a suburb of Atlanta.

I had an easy pregnancy with our first child, James. However, the forty-plus-hour labor was the stuff of horror movies. I had a completely drug-free natural birth, until two hours before he was born. Then I had drugs for the grand finale. One epidural, one round of Pitocin and out popped an almost nine-pound baby boy. The Expert and I left the hospital only twelve hours after he was born, because I wanted *out* of that hospital and *into* an Arby's roast beef sandwich and curly fries.

James was a cute baby who looked just a little like an old man with a side-part. He was cranky like an old man, too. I was breastfeeding constantly. I was dog-tired. After three months of new mothering, feeding this strange old-man baby and waking up every two hours, I slugged my way back into the office, hauling my gargantuan breastpump and wearing stretchy pants. (Not that I minded the stretchy pants.)

This was when the Fat Stranger made her debut appearance.

In the *Groundhog Days* of the working stiffs, I woke up at 5:30 each morning, pumped, dressed and fought Atlanta traffic. I worked nine hours, ate lunch at my desk, pumped twice, spent hours and hours in traffic and then picked James up from daycare.

I talked to the Fat Stranger on my commute into work. I would mumble things to her, stream of consciousness crazy, Faulkner-like: *This is not how I thought motherhood would be. Why does this kid cry all the time? How can I continue to work like this? I mean, how fat can I get before someone says something to me? Are the authorities going to commit me because I am ballooning up to the size of a whale? Would I be required to buy an extra airplane seat right now? Pitiful. I'm so gross...Ooooh! Snap. There's Dairy Queen...*

<u>2008</u>

One very special *Cinco de Mayo* Monday when James was barely six months old, I had another *Groundhog Day*. I was drenched in sweat by the time I picked up James from daycare. It was only eighty degrees outside, but I was four thousand pounds. My feet hurt because I had spent the day in court, traipsing my fat ass around downtown Atlanta in a too-tight suit paired with too-small heels.

I tossed off my shoes and plopped James in his ExerSaucer and began my afternoon ritual: empty the diaper bag, refrigerate breastmilk pumped during the day, eat whatever was in sight, start laundry, eat some more, answer work emails on the BlackBerry.

On that day, the Expert was home early. And I will never forget the next moment as long as I live.

I was standing in the kitchen, eating butter crackers (flashback to my childhood) and watching James bopping around in his ExerSaucer. My mind started to wander. *I wonder when Memorial Day is. Is it the 19th or the 26th? If it's the 26th, then I think the Expert will be here and we'll go down to see my folks. That's only, what, two to three weeks? Like 20 days. 20 days. 19 days? 19 Days....*

I gasped.

I began counting. *Twenty-eight, twenty-nine, thirty, thirty-one, thirty-two.* That kind of counting. The ticking in the mind. *Thirty-three, Thirty-four... days.* The pause.

I was late.

Yes, *that* kind of late. I looked at James. He grinned a four-toothed grin at me. I looked at the Expert, typing away on his computer.

"I have to go to the store," I screamed suddenly.

The Expert jumped. I apparently screamed pretty loud. "Why?" he asked.

"Uh, we need diapers."

"No, we don't," he said gesturing to the enormous box in the laundry room.

"Oh, yes. Yes, yes we do," I was grabbing at my purse, my keys.

"Okay, but I think I saw another whole box—"

"—we need diapers! Watch the kid, okay?" I screamed, already halfway out the door. I pulled the door to the apartment shut and I almost fell down the stairs, I was trucking so fast. I drove the three blocks to Walgreens, hopped out of the car and scurried down the aisles until I found what I was looking for.

Five minutes later—okay, that's a lie because I also went down the street and got a large strawberry milkshake with whipped cream...so, fifteen minutes later—I was back home. I locked myself in the bathroom with my milkshake and a First Response pregnancy test.

I looked at the Fat Stranger in the mirror and thought, *Oh no no no no no no no no no.*

Everyone knows the instructions. Pee on the stick. Wait three minutes. If two lines appear, then you are going to be a lunatic. Depending on your place in life, you want the two lines or you don't. I am not sure if anyone is really middle-of-the-road on these kinds of things. I peed on the stick. By the time the pee hit the indicator window: two pink lines. *Two pink lines. Two pink lines.* I did not even have my allotted three minutes to breathe.

Two pink lines.

I wandered out of the bathroom with the magic life-changing pee-stick in hand. James started screaming from his post in the bouncy thing. *Time to feed the squealing baby bird again*, I thought. The Expert glanced up from his computer. I waved the First Response in the air from across the room.

"What is that?" he asked. A glimmer of recognition flashed across his face. "Oh," he said.

I nodded, tears welling up in my eyes.

"Oh?"

"Yes," I said.

"Oh. Oh!" His eyes roamed over to the screaming baby. "Oh."

"Yeah," I said.

New Year's Eve, 2008

Once the shock wore off (four months later), I was happy to learn that I was having a baby girl. I was actually thrilled to be welcoming a new member to Team Girl in the house. In celebration of Team Girl, I ate cheesecake almost every night.

Only fourteen months after James was born, I was experiencing *déjà vu*—sitting in the same labor and delivery room as I had with James. The Expert went off to find himself a sandwich, figuring the pony show would take as long as the last one.

"I can wait here for a while," he said.

"No, go on," I had told him, "It'll be awhile before they give me the epidural. Go eat."

I refused to suffer through that natural labor garbage again. I had been in that same room fourteen months ago, for the love! Keep your judgments to yourself. I had not forgotten that pain. I was tired. I wanted the girl child outside of my body. I asked for an epidural *immediately*. Five seconds after the Expert left, the anesthesiologist arrived to give me the epidural.

Ooops. I was on my own.

"Hi, there. I'm Dr. John Malkovich [okay maybe that wasn't his name] and I am here to give you the epidural. Please sit up and turn around," he said.

He looked at my spine area.

"Oh, I see the spot where you had the last epidural. We'll just go in there." *Yeah, I bet you see it. It was yesterday that I had that other kid.*

"Fine by me," I said, noting how ridiculously skinny and bony Dr. John Malkovich was.

"How are you feeling?" he asked. I leaned back and looked at him. *What a doofus. Glad I am letting this joker stick a needle in my spine.*

"I'll let you take a guess," I said.

"Uhmmm, hmmmmm. Okay. What's your height and weight?" Dr. Malkovich asked.

I mumbled something.

"I'm sorry, didn't hear you," he said.

I mumbled again, "Five seven and a half."

"Okay," he said. "And your weight?"

I mumbled again.

"Ma'am, I need to know your weight—"

"—Two eighty!" I screamed.

He jumped. Then looked at me for just a second in disbelief.

"Two hundred and eighty pounds," I whispered, embarrassed.

He eyed me carefully.

I started babbling, "Yes, I know, two hundred and eighty pounds is horrible. I know I know I know *I know*!" I squealed, "But the sooner you get this baby out of me, the sooner I will not weigh exactly that!"

Damn all that cheesecake, I thought.

Minutes later, I was relieved from the contractions. But the effing fantastic thing about epidurals on larger women? Sometimes the epidural does not completely work. I guess the fat absorbs the fun and stops at a certain boundary. So while I had the joy of feeling complete relief from the contractions in the belly region, come push time…well, I was not so lucky. *Bonus!*

A few hours later, out flew a New Year's Eve little girl, Stella. She popped out with dark black hair and looking completely of Chinese descent.

The Expert looked at me in confusion. *Awesome,* I thought. *He thinks she's not his baby. Wonderful. Great. Super.*

"Do you think I found someone else to have sex with me, looking like this?" I wailed at him. "She's your baby!" *She was the cutest little Chinese baby I had ever seen.*

"Good point," the Expert muttered.

Little Chinese Stella was a content baby, and James was pretty thrilled to have a sister. My mom brought me a picture of herself as a baby. She looked

Chinese when she was little, too. That made the Expert feel better about being the real baby daddy and all.

<u>2009</u>

Suddenly, these two incredibly small, furry people, fourteen months apart and virtually helpless, were in our lives. All the time. And yes, I meant to say furry. I had no idea that kids can come out furry. But the fur was the least of my worries. I was most shocked at how the kids never went away. Ever. There they were—every night and day.

The Expert and I trudged along. We moved out of our tiny apartment and began to fill a modest house in a crappy neighborhood with kid junk: diapers, bottles and squeaky toys. Topping the junk with full-time work, more breast-feeding, traffic, a new mortgage, sleep deprivation and unbelievable amounts of fat was alarming. Really, the fat was most alarming. So much fat. And stretch marks.

Where did all this fat come from? I'm sorry, am I sprouting new stretch marks? Is that a freaking whisker on my chin? Who is this Fat Stranger? Ew, that is disgusting. It is a freaking whisker! Effing fantastic! Bonus! Groundhog Day! Wooooo freaking hoo.

The Expert worked for an Australian company and traveled constantly during the first year after Stella was born. In one of the Angry Fat Stranger moments, I counted up the days and the Expert was absent for four entire months of 2009. Yes, I know there are military wives who are far worse off, yes yes yes, I know. But he was not serving our country. He was serving the Aussies. And I was playing single mom to two kids under two, working a miserable job full-time and then some, and frankly, I was losing my mind. The Expert's first trip Down Under was when Stella was only two weeks old. I was the walking dead.

The Fat Walking Dead.

When I returned to work after six weeks of maternity leave, I was a complete disaster. I was enormous, sleep-deprived and angry. So angry. I constantly thought: *I am not a good mother. I can't handle this.* I felt absolutely hopeless. I did not know what to do or how to make myself feel better. When could I find the time to exercise? To eat well?

In a desperate attempt to find some sanity, I signed the Expert and myself up for a 5k race, only my second race ever. We had two months to prepare for it. He and I both tried to walk/jog/run over the next two months, but of course, there was no time. We found time to "relax" with wine and pizza and television when the kids were quiet, but we found no time for running.

Despite the crappy training schedule, we still finished the race. I will not lie, however. The experience was humiliating and heartbreaking. I finished in just under forty-minutes, but completely breathless and struggling. I was heaving. My chest hurt. My pace was somewhere over a thirteen-minute-mile and I was sick. By noon, I was dizzy and nauseated. So I drank three beers and took a nap. I physically felt terrible for two days.

I was not particularly hopeful about running or doing better after that race. I was unsure how to handle my feelings of hopelessness and stress. The day after the race, I had bruises on the bottom of my feet from just those three miles. I was still very heavy, hovering somewhere around 240 pounds.

I knew one thing: I really, really, really did not like the Fat Stranger. I did not like that she was unable to run. I did not like that she was shopping at the plus-size clothing stores. I was getting angrier and more hostile by the day. I hated the Fat Stranger to the point of tears and a Big Mac. I hated her even more when a co-worker returned from her maternity leave, looking like she'd had a tummy tuck and had been raising her newborn on a spa vacation.

I wanted to kill the Fat Stranger. Without killing myself, of course.

THINGS BEGAN TO CHANGE:

DID SOMEBODY SAY LUNCH?

Six months later, the Fat Stranger was still hanging around. On one particular morning, the baby monitor rattled loudly with Stella's screams. She was eight months old. Shortly after, James (almost two) started wailing too. The Expert was frustrated because he was heading out of town on business. I was frustrated because I had slept about three hours and I had forgotten to pick up my dry cleaning the day before. The dry cleaning which had my only size 20 suit. The one suit that actually fit me. The one suit I needed for court that day.

I dug deep in the closet and found a too-tight size 16/18 hideous brown number with a super tight waist and a miserable high-water pant. The children did not poop or throw up on me before I left, so I considered that a win of a morning. As I drove towards the courthouse in downtown, I received an email from my assistant on my Blackberry: *Hearing postponed. Judge had family emergency.* (The first of a series of serendipitous moments that changed my life.)

An hour later, I was at my desk with my breastpump shoved neatly in a drawer and my fingers flying fast and furiously across my computer keyboard. I felt okay, although my stomach was hurting from the tight pants (or was it the Egg McMuffin with two hash browns?). An email hit my inbox around nine o'clock:

Lunch and Learn Session Today
Noon
Large Conference Room

Hot dog! Did somebody say Lunch? Those lunches had the best box sandwiches with chips and cookies. I hit the reply button and locked in my reservation for the meeting. (Second stroke of serendipity!)

One minute before noon I hovered outside the conference room, taking in the scent of the glorious cookies. Only then did I realize that the lunch session was presented by the gym located downstairs. *Great,* I muttered. *Gym membership sales. Super. Super. Super.*

I listened haphazardly and smacked on my sandwich thinking, *Yeah, these dumb people thinking I have time for this. When am I going to workout? When? When? When?*

"5:30 a.m." said the leader, "The club opens at 5:30 in the morning."

I snickered to myself. *And these gym memberships are always year-long contracts and I am not going to be stuck in*—but she read my mind again.

"The membership is month-to-month with a thirty day cancellation policy."

Smartass fit lady, I thought, reaching for another cookie.

As I listened to the presentation, I thought, *well, maybe I should join this gym. I could come to work a tad earlier, avoid traffic and shower at the gym.*

Maybe.

By the end of the Lunch, I had Learned myself a sandwich, chips, three cookies and a gym membership. I was a member. The sign-up included a free gym bag. *Bonus!* (Serendipity Number Four!)

After the meeting, our firm's CFO walked over to me. "I am glad you joined the gym. I'm a member too."

"Oh yeah?" I said.

"It's a great gym. I could show you around sometime. You know, I could show you how to use the weights and the machines. Show you how to work-out," he offered.

I stared at him. *Did he really just say that? I could "show you how to workout"?*

Then I heard an explosion. Inside my head. *Boom!* I nodded numbly and turned away whispering, "Thanks."

I suppose that I appreciated the gesture. The CFO dude was simply trying to be nice, helpful. *How nice. How nice. How nice,* I repeated in my head in between head explosions. *Boom! How nice!* But I was incredibly humiliated.

And oh, was I mad! *I had once been an athlete, a weightlifter! I knew my way around a gym, especially the weights! Who did he think he was?*

To make matters worse, one of my friends overheard the CFO's comment and shouted, "No way dude, Meredith used to be some big deal weightlifter!"

I turned beet red.

He looked at me, "Oh. Oh, really?"

Boom! Boom! More head explosions. Horrible. I realized that my *past* athletic prowess was completely lost on others. The prowess was lost, because said prowess was actually invisible. Ten years had passed since I had touched a weight. I apparently looked as if I had never even heard of a gym. My feelings were hurt. I was mad at our CFO. But I realized, he was just stating the obvious.

I Showed Him.

I stewed the rest of the afternoon at my desk, and stewed during my miserable commute home. *I could...show you how to workout...Hurmph! Boom! Boom!*

I walked in the door to our apartment and stripped off my tight brown suit. I massaged my belly skin where an imprint of the waistband made a mark, cursed the Fat Stranger and slid into my stretchy pants. I was ten minutes late getting home, so the babies were thrown at me as our babysitter ran out the door. James started screaming as I fed Stella. The house was a mess. The noise was epic. I was crying and stewing and battling the children. My Blackberry was going *Ding! Ding! Ding!* I was living in an actual zoo.

Amidst all the tangible chaos, all I could think about was the CFO offering to show me around the gym. *Dammit! Damn him! Damn all of this!* I was mad. Mad. Mad. *Boom! Boom!*

I was so mad that I dialed Pizza Hut.

An hour later, I had five pieces of stuffed crust pizza in my gullet, washed down with two beers. The Expert came home a little while later and finished off the rest.

"Hey," I said to the Expert after we put the kids down to bed and planted ourselves squarely in front of the television, "I joined a gym today."

He looked at me. Then he looked back to the television. Silence.

"I got a free gym bag."

He would not look at me. He did not say anything. He didn't have to. I knew what he was thinking. Aside from his concern for the *cost* of the gym membership, he had utterly lost faith in my ability to do anything athletic. I never realized his disappointment in me until that particular moment. I saw it in his eyes. He did not mean to show it. His disappointment was not deliberate. It was not hateful. It just was.

Apparently, the Expert did not like the Fat Stranger either.

The Spark

The Expert and I did not speak the rest of the night.

I retreated to our bedroom, hurt and angry, but with a fresh beer. *This is my last beer ever*, I thought. I threw my brand-new gym bag on the bed. Slowly and muttering to myself, I dug through drawers, filled up little bags of toiletries and packed for the gym the next day. I found an old water bottle. Finally, I tucked my shiny new gym membership card into the corner pocket of the bag, set my alarm and fell into bed.

I woke up a little earlier than usual. The house was dark and quiet. By the light of the closet, I threw on clothes and sneakers, leaving the Expert and babies sleeping soundly. The traffic was nonexistent at that time of morning and I made it to the office in around twenty-five minutes, a big improvement from the usual hour. Instead of plopping down at my desk, I dropped off my purse and headed downstairs to the gym.

It was September 11, 2009. I was petrified of the shiny new gym. I scanned my membership card and picked up a group fitness class schedule. I browsed the schedule.

Spinning® Class

Indoor Cycling

6:00 AM

Instructor: Gerry

I glanced at the clock above the membership desk. *Bingo*. In my college days, I had attended a few indoor cycling classes. Sounded like the best plan I could muster that early in the morning.

I walked into the cycling studio about fifteen minutes before the start of class. The room was wrapped in mirrors and buzzing like Macy's on Black Friday. Music was playing over speakers, bikes were whirring. I spotted only one open bike near the back row and I snagged it. I fumbled with raising the seat on the bike, raising and lowering the handle bars. When I figured it out best I could, I sat on the bike and fitted my feet into the cages on the pedals. My rear end immediately hurt from the pressure of my weight. I was already out of breath as I began to pedal.

I finally looked around.

The men and women spinning away on their bikes were wearing teeny tiny shorts and tanks. I was the fattest person in the room by a good sixty pounds. I was also the most fashionable person in the room wearing an extra-large gray t-shirt with some fat lady leggings. My eyes scanned the mirrors.

Then I saw her.

The Fat Stranger. Only this time I did not acknowledge *the Fat Stranger.* Instead, I looked into her eyes and chose to acknowledge the *person* who was really there. I acknowledged the sad and miserable woman, hiding behind the fatsuit.

Ugh. *Me.*

I turned my eyes away from the mirror, blinking and resolving to keep my eyes straight ahead for the remainder of the hour. The instructor was prepping his bike at the front of the class. I guessed he was the Gerry from the schedule.

I noticed a few things about this Gerry guy straightaway. He was ridiculously fit. He was ridiculously good looking. And he was clearly a cyclist or a reality television star (or something equally as fabulous). I knew a little about cycling because the Expert always made me watch the *Tour de France*, so I could just tell. That and the shaved legs, marbled quads and tight shorts.

Another thing about Gerry: he was very loud.

"Good morning," Gerry shouted. I looked up and braced myself.

Everyone shouted back, "Good morning!" I glanced around again. *This place is a freak show,* I thought. Most everyone in the class was fit, regardless of their age. Fit fit fit. I was an outsider. I was fat fat fat. Gerry looked directly at me. I guess I stood out. Going forward, I avoided eye contact at all costs.

From the front of the class, he congratulated someone who had just finished an Ironman. Everyone clapped. *Ironman? The movie?*

He gave a quick overview of the plan for the class and punched a button for the music. I stared at his spandex shorts and thought, *Those are very tight pants. Only a man in that kind of shape could wear something so ridiculous and still look like a god.*

"Close your eyes," Gerry said. I snapped back to reality from the boom of his voice, my legs beginning to burn from the few moments I had been pedaling.

"Think about what you want to accomplish today," he said. "Leave everything else outside. For the next hour, be here. Be here now. Be grateful."

The music was loud. I was grateful for that. No one could hear me huffing and puffing. I loved the song blaring through the speakers. I was in a crowd of freakishly ripped people, but I was completely alone. I felt an intense loneliness. I was so lonely, so sad that I could taste it.

After the prior night with the Expert, the shame of my unfitness, the weariness of being a new mother twice over, the hatred of being a lawyer, I was left with nothing but disappointment in myself. Tears filled up my field of vision and rolled down my cheeks. I wiped furiously at my eyes, but the weeping continued. My face was so hot and I tried to prevent scrunchy-cry-face from happening. I could see my reflection in the mirror out of the corner of my eye. Nope, scrunchy-cry-face was happening. I was embarrassed for crying, but I was more embarrassed at the person I had become. Not just physically, although my fatness played a large role in the comedy theater of my situation.

But I was embarrassed for the *whole* person I had become. Angry. Fat. Isolated.

Be here. Be grateful.

I struggled with the pedals. I continued to move my legs, cycling through three or four songs and huffing profusely. Gerry shouted motivational words across the room. The music resounded loudly, until one song line hit me in the gut. I had heard the song a few times before, but had never given the lyrics much thought. In the cycling studio, it seemed that I was hearing them for the first time.

*"Do you know that every day's the first
...of the rest...of your life..."*[ii]

The tears came again. My exhaustion, my stretch marks and my ferocious hatred for the Fat Stranger were washed away. All of the serendipitous moments of the prior two days (*Boom! Boom!*) had culminated in Gerry's cycling class.

In place of the anger, I felt a Spark. Yes, it sounds like total cheeseball-flimflam, but I felt a Spark inside my core, a comforting warmth and then a fire of sorts. For the first time, I understood that every day was *literally* a new day and the first day of the *rest* of my life. That small understanding changed something inside of me.

My responsibilities (marriage, work and children) fell back on me when I walked out of the gym. But during that one hour in *that* class, I was *somewhere* else. I was *someone* else. *Was cycling class always that freeing? Would I be able* to escape and figure out who I was if I came more often? Would more exercise give me that peace? Was this really something special? Was it a double rainbow? What did it all meeeean???

On that day, I met the Fat Stranger with open eyes and a grateful heart, and I decided I would begin to like her.

EARLY 2010

I continued to go to Gerry's class off and on. I loved the class, but I did not change a single bad habit. I went to the gym to run sometimes, too. The Fat Stranger and I became friends alright. My standard week's schedule looked like this:

> <u>Friday</u> - Early morning cycling class. Bagel with egg for breakfast. Eat nothing else all day. Mexican, margaritas, beer and cheese-covered-deliciousness for dinner. Followed by ice cream and handfuls of Goldfish crackers until bedtime.

> <u>Saturday</u> - Recover from Friday night's fun. Take kids to breakfast. Eat greasy meal to soak up the alcohol. Take kids to ridiculous all day outing like the zoo or aquarium, then eat greasy lunch. Ice cream. Put kids down for a nap. Dinner, wine and more ice cream.

> <u>Sunday</u> - Recover from Saturday night's fun. Similar to Saturday except add "clean the frat house" and "wash all the clothes." Most importantly, declare Monday as the day to get in shape and eat well.

> <u>Monday</u> - Go to gym early in the morning, eat cookies by noon and declare Mondays too stressful to make any real, calculated life changes. Drink wine at dinner (and after dinner) to tolerate the return to work on Tuesday.

> <u>Tuesday-Thursday</u> - Wake up ass-crack of dawn, get dressed, deal with kids, fight traffic, fight clients, fight my urge to murder everyone in the legal profession, fight traffic home, fight toddlers throughout dinner, sometimes fight with husband, and then drink wine so I could wind down, eat ice cream / Reese's cups and drink more wine, so I could stomach doing it all again the next day.

(Why was I so tired? I did not understand.)

I was still miserable, even with my magical love for Spinning class. I was now friends with the Fat Stranger, but I was a little too friendly with her.

Instead of just making friends with her, I was making *peace* with her. I was letting the Fat Stranger run my life, instead of the other way around.

THE EMAIL: SUMMER 2010

On a Saturday night in June of 2010, the kids were asleep. The Expert and I were chilling on the back deck with a couple of Heinekens. As I cracked open my fourth beer I said to the Expert, "I don't know why I am so unhappy."

"Yeah," he said, "I don't know why either."

The Expert is a lot of things, but unhappy has never been one of them. He's just never been the type to complain or get melancholy. He's definitely the Tigger to my Eeyore.

"Maybe you should figure out why you are unhappy," he said.

"Yes, I would like to do that," I said. "And I have a sneaking suspicion that it has to do with me being fat. And this beer."

"But the beer is delicious," he said, smiling.

"Yes, but this fat is not," I said grabbing my overflowing gut.

"What about that cycling instructor guy?" the Expert asked.

"Gerry?" I asked. "What about him?"

"Didn't you say he was some sort of coach or trainer?"

I thought a minute and went inside to grab the laptop. A few minutes later, I found Gerry's website and started reading.

"You should ask him to help you," the Expert said.

"Really? He's really fit and looks busy and I think that——" I protested.

"——Do you want to change or not?"

I thought for a moment. The Expert was right. After five beers, I was brave enough and sent the Email to Gerry, asking for help. Help with my fitness. Help with my fatness. Help for a change. Just plain help.

The next morning, I woke up to find an email in response. Gerry congratulated me on my desire to change and agreed to talk with me after class on Friday. I was nervous, wondering if I had done something incredibly stupid.

I CAN DO A TRIATHLON! WAIT. RIGHT NOW?

Gerry and I spoke on the Friday after The Email. I arrived to Spinning class early and he made eye contact with me and waved. I had never talked to him before, even though I had been rolling into his class for almost a year. He must have figured out *who I was* based on the fact that I was the only fat chick in his class. As we talked, he explained that he coached triathletes.

"Are you interested in triathlon?" he asked me.

He was very close to me and it made me super nervous. I was even more nervous because he seemed to be a close-talker. *People think I'm this crazy close talker, but really I can't hear very well*, he later explained to me. Well, at this point, I was thinking, *Look, you crazy cute close-talker triathlete man, please take a step back or I am going to pass out from nervousness, high cholesterol and your general badassery.*

What did he say? *Triathlon?*

He looked at me.

"Um. Huh," I stuttered, completely confused. I knew what triathlon was. At least, I thought I knew what it was. The fancy fit people had shirts with swimmers, bikers and runners plastered all over. But I did not know what to say.

So I said, "I hadn't really thought about triathlon."

"You could do a sprint triathlon. Right now. If you wanted to," Gerry said.

I must've stared at him like he had three heads.

"You could!" he said. "I see how hard you work in class. You *could*."

I still looked at him like he was crazy.

At that moment, I was not sure that I could (or wanted) to do a triathlon. I was not sure if I wanted to talk to this clearly nutty Ironman anymore. Swimming, biking and running? That sounded… hard. And not very fat-friendly.

I was not convinced that triathlon was even possible for me, despite Gerry's urging. I left our first meeting feeling a tad deflated. Not because of anything Gerry said, but because deep down in my gut, I knew I'd be flailing again before the end of the day.

Cheers! Bring on the beer.

Be Bold, Set Goals

Turns out that less than seven weeks after my conversation with Gerry, I decided to make a run at triathlon. And that's when I made the Decision. So I guess, yes, I can thank (and blame) Gerry for my leap into triathlon.

He believed in me, and I started to believe in myself.

I Have a Point. I Swear.

So why did I just tell you my entire life story? Because I have lots of free time, of course. *Ha.*

Well, I believe that all women share similar struggles. For example, I have many beautiful friends with banging hot bodies. I would kill to live in their bodies, just for an hour or even ten minutes (I would take off all my clothes and run through my office buck-naked during those ten minutes, too). It pains me to stand by and watch those women pinch their non-existent bellies and groan, *Ugh, look at this fat!*

So, regardless of your size and place in life, I am willing to bet that you might be living in the skin of your own Fat Stranger or Unhappy Person. Maybe you run through Size Two Land, but you are miserable counting every single pea you eat. Hell, maybe you even have your own shiny Expert to boot.

I tell you about my timeline so you can see where I have been and how far I have come simply by incorporating triathlon into my life. I hope that my story will encourage you and make you believe that you can do the same.

I was living my life as a Fat Stranger and made the Decision to become a triathlete. I was clearly nuts, but I knew that I was on to something. What exactly, I was unsure. I had so much to learn about triathlon. I set a goal, but I had no idea what to do next. I was a wannabe triathlete with absolutely no races scheduled and no plan.

Gerry was around to help, but he was not my coach (yet). So I had no real resources. Plus, I had many questions. For instance: *what did I want out of the triathlon experience? What did being a triathlete really mean? How much and how often should I swim and bike and run? What is a transition? How far is a triathlon?*

Questions, questions and more questions. Because I had no idea of the answers to any of these questions, I figured the quickest way to get to a triathlon was to sign up for a race. Then, because I was obviously ill-prepared for a triathlon right out of the gate, I thought I could at least make some plans, read some books and start a flow chart or something.

Almost immediately, the planning aspect of triathlon resonated with me. Professional triathletes pick their races sometimes years in advance. Most human beings need a schedule and a plan, whether they realize it or not. Moms of zillions of kids rely on the whiteboard calendar. As an attorney, my calendar is my lifeline and safeguard against malpractice.

I was excited when I could put triathlon on the calendar. I could search online for races, calendar the race, color code it, count it down, Facebook it, Tweet it, and iWhatever it. Yes. I liked it.

Planning!

Types of Triathlons

The following table shows types and *approximate* distances of triathlon events. Individual races may vary slightly in distance, but the distance for each race is more-or-less as follows:

Type	Swim Distance	Bike Distance	Run Distance
Indoor Triathlon / Super Sprint	200 yard pool / lake swim	30 minute stationary / road bike	20-30 minute treadmill / road run
Sprint	400-500 yards	12-18 miles	3.1 miles (5k)
Olympic / International / Short Course	0.9 miles	25 miles	6.2 miles (10k)
70.3 Half-Ironman	1.2 miles	56 Miles	13.1 Half Marathon
ITU / Long Distance	2.5 miles (4k)	74 miles (120k)	18.6 miles (30k)
140.6 Ironman	2.4 miles	112 Miles	26.2 Marathon

THE THREE TIERS OF GOALS

On the day Gerry freaked me out by saying I could do a triathlon, he also imparted some fascinating wisdom to me about setting goals. He suggested that I start making some triathlon race goals, but that I do so by *staggering* the goals and creating tiers of ambition. "Most people set unrealistic goals for most anything right out the gate," he said. "The key to making goals a reality is to set goals you can attain. Then you build from there."

The tiered approach is basically a three-part triathlon goal management system. Because research has clearly revealed that people like things in threes (swim, bike, run—peanut butter, jelly, bread—salt, tequila, lime—chips, salsa, cheese dip…oh, I better stop now)…anyway, the three tiered goal system is harmonious.

For the purpose of the Every Woman triathlon journey, the Three Tiers of Goals are:

Quick Goal Race	*1-3 months*
Main Goal Race	*6-12 months*
Crazy Goal Race	*2-25 years*

The Quick Goal is a race goal with a two-or-three month turnaround. You will want to have several Quick Goals during the year to keep you moving and shaking.

The Main Goal is the big deal race of the year. This is your big race, the semi-scary goal. Ideally, this would be the end of the season or end of year finale. The Main Goal is the thing that motivates you every day in your training. When people ask you what you are training for, the Main Goal is the race you shout out.

Finally, the Crazy Goal is just that. *Cuh-ray-zee*. Absolutely huge, mind boggling and seemingly never-gonna-happen.

THE QUICK GOAL: 2-3 MONTH PLAN

With the Quick Goal, you are setting yourself up for a quick win.

> *As the Expert says,*
> *"Everybody needs a win sometimes."*

The Quick Goal is a reasonable goal that, with a little steady work, you can easily attain in two or three months. Three months is an eternity in the fitness world. Trust me on this! You will be absolutely amazed to see the progress you can make in twelve weeks *if* you are diligent.

The point of the Quick Goal? Pure and simple two things: Confidence booster! Habit former! By setting this goal and working towards it, you will get into the habit of working out and form a good trajectory for your future. Then when you complete the goal, you will feel great and want to continue! You are setting yourself up for big things in the future, but you schedule these happy Quick Goals to boost your mojo.

So what should you plan for your Quick Goal? I propose asking yourself some questions and evaluating your current fitness state. For example, if you can walk for twenty or thirty minutes right now, then sign up for a 5k (3.1 miles) race for three months down the road. For a person new to fitness, I think a 5k is a great place to start. If you were to walk 3.1 miles, it would take you close to an hour to complete. If you slowly jog it, maybe forty minutes.

When I considered *my* Three Tiers of Goals, I was forced to look at my general fitness. I had to assess my long-term training goals and formulate a schedule. I forced myself to honestly self-assess, even though it was painful. I knew that I could run/walk a 5k within a month or two. I was big and miserable, but I knew I could do it. I had done it before. It wasn't pretty, but I knew I could do it again.

The Swim Bike Mom (and now, the Every Woman) mantra is "just keep moving forward." Planning for your first goal is a solid movement forward. We like it! We like it!

RUNNING DISTANCE CONVERSIONS	
Kilometers / Type	*Miles*
5k	*3.1*
10k	*6.2*
20k	*12.4*
Half Marathon	*13.1*
Marathon	*26.2*

Here are some questions to ask when you are planning for the Quick Goal:

- Can I walk for 15 minutes now?
- Can I jog a mile?
- Can I walk three miles?
- Can I jog three miles?
- Would any of those things kill me?
- How long has been since I've exercised?
- How long will it conceivably take me to run/walk/jog three miles if I work at it, with a plan in place?
- If a gun was pointed to my head, how far could I run right now, today?

Please forgive me—I will use the gun-to-the-head analogy quite often. Perhaps there are easier ways to set goals than violent weapon imagery. But I find the gun-to-the-head proposition pretty effective.

For example, if someone walked into my house, held a gun to my head and threatened to kill me and my family, stating, "I will kill you *all* right now unless you put on your shoes and run ten miles without stopping"—then I believe I would run ten miles without stopping. I cannot say the same about twenty-eight miles. I would definitely *try*, but I absolutely do not believe I could run twenty-eight miles without stopping. Right now? No way. My poor dead family. Poor dead me.

I believe that *anyone* can run/walk a 5k within twelve weeks. So what if you can only walk for five minutes right now? Well, I believe that you can walk for ten minutes next week. And fifteen minutes the next week, and so forth.

The 5k distance is absolutely doable for your first race, no matter who you are. I will repeat: *No Matter Who You Are.*

Now, you may not be able to *run* the entire race, but you can certainly walk it and more than likely, you will run-jog-walk it. You can certainly move forward one step at a time, keep moving and cross the finish line. If you plan well, you might be able to run the whole thing for your very first race. If you have never in your life run a 5k, then *who cares* if you walk the race? Who cares if you jog it very slowly? Tons of people walk at races. Just go to a marathon and watch it. You will feel better knowing that even the marathoners spend time going slowly, catching their breath.

How you "run" your race is *up to you.* Don't forget it. This is your journey. These goals are *your goals* and you must not ever compare your goals to anything other than those ambitions in your head. Also, please note that when I use the word "run," I am using it for simplicity's sake. I am very slow. I barely jog. I say run because "Swim Bike Jog" doesn't have the same ring as "Swim Bike Run."

Some of you are coming to the table with some running experience already. My advice to you is to use the gun-to-the-head analogy and schedule that distance race for 2-3 months out.

I made my Decision and I planned for a 5k about ten weeks later. Then, I registered for it. I finished it. And the rest is history. Or something like that.

My First Quick Goal

On the first Saturday in October 2010, I left the house before the sun came up. A good fall chill was in the air. I picked up my race packet and retreated to the car to get warm. To be honest, I was nervous. In the past two months, I had run 3.1 miles on the treadmill, but not outside (and consequently, never on any hills).

I only had a few goals etched in stone: 1) run the entire race; and 2) finish in less than forty minutes. Forty minutes is about a thirteen-minute mile— meaning that it would take me about thirteen minutes to run *each* mile.

The first half-mile of the race was a steady incline, followed shortly there-after by another quarter-mile incline. I was sucking serious wind right from the start. But I continued to run. My heart pounded in my chest and I was breathing heavily. My legs were lead and everything hurt. But I finished. I finished in thirty-eight minutes and forty-three seconds (00:38:43). I jogged the entire race and my pace came in slightly faster than I had hoped, at a 12:30-minute mile.

Quick Goal #1: Check!

The funniest memory of the race was seeing a super-fit guy crossing the finish line at the same time as me. Then I realized that he was finishing the 10k (6.2 mile) race at the same time I finished 3.1 miles—I was a tad embarrassed, but I snapped out of it. I realized that I had a lot to be proud of! I had woken up early, laced up my sneakers and passed through the finish line without crawl-ing. That was a victory—a victory that my Fat Stranger could not have foreseen.

Not only was crossing that finish line a victory, but it was symbolic. My race number was 2010. As I crossed under the "FINISH" banner, I looked down at my race number.

2010. The year everything changed.

MY SECOND (WAY TOO QUICK) QUICK GOAL

I tend to do most things a little too quickly. In deciding to become a triathlete, I fully intended to take time to become acclimated to triathlon things—to go slowly, to learn.

But my first Quick Goal felt amazing! I wanted more! I began to look for the next month's goal. *Maybe I could do a sprint triathlon! Maybe!* I searched online. It was October. I learned that triathlon has a "season" which is pretty much over in October. I would be forced to wait until spring to do an actual triathlon.

Humph. I could do another 5k, I thought. *That would be practical.* But something haunted me. I was scared. I was scared that the Fat Stranger would get comfortable in the winter sweaters, eating the Christmas cookies, and I might lose momentum.

I was terrified that I would lose my way.

Then I saw it.

October 10th. 10/10/10. The last triathlon of the Georgia season. Appropriately named: *The Last Chance Triathlon.* I panicked. *My last chance! My last chance!! My laaaaaast chance!*

I had only actually ridden my bike *three* times since the Decision. I had been Spinning many times. I swam a few times. But my thinking was: *Last Chance! Now or never!* Not my smartest move, but I had seven days to get ready for my first triathlon. (Do as I say, not as I do.)

A couple of things about jumping into the first triathlon so quickly: it *was* way too soon. I *did* hurt myself, and I am still plagued with that injury. I also had the most humiliating race experience to date, as you'll read later.

But to say I was "bit by the triathlon bug" would be an understatement. I was eaten *alive* by the triathlon bug after that race. And I would not trade it for the world. Triathlon is a massive learning process. I am *not* advocating jumping into a first triathlon as hurriedly and as stupidly as I did. At the same time, I *am* advocating stepping out and embracing the fear factor(s) you may have. Because really, the fear is the worst part to something new. The brain in between your ears will be your absolutely biggest—and worst—asset during this journey. Do not let your mind bully your body. If you are often held back because of *fear*, begin to tackle that fear in your mind. Work hard to push through it.

THE MAIN GOAL: THE ONE YEAR-ISH PLAN.

The Main Goal can be anything in the world, but it should be something that a gun-to-the-head could *not* make happen today. The Main Goal is something to complete in six months to a year.

If your goal is to become a triathlete, but you are very new to fitness, then your Main Goal could be a sprint triathlon. If, for example, you had only ever run a 5k and had never swam nor biked, then setting a goal for a sprint triathlon nine months down the road would be a very (very!) attainable goal. Or, maybe running a 10k and focusing on a single sport like running is easier to digest before tackling a triathlon.

Up to you! This is *your* path! What would *you* like to achieve? No matter the Main Goal, the goal should be something feasible for you to accomplish in a six months to a year.

I set my Main Goal as completing an Olympic Distance triathlon. After I had finished my first sprint triathlon, I made the leap and set my Main Goal— so I had been training nine months by the time Olympic race day arrived. At the time of my Decision, I could not swim a mile, bike twenty-six miles, or run a 10k (the respective distances of an Olympic distance triathlon). I could not do any of those three *alone*, so I definitely could not do one right after the other in a race. Still, I figured that I had time. (Turns out, I was right.)

You may be a tad saner than I was in my goal setting, choosing to dial back the Main Goal a little. Then again, you may choose to hit the road like a maniac. The Goal Setting stage is also about self-analysis. What kind of personality do you have? Are you a pressure cooker? Do you need the heat to make things happen? Do you prefer more of a slow move towards things?

Yes, the Every Woman journey is about making bold moves and strong decisions, but that does not necessarily mean rushing into your goals. Just the exercise of setting the goals is part of your self-analysis. One of my big weaknesses is rushing into everything, so I will not be giving advice about *timing* of goals. I certainly cannot advocate moving slowly towards goals—I would be a terrible pot, preaching to the kettles of the world.

But I will advocate the importance of reaching outside *your* comfort zone in creating your Main Goal. You must s-t-r-e-t-c-h to grasp something worthwhile.

In creating your Main Goal, you should also put your money where your *mind* is. If you set the Main Goal, then register for it. Pay your money, mark the calendar and tell someone.

BE KIND TO YOURSELF.

Tell someone who will be supportive of your goals, if possible. Obviously, we all have different circumstances and people in our lives. Some of us have supportive spouses, friends and family. Others have buttheads for family members who beat them up emotionally at every turn. If you have no one in your life who will support your new quest, then *your* resolve must be strong from the outset.

If you are unsure if you can withstand hurtful comments or stares from others, then keep your goals quiet until you are certain you have become strong enough to tolerate the negativity. You may be starting this voyage from a place of rawness, a place resulting from years of fatness or sadness or defeat. Remember to take care of yourself and *treat yourself gently* as you begin.

I can promise you a few things: You *will* fall down. You *will* struggle. You *will* question whether the triathlon decision is worth it. Others *will* make fun of you. They might say cruel things to you: *You will never be a triathlete, who are you kidding?* Do not forget you are experiencing a process. Do not give up on yourself.

During this progression, you will be learning about a sport, but you will also be learning about *yourself*. You may not like the person you have been for many years. You may be filled with regret. Strangely, triathlon will help you work through these emotions because you will be experiencing yourself in a new way. No matter where you start and where you go, remember four words: Be. Kind. To. Yourself. Your journey will lead you to the person you want to be.

On the path to the Main Goal, continue to set up new Quick Goals every month or so. Again, this is about setting up and experiencing the small wins and obtaining small successes. You will naturally see your 5k races feel stronger, get faster, and become more fun instead of frightening. These Quick Goals will help build your sense of control, strength, determination and success.

You may be starting this journey from a place of rawness, a place resulting from years of fatness or sadness or defeat. Remember to take care of yourself and treat yourself gently as you begin your journey.

THE CRAZY GOAL: THE 2-25 YEAR PLAN.

The Crazy Goal is something mind-boggling—something that you cannot imagine in your wildest dreams actually completing.

From the beginning, I liked the idea of tiered goals. I really liked the Crazy Goal. My problem (well, one of many problems) is that my whole life I had habitually set what should be long-term goals—and expected them to happen quickly. For example, every winter I declared that I would lose weight and squeeze into a Size Two by the summer. This is not a Crazy Goal. This is a stupid Quick Goal.

Draw the distinction now, because it is important! You can set Quick Goals, but they should be *reasonable*. You can set ballsy goals (the Main Goal), but it should also be reasonable (even if scary) and eventually, gun-to-the-head attainable. Likewise, the Crazy Goal is something that you really have a hard time imagining—something that if you finished, you would expect someone to film a documentary about you. *But* because of the nature of the Crazy Goal, it is automatically a *long term goal*. Not a quick result deal.

The Crazy Goal is something that has a glimmer of desire and appeal. For example, if I had said: *I would like to wear a size 6 (not 2) in three years*, this might be a good Crazy Goal for me.

From the get-go with my triathlon goal setting, I thought of the Ironman race as my Crazy Goal. 140.6 miles of pure movement, crossing the finish and hoping Mike Reilly would say: "Swim Bike Mom, you are absolutely insane, but you are also an Ironman!" Interestingly, my nutty 140.6 dream has now morphed into my next Main Goal. I have paid my race registration fee for 2013 Ironman Coeur d'Alene. (*A full Ironman. Holy guacamole.*)

Before you realize it, the Crazy Goal becomes closer to being possible. This is precisely the point of the tiered goals. Once the crazy becomes sane, you are ready for even more crazy. You will be consistently moving forward, towards something bigger and better, while never blowing the bigger dreams by impossible expectations. As long as you remain focused on the Quick Goals, with an eye towards the Main Goal (obviously increasing or changing your Main Goals each "season" or year), the Crazy Goal creeps closer.

How exciting is that?

CORNER OF QUICK AND MAIN: SHOUT FROM THE ROOFTOPS.

Part of your bold Decision is telling others about your plan. I concede that this may be the most terrifying part. I walked into a job interview two months before my first Olympic distance race. I told the managing partner of the firm that if I were to be hired, I would need a few days off in May for a race.

"What kind of race?" he asked.

"Oh," I said, "you know, just a triathlon."

"Oh, that's good," he said. "Are you doing a sprint?"

"Well, actually it's an Olympic distance."

An ever-so slight pause. "Wow. How far is that?"

"Well, about one-mile swim, twenty-six on the bike, and then a 10k run."

A bigger pause and a strange nod. "Well, that's good." Pause. "Er, good luck."

Be prepared for the doubtful looks, the questioning eyes from others around you. I do not think it is necessarily malice, but oftentimes the looks are more…confusion. Terror. Curiosity. Disbelief.

At the time you set your Goals, you may not look like you can walk to the car without falling down. That's fine. Do not tell people that you have decided to become a triathlete, which will certainly result in some nutzo stares. But telling others about your *race plans* is important. Once the phrase "I have a race that weekend" leaves your lips, you will feel things begin to change within yourself.

KEEP THE CRAZY TO YOURSELF.

As far as the Crazy Goal is concerned, write it on a piece of paper and slip it into your sock drawer where you will see it sometimes. Tape it to the bathroom mirror. Make it your phone screensaver. But don't tell others about the Crazy Goal (unless they, too, are crazy). Once you begin triathlon, everyone outside of the sport will already think you are a loon. Leave well enough alone. The Crazy should stay in your head (for now) or be shared only with the small group of fellow triathlon crazies that you will later meet.

> *"You're only given a little spark of madness.*
> *You mustn't lose it."*
>
> — ROBIN WILLIAMS

TWO

Getting Started in Triathlon

I MADE THE DECISION.
I SET THE GOALS. WHAT NEXT?

My next question after my Decision was: what did I need for triathlon? What did I need *to do* for triathlon? Well, for starters, I needed to swim, bike and run. But I would worry about that later. So instead of worrying about the actual sports and how in the world I was going to make my Fat Stranger do the swim-bike-run, I chose to work with what I knew: reading and sitting.

I began reading and reading and reading about triathlon. I accumulated a few books for beginner triathletes, books about sprint triathlons and checklists for necessary gear. I picked up a copy of Jayne Williams' book, *Slow Fat Triathlete*[iv] (henceforth known as "SFT"). Oh, SFT was a fire starter. The tagline for that book is "Living your athletic dreams in the body you have now." She obviously wrote that book just for me. Obviously.

I had been holding on to this ideal: *If I lose weight, then I can run. If I lose weight, then I can do a race. Then maybe I will wear cute clothes to the gym.* SFT basically said to forget that ideal. Become who you want to be *now*. In the body you have *now*.

I can't take credit for this philosophy, but I can tell you that the Every Woman philosophy is definitely built on the SFT philosophy. *What are you waiting for? Be who you want to be now! Go go go!* If you wait, then it will never happen. I promise you that. Change causes change. That's, interestingly, how it all works.

I am a bit of a Type-A personality. The SFT philosophy feels a little more relaxed than ole Swim Bike Mom can be, even on Valium. Not that I'm on Valium. For starters, I believe in whole body, soul, family and job *immersion* into triathlon. Not like a cult. (You don't have to stop reading here, Mom.) But a whole-heart, healthy immersion—a schedule and a goal setting plan that becomes a big part of your everyday life. Incorporating triathlon into the threads of your life is an important component to successes in triathlon *and* life, no matter how small those successes may be.

I also believe that changing your body (or wanting to change your body) is *not* a bad thing. I believe that you should get moving *right now*, but I also see no harm in wanting to wear a bikini or desiring to have a six-pack under your shirt. I also believe that you must celebrate the body you have now, not for the way it *looks*—but for the awesome things it can *do*. Triathlon will bring that to your life. You will see.

For some people, having triathlon as a weekend fun "hobby" is enough. You may be okay with a few races here and there. And that is great! Every little bit of dedication and inspiration is life-changing. But I swear, for the true Every Women of the world, triathlon becomes a *necessary* schedule and foundation for a hectic day-to-day life. The immersion method is healing, methodical and cathartic. You will want to kill far fewer people in your daily life if you buy into the sport—hook, line and sinker.

Triathlon also walks hand-in-hand with your spiritual foundation. I promise that you will talk to your God more than you ever have before. *Dear God, make this run stop. Dear Lord, I swear I will never eat again if you can just make this hill climb end. Heavenly Father, please take away my bicycle so I no longer put myself through this pain. God, please let the pool be closed today...*

So while I will often draw on the SFT ideal of tri-ing in the body I have now, the Every Woman philosophy is a whole-life method—a little more extreme. The Every Woman way takes into account the wife, mother, and employee balance that triathlon will conquer and make better for you. Be who you are, most definitely. But strive to be the best *you* possible. Move forward in the body you have now, yes. But dream bigger dreams for yourself than the outside world can imagine or understand.

Start in the body you are living in right now. Do it for *you*. And no one else. Then go a step farther…and dream big.

THE GREAT GYM CAPER

GET FREE COOKIES

One thing I did correctly during the beginnings of the Every Woman journey was take advantage of the free cookies. I heard about that Lunch & Learn where I discovered the gym membership. Even though I did not decide to become a triathlete until much later, the gym was the foundation.

At said Lunch & Learn, the saleswoman gave me free cookies and a gym bag for joining the gym. Ironically, my never-ending quest for snack food walked my fat butt right through the doors of a gym. Take advantage of a deal for the sake of the deal. Gyms run deals all the time. Look for them.

GET A GYM MEMBERSHIP WITH A POOL.

A pool is a bigger deal than you may realize in the early stages. You will need a pool if you are thinking of triathlon (ah-hem, *swim*, bike and run). So get a gym with a pool. The ole YMCA usually has a pool (bonus: with lifeguards) and a very reasonable membership plan. Sometimes, if you have friends join you, they may have reciprocal discounts.

THE MEGA GYM

If you live near and can afford the Mega Gym, go forth and be a Mega Gym member! I promise you won't be sorry. A Mega Gym is one of those giant chain gyms like LifeTime, Bally's or LA Fitness.

First, the Mega Gym will have large pools with lap lanes. Waiting on a lap lane for swimming may remain a necessary evil, but the Mega Gym lanes rotate more quickly. The Mega Gym is less likely to have the infamous "Pool Closed for Cleaning" sign propped up for weeks on end. (Nothing will bring on the triathlon rage like a scheduled swim and a closed pool.) The Mega Gym possesses the resources and staff to tend to pool maintenance, so the pools are simply cleaner and closed less often. (Perhaps because the one million members would revolt.)

Additionally, the Mega Gym will often have swim equipment, such as kick boards and pull floats, readily available for your use. This doesn't seem like a big deal until you are juggling high heels, a suit and a wet pull float under your arm on your way to work. I speak from experience. Dry suit + wet pull float = ridiculous morning.

The Mega Gym will have numerous group fitness classes, lots of open door time (often 24 hours) and state of the art fitness equipment. The Mega Gym will usually have multiple locations, so you can get into all locations with your one membership wherever they may be located If you are a traveling employee, this is the shizzle.

Finally, the Mega Gym will usually have childcare (aka, babysitters!). This small factor will become priceless (if you have kids). The fact that someone at your gym will play with your rug-rats while you catch an hour long swim and quick run is one hundred percent worth the extra coin. The kids will be exposed to fun activities and get in the habit of seeing Mom swim, bike and run.

The Swim Bike Family works and lives in three different cities, so we actually possess membership cards to three gyms. Yes, I understand that is pure insanity. But with three gyms, one in every city the Expert or I could drive through at any given moment, we cannot find a real excuse to skip a workout. "Oh, I just can't get to the gym today." *Wrong* (insert buzzer sound here). I understand that three gyms are insane. I did not claim triathlon to be sane (or especially cheap). I'm sorry in advance.

But you will be surprised how much money you save not ordering Pizza Hut. It will easily pay for your gym membership(s). 1 large delivery pizza ordered every Friday night = $15 x 4 = $60 a month. That's the difference between the YMCA and the Mega Gym…for your entire family. If you eat out more than once a week, start running those numbers and you'll have the money for your new road bike.

Just saying.

THE 24-HOUR DISCOUNT GYM

I love the 24-hour fitness places (like Anytime Fitness or 24-Hour Fitness). But usually those gyms don't have pools. You need a pool if you want to swim, obviously. If you can find a pool for free somewhere else (neighborhood pool, etc.), then the 24-hour gyms *sans* pool are a good option.

GET A MEMBERSHIP TO A GYM NEAR WHERE YOU WORK.

A gym near the office? Really? Not by my house? Really. By your office, job, fabulous place of employment is where you should make your gym home. If you are a working stay-at-home mom, then a gym near your house may be easier because your job *is* at home. See how easy?

Here's why: Being a busy woman may require you to squeeze in workouts before the sane people (or your children or significant others) are awake.

In a nutshell, in the morning (once you have worked the schedule out with your significant other, your sitter, and/or your family), you will wake up, head straight to the gym, workout, shower, snack and have a short 5-10 minute commute to your job, thus beating any traffic. If you obtain a gym membership by your house it's easier to make an excuse to avoid it. *Oh, I woke up late. My commute is already behind schedule. Oh, I can sleep in if I skip.* It may not be statistically proven, but I've done both. Having the gym near the office is hands-down the better route for triathlon. Plus, if you are lucky (and this is the best part), some days in the hot summer, you can sneak to the pool on your lunch break. No, not for your swim. But to take a mental health lunch and eat your food by the pool.

You might only be able to workout after work, for reasons related to schedules, family and daycare. I urge you, however, to do your best to make morning workouts part of your routine..if at *all* possible. If not, then try to squeeze in your workout *immediately* after work—before going home and starting dinner and the kids' homework. If you can, hit the gym or the track directly on your way home from work—before the tornado of home responsibilities sweep you in. The later in the day you wait to train, the more likely the excuses ("I don't have time *now* that dinner is on the stove!") will mysteriously appear.

If you have an evil commute, then you may need to explore the two gym option. I'm not kidding, because you'll need your "home" gym on the weekends and your "work" gym during the week.

CAUTIONARY GYM/WORK TALE

I must caution you regarding the gym near the office. There may be a chance that *other* people who work in your office might also be members of the same gym. (Meaning: you can't play hooky from work to go workout).

I had not considered the other issues that could arise when I joined the Mega Gym near my firm. For example, in my weightlifting days, I changed clothes in front of people. Everyone did. But in the "real" world, outside of competitive sports, not as many people drop clothes in front of others in locker rooms. Normal people apparently do not appreciate seeing unattractive strangers in their birthday suits. So, I took the social cues and kept my nakedness to myself for most of my gym time at my work gym.

I would change clothes in the dressing rooms or the bathroom stalls for the longest while. But after many days at the gym and trying to sneak in workouts at lunch, the whole showering and hiding act became time-consuming. I was fretting about showing any *single potentially* offensive body part *and* getting to work on time.

So, because of the time crunch, my shower-to-clothes transition became: shower, wrap towel around self, run to locker, glance around quickly to see if I was likely to offend anyone, drop towel and haul butt to wiggle into my underpants, bra and clothes. This practice saved me all sorts of time, and if anyone saw me, hopefully the offense was short-lived. Or if they were offended, then perhaps my lightning speed haste to cover my buns was, at least, acknowledged and appreciated.

One lunchtime workout, just a few months after I joined a firm, I had a lunchtime swim. After the shower, I did my pre-towel-drop-look-around and saw a girl, completely clothed and with her back to me, standing a few feet away. *Nope, don't know her*, I thought, and I dropped my towel. Suddenly as she began to turn towards me, I recognized the skirt she was wearing. I pulled my towel back up quickly.

"Oh, hey!" I exclaimed.

My new legal assistant. I had complimented her on that very skirt only a few hours before.

Back and forth we mutter, "Uh um, hey, uh, how was your workout," trying to avoid the weirdness that is me standing there with essentially no clothes on. She was clearly embarrassed. I mean, I had worked at the firm for all of two weeks. Plus, who wants to see a co-worker in a towel (well, most co-workers)?

She was embarrassed and I was awkward, but really I was thinking, *Oh man, you have no idea how bad that was about to be. You would have had water cooler gossip for a hundred years with what you* almost *saw. And, boy, am I glad that I liked your skirt so much or I would have never recognized you and you would have turned around to be staring right at my boobs and…other things.*

What if I can't find FREE cookies?

What if the gym does not have any real deals? Well, then you buy the full price cookies for Pete's sake! Triathlon is about changing your life. If you have to pay for the expensive cookies, then you should pay for them. Obviously, if you can find a good deal, then you should go that route. But if you need to skip your Starbucks and budget yourself a gym membership, then you should make a budget and make the gym a priority after mortgage, childcare and food.

To My Mid-Size Town Friends

I grew up in Savannah, Georgia where no Mega Gym existed. But we had the YMCA and new gyms were popping up all the time. If you are in the midsize town, you may have to try a little harder to find gym access that works, but you can do it. The access is there, but it may not be as fancy as Mega Gyms.

Also, some smaller gyms in mid-size towns will provide exceptional comic relief, especially some of the fitness classes. After I made my Decision, I had a short membership at a YMCA in the burbs which had an early morning cycling class. I had attended Gerry's class for a while, so I was accustomed to exceptionally well-taught, cycling-driven classes full of triathletes, marathoners, and general crazy fitness people.

At this local YMCA, I walked into a whole new world of indoor cycling class. My first class was on a Saturday morning and I was one of four people in the class. The cycling instructor had no water bottle of his own and was wearing more fat than I was. I noticed that he wore a warm-up jacket, which he never removed from his body until the bitter end. The pre-class playlist consisted only of Winger and Twisted Sister. When the instructor wanted us to raise the resistance on the bike, he would shout, "Put on the work!" (And bless his heart, he taught the entire class without opening his eyes.)

Another class I took was led by a woman who had a good forty pounds on me. I am ashamed to say that I thought to myself, *Geez, why is* she *teaching this class?* Regardless, I learned my lesson after her class. She may have been "bigger," but she was also tough—her class goes down as one of the top five toughest classes of my life.

Both types of classes taught me lessons. First, the class with Mr. Eyes Closed Instructor was invaluable. I did not leave that class despite my burning desire to walk out. He taught me a lesson in self-motivation. I can admit it is difficult to love an indoor cycling class when the leader just landed from some alternate universe, but these experiences prove exactly how *personal* the triathlon journey is. I continue to learn that the *quality* of each workout is in my sole discretion. The class is always *my* ride, regardless of who is leading me. At the end of the day, each workout and training session is on my shoulders. A great, but scary thought.

Second, I learned to never underestimate people because of the way they look. I should have known better by simply being *me*. But I officially learned my lesson.

TO MY SMALL TOWN FRIENDS

Genuine small towns are tough when it comes to gyms. I lived in a *very* small town the first two years I practiced law. By small town, I mean population under two thousand people. I understand that my small town friends reading this book might be feeling pretty hopeless at this point. The Mega Gym? Hell, even a gym membership? Sometimes these salt-of-the-earth places have superb cocktail parties, but no gyms. Or if there's a gym, you might be staring at two 1990-model treadmills, a squeaky wind-propelled stationary bike and a couple of odd weights (if you are lucky).

For my small town friends, I propose a different track for you. Swim only on the weekends in the closest mid-sized town with a gym/pool. Invest your money in a solid road bike and an indoor bike trainer (discussed later). Finally, become an all-weather runner. You may not have the advantage of Spinning classes and yoga, but you have other benefits (like becoming an incredibly tough outdoor runner).

Your sacrifice may be greater at the outset, but the quiet country weekends, the lazy mornings and the peaceful scenery will make you into a great athlete. You will find no better road biking location than winding country roads. Finally, the community will love you because you will be something for everyone to talk about: *Did you know that crazy girl is doing them there tri-ath-a-lawns? See her? There she goes, running again. She's gonna have a heart attack!*

A GYM? BUT I STILL DON'T HAVE THE MONEY.

I can appreciate that times are tough. But again, *this is about changing your life.* Women will sacrifice for children. Women will sacrifice for husbands. Women will sacrifice for church, pets, co-workers, and random people on the street. Now it's time for *you* to sacrifice…for *you*.

If the gym costs $80 a month, then clip coupons to save that amount of money in groceries. Turn off your cable (we have). Figure it out, make a way. Push your sofa against the wall and get (steal, if necessary) a stationary bike and treadmill. Watch YouTube videos for crazy at-home workouts.

If you still say "I don't have the money" or "I just can't," then you are full of excuses and I am tired of beating this dead bicycling horse. I have to move on to others who are *willing* to make it happen.

Simply put, there are *ways*. Most Every Woman *is* tired, money-tight, and out-of-shape. The question is: how much are you willing to give up? How much are you willing to sacrifice to have a better life?

For now, if you can find a good deal on a gym, sign up. If you can't find a good deal, sign up anyway. Make the budget happen. Outside of food, family, shelter and gas for your car, comes gym membership and triathlon equipment. You will need the pool. Bike and run are possible without the gym, but the pool is tough. I don't know about yours, but my bathtub is not big enough for laps.

Admit when you've made a bad membership decision.

If you pick a "bad" gym and you don't find out until later, do not be afraid to jump ship and find another place. Ideally, the gym will have a month-to-month agreement, so you will not lose (much) money.

I have been through no less than five different gyms until I have settled on the routine and place that is right for me and my family. Be prepared to be flexible, but at the same time do not tolerate mediocrity if other options are available. However, sometimes mediocrity is all you've got. At that point, the master is y-o-u. Your strength and creativity will be a big part of your mental toughness.

All the Gear

Regardless of how confused I was about triathlon, I knew one thing was certain: the sport required a lot of *stuff*. I would need to budget for the *stuff* and figure out where to buy the *stuff*. Most importantly, I would need to figure out if my *bodily stuff* could possible squeeze into any triathlon-sized *stuff* on the market.

If you are a gear and gadget junkie, then you have landed on a great sport. Three sports mean three times the paraphernalia, which equates to twelve times the confusion. Here's the quick and dirty scoop on the equipment needed to head towards your Main Goal as quickly as humanly possible.

TRIATHLON ON THE CHEAP

"Cheap triathlon" is an oxymoron. But save a dollar and lose your mind, the Expert always says. Still, with a bit of creativity, the below items can hit your purse for around $300. Do not forget about eBay and Craigslist as a starting point for deals on gear either. Additionally, races will often have swim caps, water bottles and discounted gear at the day-before-race expo events.

Many of us have a bike stashed in storage and an old, ugly one-piece swimsuit. Yes, the bike probably stinks and is old as all Christmas, but it might be enough to get you through for a bit. At the bare minimum, take the old bike to a bike store and get it adjusted to fit you as best as possible. If you have access to a cycling class at your gym, then you are in a good place to start training for triathlon.

For riding, padded shorts are a necessity. Pain on the Queen will deter your return to the bike. (Who is the Queen? If you can't figure it out, then ride an ill-fitting bike without padded shorts…and you'll learn.) Investing in a pair of padded (chamois) shorts will make cycling life more tolerable. I am a fan of chamois capri leggings by Louis Garneau®. Even at my size I am wearing a women's large, which is a small triathlon miracle. Garneau sizes go up to women's 2XL and are available through Amazon.com and many cycling retailers.

Finally, even on the "cheap," you need excellent running shoes (discussed below).

> **Swim:** an old one-piece tank swimsuit; goggles ($15); swim cap ($5); borrow/rent a wetsuit for open water practices, if necessary
> **Bike:** your old bike in the garage; a new helmet ($30); water bottle ($5); access to a gym with a cycling class ($65 a month); chamois (padded) shorts ($50); find an old tire pump
> **Run:** sports bra ($20); excellent shoes and socks ($110)

Race Day: borrow a triathlon top and shorts, or get creative with your own do-it-yourself tri outfit (see below, race day clothing); borrow/rent a wetsuit if necessary

The Experience: FREE! And so worth it!

TRIATHLON ON THE SEMI-CHEAP

The next step-up in budgetary considerations would be to purchase a bike and a swimsuit.

Swimsuit? Swimsuit? The horror! Trust me, I completely understand. Still, if we are talking triathlon, we've gotta talk swimsuits.

You will want a one-piece, sensible suit (no skirts or tanks or board shorts). The shoulder and back straps should be reasonably thick and supportive. If the suit "holds you in" and feels comfortable, then it's doing the job. If you are an average sized gal, something from Athleta or Speedo® is going to suit you just fine. The larger crowd (mine) may not fit into these brands. Although one-piece swimming suits are absolutely hideous and scream "Watch out, here comes the tubby swimmer," I found a comfortable and practical tank suit at Junonia.com when I was starting out. Later, I could wear an XL Tall in Athleta suits when wearing size 14/16 clothing.

You will learn that triathlon clothing can be exceptionally undersized, which can be incredibly discouraging for us normal to larger women. Larger size tri clothing exists, but be prepared to hunt for it or to wear men's sizes. Other great places for finding larger size women's sports clothing are AeroTechDesigns.com, Amazon.com, and Junonia.com.

If your bike is a piece of crap, causes you physical pain to ride or feels "off," then you are probably in the market for a new(er) bike that fits you. Proper bike fit is monumental. The bike, of course, is your biggest investment, which is why I mentioned using the old dusty one in the garage for a bit. Still, a proper bike fit is something I cannot emphasize enough. From a motivational standpoint, if your bike is troublesome, you will hate the sport or think you are in worse shape than you actually are. Therefore, investing in a reasonable bike should take high priority. Many bike stores carry used bikes, and the folks there can advise on your bike fit. Either way: get fitted.

Excellent running shoes are absolutely non-negotiable. Find a running store in your town (or in the closest city). You should look for one of the places where the folks make you run on the treadmill while watching your gait, and where the employees look like they stepped off a twenty-mile trail run. These are the *loco* running people you can trust. Listen to what they say and buy what they recommend. Eight or nine times out of ten, they'll put you in a great shoe—and if not, they usually have great "run and return" policies if you have trouble with the fit.

Running shoes are a complete enigma to me. If I go to a store and wade through the shoes on my own, I will walk out with a flashy looking pair. However, the look of the shoe has very little to do with the performance of the shoe, the impact on my run, my knees and my desire to put another foot forward. I had a sweet pair of brand new Nikes when I did my first triathlon. Not blaming the shoes, but I did bring a hip injury into the equation. Spending time reading online about shoes makes my eyes cross, so once I realized that people out there existed to help me make the decision, it was a big relief, as well as a money and joint saver.

I won't get into the great shoe debate: minimalist, stability, neutral, orthotics, inserts, barefoot or the brands. Just go get a professional shoe fit and go from there. You will learn what makes your runs more comfortable, enjoyable and injury-free. The best way to figure out which type of shoe you love is to run in different kinds of shoes. I happen to like a more stable shoe just from the sheer impact factor (my weight). Mountain Goat runs almost on her bare hooves (she's tiny). Just one word to the group of us who are, *er,* heavier—don't let someone talk you into a minimalist or barefoot-style shoe. Starting out, the pounding will be too great on the body—you will want some sort of cushion on the bottoms of your feet. Eventually, you may decide to transition to something more minimalist, but go slowly into this transition.

The below items can hit your purse for around $750, if you get some decent bargains. Note: I have not listed the essential winter gear you may need to run or ride outside. This list is assuming that you will do most of your training indoors during the colds months, and hoping that you can catch the end of season winter sales for the next year.

> **Swim:** one-piece tank swimsuit ($65); goggles ($15); swim cap ($5); borrow wetsuit for practices in open water
>
> **Bike:** an entry level/used road bike with bottle cage ($350); water bottles ($5); new helmet ($30); access to a gym with a cycling class ($75 a month); chamois (padded) shorts ($60); bike pump ($25)

Run: sports bra ($20); excellent shoes and socks ($100); heart rate monitor ($90); Fuel Belt® ($50)

Race Day: Discount tri shorts and top ($60); borrow/rent a wetsuit

The Experience: Yes, still FREE! And so amazing!

TRIATHLON: THE BEGINNER'S WISH LIST

If you have and want to sink some cashola into a "hobby," you have chosen the right money pit. You will be surprised how quickly you will justify the extravagant expenditures for the sake of health, when really, you just want the shiny new Shimano shoes and Pearl Izumi arm warmers (in the summer). But I justify blowing cash for the benefit of my triathlon lifestyle because…*well, it's for my health.*

Repeat after me: These fancy new socks are for my health. My $170 ISM® Adamo bike saddle is for my health. Which actually, it is. A good saddle will save the Queen's health. (Again, if you don't know who the Queen is yet, you will—especially if you skimp on a good saddle.)

The below items can hit your purse like lightning, but if you have the cash to blow, triathlon is your playground.

Swim: one-piece tank swimsuit ($75); goggles, 2 pair ($50); swim caps ($20); wetsuit ($250); TriSlide ($12); kickboard ($30); fins ($50); paddles ($40); swim mesh bag ($20); hair care for swimming ($40)

Bike: road bike[1] ($1000-6500) and saddle ($200); new helmet ($100); cycling shoes ($200); pedals ($100); water bottles ($15); rear bottle cage/hydration system ($40-150); bike bento box ($25); access to a gym with a cycling class ($75 a month); chamois (padded) shorts ($90); pump ($50); tubes, C02 cartridges ($40); sunglasses ($100); bicycle trainer / indoor Spinning bike for house ($250-450); cycling jersey ($90); arm warmers ($30); shoe covers ($30); cycling tights ($60); outer layer jacket ($100)

---

1   I recommend a *road* bike for a beginner. Tri bikes are expensive, and they can be hard to handle if you are new to cycling. If you can score a tri bike for a fraction of the original price, however, it might be worth the added difficulty. Otherwise, start with the cheaper, more beginner-friendly road bike.

Run: sports bras ($100); two pairs of excellent shoes and many pairs of excellent socks ($200); GPS heart rate monitor ($400); wicking running shirts ($150); several pairs of running shorts ($150); running capris ($50); warm-up pants ($60); compression socks/sleeves ($60); visor ($25); Fuel Belt® ($50); Camelbak® ($75)

Race Day: triathlon suit / shorts & top ($150); transition mat ($30); gear bag ($75)

What in the World Do I Wear?

Official triathlon (racing) clothing is not an immediate requirement. In the beginning, you simply need clothes to wear while training. *Thank goodness.* I was horrified that first time I attempted to find a genuine triathlon suit. The 2XL women's sizes barely fit me, and apparently, that's the biggest size available in women's triathlon gear.

Off to the men's clothing with me.

When the time comes for the search for your triathlon race day clothing, remember that I share in your frustration. If you are plus-size—may the force be with you. I hope to change that issue in the future, but for now, there are ways around it as I'll discuss in the race day section.

Swim Clothing

The bad news: you cannot swim in a tankini with a skirt or board shorts. Triathlon clothing is tight and slim cut because it actually *needs* to be. The bigger and baggier the clothing, the more "drag" in the water. Baggy clothing *will* get in the way. I learned this lesson the hard way. The first time I wore a tankini and board shorts in the water, I literally pulled down my own drawers when I pushed off the wall for the first lap—the drag of the water pulled my bottoms down to my knees. (Much more embarrassing than showing my fat thighs in a bathing suit.)

Now, there are some two-piece triathlon swimsuits but I couldn't imagine wearing them because I would scare everyone out of the pool. For simplicity's sake, get thyself into a one-piece, sensible *swim*suit without skirts or shorts or tops. A one-piece ugly ole thing that holds you in and covers your boobage is just what the triathlon doctor ordered.

Yes, I am serious.

Cycling Clothing

You need semi-fitted cycling clothing. A loose shirt will catch wind and have you sporting a parachute on your back. Fitted clothing is often horrifying. I still wear loose tops to indoor cycling class, but I proudly sport my fat rolls in fitted jerseys and shorts when I am out on the roads cycling. I try to get away with a nice performance (wicking) shirt sometimes and some tighter shorts or capri pants on "fat" days. I am still very uncomfortable in very tight clothing, so I find what I can tolerate that still gives me the best performance. Then, I hope for the best and am careful about letting people take pictures and tag me on Facebook.

Regardless of what is covering my bum, you can bet that I am sporting some sort of padding in the shorts for the Queen. This padding is called a chamois (pronounced "shammy"). After a while in the bike seat (saddle), the Queen starts to hurt and grow grumpy from the pressure. The chamois pad will relieve some of this pressure and discomfort. Look for a one-piece chamois pad, as it has fewer surface seams for chafing and pain.

If I had money to spend on a single piece of official triathlon clothing for the initial investment, I would go with the chamois shorts. The padding makes the cycling experience much more enjoyable right out of the gate.

Run Clothing

Running is possible in virtually any clothing—just ask the firefighters who run full marathons in their fire garb. I prefer compression-style capri leggings for my bottoms, a good sports bra and a semi-loose-fitting wicking shirt. When I began running, though, I wore old t-shirts, shorts and pants left over from weightlifting days. Like I said, you can get by with running in most anything.

We'll talk a little more about proper shoe fit later, but plan to walk/run/jog yourself almost immediately to a running shoe store and get fitted for proper shoes. And don't pick your shoes based on color.

Good socks are like good shoes. If you purchase your shoes at a reputable running store, chances are that you will be offered some new socks. Get some good, synthetic material socks (*not* cotton, whatever you do). And yes, at fifteen dollars a pair, most are worth it, as long as you have your laundry monster under control (the monster that lives in your dryer and eats socks). Give the monster a good talking to and get yourself some nice sockage.

I'm also a huge fan of the Headsweats visors for running indoors and outside. The visor acts like a sweatband and is machine washable. The Expert and I probably have twenty between us.

Some women like hairbands. I cannot stand the pressure of a hairband on my head, but really, it's all about personal preference. Hairbands can be super sassy and stylish, so if you are sassy, then you might like a hairband. I have heard that Sweaty Bands® make great hairbands that stay put and look cute.

THE UNDERGARMENTS

A well-fitting sports bra is necessary for keeping the Girls under control during all your biking and most importantly, running. You want some sort of wicking fabric to pull the moisture away from your skin. A pure cotton bra will retain moisture, which will *never* dry out in a race and can lead to chafing. Your bra should reign the Girls in, but also be comfortable.

When you are trying on bras, do the in-place jogging test. If you jog in-place and your boobs stay reasonably put, the bra feels good and you like it—then you have a good start. If you jump and your boobs knock the dressing room door open, find another one to try. The truth of the matter is that it's hard to tell if you have a good bra until you've worn it through a hard workout. When you find a good one, buy ten of them.

Finally, what about underwear?

I have learned some interesting things about the woes of underwear as I have gone down the triathlon road. If you are on the bike for long, underwear is a sworn enemy. A front wedgie on the bike is horrendous and will make you quit triathlon forever. Also, the underwear seams will create even more issues for your parts. For now, if you want to wear underwear under your run shorts or pants or cycling shorts, go right ahead. But eventually, you'll be riding commando.

Yes, oh yes, yes, you will. Trust me.

Part of the reason I am *dying* for my mom to try a triathlon is just so I can have this conversation with her:

Mom: What do I wear under this short?
Me: Nothing.
Mom: (Look of absolute horror). Nothing?!

RACE DAY CLOTHING

The biggest triathlon mystery is *not* how to run. It is what to wear on race day. Race day clothing is a nightmare! Run screaming into the night right now, I tell you. Okay, seriously. What in the world do you wear on race day? I have tried everything out there. Okay, maybe not everything.

But here's *the* secret: find *one* thing to wear. Put it on before the swim. Then swim. Then bike. Then run. Then take it off when you get home. Are you confused yet?[2]

In a race you should aim to wear a one-piece triathlon suit or a two-piece triathlon kit. A "kit" is usually a top and bottom combo that looks fancy. Regardless of whether you have a suit or a kit, your race day clothing is designed to be worn in all three stages of the race. In other words, you do not take it off!

Magic!

With the exception of the wetsuit (if needed), you need not put *on* any other piece of clothing. This *also* means that you need *not* take *off* any clothing. You wear your wetsuit (again, only if needed) *on top* of your triathlon suit/kit. After the swim, you strip off the wetsuit, put on your helmet and cycling shoes and are ready to go. You should never (ever) show your goodies in transition area.[3] Ever. Ever. The best way to avoid showing others your *stuff* is to keep your clothes *on*.

A triathlon suit/kit is typically made of a moisture wicking material and has a pad in the short for cycling. The pad is thin, unlike the thick chamois pad for cycling, so you will want to spend some time on your bike wearing it ahead of time in order to get the Queen accustomed to less padding. But the thin pad allows the Queen's castle to dry much more quickly and not take on water like a diaper during the swim.

When you finish your swim, you will be soaking wet, this is true. But within a few minutes on the bike, you will find yourself almost dry. By the time you get to the run, you will not be thinking about your wet hair. This is the true beauty of the triathlon suit/kit. You may start out hating it, but eventually, you will love it. The darn thing is just so practical.

---

2   Wearing one thing is the name of the game in shorter distance races, up to a half Ironman®. Once you are in Iron distance territory, all bets are off – I have been told you wear whatever in the world will get you to the finish.

3   In longer distance races (think: Ironman®), there are changing tents – but that is because these races last from about 12-17 *hours*. You will not need to change clothes for a 2-3 hour event.

Watch a video of the Ironman World Championships on YouTube and you'll get the idea of what people are wearing. Now, *those* people are particularly fit and wearing very tiny outfits, but the idea is the same. A challenge is finding triathlon clothing that you love. I have found that people will go through two or three suits/kits until they find "the" one they love.

An even bigger challenge arises if you are a size 12 or larger. For these sizes, I recommend starting with Louis Garneau brand, Team Estrogen (www.teamestrogen.com) or Aero Tech Designs online (www.aerotechdesigns.com). Aero Tech and Team Estrogen sell a wide range of plus-size cycling and triathlon clothing. Garneau also makes triathlon clothing up to an XXL women's (available on Amazon.com and All3Sports.com).

Additionally, you may want to cross over into men's tri wear, which goes up into larger sizes (check out All3Sports.com). I have found the menswear provides greater coverage and more flexibility. Sometimes the men's suits are just going to fit better due to sheer sizing issues. I can barely ever squeeze into traditional women's tri clothing, but I often find that an XL or 2XL men's suit will do the trick, and really looks just fine.

From smallest clothing types to largest (Size 16 or XXL to Size 26), you can search for your apparel from retailers in this general order: Zoot®, Sugoi and Pearl Izumi; Danskin®, Moving Comfort®, and New Balance; Team Estrogen (Terry Cycling), Nike, Aerotech Designs and Junonia.[v]

What if you cannot find anything to fit you (or that you would want to wear in public)? First of all, remember the *Slow Fat Triathlete* wisdom: *do not care about what you look like when you are moving.* Worrying about how you look will undermine your ultimate goal—finishing the race. That being said, I understand. You may think, *I cannot wear this horrible looking triathlon suit.* But you better do it, because if you are wearing something *different*, you will stand out much more than you would have imagined. And there are ways around it.

TRIATHLON SUIT: ONE-PIECE

Many manufacturers make a one-piece triathlon suit. It's typically a one-piece zip-up number that fits like a swimsuit with shorts attached. I like the one-piece suits because you do not have to worry about the top riding up and showing your belly. I also find that the one piece compression suits "hold in" some of my jiggles.

The biggest negative with a one-piece suit is the difficulty to get in and out of it for bathroom purposes. But once you learn how to pee on the move (er, through your suit), you will not have to worry about that. (Yes, I'm sorry, it's true). My favorite suit ever (which is featured on the cover of this book) is a one-piece and was purchased from Aerotech Designs online.

You can spend $75-300 on a one-piece suit, depending on the brand and material (compression, pro-fabric, etc.).

TRIATHLON SUIT: TWO-PIECE

Two-piece suits are the most common deal on a race course. If they are matchy and have team logos, they are often called "triathlon kits." Kits are very common on thin triathletes who have no issues with fat rolls and sausage legs. Traditional kits are slim cut and super tight—so they are tough for a larger-bodied woman or a beginner unaccustomed to Spandex to even fathom wearing. But they sure look snazzy—yes, even on the Every Woman. But a kit has its many advantages: you can use the bathroom much easier; you can mix tops and bottoms; and you can look super fly.

The question of one-piece or two-piece is simply a matter of personal preference. You can spend $70-$150 for *each* piece of a tri kit.

DO-IT-YOURSELF TRIATHLON CLOTHING

Say you have a fitted wicking racer-back tank that you love and want to wear in the race. For example, a good choice is the Nike Women's Shape Sport Top, which goes up to plus sizes. If you have this top or something similar, you can always purchase a separate tri short to wear and *Voila!* You will have a self-made kit of sorts. A good bottom choice (in sizes up to XXL) is Danskin Tri Short or Athleta's Spin Short.

Whichever top you choose, just remember, remember, remember—buy a *triathlon* short, *not* a *cycling* short to complete your kit. Any cycling short will turn into a swim diaper during the swim.

Tri Suit Shopping Scoop

Smaller Fit Sizing:
Zoot, 2XU, Soas Racing, Sugoi, Betty Designs (so cute, and so tiny), DeSoto (a fold-over waistband would appear to give more room, but is still teeny—I could pull the shorts up to my knees…yay)

True to Size:
Pearl Izumi, Skirt Sports®, and TYR® are pretty true-to-fit women's brands.

Brands with Looser Fit or Larger Options:
Louis Garneau, Nike, Team Estrogen (Terry), Orca, Junonia, New Balance, Moving Comfort, Danskin (you can easily find sizes up to XXL and sometimes 4XL).

Good Places to Find Suits of All Sizes:
All3Sports.com, TeamEstrogen.com, Athleta.com, Amazon.com

Good Places to Find the Bigger-Sized Brands:
AerotechDesigns.com, TeamEstrogen.com, Amazon.com, Athleta.com (a few pieces), MovingComfort.com, Junonia.com (I like the swimsuits only)

RACE DAY CLOTHING DO'S AND DON'TS

Please, please do not wear a "real" bra anywhere near this race. Certainly do not wear your lacy underwire to the swim start as your do-it-yourself triathlon top. (I have seen this first hand, or I would not write about it.)

Wear your sports bra under your tri suit during the swim if you have boobies bigger than a table top. Some suits or tops may have built in sports bras, but seriously, unless you are teeny in the tatas, be careful. If your Girls are small and your suit has a built-in bra, then you *may* be good to go. Your headlights will likely be on during a race, so going without a bra can make the Girls shine like the top of the Chrysler Building (Sorry, I had an *Annie* flashback. Favorite movie ever!). Keep in mind that while we do not care about what we look like while tri-ing, you *are* racing in essentially a wet t-shirt contest—if you are wearing white, you *might* be giving a show. Open boobness *may* be something to consider. I say just put on your sports bra under your trisuit and forget about it.

Do not wear a one-piece *swim*suit to a tri unless you are: 1) a professional triathlete; 2) 90 pounds and 4% body fat; or 3) you have a tri short over it and intend to wear it the entire race. A swimsuit plus a tri short is a decent do-it-yourself tri kit. But if you can rock the swimsuit solo or wear a two-piece tri *bikini* for the entire race, then who's to stop you? Lawd, I applaud you, actually. The thought of *running* in a bikini makes my insides shiver.

I get questions all the time: *what if I wear my swimsuit during the swim, and then throw on my cycling shorts over it?* I am not going to say you "can't" do this, but keep in mind that you will be soaking wet after the swim and putting on tight shorts (while wet) is an Olympic event in itself. Weigh the pros and cons, and make your choice. But doesn't it sound easier to pick your one outfit— and just wear that?

My simple advice: do not change clothes during a race. Do not take anything (but your wetsuit) *off*. You can argue, and that's fine. But I still say: no.

First, because changing clothes in transition is considered a newbie move and you will stand out like a sore thumb. While we don't (technically) care what people think about us (true), who really wants to stand out and look weird? Second, because it's truly impractical, frustrating *(Dry clothes! Wet body!)* and time consuming. Finally and most importantly, someone might see your goodies.

One caveat: in the beginning, I would throw on a t-shirt over my tri suit for the run only. I felt more comfortable that way and by the time I got to the run, I was dry. In hindsight, I looked silly. But at the time, it made me feel better. Sometimes you need to take care of your inner scaredy-cat in order to finish. If putting a t-shirt over your suit makes you feel better, then you should do it. If wearing a swimsuit and putting a tri short over it makes you feel better, do it. You have to get to that starting line—that's the important thing! But please note that none of the above options involve *removing* clothing.

On race day, do not wear underwear. Really. Your underwear will not dry and you will end up with saddles sores on the Queen. Be nice to the Queen.

Do practice in your race-day clothing well in advance of your race. Wear your race-day suit to open water, cycling and running. Make sure you like the fit because a clothing malfunction or discomfort on race day is a mess.

OTHER QUICK START THINGS

Aquaphor or BodyGlide helps significantly to prevent chafing on the body. I use it under my arms or near my sports bra straps and bands to prevent chafing. You can use this good stuff anywhere. On long bike rides and race days, I put it everywhere. I mean, *everywhere*, the Queen included. For getting started, it's nice to spread wherever something might be rubbing: skin on skin, sports bra on skin, etc. Chafing is horrible, takes an ungodly amount of time to heal and thus, can be very discouraging. If you are prone to foot blisters, BodyGlide Liquefied Powder is a life saver.

Another nice thing to have is a mini water bottle to carry on runs. I like the handheld ones by Nathan or Fuel Belt® for shorter runs and run-walks. The little snazzy bottle straps to your hand. As time passes and distances got longer for me, I invested in a Fuel Belt® and Camelbak® water systems, which can hold a ton of water and gels, but I did not need something that large for quite some time.

THREE

Coaching and Community

Believe it or not, having a coach is not *that* weird in the sport of triathlon. It's true that triathletes may be the only group of people over the ages of twenty-four who *do* have coaches, but you will be surprised (and in a good way) at the way a coach will change your motivation, your goals and set your mind at ease about training.

If you are not in a position to afford a coach, I would encourage you to find a triathlon club or training group for accountability. First, you will enjoy your experience more if you are lined up with others sharing your same experiences. Second, having others around will push you to do better and keep moving. Triathlon is a fabulous sport for community.

Regardless of who you find, I encourage you to find *someone* to be with you on your journey: a coach, a team, or a tribe.

TAKING THE COACHING PLUNGE

Around the same time that I purchased my first official road bike, I had a triathlon coach lined up to get me in gear. My coach was no stranger to me: Gerry. Cycling Instructor Extraordinaire. Mr. O'Ironman.

Gerry agreed to coach me to my first Olympic distance race, and I was blown away (and very grateful). He sent me a list of questions, a spreadsheet and asked me all sorts of things about myself. *What are your goals? Your limits? Your concerns?* I took time to consider my answers, to look inside and really address my goals, fears, strengths and limitations. Gerry asked about issues and things I viewed as "limiters" for my triathlon training. *Life in General*, I wrote on the spreadsheet.

On January 26, 2011, I became an official coached athlete (the term "athlete" being used ever so loosely). Originally, I was careful about writing on SwimBikeMom.com about Gerry and the workouts he gave me. First, I did not want to violate his intellectual property or rip off his triathlon genius by "publishing" his workouts.

Second, I did not mention *who* he was in my writing, because I was not certain he wanted to claim *me* as one of his athletes. After all, I was a hot triathlon mess.

Pretty quickly, I learned how awesome Gerry was (is) as both a person and a coach. He was changing my life and I needed to tell people. I wanted to share his little smart sarcastic wisdoms on the blog. I wanted to scream, "I have a cooooooooach! Meeeee! Meeee! I have a coach!"

But I was stuck. I did not want to talk about him without his consent. But I also did not want to tell him about the blog where I complained about the four thousand pizzas I just ate and published my weight for the world to read (humiliating!).

So I had to speak of my fancy coach in the abstract. I needed a nickname for him that embodied the entire coaching package. I began to tally up the things I knew about Gerry.

- Gerry likes cookies.
- Gerry likes the band, R.E.M., especially their *Monster* album.
- Gerry is tough as bloody nails.

Hmmmm. Cookies, R.E.M. and toughness. Cookies. Tough. *Coach Tough Cookie?* No, that wasn't it…*Coach Cookie Monster?* No. Not quite. R.E.M., cookies, and badassery. *Oh snap! I had it!*

Coach Monster!

One telephone conversation with Coach Monster and I learned more about triathlon than from all the books I had ingested. I had approached my training semi-correctly up until that point because I had attempted to swim, bike, and run. But other than that—I was not doing much else correctly.

I almost fell out of my chair during the first coach-athlete conversation, which ended something like this:

"Eventually," he said, "I'll want to bring a video camera and watch you run. And same for the swim."

Gulp.

"Swim?" I squeaked.

"Yes," he said matter of factly. "I have a waterproof camera."

Of course he does, I thought. *A swimsuit in front of Coach Monster? Oh, the horror.* All the weirdos at the YMCA were one thing, but *he* was another story. I had to see that man every Friday in class. I couldn't show him my flabby buns, for the love. The thought was…was…was *unthinkable.* [Note: I avoided myself in a swimsuit near Coach Monster for well-over eighteen months. I thought I might have a lifetime record, but just recently he caught me off-guard and bamboozled me at the pool before Spinning class.]

My official training plan took off quickly. The first workout was a cycling class and a two-mile run. (*What?!*)

I blinked and re-read.

Workout 1: Spinning class
Workout 2: Two-mile run

Double gulp. Two workouts? Back-to-back? What?

So I went to indoor cycling class and then I almost perished on a two-mile treadmill run. *This coaching thing is not such a good idea after all,* I thought. Coach M just about killed me right out of the gate.

In triathlon, a "brick" workout is two of the disciplines back-to-back with a tiny break in between—just like you would have in a race. The idea behind a brick is to mimic actual race conditions. For example, a bike-run "brick" means hopping off your bike, lacing up your shoes and going for a run. A swim-bike brick is hopping out of the pool, strapping on the helmet and speeding off on the bike. The term "brick" is derived from the sensation in your legs when you begin running after cycling: your legs feel like complete bricks. (Personally, I think the term "brick" comes from the desire to throw a brick at your coach.)

So Coach Monster's plan had me doing a two-hour brick workout from day one. (*What?!*)

But I did it.

However, when I plugged in my workout data into the training software, Coach Monster wrote me back: *NO no no. Not a brick, unless I tell you it's a brick.*

Oh, ooops. Yet another thing I learned. Two workouts, unless otherwise specified, just means two workouts sometime that day—not necessarily two back-to-back workouts. However, as I went along in the triathlon training process, I proceeded to brick absolutely everything. With job, kids and schedule, I could not possibly have the luxury of two workouts a day. A morning and evening workout? *Puh-lease.* I had to do it all at once. I became a Brick House.

COACHLY THINGS

Coach Monster was (is) not an in-person coach. I see him in cycling class on Fridays, I beg him to have coffee with me sometimes and we email and chatter during the week about training. Mostly, he formulates my training plan in 3-4 week blocks and sends me the workouts electronically. Usually, I cry and question his sanity. Then he tells me to suck it up and to focus.

He has always been very nice to me. *Well of course your coach should be nice to you,* you might say. Yes, I agree. It sounds simple. But I know people who have crappy, mean-spirited coaches. People who pay their hard-earned money to be berated by Ironfolks who have absolutely no humility (or humanity). I'm not sure I see the benefit derived from coachly abuse.

You can find almost any triathlete who might be willing to coach you—and for cheap. But do not fool yourself: the coach-athlete relationship *is* a relationship. You would not be friends with someone who sucked or was constantly mean. So do not put up with a mean, sucky coach. Coach Monster is very *tough*, but he has never been unkind to me.

You should benefit from and enjoy your coach-athlete relationship. Hopefully, your coach will feel the same way. (Please do not email Coach Monster and ask him if he likes me.) At a minimum, a trust component must exist in your coaching relationship. You should feel comfortable enough to be honest with your coach about your physical abilities (and limiters), your family situation(s) and your schedule. I trust Coach Monster. Although at times, I am unsure if I can trust him not to kill me via death-by-running.

The no-thinking about the workouts is a nice benefit to a coach. I wake up, read my plan and (usually) do what I am told. Of course, the fountain of endless wisdom and resources from a coach is irreplaceable. Coach Monster is married with two daughters, so he understands how women operate. Actually, strike that. He's a man who understands that he will *never* understand how women operate, and he plans accordingly. That bodes well for me (and him).

As I said, Coach Monster is very *nice*. Not only does he say proper coaching things to me like "you're going to kick butt this year," but he remains sensitive to my ability level without ever hurting my feelings. I may be fat, but he has never said, "You know, you'd be a lot faster if you lost some weight there, Two Ton." Even though we discuss nutrition and diet, he waits for me to bring it up. Once weight is in conversation play, he showers me with his advice and we discuss. I find this wonderful, because my sensitivity is then removed from the game. If I bring it up, we discuss it. If I am quiet, he says nothing. He has other athletes who he hammers about nutrition and their racing weight, because of their experience levels. He is a coaching genius to leave me to work through my weight issues on my own, all the while being a guiding force and resource to assist when I cry out for help.

Other coaches might look at an athlete like me and say, "Thanks, but no thanks. Not until you lose fifty pounds." Coach Monster, on the other hand, enjoys the challenge of the new athlete. Even one like me (challenged in the midsection and, arguably, the head).

GRASSHOPPER

Coach Monster calls me Grasshopper. Not that we are talking Kung Fu here, but sometimes I feel that way—and apparently he does too. Plus, Coach Monster regularly responds to my triathlon issues with short, declarative sentences. I often imagine him meditating in a dojo somewhere, and picking up his iPhone when an email pings. He then types short, wise things. He then places his iPhone on the dojo floor, returns to his zen-like state, all the while randomly karate-chopping anybody who crosses him.

For example, I whine about my weight issues with bold, sweeping declarations. *I will never lose weight! I will always be fat!* Well, one day I emailed him. I had declared that particular day "The Official Eat Nothing Ever Again Day."

I wrote: *Today I am fat. Today is The Official Eat Nothing Ever Again Day!*

Coach Monster replied in short email: *Not eating is the wrong path, Grasshopper, especially as we continue to ramp up the training. You must fuel properly to support your body before, during and after training.*

I wrote: *But how can I carry this body, this weight, this fat butt across a race distance?*

He wrote: *You will figure out how.*

As I read the short sentence, I imagined him clicking "send" and returning to the dojo where nine tiny ninjas awaited serious butt-kickings by his hand.

When I doubt myself, Coach Monster reminds me of just how far I have come. When I complain, he refuses to listen. When I make nasty comments about my body or my abilities, he charges me $200 per offense. (I owe him $4 million to date.)

But the talisman of an amazing coach is compassion. When I fall apart, he shows me mercy. Deep, compassionate mercy. One of my favorite Coach Monster quotes is forever on my brain: "You can do the workouts, grasshopper, as long as you get out of your own head and your own self-limitations."

And how true.

Yes, Master. *Er, Monster.*

Ten Questions with Coach Monster

What's Your Favorite Post-Race Meal?
Bloody Mary, salty fries, and a rare burger

What's on Your iPod?
R.E.M., Eminem, Linkin Park, Live, Coldplay, Snow Patrol, John Mayer, Pearl Jam, Florence + the Machine, 30 Seconds to Mars

What's Your Food Achilles' Heel?
Peanut butter. Any sweets that are baked. Cookies, pies, cakes. Anything with a crust.

Favorite Running Shoe?
By far, Brooks Glycerin 9. Best shoe I've ever run in. Wider toe box, and I love it. Lots of mid-foot cushioning.

Favorite Place to Run?
I like to run in cities when I travel. I travel fairly often. I love to run at day break and see the city as it's waking up.

Favorite Race?
Kona. There's not even a close second.

Biggest Race Pet Peeve?
This happens mostly in an Ironman race — but I hate when people lose sight about what the event is really about —they are so hell bent on achieving a time goal that they miss the whole point. That triathlon is about the energy, the experience, the hard work. I was one of those people, and I learned to let go of that. Only when I let go, did the stars align. In the end, I was wasting energy instead of being thankful. Another pet peeve: people who have transition areas the size of small cities.

Scariest Triathlon Moment?
Any and all mass start swims. I have never quit anything in my life and during the start of least three of the six Ironman races I have raced...if I could have quit in the swim, I would have. That's how panicked I was at the start. I have worked hard on relaxation techniques through the years. That and the

experience of having gone through it many times, helps me. I am wiser about where I choose to swim now. I don't get in the middle of the chaos.

Does Your Bike Have a Name?
Yes. Her name is Black Betty and she's a stealth bomber [Blue Triad SL 2012].

If You Could Train with One Triathlete for One Day - Who Would You Choose?
ChrissieWellington, no questions asked. I met her in Kona. She's amazing.

FIND YOUR OWN MONSTER

For the zillion above reasons, I highly recommend getting a coach in your ring. Even Coach Monster has a coach. If the coach has a coach, then we should all have a coach. Or something like that. Yes, having a coach costs money. Some coaches cost *a lot* of money. But sometimes, you'd be surprised—the cost per month for being a coached athlete is likely to be less than a few eating-out extravaganzas.

Now that we've established that a coach is a good idea…what should you look for in a coach?

Personality

For starters, you need to find a coach who is a good match for you, personality-wise. Can you talk to her? Do you just plain like him? Believe me, "like" goes a long way. Facebook was on to something special with the "Like" button. Interview many coaches. Can you click "like"…or do you want to scroll past or worse, un-friend?

Coach Monster is a good personality match for me. He does not let me slack, but at the same time he understands my struggles and issues. He's tough, which is also good. If I had "too" nice of a coach, I would get away with too many excuses. He's a good balance between strict and fun. Plus, we have the same demented sense of humor. When you're talking about a sport that involves peeing in your tri shorts…well, the humor helps.

Understanding Your Goals

If your coach believes you should be running a six- minute mile and you just started running yesterday, then she might not be the best coach for you. She might be a great coach, but simply not an ideal coach for a baby triathlete. Some coaches may have been tri-ing for so many years that they have lost a grip on what it means to run a twelve-minute mile (on a good day).

Your coach should recognize your goals, no matter how crazy. But your coach should also understand your life, your family and your (true) limitations. By "true" limitations, I mean your working hours, number of kids and the like—not your lame-o excuses as to why you could "never" become a triathlete.

As I mentioned, even Coach Monster has a coach. In his coach, he looks for a "combination of expertise, perspective and empathy. In my coach, I want someone who has either been through what I am going through…or is simultaneously going through it with me, like Ironman training. I want a coach with the same triathlon-shaped scars. I want a coach that has fought on the same battlefield. And someone who is passionate."

EMPATHY

I learned about Coach Monster's empathy up-close-and-personal during my first open water swim and subsequent panic attack, detailed in Part Two of this book. Basically, I freaked out in the open water and luckily, Coach Monster was there to talk me through the fear. Another coach would have likely given up on me on that day, in that cold water with my fatness floating around in my wetsuit. The empathy Coach Monster showed me, however, was incredible.

I recently thanked him for that experience, for not giving up on me. He shook his head and would not let me talk about it. Then he just shrugged his shoulders and said, "I have been there. I have had panic attacks in the water. Mine just happen to be with 2000 people around me [in an Ironman] and I couldn't turn on my back and float. I had to swim or be swum over. But I know how *absolutely* terrifying the open water swim *can* be. It's not a joke. It's real."

He continued, "But I also know that when an athlete faces her fears, there is an amazing energy there—it's like a drug—the energy itself is very uplifting. One of the reasons I like working with new triathletes is because they come to the sport absolutely scared to death. But during the process of training and racing, they find a way to dig down deep inside of themselves. They are able to face their fears. Then they find out: the scary dragon isn't that big."

For the record, the open water *is* a dragon. But Coach Monster is right: with a little practice, the dragon becomes a baby one. *Ooooh, look at that cute little open water baby dragon.*

CATALYST

Coach Monster's goal is to be a *catalyst* for his athletes. "I don't have any magic formula to my coaching," he explained to me. "I really simply try to bring *out* what is already *inside* in the athlete. I'm not trying to put anything *into* the athlete—I'm trying to pull it *out*.

"Triathlon is a servant, not a master—triathlon should be a means to self-discovery and self-actualization. It should *serve* your life, not *master* it. Many times a new athlete may not see what's inside of her, or how strong she is. She may be her own worst enemy."

(This was the part of our interview where he pointed at me. *Hurmph*.)

Your End of the Bargain

As coached athletes, we have a duty to *try* not to drive our coaches up the wall. Note that I said "try." I did not let Coach Monster comment on this section, by the way. I mean, I *know* that I shouldn't call Coach Monster at three o'clock in the morning freaking out about my run. So I *try* not to call (sometimes I just email and text six or sixteen times in a row).

We also have a duty of hard work. If you are paying money for a coach, then for Pete's sake, pay attention to the coach and work hard. Coach Monster finds the most difficult part about *being* a coach is getting his athletes to "buy into a *process* instead of just an arbitrary time goal." In other words, an athlete should see the long-term goal, not just "Oh, today's run was sooooooooo slow."

One of Coach Monster's biggest pet peeves? "I cannot stand an athlete's lack of ownership and 'buy-in' to the process. I do not like excuses. Saying the right words and not following through with the actions is a huge pet peeve, probably for any coach. I would prefer honesty. I would rather the athlete say, 'I *will not* do that workout' rather than saying, 'Yeah yeah, I will do that' only to come up with an excuse later as to why it didn't get done. That is wasting *my* time and *their* money."

He said, "It's pretty simple. I love to coach because I am helping people and facilitating achievement of things they never thought they were capable of achieving! It's a thousand times more fulfilling for me to facilitate their dreams, than for *me* to achieve anything as an athlete. And I'm a competitive athlete and I want to do well! But when I work with someone and they get beyond their limitations and it creates a snowball of energy and achievement—that's why I coach."

Join Triathlon Club or Team

As a beginner, a local triathlon club or team may be just what you need to get moving. For starters, you will immediately meet some of the most crazy people in your area (the triathletes). Once you join a club, you will have access to coaching, training programs, group rides and events (oh, and fancy triathlon suits for races!). Joining a triathlon club will give you the accountability factor that otherwise might be missing.

Additionally, if you can't stand the thought of training alone, this is *definitely* the way to go.

Organizations like Team in Training (www.teamintraining.org) provide coaching and training in exchange for fundraising. If you are interested in making a difference *while* you learn to tri, you might benefit from Team in Training or a similar organization.

COMMUNITY SUPPORT: FIND YOUR TRIBE

Triathlon is probably the most amazing sport to find training buddies and community support. Even if you have a coach, you will need support, friends and a think-tank of like (insane) minds to help you along the way. Women are incredible (of course); but women triathletes are the most incredible group of people in the world. I am convinced of it.

Tanya Maslach is one of my new(er) triathlon pals. She is the Founder of GOTRIbal, a social online and offline experience for women leading active, adventurous lifestyles. (www.GOTRIbalnow.com). I picked her brain a little about the importance of community and accountability for the beginner triathlete.

A Message from GOTRIbal

by Tanya Maslach
Founder of GOTRIbal
(www.GOTRIbalNow.com)

I can remember the day I was swimming in Hawaii when my lane-mates suggested that I try out triathlon. My lane-mates were women who were absurdly accomplished in the 140.3 mile distance and could whip out a 10K run in 36 minutes with their shoes tied together. One friend, in fact, had exited the water as the first person (male or female) in one of the Ironman [races] she did and was a top 10 finisher (overall) at the World Ironman Championships...

But mostly, I loved these ladies because they were as funny as they were fierce. I just dug them. When I figured out the only way I was going to *see* these women was when I trained with them, I succumbed to their pressures to sign up for a triathlon.

And, the rest is history.

In fact, I laugh now—as hesitant as I was to do something as absurdly difficult as multisport, I now lead a company designed exclusively to encourage women to take on adventures that challenge their own "I can't" stories...

I could rattle off research studies about the importance of community and accountability for the beginner triathlete, but that would make you want to put ice-picks in your eyes. Instead, I'd rather tell you a story.

Whether you are a beginner or not, community, and the sense of accountability that comes with it if you're an active member, is the bedrock for your growth, learning, and development. It's also a place for unconditional support and caring.

Two years ago, a woman in GOTRIbal was driving down the road and saw another woman jogging in the opposite direction. This GOTRIbal member, Sue [not her real name], was still in her work clothes, but turned her SUV around, parked it and ran (in swanky boots, no less) to catch up to the woman. Sue had lost some 100 [pounds] in her active lifestyle journey and she was going to share that joy and pay it forward to this woman who was trying to do the same. So Sue jogged alongside the woman and told her how she admired her courage for running alone, on a desolate road, even as she could have felt embarrassed for doing so.

Sue shared that she had been overweight once too, but was enjoying a fabulous lifestyle around running, swimming and biking, and invited this woman to join her in the journey. Sue told her about all the women in GOTRIbal, the coaches, the advice, the community that was there to support her and how she had started a mini-Tribe in the Washington area for women like her to get together, socialize and work out together. And from that meeting, the community welcomed another member into their tribe.

I have so many of those stories I could write a book on them. In each, I've been amazed to see the power of the unconditional service and support that community has on positively impacting and transforming another member. The most powerful impact was the self-confidence, strength and health of mind, body and spirit members received in their relationship with other community members that ultimately helped *them* to do something they didn't believe was within their power. True communities that watch out for their members, care for them, serve their interests with humility and inclusivity, are tribes. Their influence, strength and power for supporting and developing their members is unparalleled in history. They are families. And families help their members do things they think they can't.

This is true whether in health, sport, profession, or otherwise. I could have never fallen so in love with multisport without my girls in Hawaii. Even as they trained and raced faster than I, they always invited me on every training ride, every race, every adventure. They taught me tricks, helped me get into weird training and racing outfits, introduced me to people who helped me ease the financial burden of the new sport, and took me under their wing every step of the way. Sure there was smack talk. But there was never catty, petty one-upmanship. These ladies were my community.

They made me accountable for doing that first triathlon. And when I crossed the line smiling from ear to ear, even crying with excitement and pride, they were there to help me get off my husband's mountain bike and into something a bit more comfortable before I decided multisport maybe wasn't my bag.

FOUR

Safety and Smartness

Before we dive into the nitty-gritty of triathlon, I beg a commitment from you. I want you to promise that as you embark on triathlon and training that you will:

> *Be Smart*
> *Be Safe*
> *Become a Student*

BE SMART

One definition of "smart" is to be "mentally alert."[vi] At all times during your training, you should practice mental alertness. You must be cognizant of your surroundings, your body and your mind.

Part of the challenge, especially as a beginner, is to keep tabs on your technique, your energy levels and your health. Make sure that you are feeling okay during your training sessions. At the same time, you must be smart and remember that hard work is the only path to success in your triathlon goals. *Does it really hurt, or are you just uncomfortable with the heat and the sweat? Can you push through and finish that last half-mile?* Be smart and know your limits, but at the same time, give yourself some credit and do not let your mind tell your body "I can't" when it certainly can.

Working hard and suffering through sweat is one thing, but heart palpitations and serious pains are another. If your knees feel like someone has busted them with sledge hammers, then stop running. If you are bleeding from the head, then you should stop pedaling (or at least slow down). If you are dizzy, sick, vomiting, pooping on yourself...just throw in the towel and call it a day. If you don't sleep well before a long ride and you feel nauseated in the morning, you must gauge if you are capable of pushing through, or if you think pushing would be dangerous to your health.

More often than not, you can push through it—*and* you will be just fine. But every so often, you will be exhausted and ill and need a break. Learn to listen to your body, but don't let your body give you lame excuses.

Be smart in your training and the smarts will translate to a safe and healthy race day. Even if not, it will make the odds be ever in your favor. (Really? Did you think I would omit a perfectly timed reference to *The Hunger Games*?) Coach Monster says that some of the stupidest triathlon decisions are made because someone is overtired on race day. Your mental alertness is important for your own safety and the safety of others.

BE SAFE

In recent times, female runners have been experiencing a targeting of sorts by sickos who want to assault our athletic kind. Do not run in the dark on a deserted road. Do not run in the wee hours of the morning without a headlamp. Preferably do not run alone. Carry pepper spray. Learn self-defense. Being safe goes back to being smart. If you feel scared on a run, go home. Nothing is worth your life.

Wear your RoadID® (www.RoadID.com) at all times when training. A RoadID is a bracelet, anklet or shoe fob that contains your personal information like name, date of birth, and drug allergies, in addition to emergency contact information. If you do not have a Road ID or similar gadget, get one and wear it when you are training.

Of course, we cannot control the actions of others. But aim to place yourself in the safest environments possible. Ride on low-traffic streets. Run in well-traveled and well-lit areas. Never swim in the open water alone. These safety measures, while they won't absolutely protect you from the idiots in this world, may lessen the chance that the idiots will find you.

I had been training for about a year when I experienced my first official run in the dark. When I say "dark," I mean D-A-R-K. Butt crack of dawn. Dark-thirty. Early as all hell. The moon was shining when I waddled down the driveway. I had my snazzy reflective shoelaces and my Camelbak, which was also covered in reflectors, so I felt pretty *reflective*. However, I was not very well *illuminated*. I could not see a thing, which was extremely risky for a Swim Bike Klutz like me. I took a busy route, with plenty of commuters frantically driving to get to the city. I had lots of cars zooming by and headlights to guide the way. But I was on the sidewalk, which was set back off the road and I could really only see well when a car passed.

Sunrise did not happen until my last quarter mile, but something about running in the dark was awesome, even though I was very tired. I had not scored more than three or four hours of sleep the prior few nights. Regardless, the run was ridiculously exhilarating, to be out in the cool air, running in the dark while everyone in my house was still asleep. I felt strong. I felt relieved to know that I was definitely not taking time away from anyone at this hour. Running in the dark was a great exorcism of the negative thought demons.

I wrote about this run on my blog, knowing full well that within minutes of posting, my mother would tell my father, who would then phone me, saying, *You can't run in the dark. It's dangerous.*

I was prepared with my rebuttal: *I don't think criminals are awake at five o'clock in the morning. I only saw a bunch of tired moms dropping off kids at daycare and a whole slew of angry Atlanta commuters.*

Looking back, that run was stupid. First, I was risking my life by running alone in the dark. Secondly, I was risking my ankles and knees by running on a path that was not well-lit. I have learned my lesson and avoided making these mistakes in subsequent training sessions. If it's not 100% daylight, I run with a light, pepper spray and a flashing "caution" pin that attaches to my belt or my Camelbak.

Yes, this a fun book, but triathlon safety is no joke. A swim course can be tough and dangerous. The bike is dangerous. You must learn how to ride your bike. You must learn the rules of the road *and* the race. You must wear your helmet. You must not ride in "packs" on a triathlon race course. You must *not* wear your iPod while riding a bike. *Ever. Do you hear me? What? You can't hear me because you're wearing your iPod? Oh, I see...*

BECOME A STUDENT OF TRIATHLON

Everyone can ride a bike, right?

No! Wrong!

Really? Yes, really. Go to a beginner triathlon and you'll see what I mean. You may think, *I can't do a race because I can't ride a bike.* Unfortunately, that has not stopped some people. And I do not mean that in a good way.

It is fine if you cannot ride a bike *today.* You will learn. But you should *not* go to your first triathlon if you cannot ride your bike comfortably and safely. If you cannot pedal in a straight line, wait until you *can* before you participate in a race. If you cannot shift gears, wait. I will cheerlead, "You can do a triathlon" until you are sick of hearing me, but you will *never* hear me tell you to just go out and try one without some experience, smarts and safety.

I am a firm believer in becoming a student of triathlon. Even though I ran out and did my first tri pretty quickly, I had absorbed and read a ton of books, blogs and magazines beforehand. I had ridden that evil bike in the past. I knew how to pump my tires, change a tube and fix a dropped chain. I was bad with clipping in and out of my pedals, but only to my own detriment (stopping and going). Once I was in the pedals, I knew and followed the rules. I knew that you must stay to the right of the road, not draft and pass within so many seconds (that was not my concern...passing), and announce "On Your Left!" when passing.

I hope that the upcoming sections on the swim, bike and run will guide you through your training, race preparation and race day. Remember to read the USA Triathlon rules for sanctioned events and spend some time devouring articles on swim starts, bike handling and race courtesies.

It's simple: just read, learn and absorb the safety measures and rules. Even when you may not be fast or close to it, you will at least be a good student of triathlon and you'll be on your way. Your family will thank you—because you'll be around to see more days of racing. And your fellow racers will thank you. More than you know.

FIVE

The Swim

INTRODUCTION BY SWIM BIKE MOM

I enjoy swimming for the most part. If you do not enjoy swimming, then go ahead and start repeating to yourself: *I love to swim. I love to swim. I love to swim.* The vast majority of triathlon success (and failure) may be attributed to your mental strength. So start tricking your mind into loving it now!

I love swimming in an outdoor pool when the sun is high noon. That way, my back browns like a biscuit. (But my front half stays pasty white, which is a nice complement to the goggle eyes and stringy pool hair.) Of course, swimming is wrought with less-than-ideal situations. Like used bandages (not belonging to you) floating in the water, hair globs (also not belonging to you) and water that is way too cloudy from a day full of munchkins tee-teeing in the pool. *Do not swallow the water, do not swallow the water, do not swallow the water.* Heebie jeebies.

So I am not helping your inspiration. I apologize.

Swimming really *is* a wonderful thing. I love smelling like a pool after a swim. Perhaps I do not use the right soap. But also, maybe I do not *want* the right soap. Smelling like the pool reminds me of the hard work I put in before other (sane) people are even awake. The smell lifts my spirits. By the afternoon, when I begin to forget the great effort I paid to the triathlon gods early that morning, I'll catch another whiff. I just plain like it. Of course, now with the common upgrades to saline pools, the traditional chemical smells are not as prevalent. Good and bad, I say.

A common saying for triathlon swimming is: *You cannot win a triathlon in the swim, but you can certainly lose it.* Practicing the swim is vitally important for many reasons. First, it is quite dangerous to slack on the swim. In cycling and running, you can stop moving, get off your bike or stop running and slow to a walk. In swimming, you better keep swimming or…well, you know.

Second, the swim start in a race is often crowded and full of intense energy. The goal of the triathlon swim should be to feel comfortable in the water and also, to swim strongly to avoid fatigue going into the next part of the race. The more relaxed and less fatigued you are coming out of the water, the better your overall race will be. If you begin a race completely terrified, with your heart racing and your mind blown, you are creating a dangerous environment for yourself (not to mention a likely bad race).

Finally, I beg you to learn to love the water. How? By convincing yourself that you do! When I was a teenager in Olympic weightlifting, my training included one lift that I hated to do. Hated it. I would dread those particular days. Each day on the drive to the gym, my mom would say, "Tell yourself that you love it!"

I would roll my fifteen-year old eyes at her, thinking, *what does she know?*

But I began to repeat "I love this lift, I love this lift" to myself before each training session. Eventually, that particular lift became my *best* and *favorite* lift. Coach Monster's triathlon advice is to use your *mind* to control your *body*. Turns out, my dear momma started me on this brilliant training even before the dear Monster came into the picture.

I WAS GOING TO SWIM!

After I decided to become a triathlete, I knew I had to swim. I had been a part of a swim team in my younger years (as in ages six and seven), so I strapped on my swim cap and thought, *Oh yeah, here I come again! Watch out! Taking on the swim world!*

I will never forget the first day of swimming as a baby triathlete in training. I had no recollection about how to really swim. *How do I put on this swim cap? Was I supposed to jump in the water or use the ladder? How was I supposed to get out of the pool? Did my goggles go under or over my swim cap? Did I remember how to swim freestyle?*

After slapping myself in the face about sixteen times while trying to put on my non-silicone, hair-tearing swim cap and situating the cap over my ears, under my ears, then over again (*is this right??*), I was ready. I was wearing my new plus-size swimsuit from Junonia. I wore my fancy new Speedo brand goggles (*over my cap? Right?*).

I eased myself down into the pool, scraping my back in the process. *Ugh this swim cap. Over the ears?* I could not figure out the swim cap to save my life. I pulled the goggles down over my eyes, and I dunked under the water. I came up quickly, sputtering.

Oh my gosh, I haven't been underwater in forever! I thought. I gained my composure.

Okay, ready! I went under again and I pushed myself off the wall with my feet, and I began to flail through the water. After five strokes, I stood straight up in the lap lane—not even halfway down the pool. I could not breathe and my heart was absolutely racing. *What in the…?* I went back under water and tried to swim to the end of the pool. I finally made it, and I grabbed onto the pool wall, struggling for air.

To say I was shocked would be an understatement. *Had I ever swam at all? Swim team? Hello?? Okay, so that was twenty five years ago…so what?? What in the…*

That day in the pool was an opportune time to give up. To think I would ever swim in a triathlon seemed impossible. But I spent that morning swimming wall to wall, resting, struggling for breath, catching my breath, and then starting again.

The next swim workout, I was able to do a little more. And with each workout…a tad more, and more.

Swimming may feel like the most evil discipline of triathlon when you start. But something is very interesting about swimming. Even if you can't swim a lick right now, you will see *big* fitness gains almost immediately in the pool—more so than on the bike or the run.

So, while the swimming may seem like the worst struggle, stay with it and push through. Because in a few short weeks, you will see your swim workout go from a pitiful 100 yards to a decent (but slow) 500 yards. A month or so after that, you'll be swimming 1500 yards without dying, and you will be amazed.

The swim stroke you want to learn is the traditional *freestyle* stroke, also known as the "front crawl." The front crawl is (should be) the fastest of all stroke options (as opposed to breast stroke or backstroke), although you *are* permitted to swim however you'd like in a race. The front crawl basically consists of using your arms, in alternating front forward motions, to *pull* and *crawl* yourself through the water. Sometimes you may feel so terrible and tired swimming, the *crawl* terminology is eerily symbolic. The arm stroke is made up of three primary movements known as the recovery, catch and pull. As your arms rotate, each arm goes through the motion of *recovery, catch* and *pull*.

I am not going to waste time *describing* the mechanics of the swim. The very best way to learn how to swim will not come from *reading*. I recommend lessons (if you have no idea how to swim), then Master's class (described in this section), and watching DVDs of proper swim technique…then, watch videos of yourself swimming *and* have an experienced swimmer watch you or your video. These are the ways you will improve your stroke—not reading my blubberings about how-to.

Now. Let's get swimming!

Swim Distance Cheat Sheet

One length of a standard gym pool is either 25 yards or 25 meters. A yard pool is shorter than a meter pool. Ask your gym manager which length pool they have.

A "length" means swimming from one end to another.

Wall |----------→-------------- | Wall

= One Length

Swimming from one end to the other and returning to the start is one "lap."

Wall |----------→-------------- | Wall

Plus

Wall |----------←-------------- | Wall

= One Lap

25 meter pool
Quarter-mile: 16.1 lengths; 8 laps
Half mile: 32.2 lengths; 16.1 laps
One mile: 64.4 lengths; 32.2 laps

25 yard pool
Quarter-mile: 17.6 lengths; 8.8 laps
Half-mile: 35.2 lengths; 17.6 laps
One mile: 70.4 lengths; 35.2 laps

INTRODUCTION TO THE SWIM EXPERT

Sylvia Marino, co-founder of the amazing Bia Sport, is a mom to three kids, a wife to an entrepreneurial husband, and a fabulous open water swimmer. She has made more than 120 Alcatraz crossings and was part of an all-women's English Channel relay team. She loves the open water and is about to convince you to love it too! Sylvia and Bia co-founder, Cheryl Kellond, are taking the world by storm with Bia Sport (www.Bia-Sport.com).

JUST KEEP SWIMMING

By Sylvia Marino
Co-Founder of Bia Sport
(www.Bia-Sport.com)

The first leg of your triathlon adventure is the swim. Whether you were born a guppy or drive ten miles out of your way to avoid a mud puddle, the water awaits you. If you feel the water is your nemesis, now is the time to embrace it and make it your friend. If you don't make it through the swim, there is no bike, no run. Swimming is your first hurdle—your first challenge, your first throw down of the gauntlet—your first chance to take the course by storm and make it your own!

Are you ready? The answer is yes!

Sylvia's Story

I didn't grow up a pool swimmer. I wasn't on the swim team. Swimming was a summer activity on the lake where one perfected the doggie-paddle or perhaps the never-get-your-hair-wet breast stroke.

At the age of 33, after having my second child, I found myself with a serious case of the "baby blues." Parts of my world were unraveling, the baby weight weighed me down in more than one way and I felt like I was destined to redefine the color blue.

On a visit to my OB-GYN, he suggested that I either go on a short-course of antidepressants or choose a physical / athletic goal for three months out. He suggested maybe a 5k run or a sprint triathlon—an activity that would get me out of the house doing something for myself and increasing my endorphins. I opted for the latter and settled on a sprint tri. I had a bike, could walk pretty fast and now all I had to do was learn how to swim.

As luck would have it, my gym was holding a program for beginner triathletes. The group met three nights a week for six weeks and at the end, we would compete in a local sprint triathlon.

I was awful at the first swim practice. Actually, I recall the experience more like a controlled drowning experiment than swimming. The coach was the winner of the Ironman New Zealand, Ironman Coeur D'Alene and Ironman Hawaii 70.3. Obviously, she was an accomplished athlete with a wealth of knowledge and encouragement. She suggested I take some private swim lessons. I was embarrassed, mortified and could have easily quit. Instead, I bought a three-pack of swim lessons before the next group practice.

After a few lessons I learned some of the basics and became more comfortable in the water. I bought a wetsuit, finished my first sprint triathlon and caught the tri bug for a year entering and finishing sprint, Olympic and 70.3 distances. At the same time, I was enjoying swimming in the open water more and more.

Once I found my love of the open water, I shed my wetsuit for good. I now swim in the traditional "swim costume" — a simple swimsuit, goggles and cap - no matter the body of water or temperature. I swam in the San Francisco Bay throughout my entire third pregnancy, which included twenty-five Alcatraz swims through fall, winter and spring.

I'm proud to call myself an open water swimmer...and I hope you will love the swim portion of triathlon!

TIME TO HIT THE POOL!

First, you must determine your swim experience level. Were you a strong swimmer growing up and on a swim team? Have you been out of the water for a while and are just a little rusty? Is your most recent swimming accomplishment doing the dog paddle to the wet bar in the resort pool? The great thing about swimming is that it welcomes all levels and ages.

If you are absolutely new to swimming, please call your local health club or YMCA to find a local Masters Swim program (www.usms.org). Once you have this information, you should contact one of the Master Swim coaches. Then explain that you are new to swimming and would like some private lessons. No one will laugh! Every coach *loves* a new swimmer and enjoys bringing new people into the sport and watching them thrive. Typically, a six-pack of lessons will give you a whole new outlook on the aquatic world.

If you haven't been in the water for a while and simply want to brush-up on your skills and endurance in the water, then you are ripe for joining your local Masters Swim program with U.S. Masters Swimming. These groups often meet mornings or evenings for hour long (or longer) workouts. While many have a monthly fee, all have drop-in fee ($5-$10 depending on the club) and most allow a free session for new swimmers to see if they like the program.

"Swimming Masters," as it is known, is a great way to gauge your endurance level, hone skills and build speed. Here are some tips when heading to Masters:

1. Upon arrival, find the coach and introduce yourself. Tell him or her why you are there and ask what lane you should use (or ask for the slow lane). You want to be in a lane with others who share your swimming level. This will help you get the most out of your workout. Do not be frustrated if the coach moves you up or down a lane over the course of a workout. Also, if you can only make it through a portion of a Masters workout before getting out—that's okay! Swimming is an endurance sport and you may need a few sessions before you can finish the entire workout.

2. The coach will stop by your lane and give you instructions...do not be shy about asking for help or clarification on instructions. Pool swimmers can have their own lingo! You'll soon be talking intervals and "going on the 5's".

3. Ask the coach for one drill or one specific element you can practice each week. This shows you are interested in improving *and* you'll find this is more economical than private lessons.

4. Focus on freestyle. Of the four swim strokes—freestyle, breaststroke, backstroke and butterfly—you want to focus on freestyle (also, known as the front crawl). This is the stroke you will use in triathlons as it will carry you furthest with the least amount of effort. In fact, many people opt out of the butterfly during masters and instead do breaststroke or freestyle. Don't feel compelled to know "all" the strokes before you start. Work on the strokes as you like—all strokes will build coordination and balance and improve your rotation in the freestyle. But remember that freestyle is your mainstay for race day.

5. Learn to breathe bilaterally (on both sides). You will have more confidence if you learn to breathe on both sides. Bilateral breathing involves breathing every third stroke and will benefit you in rough water conditions where breathing on one particular side may be your only or best option due to the sun or waves. Bilateral breathing also avoids neck issues and provides greater balance in your stroke...plus, it's just darn cool.

Many triathletes participate in Masters Swimming. Be sure and ask your lane-mates about triathlons and you'll likely find a whole new set of friends!

WHEN THE POOL IS NOT AN OPTION...

Not everyone is comfortable donning a swimsuit and hopping into a pool with others. You may not have access to a pool and are waiting for the lake to warm up. That doesn't mean swimming has to be on hold. Try a DVD such as *Go Swim Freestyle with Karlyn Pipes-Neilsen*. It's a great instructional video and includes a laminated drill guide. Best of all, Karlyn is not only a Masters World Record holder, but an amazing open water swimmer who has taught thousands of swimmers.

HITTING THE OPEN WATER

Eventually, you must swim in the "open water." That means—not a pool. I know, boo and hiss. But you have to do it! There are *some* pool swims in triathlons, but you won't ever reach your big goals if you stay in the pool. Aspects of the open water can be intimidating from water temperature and sea creatures to not being able to grab the side of the pool if you're tired or want to get out.

Depending on where you live and swim, the open water may be a lake, the ocean or a river. Clarity of the water may be great (think: Caribbean) or quite murky (think: Swamp Thing). Obviously, there are no lane ropes or black lines on the bottom of the open water for you to follow. You may think you swim straight but find quickly without the lane line or black line to follow, you are all over the place. Maybe you zigzag or pull to the right or left? This is perfectly natural, but also why you must learn to "sight."

SIGHTING

Sighting is critical in open water swimming. Sighting is not stopping; it is literally lifting your head out of the water to figure out "where" you are and more importantly, where you are going.

Every few strokes you will want to glance ahead to make sure you are on the mark. Usually, the "mark" in triathlon is one of the buoys that the race directors place on the race course. You stay focused and sight your goal from buoy to buoy, until you are at the swim exit. Sighting is not stopping, going vertical and looking ahead. It is *not* sticking your head up like an ostrich mid-stroke causing your butt to fall lower in the water. Sighting is giving a quick nod up with your head, and then returning to your stroke and breathing pattern.

CURRENTS & WEATHER CONDITIONS

Depending on the body of water where you are swimming, you may or may not have a current moving you. Being pushed or pulled by the tides or a current can ruin your plan of sighting and swimming in a straight line from point A to point B. Often you will need to sight on and swim in a different direction than your final target—you must factor in how the water will be moving your entire body *laterally* while you are propelling yourself *forward*.

Do not avoid open water training on windy days or when there are waves and chop. While the pool provides the constant of smooth water and an opportunity to refine your stroke, open water has a number of variables from wind and chop. The only way to learn how to adjust your rhythm and stroke is to practice swimming in different weather conditions.

If swimming in the open water for the first time, swim with a group familiar with your local tides or currents and body of water. A group provides confidence in the water, tips and fun! Local tri groups usually have open water practices so get your butt out of the box!

For additional information on how to move from the pool to open water, check out the DVD and website *Lane Lines to Shore Lines* (www.lanelinesto-shorelines.com) by Gary Emich, an accomplished open water swimmer. Gary is closing in on a world record 1,000 Alcatraz crossings in addition to two English Channel Relays and a Catalina Channel Relay just to name a few of his swims. As a race organizer, coach and triathlon swim director, Gary's ability to explain how to sight, how to think about open water and the challenges (or fears) that accompany it are both informational and inspiring.

EQUIPMENT

Swimming is such a great (cheap!) sport. All you need to start is a pair of goggles, a swim cap and a swimsuit. Yes, okay, there may also be the wetsuit so we'll discuss that too. Top to bottom, there are a few things one needs when swimming.

SWIM CAP

Invest in a good silicone cap! Silicone swim caps are slightly thicker than latex, and they don't pinch or pull your hair or "burn" the back of your neck. A good silicone cap is less than $10 and will last a long time. Buy a bright color—yellow, hot pink, neon green—so it is visible for swimming in the open water. Black, navy, dark green and white make it easy to lose sight of a swimmer.

Usually, a race will give you a cap in a specific color that corresponds with your start wave. "Waves" are groups of participants that usually leave three to five minutes after each other to keep the race start from being too crowded. The race cap will usually be latex—so put your silicone cap on first and then place the race day latex cap over it for the best fit.

For colder climates with water temperatures under sixty degrees Fahrenheit, you may want an insulated cap such as the Barracuda Hothead. This cap goes on first, followed by the silicone and/or latex.

Earplugs

I highly recommend earplugs. While Mack's Earplugs (www.macksearplugs. com) are popular and have a range of styles from soft silicone to aqua earplugs, find a brand and style that works for you.

Why earplugs? Well, no one likes water in the ear, infections or loss of hearing. *Huh? What did you say?* Specifically for swimmers who are in cooler waters, over time cold water can harm the fine bones of the ear and lead to permanent ear damage. Ear plugs are a simple and effective way to protect your ears.

Goggles

For swimmers, goggles become like a religious issue. Some people prefer the larger "mask" style goggles for races while others choose the traditional goggles you see on pool swimmers. There is no right or wrong choice here; it's what works for you. Be sure and practice with your preferred goggle of choice and try to avoid new goggles on race day, because you never know when a leak will happen.

Goggles should have a good fit and feel like they are suctioned to your head. If you are buying goggles in a store, ask the salesperson if you can try the goggles on before you make your purchase. Once you find a brand and model that you love—buy in quantity online to get the discount and to have in your swim bag and gym bag, as well as spares. Far too often I've found goggles I love…only to have the manufacturer discontinue the model shortly after I bought them.

Unfortunately, goggles will fog up. Anti-fog drops, wipes (such as Foggle) and sprays on the market work very well. However, spitting into your goggles and rubbing it around before wiping with a soft cloth also works and is much more economical. A third option is soaking goggles every so often in dish soap such as Dawn. Soak, rinse lightly and let dry naturally.

SWIM AIDS

Swim aids such as snorkels, fins, hand paddles or pull buoys are not allowed in races. While these make great training aids when working with a swim coach, leave them at home on race day.

WETSUIT (OPTIONAL)

Yes, I said optional. Wetsuits are not required in a race. Wetsuits *do* aid in warmth and flotation. Wetsuits also give swimmers an edge in the water, allowing the body to float higher and thus, creating less drag. However, just because you are wearing a wetsuit does not mean that you cannot succumb to hypothermia or drowning. On the other end of the spectrum, many races prohibit wetsuits in waters over 78 degrees as the swimmer can suffer from heat exhaustion. It is important to remember that wetsuits are not life jackets and should *not* be considered personal flotation devices.

Wetsuits can be expensive, so before you invest in your second skin, try on a number of wetsuits in the store to see which brands and sizes fit best. Some stores have rentals allowing you to try different brands before buying. Once you have a list of wetsuits, you can also search sites such as Craigslist and eBay for used wetsuits although these would not have a manufacturer's warranty which may or may not be important to you or worth the additional cost of buying new. Ask your triathlete friends as many know someone with a wetsuit that no longer fits or needs to find a new home.

BUYING A WETSUIT

Buying a wetsuit for triathlon is a big investment. Starting at around $150, a wetsuit should last a few seasons of practice and racing, so take your time and buy wisely. Here are a few tips to help you in your quest to find your second skin:

1. *Buy a Wetsuit Specifically for Triathlons:* A wetsuit for triathlon and open water swimming is different than a suit for scuba diving or surfing. The wetsuit has super buoyant neoprene to help you float high in the water and a slick skin exterior to help you glide. These are major and extreme differentiating features from scuba or surf counterparts. Do not try to swim in a surf or scuba suit as you will quickly find yourself weighed down and waterlogged.

2. *Thickness:* Tri wetsuits range in thickness from 1.5mm-5mm. Talk to the staff at your local sporting goods store to find out what thickness people are buying in your area. Also take into account your body size. If you are super thin (we'll try not to hate you), then consider a thicker suit to keep warmer. If you carry a little more on your frame, consider a thinner suit.

3. *Fit & Comfort:* Nothing is worse than an ill-fitting wetsuit. A loose wetsuit will fill with water and cause drag, whereas a suit that is too tight will cause excess chafing. The most important aspect of a wetsuit fit is shoulder to crotch. Proper fit in chest, waist and legs is important, but if you reach overhead and cannot get full extension because your girl-parts are being violated, then you should try a different size or brand. Also, remember that a wetsuit will become looser the more you swim in it!

4. *Sleeves or Sleeveless:* This is a personal preference. Sleeveless can allow an increase range of motion but the warmth factor will come into play. Sleeveless suits are seen more in warmer water areas. If you are unsure, go for the full-sleeved wetsuit as you may want to travel to colder water races in the future. When choosing the full sleeve, look for thinner neoprene around the shoulder area where you move the most.

5. *Style:* Sometimes the best fitting suit isn't the one with the cool-factor name on it, the color or look you wanted. Go for what fits you best as different brands fit bodies differently. With the right wetsuit fit, you'll be gliding through the water so fast no one will see that little patch of color you coveted.

6. *Business:* What type of warranty does the wetsuit have? How do I repair the wetsuit if I poke my freshly manicured fingernails (yeah, right) through the neoprene? These are considerations in play when you are purchasing a suit.

When trying on a wetsuit, it should be very snug and without big gaps or air pockets. Air pockets now = fill with water later! The zipper goes up the back…yes, I've had to tell people at the start line that their wetsuit was on backwards. I'm here to save you the race day embarrassment.

Avoid wearing jewelry or being anywhere near a sharp object when pulling on your wetsuit. Start slowly by pulling the rubbery suit on up to the knees and then rolling or gently pulling up from the *inside* of the suit to the thighs and waist before pulling up the torso and arms. Putting on a wetsuit is a workout in and of itself! Once you are the proud owner of the suit, you can use BodyGlide, TriSlide (spray) or similar balms to help the wetsuit go on easier. Spray or rub these lubricants on your feet, ankles, wrists, knees and arms to make the suit slide on like a charm.

Avoiding Chafing

Between the swim cap and wetsuit, chafing can be a problem. Chafing will leave you with painful, raw skin and sometimes blisters. To avoid this, many athletes use BodyGlide, Aquaphor or other such balms to aid in getting wetsuits on *and* to prevent chafing during a workout or race. If chafing gets you down, apply liberally! The common areas to apply are around the neck of your wetsuit and under the arms. If you find other places to lube up, just do it and keep it your own little secret.

Swimming on Race Day

The number one thing to do the day of the race is to *listen to the race briefing!* The race briefing is very important—do not roll your eyes or act bored—*listen* and take in the information as if your life depends on it, because it does.

Race directors take the time to test the course. As test swimmers for many of the Alcatraz triathlons and races, we swim the course the day before or at a day and time with similar tidal conditions. We divide ourselves into slow, medium and fast groups and swim the course and then reconcile our notes. What did we sight on? Where did we find chop or wind? What would we recommend to the race director to provide instructions to the swimmers so they have the best possible swim? Where to position kayakers and safety boats to best assist swimmers?

The information the race director gives during the briefing is for *your* benefit. Listen and if you have questions, ask or find the person giving the briefing and ask your questions. They are more than happy to provide answers.

GETTING TO THE START LINE

As previously noted, many races will start in "waves." Typically you will know your wave by your swim cap color or race number and this will be explained over and over again during the registration, race briefing and in some cases the race schedule. Other races are an all at once "go" with everyone scrambling into the water at once. Again, this part of the importance of the race briefing so listen, listen, listen and if you're still unsure, just ask.

Be sure to have your timing chip strapped securely to your ankle—not your wrist, not tucked in your suit but firmly around your ankle. Your timing chip is a part of your race packet, as will be described later, and basically keeps track of your swim, bike, run and total race time. Once your timing chip is strapped securely, ensure that you have your wetsuit, cap, goggles, earplugs… check.

You're ready!

BEACH, BOAT OR SURF?

Depending on the race and location your swim may start by jumping off a boat (e.g., Alcatraz), running from the beach (e.g., lake swims) or diving through the surf (e.g., Hawaii). Each type of start has its own unique quirks, so here's a quick primer on how to survive the swim start in any locale.

BEACH:

Typically, a beach is the easiest start. You will walk or run into a lake with little or no wave action making this splash-splash easy. Some people have a method of high marching step running out to about mid-thigh before diving in and starting to swim. Stay to the edge of the pack to avoid being overrun by the speed demons.

BOAT:

Boat starts involve jumping 5-8 feet into the water below. Swimmers line up at the exit doors and jump into the water from the boat. No matter how deep the water is, do *not* dive off the boat. You never know who else may be under you which could be as deadly as diving into a log. Jump feet first and *hold your goggles* onto your head to avoid losing them when hitting the water. Try to jump off to the side and quickly swim away from the boat once you resurface. You can adjust goggles and anything else once you are away from the boat and the flock of jumping swimmers.

SURF:

Surf starts require the most coordination. I highly recommend practicing entering the surf if you have never experienced it. There is a timing technique to running, diving under each wave and repeating the process until you have made it out through the first few incoming waves. I've sadly watched swimmers spend five or more minutes being pushed back by the surf as they were unaware of the trick to "going under" the incoming waves.

OCEAN SWIMS V. LAKE SWIMS

Swimming in a bay or ocean instead of a lake has added variables of changing tides and currents. All may have a wind factor, but lakes will have static points to sight as the tides and currents are not "moving" you. Again, this is where listening to the race briefing is vital.

In an open water ocean swim, currents will play a large part in which point you choose to "sight." As mentioned before, you will not swim towards the finish line, but rather a point *before* the finish line. This accounts for the "push" or "pull" the tides will give you. Trust the directions you are given as aiming directly for the finish line may cause you to overshoot and go off course.

Lake swims are much easier in terms of navigation. A typical course will have large orange or yellow buoys marking the course. Swim straight at the next buoy and then the next, repeating this for all the buoys on the course line until you are finished. "Turn buoys," buoys where you change direction in the swim—like heading back to shore—will often be a different color than the other buoys.

A note about wind and chop: both ocean and lake swims may have winds and more "chop" (waves) than you were hoping for. Some swimmers panic because they are suddenly out of the calm serenity of the pool. My best advice about chop is—learn to *literally* roll with it. Relax and find a rhythm that works *with* the waves and not against it. This may mean slowing down your stroke or making your stroke shorter or longer to find a timing that works. The best open water swimmers adapt to the water they're in and swim it.

DIFFICULTY DURING THE SWIM

A variety of issues can arise during the swim. Knowing how to handle these issues and not letting them ruin your race is key!

PANIC

Panic. Ugh. It happens sometimes. Just read about Swim Bike Mom's first open water swim in Part II. It's scary. You can hyperventilate. You *cannot* find a breath. Your arms and legs fail to move like they do in the pool. You feel like you'll never make it. Yes, this is panic.

> ## Making Friends:
> *A common theme in triathlon is embracing*
> *your fears and making those fears your "friend."*
> *Get used to this analogy.*
> *It will follow you everywhere!*

Panicking is one of the worst things you can do in the water. So here are a few ways to get you *out* of panic mode and *into* race mode:

1. *Count five swim strokes.* If you feel the nerves coming on, focus on the count of the swim *and* focus *only* on the count. This will cause you to slow down your mind and let your body do what you've trained it to do. Start with five strokes and then increase to ten, fifteen and twenty…until you are back in your groove.

2. *Heads-up breast stroke.* Sometimes just giving yourself a few breast strokes to see where you're going will help calm the nerves. Go for five breast strokes and then go back to freestyle.

3. *Float!* If the water isn't too rough, roll on your back and kick for five to ten seconds before rolling back over and starting your stroke back up. Playing otter can be fun and relaxing!

Remember, panic is mental so tell your mind to shut the front door…you have a race to finish!

GETTING PULLED OR REPOSITIONED

For your safety and the safety of other swimmers, the race coordinators may determine that you need to be pulled from the water or repositioned. If you are asked to exit the water onto a boat, do not argue! Race personnel aren't doing this to be mean or because they don't believe in you. They have a better view of the course and water conditions than you do and are taking this action for safety reasons. Ask if you can be repositioned further up in the pack or to calmer waters. Most races will do this, because *they want you to finish!* If you are pulled from the water for weather reasons such as thunder and lightning, you will be transported to the end of the swim and given instructions by race personnel.

ASKING FOR HELP

If you need help during the swim, simply stop and wave one arm overhead. This is the signal pilot boats and kayakers are trained to spot. They will come to you and ask what you need. Do not call a pilot or kayaker over to ask about the weather, where other racers are, what time the cutoff is or anything that is a non-emergency.

FEELING LIKE YOU'RE LAST

It may feel like everyone is passing you and that you will be last to finish the swim. Chances are, there are plenty of people behind you. Let them swim their race—you swim yours. Someone has to be last and the last person out of the water gets more cheers from the crowd than the second to last. If you find yourself in this position—relish it! You are a scenic swimmer and simply wanted to enjoy the course more than others.

Hypothermia

Cold, shivering, mental confusion or suddenly feeling warm and that you could go on forever are all signs of hypothermia. If you are swimming along and have difficulty counting to 10 or answering a simple question such as your name, chances are you're getting too cold and need to get out of the water. Note that signs of hypothermia can also appear once you are out of the water—dizziness, nausea, itchy or blotchy skin, physical weakness, and mental confusion are symptoms. Let someone know you are having difficulties and get into warm, dry clothes as soon as possible in addition to drinking warm liquids.

A Word on Conditioning and Swim Injuries

Throughout your triathlon training a great deal of emphasis will be on your legs and core—the big areas for cycling and running. In the swim, the big focus is your core in addition to your back, chest and shoulders. Strengthening your upper body will provide stability *before* you get into the pool. Therefore, don't just hit the gym thinking that your endurance workouts will cover "enough" and swimming will take care of your arms. On the contrary, not properly strengthening and stretching your back, chest and shoulders can lead to serious shoulder injury.

Swimming is a repetitive, low-impact activity—but one that relies on smaller muscles of the arm and tendons connecting through the tight space of your shoulder capsule to the larger back and shoulder muscles—all working in concert to pull your entire body through the medium of water which is approximately eight hundred times denser than air! Whew! This is no small feat and relying too much on the shoulder with improper pulling or arm position can lead to painful tears and long recovery times.

To avoid injuries, focus on strength, stretch and form.

- *Strength*: In the gym, work with light hand weights and resistance bands. Arms, shoulders, back, chest and core. From lat pulldowns and seated rows to chest press and internal and external rotator cuff strengthening—don't overwork one area more than the other. Muscle imbalance is a typical occurrence in swimmers and contributes to shoulder impingement which equals *pain*.

- *Stretch*: The best part of being a swimmer is stretching! Triceps, neck, back and chest are key. My favorite stretch: lay on a foam core roller and open your arms up like you're on a cross to open your chest; raise your arms up overhead and back to stretch your back.
- *Form*: When sitting at your desk, push your chest out, shoulders back and pinch your shoulder blades together. Learning to keep your shoulders back and engage the muscles that stabilize this posture will be a big benefit. There's no slouching in swimming.

While strength training and conditioning can help stave off injury, your technique in the water is the most important part. In a Masters program, a tri group or swim lessons, you should learn proper overall body position and rotation, and the correct position of the hand entering the water. (I like to think my hand is reaching into a bucket of popcorn—flat, fingers relaxed and wrist gently bent—but this also makes me quite hungry.)

If you start to feel a pinch in the shoulder, stop and see a physical therapist or trainer. Trying to "stick it out" through shoulder pain is likely to lead only to more damage. Don't worry—the water will wait for you to return.

SAYING GOODBYE TO "CAN'T"

A few years ago, I was lucky enough to be both a test swimmer and a swim 'angel' for an Alcatraz race. The swim angel job entails swimming with the back of the pack and looking for people who seem unsure, are having minor difficulties and in general, could use an experienced escort across the nearly two-mile crossing from Alcatraz to Crissy Field near the Golden Gate Bridge in San Francisco.

The swim started as usual with throngs of wetsuit-clad athletes nervously awaiting the horn-blow indicating it was time to jump ship. The angel 'skin' swimmers huddle to keep warm and endure questions, such as "did you forget your wetsuit?" and "are you crazy?"

After being the last off the boat and swimming a bit, one of the pilot boats pointed to a swimmer who could use a little help. I swam over to meet a lovely woman, someone who if you met her in the grocery store checkout you might not call her an athlete due to her physical size—but her heart said more. She was visibly nervous and couldn't take more than a stroke or two without stopping and stating, "I can't do this."

"Why can't you do this?" I asked

"I haven't done this before...I don't know where I'm going...everyone is already ahead of me..." She rattled off a number of excuses, none of which had anything to do with getting from point A to point B.

"Ok" I started, "most people haven't done this before, and lucky for you I have and I do know where we're going. How about we swim together?"

"I don't want to slow you down." She was looking for more excuses.

"You aren't slowing me down. I'm not here to try and win anything; I'm here to swim with you." With that, she sighed, not sure what to do. "We really need to get you moving, so how about just doing ten strokes to see how it feels?"

Over the course of the next few minutes, we repeated this drill—ten strokes and stop, twenty strokes and stop, thirty strokes—with very minor chit chat, assuring her that we were on a great course and not to worry about where everyone else was, that this was her swim.

During the swim, which took over an hour, I learned bits and pieces about her. Her parents were at the finish line and thought she was crazy for trying this. She really wanted change in her life due to an unhappy job. She never thought she would do anything like this. She couldn't even remember why she signed up to train and try.

As the beach drew closer her stroke became slower, and as if the beach was repelling her, she stopped and stared at the finish just a few hundred yards away.

"I can't do this. My parents said I can't do this. I can't believe this."

I really wasn't sure what to do, but I saw in this young woman a younger version of myself. The 215lb girl who no one wanted to date and was everyone's best friend except when it came to sports or party invitations. I knew her pain. I also knew what it was like to kick 'can't' to the curb. I grabbed her by the shoulders and whipped her around to look back out at Alcatraz, which was now close to 2 miles away.

"Do you want to know where can't is?" I asked. "You left it out there at Alcatraz. So if you want can't back, you're going to have to swim out and get it."

She looked at me dumbfounded as I continued, "I don't care who told you that you couldn't do this, but you just DID it. So screw 'can't,' and anytime you think you can't do something remember this and turn around to see just how far you've come."

She continued to stare at me, at Alcatraz, and then back at me. "I think it's time you finish this," I said.

You could see in her eyes a complete shift.

"Thank you," she said quietly.

I gave her a quick hug and she was off. I watched as she swam into shore and ran up across the finish line. With arms up in victory, she was greeted by a round of hugs.

Yes! Say goodbye to can't.

SIX

The Bike

INTRODUCTION BY SWIM BIKE MOM

Over the course of my thirty-three years, my bicycles and I have experienced love-hate relationships. As a young child, I was unable to *stop* my bike. The neighborhood trash cans all bore marks from me running bull-in-the-China-shop style into them. I would go and go on the bike and if I needed to stop, I would simply barrel into the nearest plastic curbside can. To this day, the biggest challenge for me is stopping and getting off my bike in one piece.

Swim Bike Klutz Bike Tip

Always use the same foot to start and stop
pedaling, and the same foot to put down when you stop.
This will help you gain confidence
with your stops and starts, especially when
you begin to work with clipless pedals.

After making my Decision to become a triathlete, I was determined to get moving right away. I dusted off my old bright yellow road bike from 1999 and wheeled it out of the garage. *I was going to be a triathlete! I needed to ride a bike! I was going to ride a bike! Here I go!*

My bike was a bright yellow Giant® OCR3, ancient as all hell, but with only fifty miles of actual wear on it. My early 20's relationship with my bike was no better than the relationship with my childhood bikes and trashcans. I was clumsy and spent plenty of "fun" afternoons with the Expert throwing my bike onto the grass, cursing at him because I was so frustrated. ("This is *all* your fault! I *can't* ride a $&#% bike!") So the "old" bike was essentially brand new, albeit old-*school* and super nerdy. I named the bike G-Force. The amount of force it took me to ride it was essentially 400,000 Gs.

On the first day of my determined bicycle riding, I packed G-Force into the car and bid the Expert farewell. The Expert just stared at me with his mouth open as I pulled out of the driveway.

The Expert loved to ride his bike and he had ridden for many years. In fact, I gave him a hard time about spending time *away* from me and loving his bike more, which was a great point of contention in our early marriage. So, eight years later, I was fairly certain that as I pulled out of the driveway, I witnessed some head shaking and heard some angry cursings from the Expert. I imagined him saying out loud, "Oh sure, *now* she wants to ride a bike. All those years she kept *me* from riding, but now…oh boy…"

Ugh. But I had to let it pass. Instead of dwelling on the past, I looked to the future. So I thought to myself, *I am going to ride my bike! I am going to be a triathlete! Ah-ha!*

I returned home only a short time later.

The Expert was not surprised. He was kind of smirking, actually. I walked in the door, slammed my keys on the counter and said two words.

"I quit."

"How can you quit? You just started." Eye roll from him.

"I don't want to talk about it," I said.

Okay, so I was not *really* going to quit. But quitting crossed my mind during that first bike ride. I mean, how miserable could one ride be? *Oh, pretty darn miserable.*

What was so terrible about that first ride? For starters, about a half mile into the maiden voyage, I hit a big hill. Apparently, I did not know what to do with my bike on a hill. I thought I had downshifted, but actually I was grinding out the hill in my giant gear, all the while thinking, *You have to be effing kidding me! This is cycling? Horrible!*

Then I began to feel like I would pass out. I looked at my heart rate monitor. My heart rate was in the high 180's, so I was physiologically dead. (At least, I felt dead.) My legs were also fighting against me and I began to roll backwards down the hill. Determined not to roll backwards, I teetered and cursed and instead, I fell sideways. *Riding a bike is miserable!!* I rode another twenty minutes, searching for small hills that I could navigate. But I hated every last second of it. Despite the fact I only rode about five miles, I drove home completely wiped out and defeated.

As I told the Expert my tale, I dragged him over to the bike and pointed my blaming finger at G-Force, declaring that the stupid ugly, old bike was broken.

The Expert pointed to the shifter, "This is broken?"

"Yes!" I screamed. "Or that," I said pointing to the chain ring.

The Expert rolled G-Force outside, hopped on the bike and took it for a spin. He returned a few moments later.

"Nope," he said matter of factly. "Nothing wrong with this bike."

I glared at him. But being the lawyer I was, I decided I would entertain his argument.

"How do you shift when you get on a hill?" he asked me.

I showed him, by gesturing.

"Umm hmmmmm," he muttered. "And how do you shift when you go down a hill?"

I showed him again.

"Nope. Wrong!"

"What do you mean 'nope wrong'? Boy, is that helpful!" I stormed away.

He chased after me, telling me to calm down. Then, the Expert assured me that I would have a much more enjoyable time once I learned *how* to use my bike. I was not convinced. He said I just had no earthly idea how to shift.

"When you see a big hill coming, you need to put it in the Granny Grocery Getter Gear," he said.

"The what?"

"*Ring ring!* The groceries are here!"

I looked at him.

"Like a granny bike. Like a slow granny riding a bike with a basket-full of groceries. With a bell. *Ring ring!*"

I stared at him.

He laughed, "You want to be in an 'easy' gear, like you are taking a casual trip to the grocery store. You want easy because that results in the biggest chance of succeeding up the hill and not blowing up your legs."

Recognition. I smiled.

"You were simply in the buster gear."

"Buster?"

"Yeah. Ball buster," the Expert said.

I rolled my eyes. But I understood. *The Grocery Getter Gear. Ring ring!*

With the Expert's help, I decided that I would try again. Of course, my triathlete dreams and Decision played a large part in me getting back on that hideous bike and trying again. Because I had declared that I was going to *be* something, I had to keep trying. I could not give up. Obviously, finding my inner athlete would be an even bigger challenge than I had anticipated.

But I kept going.

I may have been ready to become a triathlete in my dreams, but I was not ready for actually riding a bike. In retrospect, I wanted to quit because I was not *prepared* for riding. I had not learned how to shift gears, to corner. I had failed to learn the basics that actually make riding *enjoyable.*

The next few times I went to ride with G-Force, things *still* did not go so well for me. I crashed. Twice. I do not mean real heroic or cool crashes. I mean super lame crashes. Both times I got stuck in my clipless pedals at road crossings. I could not unclip my foot quickly enough. So my bike began teetering, my feet were clipped in, and I ended up screeching "oh noooo" and then hitting the pavement. I may as well have worn a sign: *Idiot rider. No idea what I'm doing.*

And eventually, I had a good bike ride.

The good bike ride was greatly helped by getting rid of the old squeaky G-Force. I went to local bicycle shop and got fitted for a new bike. I ended up with a Specialized® Secteur. I named her "Antonia" after my first Olympic distance St. Anthony's quest. The name "Antonia" is from Italian origin and means "priceless." She became my new bike companion. Our relationship started off a little rocky. But after three or four trips to the bike shop for minor adjustments, we became best friends.

On a particular morning in April 2011, I took shiny new Antonia for a ride. The weather was beautiful. It was one of those mornings where I woke up, drove to the trail and thought, *Yes, this is the right decision. I am glad I am here.* I pulled Antonia out of the car at 8:00 on the dot. Just me, Antonia and some water bottles whirring speedily through the morning. The ride contained no falls, no near-spills and no fear factors. Just peaceful and sweet, comfortable and safe riding.

Week after week, month after month, Antonia and I got to know each other. I learned how to clip into her pedals, to clip out and dismount safely. I learned to clean her up, make her shiny, change her tire tubes, inflate her tires and fix her dropped chain. Eventually, I did not run into parked cars and trash-cans. Cycling started out as my biggest enemy, but quickly became the sport in triathlon I enjoy the most.

When I asked Coach Monster to help me out with co-authoring the *run* section of this book (instead of the cycling section), he pouted a little. His favorite discipline, like mine, is also cycling. During our interview about the run, he told me, "There is nothing like the purity of *suffering* on a bike. It's a combination of the speed and the fact that you aren't pounding your body— you are actually *wringing it inside out*."

I told him later, "That sentence is precisely why I think you should help me write about the run, not the bike," I said.

He looked at me, shocked.

I said, "'*Suffering on a bike*'? You would scare away any sane beginner person with that kind of verbiage! You say that cycling is like '*wringing your body inside out*'? Dude, that is scary. You are quarantined to talk about running."

He smiled.

INTRODUCTION TO MCBLESSINGS, THE BIKE MCEXPERT

I asked one of my heroes, Mike "McBlessings" Lenhart, for a beginner-friendly peek into the base needed for cycling. "McBlessings" is a name greatly deserved by Mike. He is the President and Founder of the Getting2Tri Foundation (G2T), an organization empowering and enriching the lives of disabled individuals through the sport of triathlon.

McBlessings has a big heart and a super sweet smile. He has completed dozens and dozens of races, including three full Ironmans. McBlessings has served as an infantry officer in the U.S. Army, worked in a bike shop, written for *Competitor Southeast* magazine and been a Corporate America guy too. I met him through his Wednesday morning indoor cycling class, and he has inspired me through countless lessons in perspective. Through his passionate work for G2T, McBlessings is changing the lives of individuals with physical disabilities.

Go Social. Be Grateful.
Ride Happy. Clean Your Bike.

by Mike Lenhart,
President and Founder, Getting2Tri Foundation
(www.Getting2Tri.org)

I like the cycling piece of triathlon the best out of all three sports because it is *social*. Triathlon in general is a very "social" environment, but cycling especially. Group rides are so much fun and such great learning experiences for the beginner and advanced cyclist.

I have been fortunate to go to Kona (the Ironman World Championships held each year in Hawaii) twice as a handler (a person who helps disabled athletes throughout the race, notably in and out of the water, onto the bike, in transition). These elite-type experiences are *amazing*, don't get me wrong. But I get most excited about the every-day activities that triathlon enhances—like learning to simply ride a bike. With my work with G2T, I have been able to experience the spirit of the individual who just wants to learn to do normal, every-day activities again. So many of us take small activities for granted. Something as "simple" as riding a bike, can feel impossible for someone who recently lost a leg or has experienced a spinal cord injury.

For example, John is an athlete who I met at a G2T camp. He is a bilateral, below-the-knee amputee who was out of shape and out of work. He was diabetic, which was how he lost his legs. John came to the camp with his wife. She told me, "I really want John to learn to ride a bike again because that's what we used to enjoy doing before he lost his legs." And John learned to ride a bike at that camp. It was a good moment, a high.

So when I say that I love the socialization of cycling, I mean that in a narrow *and* broad sense of the word. You can do great things just by learning to ride a bike.

It's Not *All* About the Bike

As a beginner looking to purchase a bike, you have many things to consider.

First of all, the *type* of bike is a question that most beginners will face. I believe that a beginner will get more "mileage" out of a road bike, as opposed to any other bike. But really, the type of bike depends greatly on the individual's interests and needs. There are so many different kinds of bikes out there: hybrid, fitness, mountain, fat tires, skinny tires, tri bikes, road bikes.

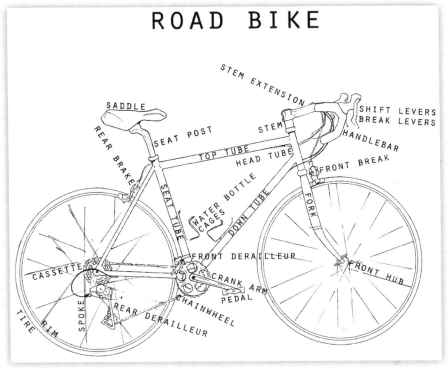

© Jennifer E. Nesbitt

If you are dabbling with cycling and your budget is low, then a fitness bicycle like a hybrid or a road bike is definitely going to be the best choice. For someone who has never cycled in her life, a hybrid may be a good entry level bike. However, if you are making a commitment to love the sport of triathlon and be in it "forever," then making the small step to an entry level road bike will serve you well. A road bike is going to be more versatile and comfortable for longer rides and for competing in races.

Bikes can certainly get expensive, but there are many ways to find good deals. First, almost all local bike stores stock refurbished bikes. Secondly, many bike stores will come down off the price if you simply ask for a discount.

The biggest difference in price point of bikes will come down to the type of frame (aluminum or carbon) and the bike components. A carbon bike will be lighter to ride but heavier on your wallet. Components are the rear and front derailleurs, shifters, pedals and type of saddle (seat). You can think about your components as three levels: gold, silver and bronze. An entry level bike with bronze components may be just fine to start, but you may have a little more maintenance and faster wear and tear. The gold standard should last you forever.

Okay, maybe at least until your next bike splurge.

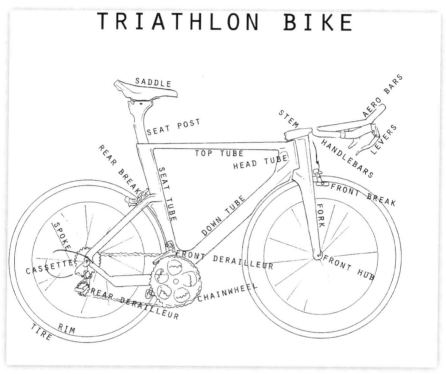

TRIATHLON BIKE

© Jennifer E. Nesbitt

GET FIT(TED)

Good cycling form starts with a proper bike fit and alignment. When you buy your bike from a reputable bike store, you will have a bike fitting. If they do not offer it, then you should look elsewhere for your bike. Do not (and I repeat), do not buy a bike without getting fitted.

Bike fits can be done in many ways—from an experienced cyclist "eyeing" your position and making adjustments, to precise measurements, and all the way down to fancy sensors and computers. Regardless of how you get fit, this is one of the most important steps in your cycling process.

Swim Bike Mom Says, "Get Fitted!"

I can attribute a lot to a good bike fit just from my personal experience. G-Force was not a good bike in general, and it certainly did not fit me well. Antonia was a better bike, but more importantly, she was a great fit, so we got along well.

Having a good bike fit sets you up for not only comfort, but also for success in your riding. If you are positioned well, you are using the most power possible in your hips and legs. A mere fit can turn you into a more efficient and powerful rider.

For most cyclists, there are three points of adjustment on the bike: seat height, saddle position and handlebar height. First, regarding the seat height, you want your leg to be extended out at the bottom of the stroke so that there is a slight bend in the knee. If your saddle is too high, you will have issues ranging from loss of power in the pedals to knee and hip injuries.

Next, you want the horizontal position of the saddle to be comfortable. This means that when your hands are on the handlebars, you want a slight bend in your elbows and also, relaxed shoulders.

Finally, the adjustment to your handlebar height will make up the last basic point of adjustment. Some triathletes like the handlebars lower (for more aerodynamic positioning), but it's really up to the cyclist depending upon his or her comfort level.

I cannot stress enough the importance of a proper bike fit. Failure to obtain a good fit will result in discomfort on the bike *and* expose you to *unnecessary* injuries. You may need many trips to the bike store to "get it right," but embrace it. Just make sure you are diligent and strive to get that fit perfect. A bike, believe it or not, *should* be comfortable. So many of us have ridden uncomfortable bikes in the past that we may not believe a comfortable bike is possible. But I promise—it is! Just work diligently to make sure you get there!

TUNE IT UP

After the first six months or so of having your properly fitted, new (or "new to you") bike, take it back to the shop for a tune-up. The cables on the bike will begin to stretch out after this period of time. Also, you may find that your saddle height or other areas might need adjustment. A good time for your first scheduled tune-up is around six months. The bike shop will adjust and work with you to tighten up your cables and make any additional adjustments to your fit. After that, once a year is a good marker for future tune-ups.

Getting Ready to Ride

You've got your bike and proper fit—now what? Are you ready to hit the road? Are you nervous? Where is a good place to start?

Indoor cycling classes are a good foundation for cycling. Spinning, as described in more detail later in this chapter, will aid in your cycling base building and get some fundamentals into your system. These classes are a good place to practice your form and cadence. However, "riding a bike to nowhere" is a different experience than feeling the wind on your face and actually moving down a road. Therefore, while training in cycling class is definitely beneficial and I believe necessary, especially in the colder months, you must get yourself out on the road and on your bike.

Group riding is a good idea for beginners. While riding in a group will be scary at first, it is something that must be conquered if you ride regularly and race. Furthermore, having a regular group ride may help for the sake of accountability. The more you ride with better cyclists, the better you will become, naturally. For starters, you should find some beginner rides—often called "no drop" rides. No drop means that *no* cyclist (even you!) will be left behind.

Understanding the rules of the road and being comfortable with cycling on the road is very important. Even seemingly secluded trails can get crowded and you need to learn how to maneuver. It is important to follow the rules of the road—just like in a car. Remember to be aware of your surroundings and be cautious. If in doubt, stop, look and listen.

There is no substitute for time actually spent on the bike. The more you ride, the better you will become and the more comfortable you will be.

The Swim Bike Mom Quick and Dirty
Rules of Triathlon Cycling

Most of the cycling rules in a USAT (USA Triathlon) sanctioned event are summed up below, but be sure to check the full rules and updates on the USAT website (www.USATriathlon.org):

Wear Your Helmet
If you are on your bike (even before the race), you must wear your helmet with the chin strap fastened. Failure to do so can result in a disqualification. Don't be a dingbat. Wear your helmet and strap it on.

Ride Nice
Be courteous and professional and nice. Otherwise you can get disqualified for Unsports(wo)manlike Conduct. Don't be the Dennis Rodman of triathlon.

Ride Right.
You must ride to the right of the road and complete all passes on the left. Passing on the right can result in an Illegal Pass penalty. Imagine if you were driving a car. You wouldn't pass on the shoulder of the road. Don't do it on your bike.

Drafting Penalties
1) Triathlon (with the exception of a specific type of races) is a non-drafting sport. This means that you are not permitted to ride closely behind the rider in front you. According to USAT rules, you must keep three bike lengths distance between yourself and the rider in front of you.

2) If you attempt to pass, you must pass the rider in front of you within fifteen seconds or a penalty will be assessed by a race official.

3) Overtaken Penalty. If you are passed, you must drop back and allow the three length distance to resume. You, as the rider who was just passed, are responsible for ensuring that you drop back.

*No Illegal Position or Blocking. Do not ride on the left side of the lane without passing. In other words, don't be a butthead who is holding everyone up — it's against the rules (and annoying).

*Usually these penalties are distributed as time penalties. The other penalties may result in DQ. That's "disqualification," not Dairy Queen.

WHAT ABOUT CLIPLESS PEDALS?

Clipless pedals allow your bike shoes to slide into a clip, so you are essentially attached to your bike. While the idea of being attached to your bike is scary—it is actually quite important, because you are able to use the power of the upstroke in addition to the down stroke. When riding a traditional bike, you are only pushing *down* on the pedals. With clipless pedals and cycling shoes, you are using the full, circular range of motion.

I think clipless shoes are good to use from the very beginning. Most pedal systems have a tension system where you can set the tension, making it easier to clip in and out of the pedals. It will be good for the beginner to set the tension light to get used to starting, stopping and clipping in/out of the pedals.

With clipless pedals, you will get about 30% more pedal stroke efficiency because you are using the *entire* pedal stroke—meaning you are *pushing down* with one leg while *pulling up* with the other. Without the pedals, you are just pushing down and the other leg isn't doing anything for you, but hanging along for the ride.

Ten Questions with McBlessings

What's Your Favorite Post-Race Meal?
A good burger. After a race, I am thinking that I did something "ultra good" (racing), so I want to do something "ultra bad!" The next morning, I wake up and say, "Oh my goodness, I feel gross," and I get back on track.

What's on your iPod?
I have a lot on my iPod. I teach cycling, so I have songs that people are familiar with. I have found that if people are familiar with the music, they work harder in cycling class. I have country, pop, contemporary and even some classical on the iPod, though. Well, really it's mostly pop.

What's your Food Achilles' Heel?
Peanut M&Ms. I could eat a whole bag.

Favorite Running Shoe?
I was a Nike guy for years. Lately, I've switched to Karhu brand. They have bright colors, which I like. I know you shouldn't pick your shoe for color...but I like that too.

Favorite Place to Run?

I like to run on the beach.

Favorite Race?

My favorite race distance is the half Ironman or full Ironman because there is a lot more to strategy involved in those distances. You have to think about the nutrition, and transitions, and the strategist in me likes to do that. My favorite race to date is the Gulf Coast Triathlon (70.3 distance).

Biggest Race Pet Peeve?

I don't like the triathlon Prima Donnas. I like to just get out there and race.

Scariest Triathlon Moment?

I've been racing for 7-8 years now, but I had a scary moment just last season. I had a wetsuit that had been boxed up all winter. And I had put on some weight. When I started swimming, my neck seized up and I hyperventilated in the water until everyone passed me. It took me a while to gather myself, and I was the last one out of the water. I was scared. But it was good, because it reminded me, "Don't get too cocky."

Does Your Bike Have a Name?

No. (laughing) Just "bike."

If You Could Train with One Triathlete, for One Day... Who Would You Choose?

I work with people with disabilities through the Getting2Tri Foundation. I have met so many heroes! But there's a guy, who is not a triathlete, but he's a long distance runner. His name is RichardWhitehead. He's a bilateral amputee (missing both legs above the knees). I ran the Georgia marathon with him a few years ago. He's an amazing guy and I have recently thought, I wish I could do that again.

SWIM BIKE MOM SAVES YOUR QUEEN

(Swim Bike Mom here. I figured I'd let McBlessings off the hook for talking about the Queen).

Extended periods in the bike saddle are hard on your rear end. When I say your rear end, I really mean your buns *and* your lady parts. Plain and simple, the Queen will start to scream after so many miles. The best way to deal with this issue? Ride more. Seriously. The Queen is a lazy diva who must be whipped into shape and only time in the saddle will save her! God save the Queen!

That being said, be nice to the Queen. Get her a good saddle, proper bike fit, comfy chamois (padded) shorts and lots of Aquaphor or other lubricant to keep her happy. If you are noticing that the Queen goes completely numb while you are riding, then you are ripe for a nose-less saddle like the ISM Adamo Road saddle or the Cobb saddle. Basically, these seats remove the pointy part of the saddle, which in turn, takes the pressure off the Queen and her castle. I have been riding with the ISM Adamo Road saddle for almost two years and I love (love!) it. Although the Expert does not have a Queen, he uses the Adamo too and says it helps with the Jesters.

In the beginning, you may need a padded seat cover. But please, I beg you, do not rely on this. And get it off your bike as soon as possible, because it looks silly. With a proper bike fit, you should not need the extreme padding (which will also interfere with the efficiency of your pedal stroke). Plus, you want to get the Queen in shape, remember!

Sometimes you can develop "saddle sores." Saddles sores are actually skin issues on the Queen or her backyard neighbors, the Humps. Saddle sores can appear from too much unnecessary chafing and movement (forward, backward, side to side) in the bike saddle—which is precisely why a good bike fit is paramount. If you are too high in the saddle, your body and hips will move too much and you are ripe for sores.

Also, keep the Queen clean and lubed up and wear a one-piece chamois pad while in the saddle. Sometimes a chamois pad can be made with two or more pieces, causing additional friction and discomfort.

And while it may be entirely too much information, I *do* know that the Queen is a better cycling partner when she is completely bald. Less chance for ingrown you-know-whats and ripped-out-you-know-whats. Just saying.

Now, we'll move on.

© Birds Eye View, Inc. | Tricyle Studios

HOW TO RIDE YOUR BIKE

As a beginner triathlete, I was scared to death of riding my bike; flat roads, hills, traffic—it did not matter—all of it was horrifying. I slowly became accustomed to riding on a safe, flat trail. But I continued to remain terrified of climbing hills. Terrified.

In the early days, I would see a hill coming and I would turn around. Leave. *Adios!* Same deal once I purchased Antonia—still terrified of the hills. The bike was not the problem. The problem was not the size of the hill, because I would run from *all* hills. The problem was *me*. I had not learned to ride efficiently and it made me scared to climb.

However, after over two years of going to Coach Monster's Spinning class and hearing things like, "It's a beautiful day to climb on a bike!" or sometimes, "You must make friends with the climb!" And even, "What a wonderful morning to suffer!"…well, some of those little mantras began to sink in a little.

Arguably, riding your bike has less to do with the actual bike than you might think. If you have a decent bike, then really, the rest is up to the *rider*. Cycling, like swimming, is much about technique, form and a little bit of coordination. To be an efficient cyclist, there are rules of the road and ways to do (and not to do) the second sport of triathlon.

MAKE SURE YOU ARE READY TO RIDE

This goes back to your bike fit, bike bag and all your gear. Take the bike for a few test rides around the block to make sure that everything feels right. Practice shifting gears a few times. Sometimes the ride around the block will save you a lot of trouble on the road.

PURPOSEFUL SUFFERING

Coach Monster has copyrighted, patented and bottled his idea of "Purposeful Suffering." In other words, we are embarking on training days to suffer… purposefully. He swears by "making friends" with the pain, the hills and the hard rides. You set out to suffer with a purpose. You suffer. And suffer. And through the suffering, you make the improvements happen.

A great tip from Coach Monster is: "Acknowledge that the suffering is about to commence. You should prepare your mind to focus on the effort. Embrace the purposeful suffering. Make best friends with the pain. Love it."

Because the truth is—sometimes riding just sucks.

"WHERE CAN YOU RELAX?"

Coach Monster screams in class, "Where can you relax?" I usually first think, *I can relax back on my couch at home. Or on a beach in the Bahamas. Silly Monster.*

But "where can you relax?" is a question to remind you to keep your body in a calm and relaxed state when riding. This means keeping your elbows relaxed and your shoulders down. Keeping your upper body completely relaxed— right down to your face muscles—saves energy and makes the bike ride easier.

Do not lock your elbows. Do not clench your hands to the point of white knuckles. Do not scrunch your face. Do not grind your teeth. Keep everything up top relaxed and you will be amazed at the energy it saves on the bottom (and the next day!). I was not naturally able to relax. (What a surprise.) But now, I practice relaxation everywhere, including cycling class and when I am in the car in Atlanta traffic.

As you are going uphill, keep your chest open, with your elbows close to your body and kinda loosy-goosey. When you are riding, ask yourself the simple Coach Monster question, "Where can you relax?" You will likely be tensing something, and this will be a good reminder to find the place of tension, release it and save energy.

This small tip makes a massive difference.

Learn Your Gears

Whether you are riding on flat land or in the hills, you must find right gear(s) for your terrain. Gearing takes practice. Period. Take your bike on rides and practice, practice, practice. That is all.

Okay, so that is not *all*.

Hill riding is especially challenging for a beginner because of the intricacies of learning to gear. When you see a hill on the horizon, do not turn around and go the other way—like I used to do. You must learn to enjoy the hills, and part of learning to love them is learning *how* to ride them.

Most standard road and triathlon bikes will have two front rings: large and small. The large gear will serve you well on downhills and flat roads; the small gear is for climbing, heading out of transition and general starting after stopping. (Tip: it is easier to "go" in an easy gear. When you are approaching a stop light or sign, you can shift into lower gears to make the re-start easier.)

You want to get in the lower gears to climb a reasonably steep hill— meaning you want your bike to be in the smaller front chain ring. However, do not slam the bike into the lowest gear when you see a hill coming. That will make a mess and cause you to overspin, possibly topple over and make a fool out of yourself. (I am not sure how I know this. I take the Fifth.)

Finding the right gear for each particular hill takes practice, but eventually you will instinctively know where you need to be gear-wise. I find that, with the larger climbs, it helps to make a move with your gears *before* you are on the hill and being devoured by the mean nasty hill. As a rule of thumb, you do not want to be pushing too hard uphill (grinding in the big chain ring, blowing up your leg muscles and knees by struggling to turn the pedals)—nor should you be spinning out of control (slipping into the small ring too early, pedaling wildly and bouncing all over the place). All of this takes practice.

If you can buzz up a short hill quickly and it will not blow up your legs, then do not waste your time fooling with the gears and just pop over the hill. If you grossly underestimated the hill, and when you are halfway up you realize you are about to be in fall-over-type-trouble—you may want to pop out of the saddle and get over the hill that way.

Pop out of the saddle? What?

Sometimes it may be easier to stand and pedal to get over short hills. This is known as "popping out of the saddle." Sounds like splitting your pants, but it's not. Think: Tour de France.

This takes a little practice and should be used sparingly because it can take a toll on your legs on a long ride.

Your bike should be fitted with the proper cassette for easier (read: beginner) gearing. Make sure you ask your bike store for a beginner cassette, so you have many options and easy gears to help you over the hills. Nothing will ruin your day faster than "professional" equipment and a giant hill. (I have learned this. Also. The. Hard. Way.) Coach Monster recommends an "11/28" cassette. If you have no idea what that is, never fear—just ask your local bike dudes. They will know (and if they don't, then find another bike shop).

Practice your gearing. That is (really) all.

"PUSH YOUR BUTT BACK!"

When you see a hill coming, stay seated and push your rear end towards the rear of the saddle. Be careful not to push your butt *off* the back of the saddle. In cycling class, Coach Monster screams, "Push your butt back!" when we are riding simulated hills.

The point? As you drive your feet downward on the downstroke, you will be engaging your quads (front leg muscles) and glutes (your bun muscles) to push forward. When your butt is back, you are in a position of greater power.

Also, remember to lean your upper body ever so slightly forward to keep your center of gravity in…well, the center.

Repeat Eminem Lyrics.

Another cycling tip is to repeat rap lyrics when the ride gets difficult. Okay, so this is a silly tip. But somehow repeating the rhythmic lyrics to "'Till I Collapse" in my head gets me up any hill much faster.

"Keep Your Head Up!"

Coach Monster strikes again with this tip. When you are riding, you should keep your head up, eyes wide and chest open. Do not look at the ground. Do not look down at your bike. Keep your head up to allow your airways to remain open and get oxygen to those punished lungs. Not to mention, you really should be looking ahead at the road at all times.

Keeping your eyes on the road does not mean looking on the road directly in front of you. Just as if you were driving a car, you should look *down* the road, so you can take in all the dangers, conditions and scenery.

At the same time, you still want to glance directly in front of you to make sure there are no potholes or dangerous gravel in the road. I tend to scan my eyes further down the road every so often to ensure the road conditions are good so I have time to avoid bad pavement or rocks if necessary.

I try my best to keep my head up all the time. Unfortunately, I have been caught on camera in most race photos with my head staring down at my feet. I am a repeat offender.

Downhills and Braking

Riding a bike is dangerous, more dangerous than many of us realize. Some good tips I have received from the Expert (who is actually a very good technical cyclist and mountain biker) and others: err on the side of caution and slower speeds, especially on a downhill.

Even if you are flying downhill like a bat out of cycling hell, do *not* suddenly grab your brakes or squeeze them too hard. An important tip is to *ease* into braking. When you are headed downhill, your body's center of gravity is towards the front wheel. Do your best to keep your butt back on the seat as much as you can in order to keep your center of gravity *away* from the front.

Brake carefully, lightly and steadily to control your speed on a downhill. Be careful with your front brakes: if you use excessive front braking you risk going over the handlebars. And by "going over the handlebars," I mean *your body* flying off your bike, *over* the handlebars and *onto* the pavement. (Eeeek.) On bikes sold in the United States, the front brake will typically be the one you squeeze with your left hand. But you can confirm by simply squeezing and looking at your brakes. The one that moves when you squeeze? *Ta da!*

When you are approaching a turn, slow down and brake *before* you turn the corner. This is the same concept as driving a car. You do not take a corner in a car on two wheels and *then* apply the brakes. You slow down first, then turn. Same principles apply on a bike. Be sure to release the brake levers as you turn. If the front tire hits some loose sand or rocks around a corner *while* you are braking, you can cause the front tire to lock down and the bike to slip out from under you. Learn to ease into braking and use more pressure on your back brake.

A good habit is to rely most heavily on the back brake. I tend to use the front brake *only* when I am cycling in a straight line—like on a trail. This is more of a habit-forming tip, which will prevent you from using the front break in a sudden or emergency situation. If you stay off the front brake, then you will have less chance of throwing yourself over the handlebars in a panicked moment.

DON'T TAKE THE DOWNHILLS "OFF"

Within the bounds of safety, Coach Monster urges that if you can keep pedaling and working hard *downhill*, you will have a speed advantage over riders who take the downhills "off" in order to rest.

To use this tactic, you need to put your bike in the bigger gears (large front chain ring) to get the benefit of the downhill *and* the pedaling. Not only will this give you a time advantage, but you will become a stronger cyclist because—well, you're simply pedaling more.

"PERFECT PEDAL STROKES!"

By using those clipless pedals for what they were designed, you are able to put more power where it matters and become an efficient cyclist. Coach

Monster reminds us in Spinning class to have "perfect pedal strokes." This means keeping your feet *flat* in the bottom of the pedal stroke, like scraping gum off the bottom of your cycling shoe. If you are riding on your toes or with your toes pointed down, you are engaging the wrong muscles and losing power. A way to tell: do your calves *absolutely* kill you after a cycling workout? You are likely "toe-ing up" and engaging the wrong muscles. Engage your hips on the upstroke to maintain a perfectly engaged, circular pedal stroke, which is a push *and* pull motion.

In other words, use the entire pedal stroke to your advantage. Up and down. Up and down. Do not just stomp your feet downward—also remember to pull upward on the pedal. See? Perfect circles.

Keep Your Knees In.

"Ride with your knees pushed close together—not touching, of course—but reasonably close. Your knees should be within the distance between your shoulders," McBlessings said in an interview.

"If you saw a car come down the highway and the two front doors were open, that wouldn't be very efficient (not to mention dangerous). Same deal with riding your bike. Keep the knees in. Otherwise, you're like a circus unicycle rider!" Not only will you look funny, but you will be losing power and risking injury, especially to your knees and hips.

Do Some Drills (on a stationary bike)

Working on cycling "drills" like swim drills will help improve your form and power in the saddle. There are many different drills, but a Coach Monster favorite is the single leg drill. Just as the name indicates, you will use your one leg to pedal and allow the other leg to "come along for the ride." By using one leg, you are able to detect weaknesses in your pedal stroke and work on strengthening the weaker leg.

Now That I Know *How* to Ride...

The next question was where in the world *should* I ride?

I highly recommend calling your bike store and asking where you can find a good, yet safe (relatively low car traffic) ride. You can also spend some time with Google and ask it where some fabulous routes are located. Many cyclists post their favorite riding routes via Map My Ride (www.MapMyRide.com), and you can download their hard-working route(s) and see if their favorite places are a good fit for you in both location and distance.

Some cities may have the "Rails to Trails" paths like Atlanta's Silver Comet Trail, which is closed to *road* traffic. Only walkers, runners, strollers, roller-bladers and cyclists are allowed on these trails. Immediately, you will have a reasonably safe place to ride. Of course, you must still be careful—no ride is completely safe.

Bear in mind that you may need to drive ten or twenty miles outside of town to find a safe place to ride. Invest in a bike rack for your car and *go*. The safety factor is worth the investment. Constantly fearing cars and traffic lights will put a damper on any ride.

Always remember to put safety ahead of all concerns. Riding in traffic is daunting even for experienced cyclists, because we are all at the mercy of the drivers on the road. No matter how careful we may be, *other* drivers and cyclists may not be as careful. Not to scare you away, but do your best to find a "safe" path, especially in the beginning.

SAFETY AND GROUP RIDING TIPS

- Wear your helmet.
- Wear your RoadID.
- Do not ride on the sidewalk.
- Do not ride with headphones.
- Do not talk on your mobile phone (!).
- Pretend you are a car. Ride on the same side of the road as the cars, *with* the traffic. For example, in the U.S., you will want to ride on the right side of the road.
- If you are riding with a group, use signals such as pointing at the road below to indicate to the riders behind you that there is something in the road (e.g., pothole, crack, debris). This will help the people behind you avoid dangers that you can clearly see.
- Use hand signals for turning.

- If there is a car coming up from the rear, shout "car back!" to the riders in front of you to let them know. Same with "car up" to signal there is an oncoming car before a turn or stop.
- If you are at an intersection and the road is clear to cross, you can shout "clear!" or "clear right and clear left!" and proceed to cross. This will signal to the riders behind you that it is safe to cross so they do not have to clip out of their pedals. Of course, you will want to be certain that it is, in fact, clear. Additionally, make sure that they are just a few seconds behind you, because obviously "clear" can change pretty quickly.
- Learn to "hold your line"—meaning, learn to ride in a straight line.
- Look over your left shoulder every once in a while to check for cars, other riders, etc., but learn to do so without also veering in the direction that you are looking. This takes practice, because our bodies want to steer the bike in the direction of our heads, so practice this often.
- Stay as far right as you possibly and safely can. Note that when the roads are wet, you should stay off of the painted lines, because they are slick when wet.
- No "cross wheeling." In other words, don't ride too close behind *and* to the *side* of another rider. If they veer to the right and you are too close behind and to the side, then your front wheel may get caught in their *rear* wheel and cause a crash.
- It is fun to ride side-by-side and chit-chat with your friends. Keep in mind that this is (technically) poor cycling etiquette and annoying to the cars and trucks sharing the road. At the same time, this is part of the fun of group rides. Just bear in mind if you are on a well-traveled route, you "should" ride in a single file and save the side-by-side rides for empty country roads.

Indoor Cycling

Bike Trainer

You have the option to purchase a bike "trainer." A bike *trainer* is *not* a human being who yells at you like a boot camp sergeant. Rather, a trainer is an indoor mechanism that allows you to ride your bike indoors. Without going into nauseating detail, you can basically attach your bike upright to the trainer. You then can ride *your* bike just like a much-harder-to-pedal stationary bike. You can find a good trainer for a couple hundred bucks, or you can invest your life savings in one.

Bike trainers are especially important if you live in severe weather climates. In Georgia, we are technically able to ride all year round, because we rarely have snow or ice. That being said, a ride in February is freezing, so even the Southerners tend to stay indoors. But if you live in a place with snow and ice, you should *definitely* look into getting a bike trainer. The trainer is also good for rainy days. Eventually, you might decide to tackle some rainy day rides. However, remember safety first! Riding in the rain takes some experience and you should put your health and well-being first. In rain, snow, sleet and hail, the trainer allows you to ride and watch television at the same time!

The benefits of working out on a bike trainer are many. Because you must keep a consistent force on the pedals (or the pedals will stop spinning), it is rumored in the bike community that two hours on the trainer is like putting in three hours on the road bike outside. Additionally, you can use the bike trainer to work your cycling drills.

SPINNING® CLASS

I thank God for Spinning class. I feel so very safe on a bicycle that stays in place. Of course, your bike trainer also stays in place, but you don't have the same cheerleading effect as in a cycling class.

So you might ask: what in the world is Spinning class? It's basically a group *indoor* cycling class.[vii] An instructor sits at the front of the class on a special stationary bike (described below) and faces a group of bikes and riders. The instructor structures a class to *feel* like a bike ride. You use the resistance knob on the bike to increase the resistance (simulating a hill climb) or release the resistance (downhill or flat road). The instructor usually has upbeat music playing and instructs the class for fifty minutes to an hour.

The bikes are often the Spinner brand bikes, but there are many, many different brands of indoor cycling bikes. An indoor cycling bike, for those of you who have never seen one, is a stationary bike, but not the kind you see on the gym floor. These bikes are equipped with "flywheels" that better simulate an actual bike ride. Also, the bikes are more ergonomically situated to a road bike than the traditional fitness stationary bikes. For me, Spinning class is the next best thing to being on a bike ride.

FAT BOTTOMED GIRL

Coach Monster often plays the song "Fat Bottomed Girls" in his cycling class. I told him awhile back that I did not like that song because I was the only fat bottomed girl who attended his class—so when he played it, I felt everyone staring at me. *Oh, there she is! Our token fat bottomed girl!* To add salt to the fat-bottomed wound, the song is usually an "out of the saddle" song, meaning I am standing up shaking my fat bon-bon. Even worse.

"Please don't play 'Fat Bottomed Girls' in class," I begged.

He brushed me off, told me I owed him $100 for my self-deprecating humor and ignored me. In fact, he completely defied me! The "Fat Bottomed Girls" song made its appearance in the very next class. There it was. Staring at me like a one-eyed cat. I glared at Coach M.

Fat-bottomed girls you make the rockin' world go 'round...boom boom boom boom...

But then the song came to a screeching halt. Nothing. No music. Silence. iPod technical failure.

"What was *that* all about?" asked Coach Monster to the class.

He looked at me and winked. *Argh! That guy!*

He started the song over again. *Fat-bottomed girls you make the rockin' world go 'round...boom boom boom boom...*then, screeching halt.

Then, I smirked a little. I had put a secret hex on that song the second it started. *My powers were stronger than I thought! Ah-ha!!* I winked back at Coach Monster, who, flustered, turned his iPod to the next song.

So my fat-bottomed tale is humorous, but I understand how hard it is to sit on a bike and jiggle all over the place when you are starting out. The best advice I have: *Get over it.* Do what you have to do to avoid the mirrors. Sit in the back. But do *not* stop attending class just because you think you might look foolish on the bike. You will begin to look better and better each week. Before you realize what has happened, you may still be the token FBG (Fat Bottomed Girl), but you'll be sitting on the front row heckling the instructor about his music. (That's when the fun really begins.)

INDOOR CYCLING FREAKS

Indoor cycling can be full of creeps and freaky people. And I do not mean the instructors. Instructors are one thing, but I am beginning to think that the *participants* in a class are sometimes a bigger issue than crazy instructors.

As a beginner, you may not know what to do in a Spinning class. Do not be afraid to ask for help. Instructors love engaged (properly engaged) participants. Instructors show up each morning to help you! Ask questions. Ask the instructor how to set up your bike and what the class rules may be. Never be afraid to ask questions before or after class. (But do not yell out questions *during* class.)

I have had some bad indoor cycling experiences to date. Yes, a bad instructor is lethal. But really, the workout is about gathering yourself and putting in the sacrifice no matter *who* is leading. And that is hard sometimes. Not everyone has access to a Coach Monster's or McBlessings' type of awesome cycling class. Sometimes you must make the best out of a horrible class, full of freaks. Now, I may not be an expert on all things indoor cycling, but I can help you avoid being *that* person: the Indoor Cycling freak.

Swim Bike Mom Indoor Cycling Etiquette

Dear Cycling Freak,

I have been watching you in class for some time now. I am worried about you and those of us around you. I thought I would give you some tips for etiquette in cycling class. Perhaps you can use these tips, so we are not all forced to continue sitting next to you and fretting.

Add Some Resistance.
My tailbone hurts just watching you in your too-tight shorts bounce all over the place. Your legs are turning so fast and furious; you are bouncing all over the place like "bike popcorn." Tighten that resistance knob down a little or you will be way too sore for your scheduled Brazilian wax.

Personal Space.
Yes, in the Tour de France, there is a pack of riders who huddle together and ride together in the Peloton. Here? In class? No. Do not move your bike closer to snuggle up next to me. This here is an enormous room. Roll your bike over four inches.

Extreme Clothing.
In the winter, you should not wear a warm-up suit, gloves, and a beanie in class. Really. I can't concentrate. I can't take my eyes off of you, because I am waiting to jump off my bike and perform CPR when you fall out from heat exhaustion.

On the flip side, I am nervous about your summer wardrobe of bikini top and tiny-crotched hot pants. I'm scared you're going to flop something out onto the handlebars, and I might scream. Please just wear a tank top or something. Please. I really don't ever want to get on that seat after you...

Wipe Up your Mess.
If you sweat, clean it up. If you puke, clean it up. If you have other leakages, wear a nappy. If you blow a snot rocket in class, you are banned from class. Were you raised in a barn?

Hold the Beans.
Look. We all fart. And an occasional public slippage is a part of life. But you get one. One toot, per class, per person, max. If you are letting 'em rip through the entire class, get off your bike and go handle your business in the potty.

Stay Home.
Why did you wake up at 5am to come to class and pretend to workout? Why are you chattering with your neighbor? Why are you on your cell phone? Why do you look like you are strolling on a beach? Why aren't you sweating...at all? Stop it. Go home! Get out your big bike with a bell and go for a cruise. But give that Spinning bike to someone who is going to use it.

Wear Deodorant.
I don't care how Matthew McConaughey you are. You smell like feet. Correction: you smell like ass feet. Do something about it. Please. We all have to ride around you.

Wash Your Clothes.
Seriously, do you ever wash your workout gear? Wash your pants or stay home. This is another version of "you smell like ass feet," only this time it's your clothes that smell like ass feet. Clean them. We are not in the desert. I understand that sometimes you won't find out until you start sweating that your clothes stink.

This happens to me too, and that is okay one time. But fix that stinky shirt before the next class, or throw it out. If you can afford LifeTime Fitness, you can afford running water and soap.

Gloves. Really?
It's an hour long class. Please do not wear gloves. Hands sliding off the handle bars from your sweat? Then use a towel. There are no arguments in this world that will convince me that gloves in an indoor class are kosher.

Don't Yell Out Inspirational Quotes.
If I hear "Pain is Temporary!" shouted from the indoor cycling peanut gallery one more time... The instructor should shout inspiring things—that's why we wake up in the early morning and trudge to the class. But, you are not the teacher. So...shhhhhhh.

Sincerely,
Swim Bike Mom

COMMON CYCLING ISSUES AND HOW TO AVOID THEM

GOD SAVE THE QUEEN

I have been through this in nauseating detail. But for a refresher: get the Queen a good saddle, lube her up and get a good, one-piece chamois padded short to wear. For all of the above, she'll thank you later.

ROAD RASH

Road rash is slang term for the scrapes and abrasions resulting from your sweet lady skin hitting the hard, evil pavement. How to avoid it? Don't fall. But if you do fall, get up quickly, smile and blame it on your riding partner.

Hand and Foot Numbness

Numbness in the hand resulting from cycling occurs often in the small and ring fingers. This numbness may be caused by too much or too long of a pressure on the handlebars. Keep your upper body as relaxed as possible during a ride. Do not ride with your hands gripping the handlebars like death, with your elbows locked and shoulders to your ears, or with your jaw clenched tight. Relaxation nation, dude. Ride free. That might help the numbness factor.

Foot and toe numbness may also become an issue. This may be caused by improper bike fit and equipment. Sometimes if you are too far back/forward/up/down in the saddle, it puts pressure on your nerves and causes numbness in the feet.

Another possible option causing the numbness might be the position of the cleats (the snap-in clip on the bottom of the bike shoe). Moving the cleat as far back on the shoes as possible (towards the heel) may help. Your shoes may be too big, too small, or the toe straps too tight.[viii] A harder soled bike shoe might also help alleviate numbness.

Lower Back Pain & Knee Problems

Many lower back and knee pains from cycling go back to bike fit and shoe fit. If you have had your bike fitted by a professional *several times* and are still uncomfortable or having back and knee pains, then you should go to *another* professional. And if that fails, then to your doctor. Then back to another professional.

Remember to relax. And do not ride like a circus unicyclist—keep those knees in and that will prevent potential knee pain.

Cramping on the Bike

Remember to stay hydrated while you are riding. Cycling is the longest discipline out of the three and you may be out in the heat and sunlight for hours. Get extra water bottle cages, fill your bottles often, use hydration tablets (example: Nuun or Fizz) and drink. Lack of hydration can lead to cramping and worse, as detailed later.

BASIC BIKE MAINTENANCE

BIKE MAINTENANCE GEAR

On your bike, you should place a small bike bag under the back of your saddle with the following inside: multi-tool, tire tube(s), tire lever(s), CO_2 cartridge(s) and a CO_2 dispenser. These simple tools will help with minor bike repairs on the road, including changing a flat. You can purchase all this gear at your local bike store. Make sure you ask for the proper size tubes and cartridges and that it all fits inside your small bike bag. If not, there are options to attach cartridges to your bottle cages, or you can ride with a tube in the back of your cycling jersey.

For cleaning your bike, you'll want degreaser, a chain brush, a bucket and lubricant specific for your bike. Colder weather riding will require a wax-based lube, whereas summer rides will fare fine with an oil-based lubricant.

KEEP IT CLEAN

McBlessings told me recently, "You can tell a lot about a person from looking at her bike. Be good to your bike and she will be good to you! A big part of being a good citizen bike owner is simply keeping the bike clean after any long ride (*all* rides is preferable)."

I was scared that he might have seen my dirty bike, so I asked him to give me some great hints about keeping the bike clean.

"A good way to clean the bike is to find one of those standing bike racks (like you see in a bike shop). You can put your bike up on the rack and spray it down with a garden hose. Get a bucket of soap and water (dishwasher detergent works fine), sponge and wash it off." [Swim Bike Mom Note: I haven't purchased a bike stand like McBlessings mentions, but I *do* have a hitch and bike rack on my car. So I simply put my bike on the car rack to clean it – does the trick! Now, my car gets a little dirty…but priorities, priorities…]

"The goal is to remove the dirt and grease from the bike. When you look at the chain, the black grease is dirt and grime—which is not a good thing. After you soap and rinse the bike, you can use the degreaser from a bike shop and spray it on the chain. Once on the chain, let the degreaser soak a few minutes. Then you can use the chain cleaner brush [from a local bike store] to remove the grease. Once that is complete, the chain will be clean and shiny.

"After the bike is clean, you want to re-grease the bike with new, fresh lube. Start with re-lubing the chain. You can use a lubricant (White Lightning, etc.) from any bike store. Drip this lube on the chain as you rotate the pedal around and shift gears. This will spread the clean lube around the gears and the chain. Additionally, put the lube in the pivot points on the derailleur and shifters. Wipe off any excess lube."

A Swim Bike Mom Public Service Announcement

Ladies, you may love your long, fancy manicured fingernails, but riding a bike with long nails may not love you. At a minimum, get rid of any acrylic nails. If you ever need to change a tire tube, you will snap off your acrylics at the elbows.

SWIM BIKE MOM CHANGES A TUBE

A bike tire consists of a tube *inside* of the outer rubber tire. The tire holds the tube onto the rim. The tube is what you fill with air. I am not being condescending. I am being serious. I had no idea that in order to repair your tire tube, you had to get the tire tube *out* of the actual tire. Something ridiculously difficult to do, by the way.

A "flat" is actually the tube inside of the tire being punctured, pinched or a victim of explosion. (I do not kid).

I hate to stereotype, but most women are *boobs* at bike maintenance. No matter how many pink books people write about bike maintenance for women, I will never get it. And from chatting with so many women, I think the feeling is mutual. I have no real idea how my bike works. I figure once the kids get in school and I quit the legal profession, then I will have more time for figuring that out. Regardless, I try my best to learn the basic-basics, like changing a tube and fixing a dropped chain.

I figured before my second Olympic distance race, I should probably refresh my tube-changing skills. Suffice it to say that forty-five minutes later, I was covered in grease, the curse words were flying and I was almost in tears—and no tube had been changed. The back derailleur situation was absolutely befuddling. My CO_2 dispenser was apparently for a mountain bike or a four-wheeler or a horse (nice work, out-of-town bike shop, recommending that *expensive* contraption to the dumb baby lady triathlete).

I was thankful that the Expert did not mock me too badly when I tackled my tube changing independence. I appreciated him shouting things like, "No, not like that" and nicely telling me to calm down, be a big girl (thanks) and that I needed to know how to maintain my bike. I also appreciated him pretty much telling me exactly *how* to change my tube.

Changing a tube is like surgery, I thought as I was trying to get the wheel back on Antonia. *Well, not actually. I never could have been a surgeon.* "*Nooooo, I can't see the vein!! The blood! The blooooooood!*"

After way too much ado, the tube was changed and I was feeling rightfully proud.

I said, "Ta da!" showing him my bike.

"Ta da, what?" the Expert said.

"I did it. The tube is changed. I did it!" I squealed.

The Expert smiled, "Well, you don't know if you've changed it *correctly* until you ride it."

"What?" I asked.

How to Change a Tube

by The Expert

My wife is scared of her bike. She does not want to touch her bike unless to hop on it quickly and ride off, hoping she does not teeter and fall down in a crosswalk. Our conversations at the beginning of her triathlon dreams frequently went something like this:

Me: *So you want to be a triathlete, but you are scared of your bike?*

Her: *I am not scared of my bike.*

Me: *Then clean it.*
Her: *I don't want to clean it. It's greasy.*
Me: *Do you want to know how to change the tube before your race next weekend?*
Her: *What is the tube?*
Me: *Here* (pointing).
Her: *That's a tire.*
Me: *No, the tube is inside.*
Her: *Why do I need to change something inside my tire?*

Indeed. I pat myself on the back for making her less scared of her bike. I pat myself on the back for teaching her to change a tube. But do not fool yourself with all her Swim Bike Mom trickery: if *I* am anywhere within 100 yards of the house and she has a bike issue, I can hear her squealing my name for help. It's not that she *can't* fix the bike issue… it's just…well, *it's greasy.*

The first step to change a tube is to find someone else to do it. That would be my wife's advice. But ladies: you must learn to change a tube because in a race, you will be completely hosed without the knowledge. Practice and practice it.

If you are lucky, you will only experience flat tires on the front wheel. Why? Because the front wheel is much easier to remove.

To remove your front wheel, face the front of your bike. See where your wheel attaches to your frame? Hold the silver bolt on the left side and unhinge and twist the lever on the right side. Once it is loose, then you can lift your bike off the wheel. Hold the wheel with your left hand, and with your right hand, pick your bike *off* the wheel.

As far as changing a rear flat, this gets a little more complicated—not so much taking the wheel off, but putting it back on. To remove your rear wheel, turn your bike over so that it is resting upside down on the ground. Ensure that the rear gear is on the smallest chain ring (large cassette, small chain ring). Just like the front wheel, loosen the axle and take the wheel off the frame. Take care to shimmy the wheel out of the chain and the gears.

To change the tube, you should open the air valve on your tire and release the remaining air from the flat tube.

The next step is to remove the tube (the inside layer) *from* the tire. To do this, you should have tire levers in your handy bike bag. Use the small or thin end of the lever and put it between the tire and the tire rim. Pull the lever downwards. You can then clip the hook end to the nearest spoke. You can repeat this with up to three levers, but the idea is to get one side of the tire completely free, so you can remove the tire from the rim.

Pull out the flat tube. At this point, you may want to check the inside of your tire and see if there is anything that *caused* the puncture still inside the tire (nail, gravel, etc.). Once it is clear, pull your new tube out of your bike bag.

Take the new tube and insert the side of the tube with the stem through the appropriate place in the tire. Carefully place the valve through the hole in the rim and pull the tire over the rim. Now, this is the tough part on the fingers (and where you do *not* want to have those long fingernails). You have to slowly work around the wheel with your fingers and pull the wheel over the rim, making sure that the tube inside is not pinched or encumbered. (Once you have the tire on is when you will inflate it.) The last part of the tire will make you scream, but you have to put some "oomph" behind it.

Once you are certain that your tire is back on correctly, the tube safely and pinch-free inside, then you can use your CO_2 pump and cartridge to re-inflate the tube.

Then you simply put your *wheel* back on the bike. Easy for the front and requiring some shimmying in the back.

Of course, this process is difficult to explain, so it helps to have a bike-savvy friend show you in person. You can also take a bike maintenance class from your local bike shop. Hands-on experience is the best way to become efficient at tube changing.

SEVEN

The Run

INTRODUCTION BY SWIM BIKE MOM

Running has always been weird for me. I flail or look like Phoebe from that episode of *Friends* where she runs in Central Park. My legs do not leave the ground quickly or smoothly or easily. I lumber around, moving in some zombie stomping motion. Even now, after achieving some pretty big goals, I still look all ogre-like. So I do not run like the wind. I do not run like a breeze, even. But I *do* run, and that is something.

My running was so bad growing up that my dad tried to correct my form and then eventually gave up. My dad was a big shot runner in high school and college, so he wanted to get me straight. I was hopeless. He never meant any malice by it, but years later in conversation, my dad would say, "Well, you *never* were a good runner." Now it's a joke in our house, because Dad can't really say that anymore—I may not be a "great" runner, but finishing a couple of half marathons and a couple of half Ironmans certainly qualifies me as a "good runner." *I think.*

I came to running as a natural born couch slug. Before my Decision and before that first magical Spinning class with Coach Monster, I had tried to run. A few times, actually. As I mentioned before, I had signed the Expert and myself up for that first 5k. Stella was very little, like maybe three months old. I needed to get my first run in.

My first run since the Size Ten days took place at 9:30 p.m. on a random weeknight. I fed Stella. I got in the car. And I darkened the gym's door for the first time in probably five years. *Quiet. Ah. Peace and quiet.* I was wearing my old sneakers. The place was empty. I eyed the treadmill. I turned it on and started moving.

The first big run did not go as planned. The workout was over almost before it began. I ran for four *minutes* on the treadmill, slogging around my baby weight, jiggling all over creation. *Four minutes.* I was at a 3.7 pace on the treadmill. Four minutes. And I was sucking wind like someone had tried to suffocate me and I had finally succeeded in knocking them away.

The aftermath? The next day? Well, I could not move. I could not carry my baby girl up the stairs without crying because I had bruises on the bottoms of my feet. I was depressed and heartbroken.

Who cannot run for four minutes?! I remember saying into the mirror with tears. *Who?!* The answer was: *Me. This girl. This girl can't run for four minutes.*

But I am not that girl anymore. Over the course of the next few years, I plodded along. I walked. I ran. I jogged. I slogged. I sprinted very (very) short distances. I quit running. I declared I wouldn't do it again. But I ran some more. I started with a 5k. I did a few more. I did some triathlons. I did some 10ks. I did some more triathlons. Then the half Ironman. Then the half marathon (yes, my first half marathon was in the half Ironman).

© Swim Bike Mom

And in case you haven't been around long, I am not skinny. I am not even what you could call thin. Hell, I am way fatter than "average." I am a size 12/14 (on a good day), but I run.

If you are starting out or if you feel like absolute crap about yourself, you can choose today to change. Even if you want to cry every single morning because of the shape you are in, you *must* start *somewhere*. And lucky for you— today is the day to run!

Eventually, if you are consistent, you will be one of those crazy people who love to run. I can call you crazy because I am one of you. I'm Meredith and I am no natural born runner and I love to run.

> *Even if you want to cry every single morning because of the*
> *shape you are in, you must start somewhere.*
>
> *Today is the day to run.*

Four words that the Expert and my Dad never thought I would say: *I love to run*. But these are words they are *so proud* to now hear me utter.

Recently, my dad watched me participate in a sprint distance tri for the first time. He was blown away, not because I was fast (I wasn't)—but because I was *faster* than many, many (many) girls *half* my size. Not only that, but I grabbed 4th place out of twenty-two Athena racers. *Wahooooo!* Fourth place in an event that was one-third running. Go figure. He was so proud, and I was proud that he was there to see it.

And even more recently, my parents were able to watch my second half Ironman finish. I'm pretty sure they were unable to recognize their own daughter...*She is running in a half Ironman? What in the heck?*

The lesson? People *can* change. And people can change for the *better*. And with triathlon, you will change. Learn to love who you are becoming. By making small steps, you *are* changing. Learn to appreciate the journey because it is *your* journey.

Every day will get better. Each day *you* will get better, inside and out. Your runs will get longer and stronger. And you will be a runner. That's good stuff.

INTRODUCTION TO THE MONSTER RUN EXPERT

As I traveled my journey with Coach Monster pushing me along with his magic triathlon cattle prod, I never told him about my blog. *Well, not really.* I mentioned it in passing and he did not seem to pay it any mind. So when I decided to write this book, I knew two things:

First, the cat was going to be out of the bag with regard to the blog. I couldn't hide much longer behind my computer.

Second, I needed Gerry's wisdom for the book, so I would be forced to come clean about my pet name for the Monster.

Uh-oh.

As I feared, when I disclosed the "Coach Monster" nickname *to* the Monster…he immediately rebelled.

Then I told the blogosphere about Gerry's hatred for the nickname…and *everyone* turned on *me* for even thinking of changing his moniker. Email after email poured in: *You cannot change Coach Monster's name! He's a triathlon Monster! He's tough! He's sweet! He loves cookies! We love it! We looooooove him! I need my own Monster! Where do I get a Monster? I wanna Monster tooooooo.* (It was a tad insane, really. I was all, *Come on ladies, get a grip!* Then I was like, *No, he's my Coach Monster. Mine!* Anyway…)

I even took votes for new nicknames. And "Coach Monster" continued to reign supreme.

Gerry's concern about his "Monster" nickname was that he might be perceived as a crazy, mean coach. But as you all know by now, that is not the reasoning behind the nickname. In place of Coach Monster, he proposed the nickname "Coach Purposeful Suffering." Coach <u>PS</u> for short. *I was thinking about it.* But only because I could call him Coach <u>P</u>ain in the <u>S</u>addle. *Might work.*

Regardless of his nickname or non-nickname, Gerry Halphen is a triathlon mega monster. He began his triathlon career in his mid-thirties, looking for a way to extend his ability to train, compete and stay fit. To say that it was a humble triathlon beginning, especially in swimming, would be an understatement. When Gerry began, he quite literally could not swim twenty-five meters.

Despite the challenges, Gerry worked extremely hard and engaged in a lot of what he calls "purposeful suffering" to achieve some of his ultimate goals: qualifying for and competing in the World Championships for both the full Ironman (Kona) and the 70.3 distance. Along the way, he met many incredible people and became so passionate about the sport that he became a certified

USAT coach. As both an athlete and a coach, Gerry has helped athletes of all ages, backgrounds and ability levels to achieve their triathlon goals. He lives in Alpharetta, Georgia with his wife, Christy, and their two daughters, Emily and Olivia.

I pull quotes from his cycling classes for my desk at work. I write his wisdom(s) on my hand when I am having a tough day. I have seen him race a half Ironman. I have seen him suffer to the point of collapsing. The dude is the real deal. I am thrilled that Gerry (*the Coach Formerly Known as Monster?*) has agreed to share his wisdom on the third (and most wicked) discipline of triathlon: the run.

GO SLOW TO GO FAST

by Gerry Halphen
Thrive Performance
(www.ThrivePerformance.com)

You must remember two very important things when you begin a running program, especially in triathlon:

> Go Slow to Go Fast
>
> and
>
> Focus on *Quality* Instead of Quantity

What does "go slow to go fast" really mean? It means to take your time, build a solid foundation of good running form, and develop the proper running habits. As a beginner, you should not attempt to go from the couch to a marathon in a week. It will not work. That's like the binge diet of triathlon training. You may run twenty-six miles, but you'll certainly end up in the ER.

Going slow *does* work. If you structure your training in a methodical way, the simple adaptations to your body will happen to make you a better runner. Eventually, the speed will follow. This methodology takes time and patience to build and varies by individual. Many different things may impact the progress—such as bodyweight and stressors in life. But this method is proven: if you have enough time and go slowly, your body will adapt over time and what appears to be impossible—will become real.

The next important component is to maintain high *quality* workouts. If you can give fifteen minutes of high quality, then I will take that any day over an hour of crappy effort. If you focus on the *quality* of your time in your running shoes, eventually, the *quantity* will take care of itself.

THE GEAR

Go to a running store that will take time to do a shoe fit. Experts at excellent running stores will watch you run on treadmill or run outside the store before attempting to put you in a shoe. They will use their analysis of your gait, footstrike and other factors to put you in the right shoe which makes all the difference.

Different theories exist about how often you should replace your shoes. I have found that having a rotation of running shoes is nice. Once you find a pair you like, then purchase a few pairs and rotate them. Typically, the rule is to replace shoes every five hundred miles, but this will vary wildly depending on footstrike, shoe and weight of the athlete.

Your choice of sock is really all about feel. Some athletes like ultra-thin socks, some like more padding. You will know after trying a few pairs. Regardless, you will want to pick up a specialty running sock, not just a typical cotton tube sock. Whether you like thick or thin socks, a running sock will be made of more breathable material that will help to prevent chafing and blisters in the long run.

RUNNING SURFACES

As a new runner or triathlete, running on a mixture of surfaces is a good idea. This includes running on a trail, other soft surface, treadmill *and* pavement. You're better off starting with a majority of your runs on soft surfaces, but you must mix in the pavement because most races take place on pavement. This does not mean that you need to zoom on the pavement. You still need to go slow to go fast. If you spend too much time on the pavement to start, you can injure yourself from the pounding. Be smart about where you run and listen to your body. Still, remember to work in the pavement running, because if you run on nothing but soft surface, then your legs will break down on pavement in a race.

I know some people who do all their training on treadmills. As a coach, minute for minute, a treadmill creates a precision with training that you simply cannot obtain from outside running where distractions like cars, stop lights, etc. can disrupt a run. Further, if you are pressed for time as most women are, the treadmill is the perfect solution. You get up to speed quickly, you have to hold the pace, and you can vary your "terrain" as needed.

Also, I must add a note about safety. In the wee hours of the morning, you may find running outside to be peaceful. But safety must be your priority. Running inside on a treadmill may be a safer choice before the sun is up. Additionally, while running alone is cathartic, always remember to wear a headlamp, to have your cell phone and to use common sense in the wee hours. Using the treadmill can eliminate these issues.

You'll hear people call it the "dreadmill." They'll whine, "I can't run on the dreadmill for more than twenty minutes!" The longest run I have done on a treadmill is twenty-two miles. Was it mentally draining? Of course it was. Running on a treadmill can make you want to poke out your eyes. Which is precisely the point of doing it! To build *mental endurance*.

If someone tells me that they cannot run for more than thirty minutes on a treadmill without going crazy, but yet they want to finish an Ironman race, I have to stare at them a little. I will say, "You might want to pick a different sport. If you cannot use a treadmill and find a place in your mind that is immune to the loneliness, boredom and fatigue, how are you going to do that in a race?"

RUNNING FORM

Like shoes, there are many theories about running form. Especially for a beginner, I firmly believe that it is more important to go out and be active and get some miles in your legs than to have the perfect form. If you are waiting on the perfect form, then you will come up with the excuse, "I can't run because my form's not good."

At the same time, you need to balance the mileage with the *quality* of your workout. There it is again: *quality*. Good running form makes you a more efficient runner. Being efficient saves energy and allows your mind to be present, working and sharp when you need it.

If you get super fatigued from the beginning, your central nervous system begins to wane, and you can make bad decisions, both in training and on race day.

Some helpful things to remember that will improve your running technique:

1. Work on your core and lower back strength.
   Maintaining a strong back and core has everything to do with maintaining posture and proper form. The back and the core are often components that people neglect, but they are quite literally the center of power. By engaging your core your legs will not suffer (as much). Therefore, when it comes time to run, you have better running form.

2. Keep your feet underneath your body.
   Your stride should be reasonably "short," meaning to keep your feet under your body. If your stride is too extended (too long), this will add stress on your back, knees and hips. If your feet remain *under* your body, then you will turn over your feet more quickly and propel yourself forward faster.

3. Foot Strike
   There are many different arguments on heel strike versus foot strike. Again, it is important for a new runner to hit the road and begin moving. Still, working on keeping your feet beneath you during the run will help prevent a hard-to-break heel strike habit later. The heel strike, if it is deliberate enough, will serve to actually slow you down and "brake" your run stride.

4. Relax your body.
   Like on the bike, you want to relax your upper body, right down to your jaw. This includes your hands.

5. Posture
   Have excellent posture but you want to lean your body ever-slightly forward *from the ankles*. In other words, picture a straight line from your ankles through your body. That line should stay straight and rotate slightly forward during your run.

6. Get rid of the chicken wing.
   Keep your arms close to your body and don't flail them around like a chicken. (Ah-hem, Swim Bike Mom).

7. Consider Giving Galloway a Try.

    The Galloway Method[ix] of running has proven some great results for beginners and advanced athletes alike. Basically, Galloway is about incorporating walking breaks into your running sessions (and races). You can run for five minutes, then walk for one minute; run for a mile, walk for a minute—whichever combination you choose is up to you. The secret to the method is consistency, however. If you decide to walk one minute every ten minutes, then stick to that plan and implement it. If you can't stick with that method, then I recommend against using Galloway because it could become a cornerstone for inconsistency and an easy way "out" when the running gets hard.

ADD DRILLS

To improve your form, basic running drills may be incorporated into your training. The internet has an endless catalog of videos for various running drills, most notably the "100 Up" by Chris McDougall featured by the New York Times online.[x] Another great drill is the "Butt Kick." Butt kicks are just as they sound. Standing in place while keeping excellent posture, spring to your forefoot and with the other leg kick your heel towards your rear end. Your arms should be positioned like you are running. Three sets of ten kicks is an excellent starting point.

BUILDING YOUR ENDURANCE

One of the most common misconceptions is that you have to go hard all the time to improve. The more I do triathlon, the more I have come to understand just how important low intensity training is. As I mentioned before, you want to *go slow* in order to *go fast* later.

This method of training is based on heart rate zones. You monitor your zones through the use of a heart rate monitor (usually worn on the wrist) and a chest strap (which fastens around your chest, just under the bottom of your sports bra band). The chest strap reads the heart rate and transmits the data to the watch. While there are several methodologies for structuring heart rate training, ranging from 4 to 7 target zones, I've included the simpler 4 zone method below for illustration purposes.

Maintaining your runs in Zone 2 or approximately 70-80 percent of your maximum heart rate (or 80-90 percent of your lactate threshold) will build endurance. Lactate threshold is determined by a test called Blood Lactate Testing (BLT) and is the most accurate way to determine your specific heart rate zones.

If all else fails, you can broadly estimate your Heart Rate Zones by: using 220 minus your age for your maximum heart rate. While most fitness practitioners agree that this method is crude and can be off by 10% or more, if you are just getting into exercise, it is a place to start. As you get more into the discipline of training and if you want more precision with our heart rate zones, I'd recommend getting a BLT conducted.

Heart Rate Zones

Zone 1 - active recovery, beginner programs (60-70% of your max heart rate)

Zone 2 - endurance and aerobic base building (70-80% of your max heart rate)

Zone 3 - aerobic and anaerobic combination (often I refer to Zone 3 as "no man's land" because you are not completely aerobic, nor are you anaerobic; 80-90% of your max heart rate)

Zone 4 - anaerobic threshold (where a beginner does not want to be; 90-95% of your max heart rate)

Again, the BLT is the best way to determine your proper Zones!

However, if you *must* use the broad estimator, here is an example using Swim Bike Mom: 220 minus her age (33) is her *estimated* maximum heart rate = 187 beats per minute. Based on 187 as a maximum heart rate, her zones may be calculated as follows:

Zone 1: 112-130 (60-70%)
Zone 2: 131-149 (70-80%)
Zone 3: 150-168 (80-90%)
Zone 4: 169-177 (90-95%)

In order to improve endurance, you must build both your aerobic base *and* your anaerobic (muscular) endurance. You improve your *aerobic* endurance by going slowly, staying in Zone 2, particularly *low* Zone 2, during your runs. This practice will expand not only your aerobic capacity, but it will allow time for your body to adapt to the training, the movements and the shock you might be putting it through. By the way, as an added bonus, this time is low Zone 2 will also maximize your fat burning as your body can/will use fat as a fuel source at this lower level of exertion.

Conversely, you build your *anaerobic* engine by going hard. Therefore, by expanding and working both systems—you have two stronger engines.

As an example of aerobic training, during the off-season many professional German male triathletes "go slow to go fast." During this time, they will cap themselves at 15-16 MPH on the bike. For a pro, 15 MPH on a bike is very, very slow. This caliber of athletes is accustomed to riding 26-28 MPH in races. However, these professional men train this way because they are seeking to build their aerobic endurance.

It is rare to find an athlete, especially one who thinks she's fast, who can agree to turn down the "heat" and run slow according to a low Zone 2. But this type of training pays huge dividends.

There is another method of training intensity monitoring called RPE, or "Rate of Perceived Exertion." This method is based on how you feel. The correlation is typically as follows:

Heart Rate Zone	RPE
Zone 1	easy
Zone 2	moderate
Zone 3	slightly difficult
Zone 4	extremely difficult

This may be a good way to train as a beginner, but I recommend from the start using the heart rate method, as it will yield more accurate results. That being said, you should always be in tune with your "perceived exertion" and adjust accordingly.

As a new triathlete, you will want to spend plenty of time going slow. Even later as you get stronger and faster, you will want to continue to incorporate slow runs into your training. Slow runs continue to improve your aerobic base as well as allow you to focus on smooth, clean running form. You will want to also incorporate short, fast runs and hill workouts, which will increase your muscular strength, improve your foot speed, and build your anaerobic engine. It's training *both* the aerobic and anaerobic engines that yield the best long-term results.

Warm Up to Run

I do not believe in static stretching before a run. I prefer walking or jumping jacks or neuromuscular drills before running and then, stretching after. Stretching *after* a run is far more important.

Staying Injury-Free

The easiest way to stay healthy and injury-free is to limit the frequency of running, particularly the frequency of *intense* running. You do *not* need to run as much as people think. For example, since I started this sport ten years ago, I have gotten faster every year—by running no more than three times a week. And that includes my Ironman training. What you do in those runs will vary depending on what distance race you are attempting, but the key point is that *quality* trumps *quantity*.

> ### Amazing!
> *You do not need to*
> *run more than three times a week!*

Additionally, most bodies have difficulty tolerating running more than three times a week—the body may break down and open itself up for injury. Regardless, no matter how much or how little you are running, you need to listen to your body. If you are hurting or exhausted, then you may need some recovery time.

Remember to work on your strength training and core. I have included some different types of exercises below. The type and duration of strength and core should change throughout the season, but it should always be a mainstay of your training.

I also recommend ice baths after any effort beyond an hour. Yes, I said ice baths. While horrific and medieval, ice baths are absolutely essential.

Finally, find the new love of your life: the Foam Roller. Trigger Point Therapy makes a wonderful roller product called The Grid (www.tptherapy.com). Using the foam roller is a form of self-massage and myofascial release that works like a deep tissue massage. This practice hurts, it makes me want to cry, but I firmly believe that the foam roller is a training longevity tool.

If you do not know what an IT Band is now, you will. The IT band stands for the ilioltibial band, which is a "band" of tissue that runs along the outside of the thigh, over the hip, down the knee and below the knee. The IT band keeps the knee stable during walking and running. The only thing to *help* the IT band when it starts to act up is to exert pain *on* the IT band: to roll on a foam roller; to get a deep tissue massage; to embark on ART (Active Release Therapy[xi]); to roll on a lacrosse ball, tennis ball, baseball, or Trigger Point Ball; or do whatever you can to punish and work that IT band loose.

RUN WORKOUTS

I recommend a simple breakdown for the three weekly run workouts:

Long Run
Moderate Run
Hard Run

THE LONG RUN

This is your aerobic building run/jog/walk which consists of going long and slow, in a low Zone 2 heart rate zone. The long runs are known as "base building" runs and they create the foundation of your aerobic system.

Remember: you go slow and long in order to go fast. On the long run workouts, you should focus on your heart rate and your running technique. If you cannot run *and* keep your heart rate in Zone 2—then you should walk (as fast as you can) and focus on your heart rate staying in Zone 2. You will build up to a jog eventually—and yes, then a run.

The benefit of this workout is to build your aerobic base. This base will be built by keeping your heart rate under control—again, even if this means walking. You want to keep the mileage *high*, and the heart rate *low*. Focus on the quality of each stride.

THE MODERATE RUN

On this particular workout day, you should incorporate some increases in pace and also, where possible, hill work. The purpose of the moderate run is to use both your aerobic *and* anaerobic engines.

For example: complete a thirty minute workout, with every five minutes picking up the pace or going uphill for one or two minutes, holding steady, then dropping down for a few minutes of recovery. Repeat until the thirty minutes is up. As you get more advanced, you can add longer intervals, steeper hills and/or less recovery.

THE HARD RUN

"Hard run" is a relative term depending on your experience level. If you are a brand new runner (or even walker), intensity means one thing. If you are a seasoned 800 meter runner on a college scholarship for running, intensity means something else. It is important to have a clear idea of your intensity levels and to remember that yes, it will be hard. But a "hard run" is hard regardless of whether you are a newbie or the experienced athlete. Hard depends on your *personal* level.

Also, it is worth mentioning that as you are starting out, you may want to stick to the slower runs for a few months, because they will feel "hard" enough. Just keep moving along at the slower pace and eventually, you will be able to differentiate between the three types of runs.

If you build your aerobic base and then omit the moderate and hard runs, your anaerobic (muscular) base will decrease as well as your running potential. While these two types of runs add variety to the training and make it more interesting, they also serve to confuse your body and prevent the ever-dreaded plateau.

With regard to completing a run as long as the "race distance" *before* your race, this absolutely depends on the athlete. For example, do you mentally feel the need to run a 5k before you do a sprint triathlon? I believe you can benefit from having run four or five miles before a sprint triathlon, but it is not essential. Most athletes benefit from knowing in the back of their mind that they can do the same distance of the run in the race *before* race day. At the same time, you can certainly run a 5k in a triathlon if you have run 3.1 miles in training.

The sum of the parts is greater! If you maximize the quality of all three events (swim, bike and run), you will be rested and can feed off the adrenaline of the race. One of the key sayings in triathlon is: The hardest part is getting to the *starting line*. That also means getting to the starting line intact, without injury.

THE BRICK WORKOUT

As explained earlier in this book, running immediately after you bike is known as a "brick." This is an important component of your training because the brick workout simulates the physical and mental stressors on race day. You must train your legs to get accustomed to the feeling of coming off the bike and immediately running. Trust me—it never feels "normal"—but the more you do it, the more easily your body agrees to adapt.

After you have built a solid aerobic foundation, I recommend making one of your run workouts a week as a brick: where you run anywhere from one to four miles *after* your bike workout. This varies from race distance to race distance, but a sprint and Olympic distance would be served well with this rule of thumb. The distance is not as important as the body adaptation to the feeling of "bricks" in your legs as you run off the bike.

SAVING YOURSELF FOR THE RUN IN THE RACE

The energy for the last part of a triathlon is all about mental preparation and mental control. You must control your output on the first two segments (the swim and the bike) with the knowledge you still must complete the last segment of the race: the run.

In training, utilizing the "brick" workouts will help your body learn to adapt to the cumulative fatigue of running when you are tired. The brick workouts are a strong foundation for being able to tolerate and adapt to the run at the end of the race. Using your mind to control your body starts in training, and adapting to the fatigue is another part of this.

==

TRAIL RUNNING

Trail running for ole Swim Bike Mom has not turned out so well. I'm too clumsy. Or not goat-like. Lucky for all of you, I have a mountain goat for a good friend, and she's full of goatly running tips to get you to the trails without hurting your hooves.

INTRODUCTION TO THE MOUNTAIN GOAT

Liz George, who I affectionately call "Mountain Goat," was a partner at a mid-sized law firm and wasting her life away to billable hours. She recently escaped the drudgery and now works in private practice with her husband at his Atlanta-based practice, The Shah Law Firm. Mountain Goat has been running for over seventeen years. However, it wasn't until she moved to Atlanta and became a lawyer that her true love affair with running really began. Mountain Goat is a frequent age group winner and has several overall wins here and there. Most recently in 2012, Mountain Goat came over to the "dark side" and finished her first triathlon—the Atlanta Iron Girl. She said, "I would have never completed it without the help of Swim Bike Mom.

Suffice it to say that goats are better on their hooves than they are in the water or on a bike!"

To which I say, whatever. She darn near beat me.

THE URBAN MOUNTAIN GOAT'S
TRAIL RUNNING TIPS

By Elizabeth George
Attorney, Mountain Goat and Bad Ass Trail Runner
(www.UrbanMountainGoat.com)

Apparently I eat, train and run like a mountain goat. However, as a resident of Midtown Atlanta I am often restricted to an urban environment. But fear not! Whether you are a mountain dweller or a city slicker, you too can eat, train and run like a mountain goat!

Growing up, this Goat was an awkward youth, sporting big glasses, a crazy wardrobe and a full blown mustache and uni-brow. I was forced to endure taunts due to my "uniqueness." I misguidedly tried to fit in by trying out for cheerleader and other conventional things that "cool kids" did.

After much failure and disappointment, a girl who lived nearby encouraged me to join the cross country team and introduced me to an activity that would make high school bearable, teach me to be comfortable in my own skin, and would to help me persevere through other tough times in my life. Despite being a bit pudgy and a just plain awful runner, I found solace on the trails and was embraced by my teammates. I soon learned just how awesome runners are—and just how life-changing a great run can be.

> *"The woods are lovely, dark, and deep,*
> *But I have promises to keep,*
> *And miles to go before I sleep,*
> *And miles to go before I sleep."*
>
> — ROBERT FROST

WHY TRAIL RUNNING?

So why do you want to trail run?

In our modern society, just about all of us work indoors trapped at a desk for hours on end. To make matters worse, when the day is over, we get inside our cars and sit, trapped for more hours. After a horrible day there is nothing more liberating, satisfying or freeing than a jaunt through the woods. No traffic, no noise, no fumes, no crowded sidewalks and stoplights.

As humans, when things get too much or we need an escape, we always have this urge to get back to the basics. Nothing is more basic than a run through the woods. The last few years have been tough with the downturn in the economy. People are under a lot more stress—and more people are dissatisfied with where they are in life. Not coincidentally, trail running has become more popular in recent times as people are looking for an escape and for something more basic and simple.

Even if you're a triathlete or a runner or cyclist who has been training for a while, it is easy to get bogged down in the monotony of training plans, workouts, equipment and expectations. If you're bored with running on the

treadmill or the roads, trail running may just be the answer you've been looking for. Also, you can use the trails for your long slow runs or recovery runs.
Embrace the hills and use them as prep for climbing on the bike. Just slow
down, breathe deep, and enjoy the moment with just you and Mother Nature.

Aside from saving your sanity, trail running could help save your body too.
Trails tend to be softer surfaces causing less impact with each foot strike. The
terrain of a trail varies, and the uneven surface causes your foot to come down
differently with each step resulting in the use of more and different muscles
from your core, to legs, back, glutes and feet. Using different muscles equals
less repetitive motion and results in less injury!

So what do you have to lose? Go forth and run my little goats!

WHERE TO TRAIL RUN?

So you're ready to give this trail running thing a try—but where do you go?
Truly, the easiest thing to do is an internet search for hiking, mountain biking
or rail (read: softer, flatter) trails in your area. The National Park Service has a
great system of trails, and likely your state park system does too. Local nature
preserves, botanical gardens, and parks often have trails too. If you've checked
all these places and are still stumped, ask your local schools where the cross
country team runs. Most cross country courses are partially off-road, and
some of our local high schools have beautiful courses on campus that are open
to the public.

WHAT DO I WEAR?

What you wear out on the trail is going to depend on the type of trail you're
about to tackle. If you're going to be out in the sun or wind, don your favorite
visor, sunglasses, hat, windbreaker or other gear just as you would out on the
road. Don't forget to wear sunscreen and bug spray as well.

If you're going deep into the woods or a very heavily-wooded area, you
may want to opt for a longer sleeve and longer pants as well to protect against
bug bites and itchy plants. If you live in a colder climate or where weather
is more uncertain, make sure to layer up so you're prepared for anything.
You'd be surprised how quickly weather can turn on you when you're in the
mountains!

Make sure to wear synthetic, moisture-wicking socks. If I know I'm going extra-long or that my feet will be getting wet, I like to apply a layer of liquid powder to my feet first before putting on my socks. I ran thirty-four miles with no socks and lots of BodyGlide Liquefied Powder and finished without a single blister!

Do you need trail shoes? This depends on the types of trails and the frequency you run those trails. If you opt for soft-packed, non-technical trails—a park trail, a crushed limestone or gravel trail, a woodchip or dirt trail, rail trail, or fire road—then your usual running shoes will do just fine. However, if you plan to trail run more often or navigate trails with more rocks, roots, stream crossings, mud, etc., then you probably want to opt for a trail-specific shoe.

Trail shoes offer three advantages: 1) stability; 2) traction; and 3) protection. A true trail shoe will have a thinner, denser midsole so that you feel lower to the ground, allowing better responsiveness to avoid twisted ankles and trips and falls (ah-hem, Swim Bike Mom).

For most terrain and most people, a hybrid shoe will work well. If you're looking to take on tougher terrain that is rockier, rougher, and muddier than you will want a shoe that can stand up to that sort of terrain and properly protect your foot. You'll want to look for a shoe that has greater traction with bigger lugs (the cleat-looking things on the bottom). But remember, bigger isn't always better and these shoes can be clunky and weigh you down.

Last, but not least, if you plan to be out on the trails for a length of time or to tackle trails that are rockier and have more debris, you will probably want to invest in a pair of gaiters. Gaiters are like little skirts worn over the shoe at the ankle to keep all the yucky stuff from the trails out of your kicks!

What do I take?

When you're first starting out, keep the run short and the equipment to a minimum. If it's hot, you're going to be out for an hour or more, or you are unfamiliar with the trail, you want to take a water bottle. I recommend something like a small hand-held Nathan bottle, a Fuel Belt with bottles, or a small Camelbak. Take your cell phone with GPS. If you're going to be running alone in a secluded area, you may want to consider pepper spray. If you're new to a trail or are unfamiliar with the territory, the best thing to take with you is likely a friend who knows the turf!

What do I eat?

Bringing along some sustenance is a good idea for any efforts over an hour. While the usual gels and sports drinks are fine, I find that "real" food performs better out on the trail. Good trail noshings: PB&J, hummus on gluten-free crackers, plain cubed potatoes, pretzels, fruit (fresh and dried), nuts, Larabars and Kind granola. My favorites are usually grapes, oranges, pretzels, cashews and dried fruit.

As far as beverages go, Nuun tablets in water are great. They have all the electrolytes and none of the sugar, and are convenient to carry.

Trail Lingo

Out on the trail, runners have some specific lingo, which can be quite confusing at first. You read a race description talking about sweet singletrack, switchbacks, technical sections, and all sorts of other crazy things that make your head spin. Here are the basics:

Trailhead – This is where the trail begins. Typically it will be noted by a sign of some sort usually containing a cryptic map of the trails ahead.

Technical – A trail may be described as "technical" or different degrees of technical. "Technical" refers to the level of rocks, roots, steep drops, crazy climbs—more or less trails where there are more obstacles and more chances of falling if you aren't paying attention.

Singletrack – A narrow path or trail. Read: only one person at a time is gonna fit. Makes for a fun race start. (Similarly, *doubletrack* is trail wide enough for more than one runner and often less technical).

Switchback – A 90 degree or greater turn. Somewhat of a "Z" trail that makes going up steep inclines, making them easier but longer. They cut across hills in runnable grades making them longer but more manageable. Lots of fun out on the course!

Ultramarathon – Anything over marathon distance. A race reserved for crazy people who really love running. Super fun because the aid stations feature foods such as sugary soft drinks, pizza, candy, and cheese curls.

If you're lucky, maybe the race director will bake homemade chocolate chip banana nut bread.

Railtrail – A railway easement converted into a multi-use path. Typically long and flat. Great for beginners or for getting in that long run or ride.

Fire Road – A road maintained chiefly for emergency vehicle access. Trail big enough for four-wheelers. Usually just like a regular road except hard packed instead of asphalt and are great for beginner trail running!

LSD – "Long Slow Distance." Perfect for the trails!

TOTF – "Time on the Feet." In trail running, and particularly in ultrarunning, it's all about the time you spend on your feet in training more than the miles covered.

TACKLING THE TERRAIN

Trail running is about the journey, not the destination! For this reason, go slow. Don't go out of the gate with the pace you would when running on the road or "the dreadmill." Slow down and be aware of your surroundings—and enjoy it!

You're going to encounter many twists, turns, rocks, stumps, branches, and other natural wonders along the trail—that's part of the fun. But you won't be having very much fun if you're tripping and falling over these natural wonders. As a general rule, try to keep your eyes focused about three feet in front of you, shorten your stride, and stay upright. In time, your feet will fall naturally and get better about navigating the obstacles.

With trail running, it helps to leave your pride behind. Don't be afraid to walk steep up or downhills or particularly rocky or technical terrain.

For steep downhills, it is helpful to turn and run or walk down sideways, or on an angle in a shuffling-type motion. Some of the best trails I have run have rocky sections that were more appropriate for hiking—not running—and you need to know when to let go of your obsession over time and just tackle the course in the safest fashion no matter how slow the pace. It's important to have the right expectations when first beginning trail running, and being willing to walk or hike when necessary is an essential attitude on the trails.

Trail running tips certainly would not be complete without a cautionary word about critters. No doubt, while out on the trails, you will at some point make contact with some sort of critter. Whether it be snake, insect, squirrel, mouse, raccoon, bear, turkey, deer—whatever—you will probably come across one. Read posted signs before entering an area (for example, this Goat has learned not to ignore the Georgia State Parks signs that say "you are now entering the habitat of the canebrake rattlesnake" or the yellow jacket warnings), and be sure you are familiar with what sort of animals call the area you're in home so that you can be ready if you do happen upon one. Most critters you experience are more afraid of you than you are of them and retreat is often the best option.

MINUTES OVER MILES

When you're first starting out on the trails, don't worry so much about mileage. Set a goal time amount—do you usually go out for a three miler and it takes you thirty minutes? Then set out to run an easy thirty minutes on the trail. If you start out on the trails with time-specific goals, you'll enjoy yourself more, you'll keep at it because you will more realistically achieve your goals, the time will pass quicker, and you'll be able to just appreciate the experience and take in your surroundings.

OFF-ROAD TRIATHLON!

A talk about trail running in a triathlon book wouldn't be complete without a nod to off-road tris! Love trail running? Love triathlons? Go grab your mountain bike and tear up the trails on both two wheels and two feet after taking a dip in the nearby lake, pond, river or ocean. Lots of local race directors and organizations put on these off-road adventures, but a great place to start is Xterra Planet. They put on trail races and off-road triathlons and duathlons across the country and the world. The races range from beginner to advanced levels.

EIGHT

Rest & Recovery

I almost did not include a section in this book about rest and recovery. Why? Because for a working wife and mother and well, for a woman in general, what in the hell is "rest"? I am *never* rested. *Take a rest.* What? You're speaking another language, stranger!

Still, while sleeping in past 9:30 a.m. has not happened in over five years, I can attribute great importance to "recovery" and "rest." Running yourself into the ground, while at times feels like a by-product of being a woman, should not be an attribute of triathlon. Triathlon should *benefit* your life, not complicate it.

In order to appreciate the workout days, you must relish the recovery days. To have a reasonably successful race day, you need to train smart. That means giving your muscles, your body, your soul and your brain a rest from training.

There are typically three types of rest and recovery themes:

Rest Day

You can have a day completely *off* from training. A day off is, obviously, a day off. Take advantage of true rest days and really rest. Take care of your extra non-training errands, spend a family day or whatever will help re-charge your soul for the next day of workouts.

Active Recovery Workouts

Active recovery workouts are low in mileage and intensity. For example, these may be a day where you put out an easy spin on the bike or a slow jog/walk. Active recovery days get your blood flowing, and allow you take some much needed time to focus on your technique.

Recovery Weeks

When you follow a training plan, a recovery "week" will be included every fourth or fifth week. The recovery week will dial back your mileage and intensity *for the week*—in order for you to rest and recover properly before the beating of the next training cycle begins.

No Overtraining Allowed!

On rest days, I tend to be crabby and bloated, because I like the endorphins and sweat expulsion that training days bring. At the same time, triathlon is about balance. I still need the break, even though I am crabby about it. On a neuromuscular level, rest days and recovery weeks are vital. It's easier to "survive" the rest days if you look at them as a time to recharge and regroup for your next big workout.

Overtraining is a big danger in triathlon. You can very easily become so focused (obsessed) that you fail to listen to your body, your training plan or your coach. If you fail to insert recovery into your plan, you are at a risk for physical damage *and* psychological damage (read: complete and utter burn-out). Take a break. If you feel overtrained, take another break.

Don't get me wrong: you will be *tired* from training. You may wake up tired. You may go to bed tired. You may fall asleep on the potty. You may sleep at your desk at work (*oh, I mean…*). But there is a difference between tired and fatigued. Rest is yet another component of overall health and balance. You need to stay hydrated, mentally focused, happy (as happy as possible) and sane.

Remember, Coach Monster emphasizes the importance of *quality* versus *quantity* in training. It is far better to take a rest day (even an extra one here and there) to ensure that your next workout is the best workout possible.

NINE

Lost in Transition

THE MINI RACES IN BETWEEN THE SPORTS.

Transition was a confusing topic for me when I started thinking about triathlon. Everyone was talking about "T1" and "T2" and I had no earthly idea what that meant. *Was it something to do with a potty? I need to transition?* Sometimes. But really, transition means two things.

First, transition as a *noun*: the place where you store your bike (and other stuff) during a race. This location is usually a large, open area with metal racks for the bikes. You will likely have an assigned space on the rack for your bike, and a space under your bike to place your triathlon "things."

Second, transition as a *verb*: the action of moving between the sports. You transition from the swim to the bike. Then you transition from the bike to the run.

TRANSITION

All you need to remember to ask yourself: Am I wearing what I should be wearing for the sport I am about to do?

Goggles go with swim. Helmet goes with bike. Really, transition is like a preschool game of Memory. But the problem in the middle of a race is, you are actually thinking like a cranky preschooler—so remembering to wear the proper gear is more challenging than you might initially imagine.

The best advice I have about transition in your first few races is: *take your time*. I know it is counterintuitive to "take your time" in a race. But making a strong exit from transition is more beneficial than making a fast (and potentially clumsy) exit.

In a later section in this book covering race day, I will go into detail about the things you need for your race and how to set up your transition area—but for now, here's a quick overview of transition—the noun *and* the verb.

T1

T1 is the transition from the end of the swim to the bike.

McBlessings recommends that as you are finishing up your swim, you begin to think of your transition to the bike: *Where is my bike? Repeat the order of your transition in your head: helmet, glasses, shoes, race number belt with number turned to the back* (or whatever order you choose). This will make a smooth transition onto the bike.

Again, as a beginner, you will want to take your time in both transitions, especially in your first race. Yes, this whole thing is about *racing*. But you don't want to come barreling out of transition without your helmet and get disqualified. Take a moment to gather your composure, and ensure that you have all your gear (and wits) about you.

As I am coming out of the water, I usually take off my goggles and swim cap. If you are wearing a wetsuit, you can pull the wetsuit down to your waist as you are coming out of the water. Races will have "strippers" (woo-hoo! Triathlon is *awesome*! Okay, not *those* kind of strippers...)—volunteers who help *strip* off your wetsuit near the swim exit. You sit on your bum, lean back and they *riiiiiip* your wetsuit from your body. Fun times! Let them help you, it's much easier that way!

Once you are in your transition area, Coach Monster recommends having an extra bottle of water to spray off your feet and eyes (especially after a saltwater swim). Usually you will have mud, sand or grass on your feet from the run *into* T1 after the swim. Sometimes the race director will have a baby pool to step into to clean your feet, but sometimes you may overlook the pool or it may be crowded (or dirtier than your feet!). I have found this water bottle tip to be great advice! I love to rinse and quickly wipe my feet before putting on my bike shoes.

I normally do not wear socks on the bike because my feet are wet and wet socks are frustrating. By the time I run, I am usually dry enough to put on socks. Or, I will wear socks on the bike and then, put on fresh socks before the run. However, this is a matter of personal preference—do what works for you! Once you are helmeted, race number clipped on (use a race number belt, described later) and ready, you can head out to bike. (And no, you do not use a towel to *dry off* your body before getting on the bike. Crazy, I know. Get on that bike sopping wet—you'll survive, I promise!)

You must roll (not ride) your bike out of the transition area. There will usually be a banner or a sign: *Bike Exit.* Head that way, walking alongside your bike, but do not get *on* your bike until after the mount line.

Mount line? What?

Before the race, make note of where the "Bike Mount" line is. Most races have an actual line of tape or paint placed on the ground right outside of the transition bike exit. Sometimes they designate it with construction cones or a sign: "Mount Here." Regardless of what the line is—it is only *after* this line or designated area that you are allowed to get on your bike and ride. Do *not* mount your bike before this line or you can get disqualified. Usually the volunteers are very good about letting you know (screaming, if necessary) where to be and when to get on your bike.

The best practice is to roll your bike past this line and over to the right side (to make room for those who are flying out of transition). Clip safely into your pedals if you have clipless ones and pedal off for the bike leg. As a beginner, the race will be confusing enough. If you get nervous or confused, just move to the right side of the course (out of everyone's way) and gain your composure before moving again. But always get yourself to the right—don't just stop in the middle of *anywhere* in a race.

T2

T2 is the second transition when you finish the bike and begin your run.

Much like the way *out* of transition—you do not ride *into* transition either. You must walk and roll your bike back to your spot. As you are riding your bike towards T2, you will see a "Bike Dismount" or "Dismount Here" line. You must dismount your bike *before* this line. Sometimes the dismount line is the same as the mount line; sometimes they are in two different places—just check before you begin the race.

If you are shaky on the dismount, slow down well in advance of transition and pull to the right and take your time dismounting. Once you are off your bike, roll your bike to your transition spot and rack your bike.

At this point, you are ready to take off your helmet and bike shoes and get ready to run. Turn your race number to the front, find your hat or visor, slip on those running shoes (and socks if you are like me and bike without) and get moving!

As the Expert says when he is spectating my races: "Run and done!" That is my favorite mantra after the bike. I repeat it often: *run and done and run and done and run and done and run.....*

T3

Fooled you. No such thing as T3.

Well, actually there is. T3 is the time after the race where you wander around aimlessly looking for snacks and beer. *Beer! Beer!* (I'm sorry, isn't that the reason we race?)

Swim Bike Mom Transition Tip

Practice your transitions before race day. You will look funny in your driveway, but who cares? Better for your neighbors to think you are nuts than your fellow triathletes.

TEN

The Other Important Training Stuff

STRETCHING

What is static stretching? This is the slow, methodical method of stretching (no bouncing). You pick a muscle group—hamstrings, for instance—and attempt to touch your toes, moving as gradually as you can to achieve the best (but not painful) stretch possible. Static stretching is best saved for *after* a workout or on recovery days.

For your pre-workout stretching, Coach Monster recommends something to get the blood flowing—like jumping jacks or dynamic stretching. I ignore him completely with regard to jumping jacks. I've had two children, for Pete's sake. Maybe if I put on a diaper first... But dynamic stretching is helpful, especially in the shoulders. You essentially utilize a full range of movement, like a swim stroke or shoulder circles, and repeat to warm-up.

Stretching *after* a workout and on recovery days is vitally important. I like a combination of standard hamstring, hip flexor and quad static stretches for my lower body. Then I use the foam roller to "roll out" my IT band, hamstrings and calves. I use shoulder rolls, triceps stretches and other shoulder stretches for my upper body.

You will find that stretching is a matter of personal preference, but you must find what works for you. Find it, and use it. Stretching and foam rolling are vital to your triathlon habit.

THE CORE: YOUR CENTER OF AWESOMENESS

Immediately after Coach Monster began training me, I was introduced to the importance of developing a strong *core*. The midsection, abs and back muscles are often referred to as your "core"—these are the muscles that support your spine and keep your body stable and balanced. A tough midsection and lower back is necessary for smoothness in the water, holding form on the bike and your posture during the run. Apparently, a strong core is the secret to solving all the world's problems, in addition to being the foundation of the body. So, basically, because the core is so important, I was introduced to the hideousness that is known as... the *plank.*

While there are a million different resources available out there for core moves, core strength and the like, the most powerful out of all is the plank. I really can't even talk about a plank without feeling shame and fear. It is so hard!

It looks like a pushup on your forearms, except you are not moving. I'm sure you've seen it. If not, Google it. You'll see, and once you *do* the move, you'll *feel*.

A plank is performed as follows:

* Lie on the floor, facing down with your forearms on the floor.
* Push up off floor as if doing a push-up, but instead of completing a pushup, rest on your forearms and elbows.
* Keeping your back as flat as possible, engage your "core" muscles to prevent your stomach or hips from sagging, or your butt sticking up in the air.

There are derivations of the plank: plank with knee raises, side plank, plank with rotation. All are terrifying and core-busting.

In addition to planks, you should incorporate abdominal moves such as crunches, leg raises, crunches on a giant ball and, if you dare—sit-ups. Coach Monster likes to incorporate abs and core into my workouts no less than twice a week, year round. *I love the Monster. I love the Monster...*

STRENGTH TRAINING FOR TRIATHLON

You can pick up any issue of *Women's Health* or *Shape* magazines and find perfectly acceptable strength workouts—for looking *hot*. But interestingly enough, strength training for triathlon is *different* (and it should be).

I don't want to "bore you" with weight training and strengthening exercises here in this book, but only for one reason. I hate picking up a book about triathlon and finding half the book to be strength workouts. I'm like, "Where's the value!? I want to know about *running*, not lunges! I know about lunges! Errrr! *Fitness Magazine* has covered lunges for the last twelve issues!" So, as a beginner, if I picked up a triathlon-centered book, I wanted someone to tell me about swimming, biking and running—and that's all. But I will admit when I am wrong—and my attitude about strength training has been *wrong*.

Indeed, there's yet another discipline to triathlon: strength training. And I had to learn this the hard way.

Recently, I have been plagued with weird injuries and strange *imbalances* in my body. If right knee hurts, then my left hip starts killing me. My back, then my quads. I swear I've got a new baby hunchback from all the training hours in the saddle. And these bizarre issues did not seem to arise until I hit some major mileage in the training.

As I set out to write about strength training for this book, I sort of glossed over the importance of it. But then, my injuries got worse. Then an epiphany slapped me in the face: My imbalance issues and injuries could have been prevented *from the start* of my triathlon training.

Whaaaaat?!

And interestingly, while swimming, biking and running did, indeed, make me a triathlete, I needed the balance and foundation brought from strength training to *continue* my triathlon journey. I would not be a triathlete for long, continuing as I was. I was all out of balance.

During some sad injury-ridden times, a triathlon friend, Elizabeth, turned me on to the book *Holistic Strength Training for Triathlon* by Andrew Johnston. After I read this book and began incorporating the exercises into my regimen, I decided I definitely wouldn't bother writing about strength training in *this* book because Johnston's book is *the* strength training book specifically for triathlon. I cannot even begin to reference and cite some of the wealth of information that he provides. The book covers the *why* of strength training (and it's not all with weights!), takes you through the *how,* and then some. Take some time to pick up his book and work towards building the strong foundation you need from the beginning of your training.

One of the good things about triathlon strength training (as shown in Johnston's book) is that you can incorporate strength moves for each discipline that do *not* necessarily require hitting the weight room. Many basic strength moves are floor or standing moves (think: no weights needed; exercises such as pelvic bridge, hip extensions, flexions, twists and a variety of stances). Additionally, a big part of whole (and holistic) triathlon training includes proper stretching, fascia release and massage techniques.

Of course, there are strengthening moves *amongst* the three disciplines too. In the pool, you can increase your strength by performing swimming sets using a pull buoy or float. That move helps to stabilize the lower body and cause you to rely more on your upper body. The same can be said for hand paddles, although the jury is still out on whether these are good for beginners. On the bike, all you need is your favorite big gear on a flat road or some "suffering" in the hills. Finally, you can increase your power in the run by incorporating hill running or consistent interval training.

However, you'll be surprised how much work can be (and should be) done outside of your swimsuit, cycling shoes, and running shoes—and on the floor of your living room.

Please note that I am not de-emphasizing the importance of strength workouts by limiting this section—rather, I am recognizing strength is *far* more important and in-depth than I can (or am qualified) to cover in this book. Strength training from the ground up provides you the base and the balance you need to stay as injury-free as humanly possible, and to thrive in triathlon. So read *Holistic Strength Training for Triathlon*—it will take you through all the information you need for this portion of your training. You'll be glad you did. Promise.

BALANCE AND YOGA

BOSU®

Coach Monster often prescribes "balance" workouts for me—one-legged stuff on the BOSU® ball. At first, I did not understand the point of those balance moves. But a few spills during the year taught me that I need help with my balance and small connective tissues (ah-hem, more strength training moves).

Furthermore, running and biking obviously require pretty decent feats of balance. Many of these vital moves are also in the Johnston's book, referenced above.

Yoga

I love yoga, but hate it at the same time. I have found some hard core yoga DVDs like the Yoga-X from Tony Horton's *P90X* series. The Expert and I like to do yoga, but it's difficult to find the time to throw it into the mix.

Yoga is awesome for core building, stretching and overall mind and body connection. I find that time for yoga is tricky because there are so many other workouts to accomplish, but I do *love* the way I feel post-yoga. If you have time and want to incorporate yoga—do it. Go forth and *om.*

Coming Attractions

You would think that the next chapter should be about race day. And I would tend to agree with you.

However, there are more things to handle in your life *before* you get to race day. Important things like training with a full-time job and family, how to handle your nutrition and your mental toughness. I will cover your race day and preparation, I promise.

But first, let's talk about getting your mind, your nutrition and your family set on your journey.

ELEVEN

The Mental Game

Much of triathlon is training the mind to tolerate the pain that the body is experiencing. But you must not simply *tolerate* pain. Instead, your goal should be to embrace the pain, love it and make friends with it. Coach Monster and his Purposeful Suffering mantra is all about embracing and enjoying the pain. I thought this crazy until I began to practice it…and then saw the great results from focusing my mind to endure the hurt.

But triathlon is not *only* about enduring the beating of the training. The training is also about wrapping your head around your true strengths, learning to believe in yourself, and using the sport as a foundation for a better, stronger life. You will learn that you are stronger, faster and tougher than you ever thought possible if you stay strong of mind and just keep going.

Four vitally important Every Woman Rules must be followed with respect to the Mental Game of Triathlon:

The Every Woman Triathlon Rules

Rule #1:
Believe in yourself.

Rule #2:
Ignore those who do not believe in you.

Rule #3:
Know when to stop.

Rule #4:
Most importantly, know when to keep going.

Strength and character can be built from this sport—I believe it with all of my heart. Pushing through the pain, the doubt and the sweat to go to a new place (a run distance, a swim personal record) will reveal more about you… *to* you.

You may not believe in yourself right this second, but you must begin thinking in terms of belief. Start out with just once-a-day mind tricks. Once a day, think about triathlon and simply say, *I can do this*. No need to dwell on it, do it quickly and move on with cooking dinner or driving.

Little by little add other little affirmations to your day that will help you focus on yourself:

I am a runner.
I like to swim.
Triathlon is changing my life.
I can do this.
I will do this.
I cannot wait for race day.
Triathlon is the bomb diggity boogity. Woot woot.

Your mind is the controlling force of your entire body. Use it for your benefit!

Introduction to Life Coach Carrie

One of my newest friends, Carrie Hanson of Tempo Life Coaching, has been an amazing force during my triathlon trek. Interestingly, she has not been my actual "life coach," but she provides me very coach-ly wisdom. Her friendship has helped me through some tough times. Most importantly, she makes me think long and hard about the cookies that I eat (and *why* I am eating them!).

Triathlon as a Game Changer

by Carrie Hanson
Tempo Life Coaching
(www.TempoLifeCoaching.com)

Triathlon will change your life. Really it will. Not only will the obvious outward changes take place (can you say muscles?), but it will change you on the inside too. It truly *is* a life-transforming sport.

Everyone starts triathlon from different places in life, different athletic experiences and different self-comfort levels. And everyone experiences the highs and lows that come with this sport as well. In that way, we are all alike. We all push our bodies to some level of discomfort, we all battle the inner voice demons, we all have fantastic workouts and horrible ones, and I haven't met anyone yet who doesn't experience the post-race high. It makes no difference your time, your distance, your place...the post-race high attaches to you as you cross the finish line and it sticks around for a bit.

I started training for my first triathlon just about a year ago, and have participated in three sprints, with several more on the schedule for this season. It was my brother who got me going with triathlon.

During his first race, he experienced a panic attack during the open water swim. He said if ever there was a time he wanted to quit something, it was then. But he didn't quit. He pushed through the swim and went on to complete his race. After his race, I received a text message from him, "You must start training for a triathlon. You'll feel so good about yourself and your sense of accomplishment."

Uh, I already feel quite good about myself, thank you very much, I thought. *He's crazy.*

But of course, the seed was planted, and within a few weeks I had taken the plunge. I signed up for my first tri (three months down the road) and contacted a coach. I already had my running shoes and a bike, and I quickly set out for my swim gear. I was ready to roll.

Following the prescribed workout schedule written by my coach was easy enough. Don't get me wrong, the training was hard because I was totally out of shape and carting around a few extra pounds, but following her directives was easy. I found that having a set schedule and having to check-in with my coach kept me accountable and gave me something to focus on. I think I may have been a little lost otherwise, or I'd likely have stopped training immediately (as in the first time I hit a hard workout). But I didn't quit...I followed the schedule and felt so accomplished with each workout. I'm still amazed and pleased with myself when I think about how much time I spend training each week. It's not a crazy amount like some people, but it's a lot more than when I was hanging around on the couch being lazy.

Here is what I've come to learn over the past year: mental training is equally as important as physical training. Even for elite athletes, the mental part of the game is every bit as important as the physical part. Starting out, you might be quite out of shape and a "run" might consist of only thirty seconds of jogging (or shuffling, as I like to call it).

It's hard to not compare yourself to others when you're wheezing and feeling like quitting after thirty seconds. Keep at it though. Before you know it, that thirty seconds will turn into a minute, which will turn into two minutes, which will turn into a consistent jog/walk, which likely will turn into a full 5k jog.

I say "likely" because maybe it will not turn into a full jog. Perhaps it will remain a jog/walk. A jog/walk is fantastic though! Think about it. Any progress is fantastic. Which is precisely where the mental game comes in. The only room for comparison in triathlon is when comparing to yourself.

I still struggle with the mind games. Most of the time I am pleased with myself, with my progress, with my training, but then the bully voices in my head start to scream loudly. The voices point out how slow I am, how far behind the rest of the pack I am, how scared of the ocean I am, how hard this is and how much I want to quit when it gets hard. Let's not forget how "fat" I look in my tri clothes compared to everyone else. Yes, that internal bully is mean and destructive and tries to get the best of me.

But here's the most exciting thing about triathlon: eventually, you get stronger than those voices. The voices in your head begin to say nicer things. Or if not, you learn how to push past them and shut them up. I've found this part of triathlon to be the hardest part quite honestly, and I have also found it to be the most transformative because it overflows into the rest of my life.

Being in the back of the age group really is no big deal. Someone has to come in last; who in the world cares *who* it is? Sometimes it's embarrassing. Sometimes I get frustrated with how slow I am. But then I remember all the positives in the sport of triathlon, of the triathlon community in general…the support, the friendship, the fun, the camaraderie. I have not met one athlete, either face-to-face or in an online community, who isn't completely 100% supportive of my efforts and those around them. I may be the slowest in the group, but I'm out there *in* the group. And you can be too!

So remember, you are out there doing this thing called triathlon when so many others are afraid to even try. Stand proud, and when those voices get loud in your head, just push them aside and remember that you are out there swimming, biking, running (or walking) pushing yourself physically and mentally. Getting yourself to the starting line is where your real success is. The rest is just icing on the cake.

So pour yourself into your wetsuit, get your bike ready to roll, lace up your shoes and get ready for a journey of a lifetime!

MENTAL TOUGHNESS: THE TRIATHLON GOSPEL

by Gerry Halphen

Mental toughness is the triathlon gospel. Period. I preach this all the time. I cannot tell you how many times in a race I have passed superior athletes—because their mind has given up. And mine *hasn't*. Triathlon, particularly long distance races, is about developing the ability for your mind to rule your body, not the other way around.

Mental strength is not simply about the capacity to suffer. Your capacity to suffer will increase by training. But mental strength is also about maintaining the quality of every training session. Each and every session, you must use your *mind* to control your *body*. If you practice this principle every day, then race day just becomes an extension of your new habit. Remember: you cannot show up on race day and expect to do things you haven't done in training.

Very few triathletes practice mental training techniques. They will say "yeah yeah," but they can't tell you their specific visualization techniques or their mantras they intend to use as the race unfolds and things get difficult or "go wrong." Trust me: if you don't practice these techniques, you'll never be able to master them and use them to maximize your performance on race day.

Get a mantra. What will you say to yourself during training or a race when things "happen" or begin to get difficult? What will you say when your body feels like it can't move another step? *Just move forward. I am lucky to be able to do this great sport. Keep going strong. You are strong. There's beer at the finish line!* It does not matter *what* you say, as long as you have something to recharge your mind and keep you focused on the goal.

Visualize your race. You might be surprised to hear that you should *not* visualize a *perfect* day. Rather, visualize yourself in a positive, focused mental state *no matter what happens* on race day. Anticipate things that could happen (e.g., choppy swim conditions, a flat tire, leg cramps on the run, etc.)—and visualize yourself dealing with all of these events with a clear, focused mind and a positive mental outlook. When things "happen," as they inevitably will, you will have already worked through those issues mentally, be able to leverage your mantras to keep you going, and you'll be ready to handle the problems. Some amazing athletes claim to have a plan, but when things go badly in a race, you can see them falling apart—they do not react well. I've seen these "thoroughbred horses" on the side of the road cracked into pieces. Then there's me, the old farm mule, just plowing through by sheer mental strength and preparation.

One of the most wonderful things about the mental side of triathlon is realizing and re-discovering that most limits are actually self-imposed. If you had asked me when I started triathlon ten years ago if I would ever go sub-10 hours in an Ironman and earn a spot at Kona [the Ironman World Championships in Hawaii], I would have said you were *crazy*. At that time, I couldn't swim twenty-five meters. But I moved forward, worked consistently on both the physical and the mental portions of training, and have broken through my self-imposed limitations. You can do the same.

Again, I cannot emphasize it enough: learning how to maximize the quality of each and every training session will, by default, build the mental strength and endurance that will sustain you through the difficulties that inevitably arise. This mental edge is a rare skill and it takes a long time to develop. But I can promise you that—once you develop the skill—it's money in the bank.

===================================

Strong Mind, Strong You

Doubt: The Enemy

Swim Bike Mom here again.

I struggle with *myself* more than I struggle with anyone else. When I started training in 2010, I had to make a consistent effort to restrain myself from my typical *modus operandi* of self-sabotage. Even when I had completed hours of training, I would doubt my ability to race. During some of the harder months of training, I doubted my ability to do that first half Ironman. And I doubted it—big time.

For almost a year, I had been going back and forth with a hip injury. For a while, I experienced no real pain, but then the fresh pain would come in waves. After my first thirteen-mile run followed by a very long day in heels at work, I pretty much began to hurt all the time. I was forced to admit that my pain was real, present. But I recognized that, in my usual way of self-sabotage, I might be using the pain as an *excuse* to devalue my abilities and cop out of my big race.

There is advantage in the wisdom won from pain, I would tell myself, repeating one of my favorite quotes from Aeschylus.

At physical therapy during this time, the massage therapist dug into my hip and butt for trigger point therapy. He hit one spot that immediately brought tears to my eyes, what I call the "hurts so good" factor. He said, "You are the first person in thirty years of massage therapy who didn't scream, cry or crawl away with that point."

"Huh," I said. "Well, I only screamed once in thirty-six hours of labor and your trigger point wasn't even close to that."

He stared at me.

So I have a high pain threshold. So what? Am I bragging? No, quite the opposite, actually.

Once I understood my high tolerance for the physical pain, I realized that my doubt issues fell somewhere in my *head*—not in my *body*. I could physically *tolerate* the pain. But the question was: could I *mentally* tolerate it? Was I mentally strong enough to make it to and through my training and the big race?

> *"Fear is probably the thing that limits performance*
> *more than anything - the fear of not doing well,*
> *of what people will say.*
> *You've got to acknowledge those fears,*
> *then release them."*
>
> — MARK ALLEN

A very smart person, running coach Missy Munoz (also known as "Miss Teeny"), told me how to avoid the doubt-fear-anxiety factor in a race: "Do not let a single negative thought creep in your head during the swim or the race in general. If you feel a negative thought coming, push it out. If you are in the open water and you feel it coming, then sing a song, breaststroke, but do not let negativity in."

I responded, "Well, what if I am panicking?"

She told me, "No no no. Do not even *utter* words like 'panic' and 'fear.' Knock them out of your head now, in the beginning and in training, and while you are on the land. And do not let them return."

I began to use these quotes, phrases and sayings on a daily basis. I listened to Coach Monster and began to use my mind to control my doubts—which slowly worked to control my body.

Just Show Up

In the book *Your First Triathlon*, author and triathlon coach, Joe Friel, writes about the importance of never skipping scheduled training days. He emphasized that the level of commitment to triathlon must be hardcore. I totally agree, and I also agree with another point of his: that if you commit to getting dressed and giving your workout a promised five minutes, chances are, you will finish the workout. Then, if after five minutes, you cannot do it, stop moving, give up, because today is *not* your day. Just do better tomorrow.[xii]

I have found the five-minute rule to be fairly true. If I make the effort to wake up early, get dressed and drive to the gym, and I am a complete crabapple, usually I will snap out of my funk after five minutes. I may not be singing songs and skipping happy while I complete the workout, but usually, I can scrounge up enough fortitude to finish.

However, I have stumbled across a handful of days, outside of being sick, where I did not feel like running, jogging, walking, cycling (indoors or outdoors), swimming or floating. Days where I just wanted to be lazy for no apparent reason. But I always tried my best to *never* skip a scheduled workout. Even feeling like garbage, I would get dressed, strap on the heart rate monitor, the shoes or the swimsuit. But only a few times, I jogged or swam for five minutes and actually threw in the towel. I knew that I needed to quit when I was in the pool and ready to give up. Usually, if I get my hair wet, I force myself to make the wet hair and chlorine exposure worth it.

The best thing to remember is that walking away from the workout is sometimes okay. You made the effort to show up, you put in the attempt, and if it does not happen that day, forget about it and move on. When that happens I say to myself: *I will do better tomorrow. That's all I can do for today.*

Focusing on What I Could Do

I had a difficult time in the lead up to my first Olympic distance race because life, at that time, was very hard. The Expert and I were going through some issues with our three-year old son. Work was killing me. My commute was brutal. And then, I had added triathlon to the mix. Willingly. *Boy oh boy, I just gave myself yet another thing to do. I rule.*

However, I am not one to throw in the proverbial towel when things get difficult. Not externally, I should add. I rarely throw my hands up, scream "I quit" and walk away. Instead, I tend to *internally* self-destruct. Stress at work, sick babies, and suddenly, I find myself eating a pint of ice cream in the closet and listening to *Boys for Pele* underneath my old prom dresses. Once the pint of ice cream is scraped clean and a few rounds of *Hey Jupiter* have flashed through my head, I am back to business as usual. Only the "business" is planted firmly on my rear end in the form of fat cells.

About ten weeks the race, I was awake all night with a sick baby boy. My alarm was set for 4:30 a.m. to wake up for cycling class. Mistakenly, however, I had set the alarm for p.m. Needless to say, cycling class happened thirty miles away that morning without me. I knew that the one instance was just a boo-boo, a mistake and a life happening. I needed to stay home anyway, because the kid was sick.

But the question for the rest of the day was how to deal mentally/emotionally with a missed workout, sleep deprivation, a ton of work to accomplish and no way to do it because of caring for a sick child? The tougher question was how to do all of that without sabotaging my diet, turning completely evil and making excuses in perpetuity.

I started some positive self-talk. *Sure, I missed cycling class, but I own a bike in the garage. I can cycle tonight on the trainer after I tuck the kids away. Sure, Coach Monster won't be yelling at me from the seat, motivating me, but it's something.*

As for the food and the sabotage, I created another dialogue. *Yes, I am home today. But I don't freaking live in a Taco Bell. I can control my diet.*

Finally, with regard to the work factor: *I had a computer and a babysitter who will come in for a few hours. I can work from the house, breaking only to eat (not at the Taco Bell) and take the baby boy to the doctor. That kills two birds with one stone: being a conscientious employee and a "decent" mother.*

That small positive self-talk movement was the beginning of focusing on what I *could* do, instead of getting hung up on what I couldn't do.

My big lesson in triathlon was learning to define *my life*—to not allow life and its inevitable chaos to define *me*. Each day of training and each race experience brings this clearer into focus: *I am defining my own life. Me. I will make my life happen. I will create the life I want.*

BOTHERSOME HAPPINESS

After almost a year of training, I found myself pretty darn happy. Interestingly, my happiness actually bothered some people. And the longer I am in this, the more I find this to still be true. *Your* happiness and strength may begin to grate on people—granted, those people might not be the type of folks you need on your side, anyway, but...

You must learn to keep out the bad energy. People might be annoyed by your new-found triathlon happiness. If you have not experienced the jealousy yet, you will. Friends that were "best" friends can become borderline enemies because of their bitter sarcasm directed at your journey. Just be prepared for it. Remember: your bothersome happiness is worth the ridicule.

> "Triathlon will teach you alot about yourself. The time in the saddle, the quiet in the swim, and the pain of the run. The time in your head creates a space of quiet, a space of reflection. Triathlon will teach you things about yourself (...things that sometimes you may wish you didn't know!) ...But You have found your strength when you figure out how to handle those things. The question is: what are you going to do next?"
>
> — COACH MONSTER

SELF-MOTIVATION

Sometimes the hardest part about triathlon is moving forward when you are working out alone. For example, there will be times when you are the only spinner in the room, there is no music and it's 4:30 a.m. You may be the only runner on the path (be safe). Or, the lonely fish in the pool. You may be the only human for (what seems like) a hundred square miles.

If triathlon teaches you anything, it will be self-motivation. At the end of the day, each training session is up to you. You have the choice to push through or ship out. Do not make excuses to give yourself an "out." Keep moving forward. Every piece of food (good or bad) that you put into your mouth is your choice. Every "snoozed" second you sleep in...you got it—your choice (and sometimes, the snooze button *is* the better option).

Your life is *yours*. Training by yourself is a good correlation to life in general. Start believing in yourself. Rely on yourself. Make yourself stronger. You can do it.

FIGHT OR FLIGHT

After a race, Coach Monster often makes me talk about things I learned *from* the race. "What did you learn from the race over the weekend?" he asked me for the very first time after a heinous trail race.

I jiggled the phone nervously and thought for a minute. "That I am *way* fatter than I thought?" I asked.

He paused, cleared his throat and said, "No. Try again."

"That I have *got* to improve my run pace? By, like, alot?"

Silence.

"Get in line for the potties much sooner?"

More silence.

"Okay. So what are you looking for?" I questioned. Deep down, I knew what he wanted. He wanted to hear the guts, the actual triathlon tid-bits that would improve me as a baby triathlete and as a person. But learning experiences have never been my forte.

"Okay, okay," I said. "I have learned that this is a fighting sport. I must fight. The entire time. Fight against the doubts, the pain and urge to quit."

"That's more like it," he said. "Keep going..."

Fight

I usually deal with all of my life experiences in one of two ways: fight or flight. You may say, well, duh—that's every person's choice: fight or flight.

But that is *so* not *so*.

What about floundering, frolicking, or falling? Freaking, flailing or fumbling? See? Lots of choices, other than fight or flight.

In triathlon, I must continue moving forward, clawing and fighting, even if I am *crawling*. Moving forward may seem like flight, but it is not. The push forward and the pain is what makes *fight*. Raccs teach me to suck it up, keep going, no matter who told me *good luck with that* or raised their skinny little eyebrows at me (oh, my favorite!).

I just move forward. I fight. I stay. Fight.

Fighting is the motion of kicking away the self-doubt. When the bad mother of doubt creeps in, I show her what a *bad mother* can be.

Then, I fight the waves, the water, my goggles, my swim cap, the swimmers around me, the buoys, the sunlight, my clipless pedals, transition, my wet socks, my gears, my helmet, my shoes, the hills, the turns, the "on your lefts!", the blisters, the dehydration, the GU packets, the rocks, the dirt, the pavement, my shoes and my own horribly, uncooperative body. Fight.

I fight the urge to cry in every single race. And not from the pain. I am so moved by witnessing the impossible become possible for those around me—myself included. I am overcome with gratitude for the opportunity to be *alive*, to be outside, covered in blessings. Sometimes, I lose it and just cry. Then other times, I feel like I cannot run another 12:30 pace step. So I cry from that. But usually if I think of the heroes in this sport and not my tired legs, I cry less from the tired legs and more from the motivation. Either way, I try not to cry so much. Fight the waterworks. (I often fight with the Expert, especially when we are running ridiculously late for an event.)

Flight

When your workout or race is really over, then it's time to close the gate and fly away home. But for the most part, triathlon is a fighting sport. Sometimes, you must fly away, and call it a day, but mostly triathlon will be about the fight.

Perhaps, if you are really fast, then arguably, you *fly*. As for me? I'm more of the flightless bird type. One with really sharp talons and super bird mental games: a fighting bird. A tubby little fighting chicken...

So I urge you to find your *fight* as you embark on this sport. Because during the tough workouts and the hard races, there will come a time when you'll be *fighting* like hell to take just one more step forward.

Mental Toughness: Not Just for the Pros

Until triathlon, I had always been the type of person to focus on my weaknesses, to let my head drop. *Why am I so fat? Why don't I have any fashion sense? Why do I giggle in court when other lawyers do stupid things so that the judge glares at me over her glasses?*

For year and years, it was all about what I could *not* do. *I can't run. I can't bike. I can't clip out of my bike pedals without falling.*

I still battle the instinct to respond to almost everything with a negative light from the get-go. Maybe it's the lawyer in me talking (*we're all going to get sued in the end, so what does it matter?*). Usually, I can turn lemons into a fabulous lemon soufflé by the *end* of the day. But my gut reaction in the morning is to scream: "Sky. Falling!! See it?"

Chrissie Wellington wrote an amazing article for CNN in February 2012.[xiii] If you do not know about Chrissie Wellington, then you should swim, bike and run to the video of 2008 Ironman World Championships (YouTube. com has a version). Chrissie gets a flat tube on the cycling leg, wastes her CO2 cartridge, and yet, still goes on for the win. As of 2012, she's won the World Championships in Kona four times and has never (ever) lost an Ironman distance race that she's entered.

One of the best quotes in the article is also one of my all-time favorites: "If we let our head drop, our heart drops with it. Keep your head up, and your body is capable of amazing feats." She also wrote that when negative thoughts arise, we must "deliver these negative thoughts a knockout punch before they have the chance to grow and become the mental monster that derails your entire race."[xiv] Of course, this applies to training and life too.

The negative game I was (and sometimes am) playing is a mental beast, just like Chrissie points out in her article. With my Decision, I decided that I would not spend so much time sitting. Then I entered races and set goals. If only I had spent the last ten years saying, "yes, I can do that" or "I will sure as hell try," who knows where I would be. Probably still in the back of the triathlon pack, but I would have been more calm, happy and focused those years—instead of stressed and hopeless.

Something inside of my brain clicked at the start of this journey. I *decided* to become a triathlete. Ah! The mental component. The "yes, I can" factor!

On those long runs where I swear to my dear sweet Lord that I am about to die, I hear my brain say to my body: *You aren't going to die. The pain will stop when you stop. Just run through the pain. When you're done running, the pain will stop. But if you stop before you are done, the physical pain will become shame pain and you will have to tell your coach that you quit because "it was hard." For shame.*

If, at any time, during the year long process of getting to (and finishing) some big races, I would have truly given up mentally—if I had really doubted that I could finish those races—then I would have stalled before even beginning. Of course along the way I experienced moments where I stomped my feet, cursed and said, "I quit!" But overall, I maintained some form of mental toughness, even when my body was not tough, but just a flabby ball of mess.

I maintained the mental toughness especially during the actual race in Miami, when I jumped into a raining swim start, sick as a dog and with a nagging hamstring, and when my legs literally gave up on me at Mile 4 of the half marathon. I learned especially that one must be mentally tough to use a race Porta-Potty.

Do not kid yourself. While mental toughness is certainly for the pros and elite triathletes, mental toughness is even more important for the *newbies* to the sport.

Why?

If you are starting out anything like I did, then you are accustomed to society (and yourself) telling you that you aren't good, pretty, thin, smart, rich or fit *enough*. Therefore, when you make a crazy declaration like "I'm going to become a triathlete," and those same people who thought you were *fat* now think you are fat *and* crazy, your mental toughness is forced to either rise up or eat crow.

(I've never cared for crow.)

At the beginning of triathlon, you must be mentally tough, learn to brush off the negativity, and move forward. Every day. *Brush brush brush. Step step step.* You must go, you must move forward. You do this until one day, not too far down the road, one of the negative folks will catch you in the break room at work or in the checkout at the grocery. You may not *look* that much different in just a few months of training, but you will *be* different.

One of those negative nellies will then ask you: "So how's that little triathlon thing of yours going?"

You will respond, "You mean my big race?"

He will say, "Oh yeah yeah. How far is that race again?"

You will tell him the distance, or answer his other snarky questions. And as he's walking out of the room, he'll probably snicker and say something like, "Well, good luck with *that!*"

At that moment, you will say something that will stop him dead in his tracks.

You will say, "Oh *that* race? It was *last* weekend. Already done. I finished it. It was great."

He will most likely stand, stunned and floundering for words. Somehow, "congratulations" never seems to be one of the words that spring to mind with these people.

More like, "Oh wow" or "hmmm...that's great."

Regardless of their reaction, your mental toughness will have paid off, and it will be your turn to shine and glimmer and feel full of sparkles. Oh, and it's a kind of social revenge, too. Truth: sometimes that slight vindication makes it all worth it. While smirking smugness is not *why* we race, the "I did it" revenge factor is sometimes quite lovely.

Whatever your goal, be a mental giant! Channel Chrissie Wellington. Channel the cold beer at the end of the race. Who cares how you build the toughness, just build it. Talk down those fears from the ledge in your mind. Run a 5k. Run a 10k. Do a sprint triathlon. Register for that big Main Goal. You can do it. Make it happen. No matter your size or shape, 90% of the people in your life won't be able to keep up...and they sure as hell won't know what to say when you reach your goals.

TWELVE

Nutrition, the Scale and Self-Esteem

FOOD. A LOVE STORY.

If there is a chapter in my book that I am completely incapable of writing on my own, it would be this one. Weight, dieting, nutrition, the scale, my muffin top and self-esteem are all my sore spots. Along with the size of my arms, my thighs, my rear butt, my side butt, the post-pregnancy belly pooch (ew) .... oh, nevermind. Precisely why I am not flying solo on this chapter.

I will always want to weigh less than I do. I will never be content as the fatter version of me, just because of the way I feel when I am at a lower weight—I feel better in my own skin.

The actress, Kirstie Alley, and I—we would be awesome friends like that. When Kirstie is in her heavier stages, I always say to myself, *awww, Kirstie. I know, girlfriend, I know.* Then I root for her when she shows up in a bikini somewhere, after finding hot yoga and magic food. Then she shows up again on a magazine cover, "Kirstie Fat Again!" and I want to kill the magazine editor. *Leave my friend Kirstie alone!!* I scream, standing in the grocery checkout, eyeing the Reese's cups.

Anyway.

Even though I have been on the same rollercoaster as my best friend, Kirstie Alley, I believe in my heart and soul that I will (someday) have the body I want.

But I am also realistic.

I do not say, *Oh, I can't lose weight.* Do you know why? Because I also *know* that I have not made the necessary sacrifices to have my dream bod. Have I given up pizza? *Nope.* Ice cream? *When hell freezes over.* Beer? *Sometimes yes and sometimes no.*

To look like super trainer and guru, Jillian Michaels, you have to eat, train and be dedicated like her. I am not there *yet.* But that does not stop me from trying to be the best *me* possible. Slowly, I am learning about the nutrition journey and how to play by the good-eating rules—not for sexy legs, but for *strong* legs that will get me to the finish of my next race!

Regardless of what you weigh right now, you must move forward and work towards your triathlon goals *at your current weight.* You must start *now.* Do *not* wait until you are "smaller" to start moving. Do not say, "When I lose weight, then I will run." That does not work, and if you are like me, you might be waiting forever!

I would have wasted the past two years if I waited to be a Size 10 to run. Because I'm *still* not a size 10, and I've finished ten triathlons, including two half Ironmans. Look what I would have missed just in that time!

Go, go, go!

DON'T WEIGHT… ER, WAIT!

Get moving now, at your current size!
Do not wait for the perfect day, your perfect size, or perfect weather.
All of these things will never happen at the same time, and you'll be waiting forever to get started.

Go now!

Regardless of your size, a nice side effect of triathlon is *feeling* better, looking better and (if you're diligent) dropping pounds. If I had not replaced every single calorie I had burned over the past two years with junk food, I would be forty-three pounds lighter. At least, that's what Daily Mile said I burned through my training last year: 43 pounds.

Turns out I must've eaten thirty-five of those back.

The Swim Bike Mom Battle

Oprah Winfrey and I have one notable thing in common. I would prefer to have things in common with her such as her shoes and billionaire status. However, the thing that Oprah and I share like twin sisters from other misters is: giant arms.

I have always had big arms. (I blame genetics! That's it!) Also, I am a former weightlifter. (I blame that too!) Okay. Reality check. These arms are *not* products of massive biceps and triceps, although I feel some remaining muscles there. My arms were huge even when I was at my leanest during weightlifting. Now that I am not lean (at all), my poor arms are even worse off.

For the longest time, I suffered through sweltering Georgia summers in cardigans, long-sleeved t-shirts, and everything I could grab that was 3/4 sleeved. *Must hide the arms, must hide the arms.* I would sweat and curse and yell at the Expert who failed to start the car fast enough to get that air conditioning blowing. I would *never* wear short sleeves. I am not talking sleeve*less*, I mean *short* sleeves. Not even those.

Interestingly, as I began to train, I found that I did not have the patience for my sleeve addiction and my fat arm obsession. The demise of my sleeve fetish was a gradual thing. Triathlon does not lend itself to long sleeves. *Do I really care about these sleeves when I am wearing a giant helmet? Should I really fret about these fat arms when I was wearing a tri-suit that has turned my entire body into links of sausage?*

As I swam, biked and ran my way through the summer of 2011, I found myself swallowing what little pride I had and accepting the fact that I would sometimes be forced to go sleeveless in triathlon *races*.

However, the sleeveless status seeped into my training runs. Then, I found myself browsing sleeveless jerseys, buying them and subsequently *wearing* the jerseys on rides. A few times, I even went sleeveless in indoor cycling class (a real public place). I became comfortable *sans* sleeves in my triathlon world. And that felt pretty nice (and much cooler).

Then, I started wearing some sleeveless shirts on the weekends and on vacation where no one knew me. I was, however, especially unprepared for one particular day: I walked into to the bathroom at work. I looked in the mirror and *suddenly* realized I was wearing a short-sleeved shirt. At work. And a skirt. At work. Now, subconsciously, I remembered packing that outfit the night before to take with me to the gym to wear to work. I remembered putting that outfit on at the gym after my run. I remembered thinking at the gym: *Maybe all that swimming is paying off—my arms are less like giant, flapping hawk wings and more like baby bat wings.*

But to look in the mirror at work, and actually be wearing a short sleeved outfit (and not cringe): it was a first. Interestingly, while my diet and nutrition remained terrible, a side effect of training was gaining confidence to wear short-sleeves. My self-esteem was growing and the sleeves jumped off my arms before I even realized what happened.

KEEPING TRACK OF WHAT I PUT IN MY MOUTH

I was down about 8.5 pounds after a few months of triathlon training. I tracked calories. I watched what I ate. I avoided alcohol and I trained hard. I was certain that I had broken down the science of weight loss during this month. Turned out that I was wrong.

I continue to battle the bulge. Every day I fight with myself and my desire to bathe in a sea of delicious food, sail down a river of peanut butter and shower in a spring of red wine. Part of my weight struggle has been simple overeating. But like most everything in life, the weight game is also mental.

Three times in my life I have lost a substantial amount of weight: (1) when I was ten years old, I joined Weight Watchers and rode a stationary bike sometimes (we won't go into all the issues pertaining to a ten year-old being on a diet); (2) my brief visit to Size Ten Land when I gave up alcohol, took diet pills and ate only brown food (in addition to running and obsessing over *Tae Bo*); and (3) during a four month vegan stint with killer exercise to start off my third decade and to celebrate my 30th birthday. I lost about 22 pounds.

All the three times, the weight loss hinged on three factors:

1. No alcohol (well, not at age eleven);
2. Some sort of exercise regime; and
3. Keeping track of whatever I put into my mouth (Weight Watchers) or putting myself on restrictions so steep (veganism) that I could eat all day long and not possibly gain weight.

Swim Bike Vegan

Four and a half months before my big 70.3 race, Mountain Goat and I decided to embrace the vegan lifestyle once again. Veganism is basically a diet consisting of no animal products or by-products. If you are a really good vegan, then you buy and wear no leather goods or use household animal products. Mountain Goat was already a vegetarian. I might as well have been. If I take a bite out of chicken, inevitably, the chicken is either undercooked or I snag that horrible, nasty part of the chicken breast (I could yak thinking about it now). I find weird things in my burgers. Seafood I will forever love, being a Savannah girl. I would probably eat shrimp even as a "vegan" because a shrimp does not really seem like an animal (go ahead, call me a bad vegan).

In 2009, I went completely vegan for six months. Even made it through Thanksgiving and the holidays without dairy, meat or animal by-product. Anyway, I think of my Vegan Period fondly. I went four months without touching a single animal product, right down to my shampoo. One awesome thing about veganism: you can seriously nosh *all freaking day long* and not gain weight. I mean, can a person get fat on broccoli, apples and salad with vinegar? On lentils and black beans? On cashew cream sauce…*Mmmmm, okay maybe on that.*

Veganism is unique in the fact that I ate all day long and I lost weight like gangbusters. Veganism was also as close to a cure for my allergies as I've experienced. I am a freak of nature when it comes to allergies. I'm allergic to everything: dust, leaves, pollen, grass, trees, corn, celery, onions, wheat, and pork. I am also incredibly allergic to soy. So what can an allergic vegan eat? I'm so glad you asked! *Well, not much.* Which was the whole point.

But then one day, I fell off the wagon due to work stress and I was downing ice cream and shopping for knee-high leather boots by lunch. A month after that, I was chowing down on a burger and struggling to remember where I lost my way. And suddenly, there were the twenty-two pounds I had lost. Plus ten.

Sigh. I am not one to do anything in moderation. I do not eat or drink in moderation. Clearly, I am not one to exercise in moderation (hence, triathlon). I'm *all in* or I'm completely out. Because I "cannot" moderately eat anything, I tend to think that I just should not eat.

So my second adventure in veganism with the Mountain Goat was going reasonably well. But a stressful day brought on the cheese and it was all over. I had a torrid affair with some parmesan, a little cheddar, and a smidgen of mozzarella. I did not make it much further into the Vegan Period before I crashed.

What was it going to take to make a permanent change? I was so lost.

Food Regret

Clearly, I was hanging out with the wrong friends and working with all the wrong people. If I had real friends and real colleagues, those people would have tied me to a chair and wired my jaw shut. At a minimum, they would have slapped my hand away from the goodies in the break room at work. *Was a padlock on the break room door really too much to ask? What about making my desk into some sort of consistent, energy-creating treadmill?* "Keep running, Mere, or your computer will shut down!!"

You would not believe the snacks at a law firm. Chocolates, sweets, cake, breads, quiches—you name it—and when clients are happy, they send food, which is subsequently displayed in the break room like a cornucopia. *May the snacks be ever in your favor.* Typically, I would walk into the breakroom to fill my water bottle. Then I would see the goodies. Suddenly, my apple, protein powder and salad looked like compost.

On one particular day, the spread was insane. So I had a piece of zucchini bread instead of my compost for lunch, justifying the choice because the bread was *zucchini* bread. Next, I had some banana bread for snack (my fruit component). Of course, I had to have a slice of coconut cake (coconut is loaded with some sort of antioxidant). I had three different—okay, fine—*four* different types of junk on that day. Part of the coconut cake I wore on my right elbow for the better part of the day like the Scarlett Letter for a bad eating whore.

Food addiction. *Oh!* Another thing that Oprah and I share in common! *Yay!* Big arms and food addiction. I like healthy food. I like junk food. I feel better when I ignore the junk food (who doesn't), but I still do not understand why I cannot show enough restraint to stay away from bad food? With my huge half Ironman looming in the distance, the weight situation was starting to really be un-funny. I knew I had to get off thirty-five pounds before that race. But I could not stop eating. Consequently, I raced Miami quite heavy.

Yes, I train hard and I am (always) hungry. But the vast majority of the issue is that I am a blazing, self-destructive jackass. I was at the bottom and I did not know what to do.

So like The Email I sent to Coach Monster back in the beginning, I sent another email. I reached out for help and I scheduled an appointment with nutritionist, Ilana Katz.

70.3 NUTRITIONAL INTERVENTION

I prayed that Ilana would help me. I prayed that she would not produce wires to clamp my jaws shut. I needed some definitive answers, a *lifestyle* plan. I had been on a giant weight yo-yo for my entire life. My closet ranges from size 8 to 18. I would like to pick a size and stay there. Forever. Or at least for six months. I would prefer size 8, but I'll take 10, and live happily ever after in a 12. I've spent most of my life bouncing around size 14 like a ping-pong ball, which really would be just fine too if it were permanent. In all reality, I was simply crying out for consistency.

So what did Ilana say?

She said, "Stop eating. You are a cow."

Okay, I am kidding. But she did mention cows. She listened carefully to my eating woes and she likened my typical food patterns to…grazing like a cow. How in the world can cows get fat on grass? Because they eat all day long. That was my first problem. I *graze* around my kitchen and living room. All night long.

My second problem is that I am able to hold together my nutrition from morning until early afternoon—but around early afternoon all hell breaks loose. I get busy at work. I forget to eat a snack and by dinner time, I am starving and on a raging food binge. Ilana confirmed that I was not eating *often* enough. And when I did eat, I was definitely not eating the correct combinations of food.

So my blood sugar was shooting up and crashing down, and in turn my body was clinging to my beautiful fat cells like crack cocaine. Ilana weighed me. She callipered me. I was 33% fat. That is correct: I was made up of one-third fat. That should have hurt my feelings, but I was numb. I had known I was (at least) one-third fat for a long time.

My plan was to eat more often (e.g., have an actual "schedule"). Stay away from the garbage (eat "real" food). Eat protein at every meal. If I eat a carb, then I should snuggle it up to a protein. The plan seemed so obvious. But I had *obviously* failed to manage these obvious things thus far. So they are either in actuality un-obvious or I just needed someone to say it to my face.

The conclusion: follow the guidelines and stay away from crap. Do not stuff my face when I am stressed. Do not retreat to the starving cave when I am happy. My issues with food are tied to many emotional issues, I'm sure. But the problem with *food addiction* (as opposed to other addictions) is that a person *needs* food to survive; but yet, food (the drug) is the very *trigger* that causes the issue. So, for me, Oprah and my fellow food addicts out there, we must learn to balance the trigger, because food isn't going anywhere.

The Skinny Vault

I hope someday to write an article or blog post entitled "Update on My Six Pack" and have the post *not* be about the frosty bottles of Stella Artois in my fridge. On day four of eating as I was prescribed, I felt great. And I was trying to stay off the scale, seriously *trying*, but my obsessive, self-destructive personality was so accustomed to the following morning ritual:

- wake up
- use bathroom
- brush teeth
- strip off clothes
- weigh
- curse

I was not sure how to yank myself out of the weigh-curse scale cycle. I wanted to know my progress, but at the same time, a *lack* of progress *as defined by the scale* ruined my day. I knew I should measure progress by clothes fit, the way I felt, *blah blah blah*. Blah. Blah. Blah. (*Blah blah blah*). But the scale refused to budge, even when my *fatter* clothes were falling off of me. *Why did I care about the number so much?*

In an effort to save money instead of buying new clothes, I cracked open the giant Rubbermaid vault of "skinny" clothes (sizes 8-12) from my residence in Size Ten Land—in hopes that I could find some slightly smaller scraps to wear to work. As I was rummaging through the Skinny Vault, I came across my favorite jeans from Size Ten Land. I picked up the jeans, turning them over in my hands, holding them up in the mirror.

My self-destructive nature took over.

I was talking to myself like a crazy chick: *What if I just* try *to put on the jeans, just to see how* far *they will go up my legs? I mean, if they make it past the knees, that's something.*

I knew full well that when I was in Size Ten land long ago that I weighed twenty-five pounds less. I also knew that if I tried to pull those jeans up, I was setting myself up to be furious for the rest of the evening. But the Expert was upstairs reading with the kids. No one was watching me. I was safe. I stripped off my shorts and quickly put one leg in the jeans, then the other and I braced myself for the pull-tug-scream-suck-in motion that was about to happen.

But something very strange happened instead: the jeans pulled up. Over my legs. Over my buns. Then something even stranger happened. I pulled the front of the jeans forward. I buttoned. I zipped. I blinked. I looked in the mirror and I blinked again. I was twenty-five pounds heavier than the girl who wore those jeans while living in Size Ten Land. Yet, I put on those jeans no problem. Therefore, *ipso facto*, I had absolutely no idea what in the world was going on with my body. No idea! I officially gave up. (But not before my West Coast friends probably heard me squealing in my best Southern voice, all the way from Atlanta: *Oh Em Gee! I am wearing these jeeeeeans!*)

Plus-Size Notes

The Expert went on business trip to Germany and brought home a fabulous array of pictures on his iPhone. He took a special picture just for me (no, not one of *those!* Mind out of the gutter, ladies!). It was a picture of the outside of a clothing shop. Upon closer inspection, I noted that the mannequins were wearing women's clothing, and as I looked even closer, the clothes were sort of—well—large. Then I realized why the Expert took the picture. This particular store was a plus size women's store—and the name of the store was: *SuperWomen.*

Argh. Another one? And in Germany? The Expert knows my beef with the plus-size clothing industry. I am usually incensed and aggravated by the names of American plus-size women's clothing stores, but that one took the cake. *Mmmmm cake.* Well, it was a close second to Catherine's Stout Shop, an old Savannah, Georgia favorite. Because I have done my fair share of dabbling in the plus-size genre, plus-size store names absolutely slay me. For example: August Max Woman. The Woman Within. Silhouettes. Junonia. Hips and Curves. And Size Appeal (just to name a few).

I think I am most blown away by the "Woman Within" catalogue. Why? Well, *large* is the last acceptable prejudice (of course, this is satirical).

Now someone operates a business which by its very name states: *Oh, there's a woman <u>within</u> you. As far as the outside of you, well…that's TBD (to be determined).*

Then there's Junonia, the place where I purchased my first swimsuit for triathlon training. A *junonia* is a type of butterfly. I do not like the butterfly allusion. *You are ugly, but like a Junonia maybe you will become a beautiful butterfly … someday.*[xv] Another meaning of Junonia is a *large sea snail* that lives in deep water. The shell is usually only found washed up on beaches after a strong thunderstorm.[xiv] Yet another meaning for this blessed store name: Junonia was an ancient Roman colony located at the site of Carthage, known as a superstitious site of bad omens.[xvii]

Finally, August *Max* Woman. Sigh. Need I get into this one? No wonder it went out of business. I had to put on a cape and sunglasses to go in that place (although I did like the clothes).

I think (we) larger women are hesitant to workout—not because of the common evil theme that larger women are *lazy*—but rather because of the embarrassment. The gym is such a horrific place to put your size out for everyone to see—all that jiggling and moving. Starting to move is difficult enough, without shaking like a bowl of jelly. You jiggle at the gym, then you drive home feeling good about yourself only to check your mailbox and find one of those heinous catalogs. *Thank goodness! My Woman Within catalog arrived! I can't wait to find the woman within me! Hot dog! Mmmmmm. Hot dogs...*

A plus-size woman's first step towards fitness is monumental. If you keep going forward, despite the ugly looks from others (or yourself!), you will find that the "woman within" is also an awesome woman on the outside too. Trust me, you will get these looks from time to time. But you must arm yourself with a strong will that overpowers any real (or perceived) negativity. I say "perceived" negativity, because sometimes we're just making it up—and serving it as a dessert to our main meal of excuses. I battle issues with my size every day. *Every day.* No matter what size I am, I look in the mirror and I see a fat girl. I think I probably always will. I guess my "woman within" is a bit of a bitch.

WHAT IS THE REAL ISSUE?

A common theme in my food life is: eat like a pig all night, then wake up hating myself for spiraling out of control (yet again). *Why do I like to eat like a vacuum cleaner?* A simple explanation is that the endorphins make me feel better for a moment. But what about the real issues? The real why-do-I-eat-like-this? Why do I sabotage my training, my health and my day-to-day life for the sake of peanut butter and cookies? *Mmmmmm....peanut butter cookies.*

After almost two years of pondering, I came to a conclusion. My relationship with food was a pure and simple act of rebellion. Instead of incorporating Ilana's wisdom about food being the only thing I can actually control in my life, I often choose to rebel in a passive-aggressive way. I eat like it's my job. Then I think: *I'll show you. You can't control what I eat. Mmmmm, pizza and ice cream. I'll show you.*

But in reality, I'm only "showing" myself some extra pounds and more bad feelings.

The following tale is not a blame-your-parents moment. Rather, I am sharing because this particular moment in my life was a critical point and has great weight (no pun) in my self-analysis.

Here's the story: I was about eight years old, rocking out my prep school uniform in 1987. On some Fridays after school, my mom would take me to get a small ice cream cone or those awesome little cookies from old school McDonald's. On a particular Friday, I had a quiz paper in my backpack. I knew that the paper was going to be an issue, because I had earned a big fat "C" as scrawled in red by the teacher. As we were pulling up to the McDonald's drive-thru window, I showed that paper to my mom (my timing was off, clearly). Suffice it to say, no ice cream for me that day.

Growing up, two things were disallowed in my house: recreational drugs and "bad" grades. I am certain that my mother's actual response to the quiz grade and subsequent drive-off was: "You got a 'C.' You can do better. We aren't going to have ice cream today."

However, in my memory, I recall wheels screeching as we blew out of the McDonald's parking lot. Flames were shooting from my mother's eyes and a dark rain cloud with lightning stormed down from the heavens and struck our Buick wagon repeatedly until I cried out for mercy. That was the last "C" I received until evidence class. In law school. Seventeen years later. (Unfortunately, it was *not* the last ice cream cone.)

Do you see where I'm going with this?

Irrespective of the fact that a food-reward is probably not a good idea for a food addict, my adult stress eating made perfect sense when I recalled this childhood incident. Food is connected to my struggles with perfection, rebellion and control. Again, I am not blaming my mother for my eating issues. I cannot blame her for the four hundred and ninety-three Krystal burgers I ate as I wrote this book. (What's Krystal? *Dude.* Like White Castle, only better.)

When I earned the "C" on my quiz (imperfection), the food (reward) was taken away. In that situation, the denial of food was completely out of my control. I wanted the ice cream, but it was denied, denied, denied! #%$^! I had someone telling me that not only did I disappoint them, but *also* that I could not eat. Growing up, I was told what to do, what was expected of me and how to act in every single part of my life (control). My parents expected things of me. I was told to stay on target, always. I usually did, at least outwardly. But food? My parents could not control that! No, stuffing my face remained *mine*, all mine. I could eat! I could sneak food. I could steal other kids' Fruit Roll-ups. Every last bit and bite was mine (rebellion)!

Then, because I was a chunky kid, everyone wanted to slow down my food intake (control). But what I put in my gullet was mine (rebellion). *It was mine. Mine! You can't decide! You can't stop me from eating!* Even when I did not need food, I would eat because I was *oh so rebellious* and I was showing my parents who was *really* the boss.

And it wasn't Tony Danza. *Me. I'm the boss! I eat what I want, when I want, and how much I want. Me!*

Twenty-four years later, I am still playing these same games. Although, now I really am the boss of me, so I guess I am showing…myself…that I am the boss? *Wow.*

Maybe it's less clear than that, more societal. I am supposed to be a good mother, wife, daughter, employee, member of society. All these things are connected. All these things tell me to stop overeating. But I continue to stuff my face (rebellion). Even against myself. I am rebelling against myself. Figure that one out, Oprah. After I rebel eat, then I punish myself with negative self-talk for dessert.

My overeating is a backwards, self-destructive form of rebellious control. Backwards control? Precisely. I have it all wrong. When my life appears to be spiraling out of control, Ilana says that is precisely the time to grab the bull by the horns and take *control* of what I *can* control. Instead of rebelling, I must create a portion-controlled, systematic food world where I have complete control.

Me and the Hidden Scale

I recently posted on Facebook that I was putting away my scale. Man, people are passionate about their scales! I received *tons* of comments. Some of the readers said: yes, put it away. But then I received many comments and emails: *My scale keeps me on target. I need it. I have to have it. I must weigh to know that I am staying at goal.*

I stopped and pondered, wondering if "hiding" the scale would really help or hurt me. And I came to this conclusion: maybe scale necessity applies to those who don't have ~~30~~ ~~40~~ ~~50~~ 80 pounds to lose. For example, if I were already at my never-been-before-since-5th-grade weight of 120, then maybe I would drag out the scale and make sure I wasn't gaining it back. Maybe. But I have been tied to a scale for twenty-one years.

And I am someone who needs (desperately) to see the number go down. So, I'm not sure the scale is the best psychological tool for me, especially with training. When I have a bad ~~day~~ ~~week~~ month and I get on the scale and see ~~+10~~ ~~+12~~ +16, the number *destroys* me. After a bad weigh-in, the first thing that comes to mind: *you stupid idiot, how did you let this happen again, you are disgusting, look at you.*

As I packed up my scale to put it away for a while, I felt a sense of freedom and I knew I was doing the right thing for me. Here's how I knew: during the final ramp up for the half Ironman in Miami, I had completed a big workout: forty- mile bike ride, plus a six-mile run. I was in absolutely the best shape of my life. Even when I was thirty pounds lighter, I could not have fathomed that kind of workout. I felt strong, I felt proud, and I had a great day. The Expert and I went out to lunch after the workout. I ate a mass of food, but healthy stuff: salad, hummus, black bean burger with only half of the bread.

On the way home, I was elated, feeling that Miami was within reach. But once home, as I turned on the water to get in the shower, I stripped off my salty clothes and stepped on the scale. I was up seven pounds from the morning. Nevermind that I had just experienced the best workout of my life. Nevermind that I had downed six bottles of water on a hot day, ingested tons of electrolytes, and followed it up with a three pound, salty meal. Nevermind it all.

The scale had *spoken*. And I was crushed. And it was ridiculous.

My reaction was like giving birth to a beautiful, healthy baby and *immediately* cursing the loose skin, the weird boobs, and whatever nightmare is going on downstairs. Same thing—on that training day, my body had given me beautiful *results*. A beautiful triathlon training baby! But I *chose* to ignore what wonderful things my body had *accomplished* for the day. Instead, I chose to numbly focus on what my strong, capable body *weighed.* I chose to concentrate on the Earth's gravitational pull. *Gravity.* Gravity is what made my mood change.

The morning after I put my scale away, I woke up and I felt great. I had no number to decide how I was going to feel. Then, I had a great run. My entire day would have turned out differently if I had started with the typical self-curse of *you are disgusting.* Whether you love your scale or hate it, think about the consequences of your scale, its place in your life. Are you allowing your scale to shape your day? Your life? Your self-worth?

Words from the Nutrition Expert

So I may be a lost cause. It's no wonder that the longest chapter in this book is about food. But I will not leave you without help!

Ilana Katz, MS, RD, CSSD, is the founder of Optimal Nutrition for Life. She has really helped me breakthrough some big issues this past year with my nutrition, my self-esteem and my eating addictions. She is a triathlete and an Ironman. She has written two eBooks, *The Three Week Metabolic Boost* and *The Metabolic Burn* (regular, vegetarian and gluten-free versions), all available in the online shop at SwimBikeMom.com.

Sports Nutrition Mistakes and Fixes

By Ilana Katz, MS, RD, CSSD
Optimal Nutrition for Life
(www.ONforlife.com)

Introduction

Triathletes are interesting people. After all, we are a group of people who inflict pain on ourselves…and on purpose! What a moronic thing to do! Well, maybe we are not *all* morons. Some of us have difficult challenges to overcome—one of the highest-ranking challenges is body composition and weight management.

Another challenge in triathlon, which goes hand in hand with nutrition, is preventing gastrointestinal (GI) distress (e.g., stomach cramping, diarrhea, bloating, nausea) during training and racing. It is my intention with this section to guide you (nutritionally speaking) through some rookie mistakes, offer some effective and appropriate solutions, and hopefully fit that nutrition jigsaw piece more clearly into the big triathlon puzzle.

Weight Management

Before I offer any corrective actions, I want to make sure we are all on the same page regarding macronutrients. Macronutrients are carbohydrates, proteins and fats. Here's a very quick nutrition 101:

Carbohydrates
Athletes will refer to these as "carbs," particularly when name dropping and using fancy terms like carbo-loading. Carbs are in fact the main source of

fuel for working muscles and the brain. As a sports dietitian, I can verify that 99.9% of my regular clients will not bat an eyelid when I tell them that carbs are our friend. Without carbs, *anyone* will feel lethargic and mentally disoriented—especially athletes.

Most laymen get rather excited when a dietitian allows about 55-60% of their daily intake to be carbs, but if you are one of those envisioning cakes, croissants, biscuits and pie, although these are considered carbs, they are *not* the carbs your body will process as optimal fuel. Yes, fruits and veggies, legumes and grains, potatoes and winter squashes are the carbs I am talking about. So from now on, the word "carbs" means good, clean, unprocessed, optimal-burning fuel for the human engine.

Protein

Protein is mostly required for rebuild, repair and maintenance of muscle, organs, blood cells and immunity. Although the body can use small amounts of protein as fuel, protein is not typically a good choice for fuel. The body will revert to muscle as a fuel source when carbohydrates are absent. Why? Because fat requires oxygen, the by-product of carbohydrates metabolism, to burn.

Muscle is our most metabolic active tissue, and is thus the last source of fuel you want to burn. Contrary to popular belief, protein consumed in excess of requirements does not build muscle, but is actually excreted from the body with a by-product of nitrogen build up, needing to be cleared by the liver and the kidneys. Good sources of protein for rebuild and repair include lean meat such as poultry breast, fish, egg whites and whey. Greek yogurt and some quality protein powders (e.g., pea, hemp) are also decent sources of non-animal protein.

Fat

Fat is used to absorb fat-soluble vitamins essential to metabolic function (Vitamins A, D, E and K). Fat sources include essential fatty acids, which are required for nerve function and brain activity. Good fat sources (typically liquid at room temperature) can improve good cholesterol and lower bad cholesterol, such as olive oil, walnuts, avocado and fish oil. Whereas bad fats, which are saturated or trans fats (usually solid or semi-solid at room temperature) will have the opposite effect. These fats include fried food, butter, margarine, fat in processed food, and fat found on meat (fat on steak or poultry skin). Yes, fat is a reserve tank of fuel too—but always remember, as stated above, that fat in the reserve tank cannot be used as a fuel source, unless carbs are present to provide the oxygenation for this to happen (described in more detail further in this chapter).

Rookie Mistake for Weight Management:
"I swim, I bike, and I run. Therefore, I can eat anything, anytime."

Why This Is a Mistake:
Although you will burn many more calories with an endurance training program, it is vitally important now to focus on the origination of the calories and when they are eaten. Timing is everything! Our bodies are like any other engine: if we do not fuel optimally, we will crash and burn. With your training, you must focus on a new methodology to pre-workout eating, recovery and fueling.

I have taken part in many endurance events and given many seminars on sports nutrition. One of the most mind-boggling experiences for the new athlete is believing that she will drop weight like a bomb once training begins... only to find her weight will skyrocket instead. Why does this happen? Why? Why?

Corrective Action:
Fuel optimally each day. Fuel optimally before, during and after your workout.

You must have a plan for your daily nutrition. Weight management does not begin and end with training and race days only. The everyday lifestyle and routine is what encourages the body to adapt to efficient and effective fat burning.

Weight management also does not occur only on weekdays. If you are a "weekend warrior" in your training, sometimes weekends turn into a free-for-all eating binge. Now is the time to adapt a consistent eating pattern from Sunday to Sunday. You do not want to "throw away" all the good work you did nutritionally between Monday and Friday on weekend binges.

As far as training nutrition: do not drive your engine to its destination and *then* put gas in it. If you train without fueling optimally and then leave your engine starving after putting it through the grind, most of the calories you take in will be stored in the reserve tank (your fat cells!).

Take care to ensure that you have a pre-workout meal. This can be a couple of hours before the training or racing event, if there is enough time, or even thirty minutes prior to the workout. Depending on how much time you have for digestion will determine what type of carbohydrates (slow burning or fast burning) should be included and how much.

PRE-WORKOUT

Rookie Mistakes:

1. You include protein, fat *and* fiber in the pre-workout meal.
2. You are eating too much (or too little) pre-workout.
3. You are skipping the pre-workout meal entirely (perhaps due to gastrointestinal distress concerns, or due to avoiding extra calories).

Why These Are Mistakes:
The human body is an engine, and it needs fuel *to get started*. Pure and simple, you must put something in your tank before working out, even if it's just a little something. If the destination is far away, your body will need to be continuously fueled along the way. The choice of what you put into your tank *matters*.

Corrective Action:
Avoid fiber, protein or fat immediately before a workout. This includes meals like peanut butter on whole-wheat bread. Particularly if you are sensitive to having gastro-intestinal (GI) issues, you will want to avoid these. [Swim Bike Mom recommends peanut butter and bread before a race—but that is several *hours* before the race. We are talking about a pre-workout meal immediately before your workout).

You will want to avoid fiber, protein and fat because they can take a toll on the digestive system. Furthermore, the slow metabolism of fiber, protein and fat can cause gastro distress, especially while your heart rate is in a higher zone during training.

The only way to know what works for you and what doesn't is, unfortunately, trial and error. Sometimes you'll find more errors than you would hope. Try different things. Make notes on what you feel fueled you the best and what texture is most appealing before the workouts (especially early in the morning), and create a list of what you can and should eat before training. Some people prefer liquids (sports drinks) or semi-solid fuel (gels) before training. Others prefer solid foods, such as low-fiber breads or potatoes. The only way to know what works best for you is to try.

Additionally, your fueling should accompany a timing strategy. In other words, if you have more than a couple of hours or so for your meal to digest, slower-burning, complex carbs can be included. Also, a little protein and fiber *may* be appropriate to slow the release of the carbs down if you have some time to spare (like Swim Bike Mom's favorite pre-race meal of peanut butter and bread). When you have time to spare, some good choices are: oatmeal, apple, or even yogurt blended with ice and a sports drink. Again, it's all about what works best for you. Some athletes prefer to drink rather than eat before training, for a smoother gastrointestinal process.

If you do not have much time for a meal to digest, then thirty minutes before the start of your workout or race, you should choose fast-burning carbohydrates and avoid fiber and fat. A banana would be an excellent choice.

B-A-N-A-N-A-S!

A banana is the lowest fiber, but highest carbohydrate and quick-carb release fruit. Additionally, bananas have potassium! Ta da! A natural sports nutrition product! Who knew!

When you are short on time, you can also choose a sports gel, wafer or bar, or about eight ounces of a sports drink. There are many convenient sports drinks on the market specifically designed to digest quickly and smoothly; be careful, because some are better than others.

So you may then ask, what should I be looking for in a sports drink? There are a few things to consider. First, fluids are absorbed into the bloodstream faster when the concentration of their solution closely matches that of body fluids such as blood (scientifically, the term is "osmolality").[xviii] Concentration is the ratio between solute and water. First, a sports drink should have calories. Typically these calories are concentrated at 6-8% in relation to the water it is made with. Carbohydrates below 6% concentration have no significant impact on the gastric emptying rate (the rate at which ingested fluid is emptied from the stomach)—and in fact, empty at the same rate as pure water—which is a good thing for training and races. However, carbohydrate concentration over

8% will significantly decrease the gastric emptying rate and thus, will raise the risk of gastrointestinal distress.[xix]

Secondly, the nutrient content of the drink is important to consider. Electrolytes that play an important role in regulating fluid balance in the body should be in your sports drink. At a minimum, this includes sodium and potassium; other electrolytes are magnesium, and chloride.

Furthermore, be aware of marketing gullibility. Sports drinks are designed to contain carbohydrates (the fuel source). As such, a zero-calorie beverage (for lack of a better word) is *not* a sports drink. (Gatorade light (G2™) or Powerade Zero™). A lower-calorie, or calorie-free electrolyte drink is appropriate for use *leading up to* a long training or race day. The additional electrolytes can enhance hydration but they do *not* provide fuel (energy).

Probably among the best marketing "cons" in this area are energy drinks such as Red Bull™, Monster Energy Drink® or 5-hour Energy®. They are *not* sports drinks. And I repeat: *not sports drinks*. Similar to caffeine, energy drinks appear appealing as metabolic boosters to many athletes. Furthermore, many of them are typically marketed as *sports* energy drinks. This terminology leads one to believe that energy drinks may be beneficial for performance. The carbohydrate concentration in most energy drinks is similar to soft drinks, and is much higher than sports drinks.

Remember, for an optimal gastric emptying rate, concentration should *not* exceed 8%. The carbohydrate content in *energy* drinks is much higher than this and will delay gastric emptying, which increases the risk for gastrointestinal distress during exercise. Furthermore, *energy* drinks are not sports drinks due to their lack of electrolytes, the carbonation factor, and the overemphasized caffeine content—all factors which have potential to cause gastrointestinal distress and, needless to say, a "caffeine crash"[xx] while working out.

HOT POTATO!

If you are short on time, you can eat half of a baked, white potato for your pre-race or workout fuel. A potato (without the skin) is quick burning and natural. Add salt! The extra salt will provide you a nice dose of electrolytes.

DURING WORKOUT

Rookie Mistake:

Glycogen is the fuel source that feeds your muscle and brain. Glycogen can only be stored in the muscles and liver for a limited time. The Rookie Mistake is failing to replace this essential fuel during a workout. Many times, an athlete may want to avoid the extra calories (for weight management purposes). However, the most common reason for the dreaded DNF ("Did Not Finish") is due to glycogen depletion.

Why This Is a Mistake:

Glycogen is the only fuel that allows the muscles to work. Glycogen is the storage of carbohydrates in both the liver and in muscle tissue. You can use the terms glycogen and carbohydrates interchangeably for sports nutrition. The unused carbohydrates go into a reserve tank called "fat." The reserve tank is still necessary as a source of fuel and is burned with the aid of glycogen, during moderate intense exercise.

Without glycogen, you will inevitably "hit the wall" or "bonk." This is the terrible feeling where you feel completely out-of-body, woozy, sick and sometimes can risk passing out.

Bonking is a funny term, because where I come from, South Africa, bonking means something entirely different than glycogen depletion. However, actual G-rated, triathlon bonking is no laughing matter. If you bonk, you will not be able to move another muscle. The gas tank is empty and you will be found on the roadside (hopefully not dead—but in a seemingly lifeless and tragic state).

At this point, I do not want to hear the argument that most of us have an endless reserve tank called fat to use for fuel. Although this may be true (I still don't want to hear it), the fat reserve tank *cannot* be tapped *unless* there is glycogen present. Simply: fat may only be used as a fuel source in the *presence* of carbohydrates (glycogen)! The metabolism of carbohydrates provides the *oxygen*, or the flame so to speak, for your fat to burn.

Furthermore, if you are trying to save calories, research has proven when athletes replenish glycogen during a workout, they end up eating fewer calories the rest of the day than those who don't. So if you think you are saving calories by not utilizing sports nutrition products, you may actually be sabotaging your weight management goals.

Corrective Action:

During a workout or race, the goal should be to spare glycogen. In other words, you want to use glycogen as efficiently as possible. One of the most optimal ways to conserve glycogen is to *consistently* replace what is being oxidized. Now, you may not need to replace much during a sprint-distance race, but then again, you may need to depending on your weight and effort.

The human body oxidizes approximately one gram of carbohydrates per minute, thus equaling sixty grams per hour, so that should be your glycogen replacement goal. Thirty grams of replacement glycogen every thirty minutes is an optimal goal for carb replenishment.

Conveniently, the well-marketed sports products have about twenty-five or thirty grams of carbohydrate in one serving. For example, one gel, packet of sport beans, chews or sports drink will automatically get you this specific glycogen replacement. A strategy to ingest at least of one of these approximately every thirty minutes during a workout or race is ideal. Remember, sports drinks that are low calories or calorie free (even sugar free, meaning carb free) will not accomplish this goal.

Swim Bike Mom Workout Fueling Tips

I recently discovered that I love to eat "real" food when I am out on a long bike ride. A peanut butter & jelly sandwich on gluten-free bread or Go Raw! Super Cookies have recently super-charged my long bike rides.

Your long workout nutrition is going to literally be a game of trial and error. Try lots of things and see what works best for you.

Just bear in mind that if you are working out for <u>less</u> than an hour, you typically need <u>not</u> fuel during the workout. (Before the workout, yes. During? No.)

During a race (even a short one), I will have a gel or two on the bike and run, because I find that it helps me. I like the burst of energy.

Gels and liquids are the most easy forms of fuel to handle on the run, but the taste (especially at the end of a longer race) can make you loco after awhile.

The biggest tip: practice your nutrition during training—not on race day. Do the same in training as you plan to do on race day, and that will serve you well.

POST- WORKOUT (RECOVERY)

Rookie Mistake:
Not eating right after a workout. When you finally do eat, then you tend to eat everything in sight.

Why This Is a Mistake:
Delaying your recovery by not eating means that glycogen will be stored neither effectively, nor optimally. In other words, not only will workouts for the following few days seem less energized and strenuous, but regular, daily energy will also be decreased.

Although you may not feel hungry immediately after a workout, optimal recovery has a very small window of opportunity. The hormone acting as an appetite suppressant is at its highest after a hard-core training session or a race. However, the appetite stimulant kicks in a few hours later. Controlling the physiological drive to eat feels impossible if you haven't replenished immediately after the workout. Furthermore, the enzyme that aids in glycogen replenishment is most active for only a short window after an intense workout, and depletes progressively from there.

Corrective Action:
A ratio of at least 3:1 carbohydrate to protein should be eaten immediately after a long training day or after a race. Even a 4:1 ratio is acceptable. This strategy will not only help recovery for that day *and* for future days' workouts, but it will also enable a steady fat burn throughout the day (bonus!).

This is a great weight management strategy for two reasons. First, if you wait for the appetite stimulant to be triggered, physiologically your body will want to store everything as fat to protect itself from future starvation occurrences. You will most likely eat "everything" in sight as well. Recovering properly will prevent the fat storage! Secondly, if you do not recover optimally, you will most likely end up eating many more calories during the remainder of the day than you would have eaten had you properly recovered your glycogen. Tada, weight management!

RACE DAY

Rookie Mistake:
You do not have a nutrition strategy before the race. Or, if you do have a strategy, you throw your strategy out the window because of the free stuff at the race.

Why This Is a Mistake:

Most athletes, even those elite and experienced ones, have pre-race jitters. Adding another dimension to a race, such as gastrointestinal sensitivity, is devastating and can result in hanging out in the portable toilets during a race. Not only is a portable toilet a less-than-pleasant room without a view, but while you are *in* the room, your competitors, who have a great nutrition strategy, might be sailing effortlessly through the finish line.

Corrective Action:

Practice the most important rule in triathlon: "Race like you train, as long as you train like you race." In other words, during your training days, you should be practicing what you intend to do on race day. The rationale behind this is simple: when it comes down to the nitty-gritty on race day, far much less will be unforeseen.

Did I mention that a fiber-packed cereal is not an optimal pre-race meal? Just a little subtlety learned from experience. If you are easily enticed by freebies at a race, then make a point of checking out who the sponsors will be prior to your event, learn what will be supplied at the aid stations on the race course, and adapt those products as part of your training. This in itself is a good strategy because this will eliminate the need to bring in your own nutritional supplies.

As far as your potty strategy (and you should have one!), account for time in the morning before the race to get this very important "step" accomplished. Simply put: poo before your race. If you have a hard time with this (no pun intended,) try drinking hot water with lemon squeezed in at least thirty minutes prior to your rituals.

HYDRATION

Rookie Mistake:

Like your nutrition strategy, you should have a hydration strategy. Your nutrition strategy may go hand-in-hand with hydration if you prefer liquid calories. Nothing like killing two birds with one stone. This is precisely why a product like Gatorade™ is a scientific breakthrough in the world of endurance. However, a sports drink is *not* a beverage—and a beverage is not a sports drink. The Rookie Mistake is failing to know the *difference*.

<u>Why This Is a Mistake:</u>

Sports products are scientifically designed to efficiently and effectively move through your gut at an optimal rate. This helps avoid gastrointestinal distress.

Some products do just this. Others are pure hype. Why "hype"? After the original Gatorade™ was recognized for its brilliance, other sports products began to clutter the market. You are definitely in a state of "buyer beware"— you should trust no one hyping a sports nutrition product unless you have completed some responsible research into the product.

Any selling edge is bait for those wanting to run faster, swim further and ride harder. As mentioned, the ideal carbohydrate concentration for gastric emptying, intestinal absorption and adequate carbohydrate delivery is 6-8%. Less concentrated drinks do not provide enough carbohydrate to maximize energy provision. Carbohydrate concentrations over 8% significantly *decrease* the gastric emptying rate and thus, raise the risk of inducing gastrointestinal distress. Therefore, your optimal sports drinks will have at least twenty-five grams of carbohydrates per serving, may have some caffeine if desired (but caffeine is not the only ingredient), should not be carbonated, and should contain less sugar than fruit juice.

<u>Corrective Action:</u>

Do not be fooled by marketing hype. For example, Red Bull may not actually give you wings and 5-hour Energy might provide one minute of energy (if you are lucky). Both of these drinks are brilliantly marketed as energy drinks, but they are not *true* energy drinks. Do not forget that caffeine is only a *boost*. If carbohydrates are present, carbohydrates (in form of glycogen) are the *only* source of fuel that your muscles can use for energy. Furthermore, do not dilute your well-designed sports drinks because you are worried about the calorie density. The concentration and carbohydrate amounts are scientifically designed to avoid gastrointestinal distress.

On the point of calories, the lighter versions of Gatorade™ (G2) and Powerade™ (Zero)(the calorie-free "sports" drinks) are *beverages,* not sports drinks. These beverages are *not* the diet versions of the fully-loaded real thing, and as such, they will *not* fuel your muscles! In my opinion, these types of drinks are meaningless, particularly if you want to hydrate and fuel simultaneously.

ELECTROLYTES

<u>Rookie Mistake:</u>

Pure water can be intoxicating (and not in a good way). Pure electrolytes can be lethal (and not in a good way).

What Does This Mean?

The intoxicating and lethal aspect of water and electrolytes is technically referred to as hyponatremia (salt depletion) and hypernatremia[xxi] (water toxification). *Hyponatremia* is where sodium concentration is lower than normal in the body, often caused by too much water in the body. *Hypernatremia* is an electrolyte disturbance caused by too much sodium in the blood, often caused by a deficit of water in the body and as such, is commonly known as dehydration.[xxii]

Unfortunately, hyponatremia and hypernatremia are the leading causes of death amongst endurance athletes. My purpose is not to freak you out, but it is extremely important to understand these two dangers, because it is very easy for new athletes to get caught up in the marketing of sports nutrition products on the market, without learning how to use them appropriately.

Corrective Action:

Know your sweat rate. Are you an aggressively salty sweater? Work out all these logistics for varying conditions, especially potential race day conditions, such as hot and humid, cold and dry, or any various combinations. Even elevation may play a role here, if extreme.

On average, a person sweats between 1 to 2 liters (or 28-50 ounces) per hour during exercise. As a visual, an average size bike water bottle typically holds 24 ounces of fluid. The easiest way to measure your sweat rate is to weigh yourself without clothes before exercising. After one hour of exercise, weigh yourself again with no clothes on. Assuming you did not use the bathroom nor consume any fluids during this hour your weight loss is your sweat rate. For each pound of lost weight, you lost sixteen ounces of fluid. If you drink any fluids or use the rest room between the two weight samples, be sure to include both of these estimated weights in your calculations. *Add* fluid consumed to the amount of weight lost. *Subtract* estimated urination amount from the total weight lost.

It is always a good idea to record the heat, humidity and altitude (as appropriate) conditions in your sweat test. Repeat the test in different conditions (e.g., cool, hot, humid, dry). Repeat the test for swimming, running and cycling because sweat rates will vary for each sport and vary with environmental conditions.

While knowing your sweat rate will help you to calculate the amount of liquid you need, do not forget that you will *also* need to replace your electrolytes.

To determine how much you should be drinking about every fifteen minutes, divide your hourly fluid loss by 4 (e.g., if you lost 2 lbs, then 2 x 16 = 32 ounces divided by 4 = 8 ounces). The more environmental conditions you have tested, the more accurately your sweat-rate replacement fluid can be consumed.

Based on the results of your sweat-rate test and race day conditions, you will be able to determine the amount of electrolytes that you need to not only prevent a dangerous situation, but also prevent cramping that might lead to a DNF. Electrolytes may be in salt tablet form, pure salt, or included in your nutrition. A consultation with a sports dietitian may be beneficial to assist with your personal nutrition, especially once you begin to tackle the longer distance races.

Additionally, Jono Rumbelo, Certified Ironguides Method Coach, recommends a few tips, such as drinking frequently during training and racing to keep your hydration up. Interestingly, anti-inflammatory and ibuprofen tablets are recommended to be avoided when you are seeking to keep your hydration levels up.[xxiii]

CARBO LOADING

Rookie Mistake:
Loading up on as many carbohydrates as you can before the race.

Why This Is a Mistake:
Overeating can lead to absolute misery on race morning. The anxiety of the race, on top of equipment stress, plus a ridiculously full gut is a recipe for disaster. Additionally, adding constipation (or the other) to the mix is no fun. Carbohydrates can be rather constipating, just like stress. I am sure you understand my point.

Furthermore, even the right amount of carbohydrates consumed the week leading up to the race will cause hyperhydration to a certain degree, because for every gram of glycogen stored, three or four extra grams of water will be stored too. You certainly will feel heavier race morning even if you carbo-load optimally; why add unnecessary overeating to that "heaviness"?

Remember that the extra weight is merely because of the hyperhydration effect of carbohydrate loading. The extra carbohydrates will certainly be welcomed once the race is under way, and you will feel light again.

Corrective Action:

In addition to your general nutrition strategy, you will also want to have a carbo-loading strategy. This may not be as important for sprint-distance races, but it begins to be of monumental importance for efforts over an hour or two.

A good strategy: without changing up the amount you eat, you should shift your carbohydrate percentage closer to 90-95% about two or three days prior to race day. This means that protein and fat percentages on those few days are minimal. So most of your food sources will be from carbohydrates, but the size of the meals and the total caloric intake in those days should be just like any other day. If you have a hard time putting this in perspective, a sports dietitian or your coach can formulate an exact carbo-loading meal plan, which will probably begin a whole week out from race day.

The plans I develop for my clients also consider the taper phase of training. The taper phase is where your workouts taper from high volume to minimal volume two or three weeks out from a race. Taper time and volume will depend on race distance, as well as the importance of the race in the big scheme of things. Nutrition in the taper phase is very important to consider, because tapering means a drastic reduction in workout volume, which requires a need to tweak nutrition accordingly.

THE FINISH LINE

Eating for competing should *not* be about dieting. Racing at an optimal weight takes a lifestyle commitment with regard to appropriate and discretionary food choices. Keeping the number on the scale in perspective is *also* part of your training. Balance your efforts and your mind to keep the *why* of training in perspective. We race for fun and enjoyment—don't forget!

Of course, the celebration factor that follows the finish line is full of delicious food and sometimes alcohol. After all, that is why we do this, right? Once you have finished your race, certainly go and celebrate your accomplishment! Have a beer or two! But always remember, you can only have *one* six pack (either a six pack of beer or a six pack of abs)…the choice is yours. And never forget the lessons you learn about nutrition along the way.

I finished my first Ironman race in 2011. I have done many races and have learned a lot about nutrition not only from my background, but also from my very own races. Here are the quick tips:

- Train like you intend to race, nutrition included!
- Never (ever) try anything new on race day, *especially* nutrition.
- If you swallow most of the ocean in the swim portion of the race, cut back on the salt tablets during the ride.
- Carbo-loading does not begin and end with the traditional pasta dinner the night before the race.
- Bathroom anxiety in the morning pre-race can make or break your day: have a bathroom strategy!
- I am known for my white potato and salt tip for a race—it's a good one, promise! I was in a race eating a potato and a racer I have never met said, "You must work with Ilana, the sports dietitian!" *Well, yes! Yes I do!*

Happy triathlon!

THIRTEEN

The Tri-Fecta: Family, Work and Triathlon

INTRODUCTION

Most of the time when I tell people that I'm a wife and a mother, they smile. Then I say I'm a lawyer, and I will see a mild grimace pass across their faces. Finally, when I mention that I love triathlon, I see a horror-stricken expression, which is inevitably followed by, "What? How do you do it *all*? That's *craaaaazy?*"

To which I respond, "I'm an insomniac. I never sleep, so I have lots of time to do these things."

Part of my insomnia response *is* true. But you'll notice as you begin to balance your life, your family, your job and your training, that you will feel surprisingly *less* crazy. And the people around you will think you are *more* nuts. Also, you may tell others that you have a disorder—like insomnia—to prevent them from feeling badly about the fact that you just accomplished more before six in the morning than they might accomplish in an entire day.

Balancing family and training is tough, I will not lie. But your family can be a great strength to your training. Coach Monster says, "I draw on my family, when I am racing or in hard training sessions. I draw on them as a source of inspiration – sometimes it causes me to cry. But it has allowed me to tap deeper and deeper into sources of strength."

I find this to be true. I, too, draw strength from my family during triathlon training and races. I also find my strength is *renewed*, and I am able to be a better wife, mother and daughter after each training session. I may drop my kids off at the gym activity center wanting to put them up for sale… but after a run, I pick them up and I am so glad to see them. The difference a few miles makes.

Admittedly, some families may be a detriment to your training. This is all part of the triathlon balance. Where my family is a positive for me, my profession is often the detriment. On the other hand, I have friends who work part-time or stay at home, but their families are completely unsupportive of their triathlon goals. We *all* have different circumstances. We *all* must balance what we must balance. Once we balance, then we must balance some more.

> *In horse racing terminology,*
> *a **trifecta** is….*
> *a bet in which…the bettor must predict*
> *which horses will finish first, second,*
> *and third in exact order.*
>
> —WIKIPEDIA

Family. Work. Triathlon. The Tri-Fecta. Which horse is going to win? Does one horse have to win? Can you make them all win?

Yes. I think so!

I receive emails all the time, saying the same things: *How do you do it all? I don't have time for it! I can't possibly find time to do a triathlon!* Well. Yes, you *can*.

I often have my pompoms shaking and I'm screaming, "Yes you can! Rah rah! Shake your bon bon! Ride your bike! Yah yeah!" (And I do have my pompoms right next to me right this very second. But they are silent beside my desk.)

Because while "yes you can be a triathlete" is very important, and is my big mantra, there is more to it. This Tri-Fecta issue is also a question of your determination. The question is whether you are separating the "I cans" from the "I *won'ts*." The real question at the heart and start of this horse race: *Do you have what it takes inside of yourself to make your dreams happen? Or are you just a pile of empty, blubbering excuses?*

This topic requires a sobering reality.

This is your life, and it's up to you to make *your life* happen. Period. And it's up to you to make it happen without excuses, without finger pointing, without "can'ts" and "buts" and "well...I *would,* however...."

Women are always weighing the logistics of things: *How can I make this appointment between these hours? And who will pick up the kids? When can I find time to run? And forget swimming, who will do the laundry?*

Coach Monster says, "You have a duty to *yourself* to find a way to get things done—rather than finding an excuse for why you didn't."

Oh yes. This is pure Tri-Fecta goodness. It bears repeating.

> *"You have a duty to yourself*
> *to find a way to get things done...*
> *rather than finding an excuse for why you didn't."*
>
> — COACH MONSTER

I asked Coach Monster how *he* does it. After all, he's married with two daughters, working in corporate America (often out of town), coaching athletes and training for Ironman races. He's got a huge juggling act too. He said, "It is important to balance the needs of my family while keeping perspective that I do triathlon for fun..."

He went on, "I think we all have a tendency to get fatigued with life, with training over time and say, 'I can't train today because my family needs me now.' Now, there *are* times when things come up and those family things must be a priority. However, I believe these 'things that come up' can also be *managed priorities*. In other words, you are *tasked* with finding ways to get things done...rather than finding excuses for why you can't or why you didn't do it. For example, my personal record for a workout took place at 3:18 in the morning. I was in the pool at 3:18 in the morning so I could make a seven o'clock flight for my work. I planned, I balanced and it worked.

"This really goes back to the concept of quality versus quantity. I am a better husband, father and person when I am fulfilling commitments to myself. I come back from those training sessions almost unequivocally a better person. I am bringing a better person back to the people I love. Some would say that I am rationalizing my time away from my family or avoiding family responsibility. But I would say, 'No. Go ask my family.'"

While a 3:18 a.m. Coach Monster wake-up call may be extreme, I must say that I wake up at 4:10 a.m. every Friday to get my swim and bike brick completed. I have, a few times, risen as early as 3:45. On those few occasions, I was asleep at my desk by 3:00 p.m., but I felt like a million bucks up until mid-afternoon.

The point is that we must all begin to look at our Tri-Fecta differently. Instead of "How can I possibly get this done?" We need to say, "I will get this done, and here's my plan for how to balance it all *today*."

Day by day, we make the plans. Not broad, sweeping and unwavering plans. We may need to roll with the punches. The morning run might get rained out from a diaper explosion; *that's fine,* just get it done later *that* day. And if something tragic happens, then you move on and do better the next time. But you don't simply *allow yourself* an "out." You are better than that.

> *Instead of saying,*
> *"How can I possibly get this done?"*
>
> *...Try saying, "I will get this done,*
> *and here's my plan for how to balance it all today."*

Most of us feel guilty putting ourselves first. We are considered selfish and hardened by others; or, maybe we think that of ourselves. Maybe we are scared that people will think of us as lesser mothers and wives for leaving the family for a bike ride. Maybe you will get evil glances showing up with wet hair at a family reunion or PTA meetings.

But I say it all the time: what good are we to others when we feel like crap about ourselves? Do not worry about what others think about you. Take care of yourself. Make time. Prioritize and plan, and your Tri-Fecta will be three beautiful, manageable horses.

DOING IT ALL

One month into my triathlon training with Coach Monster, I found myself completely frustrated at home and at work. I woke up at 4:30 a.m., completed everything I was supposed to do that day, including training, plus feeding/entertaining/getting beat up by children after my workday was over. By the end of the day, I was wrecked. I was so sick of my kids acting like I was not there. I had said, "No stop that" for the hundredth time—and watched as they stared at me like I'd grown a fifth head. I was at the end of my rope, sick of doing everything for everyone. I was deadly sick of the practice of law. I was also incredibly sore from the training that morning...but interestingly, the sore muscles were the best part of *that particular* day.

I realized something fairly early in the triathlon game. Sometimes when I felt like I was losing my mind at home or at work, the promise of triathlon and training *saved* me. The promise of the next workout and the quiet and the sweat began to be a foundation of sanity for me.

I could murder the Expert right now, but at least I have a seven-mile run to think of the many reasons why I shouldn't. Coincidentally, by the time I was finished with seven miles, I was thinking of all the ways I loved the man and looked forward to seeing him for dinner.

Did that butthead partner actually ask me "did you really go to law school?" I'll slash the tires on his mid-life crisis car! I'll toss his Rolex in the river! A few thousand meters later, I was armed with the power to continue briefing and smiling (most of the time).

Triathlon is an enigma: How can something *so* painful also be relaxing and therapeutic? How can a sport save you from jail time?

I slowly began to understand the complexity of the triathlon balance and how it was actually saving my life. Saving. My. Life. When every single other thing in my life was making me bat-shit crazy, triathlon was keeping me balanced and sane. On challenging days, triathlon was sometimes the only thing that I could snuggle to and feel safe. *I love you swim cap. You are the world to me, running shoes. Thank you for loving me, bicycle.*

Of course, triathlon is not my *life*. I know that. But triathlon is an important part of my life. Like a pair of eyeglasses, swimming, biking and running made clear the blessings around me. Triathlon became the *process* that allowed me to see my life for all its good, all its blessings and all the things worth loving and living for.

I tell myself that at some point I should slow down, relax a little and learn to say "no." But when I cut out one thing, I usually just add two more things. How realistic is it for me, or women in general, to cut back? If I stop triathlon, I'll just start some other shenanigans. Then I run the risk that those shenanigans might not be as beneficial to my health. *What if I take up baking? Oh, lawd. The cookies? Mmmmmm…the peanut butter cookies?* Not beneficial. Plus, I do not think that most women can ever truly relax. So my hypothesis is that we should at least add something beneficial—like triathlon.

Triathlon is all about learning to prioritize. I do not think training for an Ironman is too much to ask out of my life. However, I am strongly convinced that cleaning my house is waaaaaay too difficult to squeeze into my schedule. Therefore, the swim workout usually wins. And cleaning the house loses. My health and training takes priority over a white-glove-clean house…sorry, but it's true. (Very, very true.)

Marriage & Serious Relationships

Marriage is one of life's greatest joys—and one of life's most enormous pains. Marriage combined with triathlon is amazing and crazy and terrible, all at once. Like a giant Slurpee—delicious and beautiful—but most often causing an enormous headache and horrors to your waistline. The same can be said for long-term relationships. Anytime you are cooped up and sharing bathrooms with someone you *love*, you will have issues.

There are three possible scenarios where you are the triathlete in your marriage or other serious relationship:

1. You are the solo triathlete in your family and your significant other is *supportive*.
2. You are the solo triathlete and your significant other is *not supportive* or is *indifferent*.
3. You are both triathletes.

Each category presents its own benefits and challenges. If you are the solo triathlete with the supportive significant other, you should count your lucky stars and never complain.

If you have the unsupportive partner, what a tough road ahead—but take the road anyway—there are ways around it. Keeping the other non-tri-ing person's feelings in perspective is important (this is your *relationship*, after all)—even if that person is unreasonable. But you may be dealing with a partner who doesn't think you should have any time to yourself.

And if you are both triathletes, be prepared for some of the strangest fights: *No, I get to swim first! Me! I'm first! Did you take the last water bottle? How could you be so inconsiderate?! What? You lost my Ironman visor!!!!?? Get off my bicycle! Those are MY gels! You are not getting a new helmet—I need one first!*

No matter which category you fall under, it is *all* a personal battle and one that you must fight smartly and strategically.

The Solo Triathlete, Supportive Partner

I have a long-time girlfriend who is a stay-at-home mom. Her husband works full-time, but when he walks in the door, she takes off for training. On weekends? She's gone riding and bricking and swimming. The dude drags the kids to the races to watch her race. He's totally cool with it. He makes posters. He cheers. He is a rarity and she's quite lucky to have this kind of undying support.

If you are in a similar situation, I think the danger is taking the saintly significant other for granted. Eventually, I would imagine he might tire of you being gone every available moment to spend time with your bike. So, be grateful for what you have, but be careful not to take advantage or create a resentment that is unnecessary in your pretty-darn-perfect training world. And you should probably do some super nice things for that partner of yours, too—and I don't mean cooking (although that is a nice start).

THE NON-SUPPORTIVE BUTTHEAD PARTNER

You are living with a non-supportive butthead. You're darn right that I don't know you and I *just* called your partner a butthead. This situation is *the worst.* You have a new passion (triathlon) that will benefit your life. But your significant other is negative, unsupportive, or abusive (or all three).

These situations call for you to be a triathlon ninja. If you are not a ninja, you will never make it to your first (or next) race. Do not attempt to stick the butthead with the kids while you go on a bike ride. Do not even bother explaining to the butthead that you can't cook dinner because you have a long run. You will be setting a time bomb.

Without delving into the issues that may be at the root of your relationship, you *must* bend over backwards to ensure that the other person is *in no way* inconvenienced by your triathlon dreams. You must complete workouts before he is awake. Learn to love the Crock Pot and cook every darn meal in it. Find other childcare for your race days. You must never leave him with screaming kids or dirty laundry while you go for a run. Sell your stuff on eBay to pay for your new triathlon suit. Don't even leave room for him to say, "How much did *that* cost *me?"* (And don't sell *his* stuff!)

Is this really fair? *Heck no, Joe!* But do you want to be a triathlete and still stay married, or what?

Remember that you cannot change the actions of others. You can only change yourself and how you react to their actions. Get up super early. Squeeze in the workouts. Find ways to make quick meals, have laundry delivered to your office or whatever it takes. Make it happen and talk about your training with others who *will* be supportive.

You must find a way for your butthead partner to have absolutely no ammunition against you. (If you are in an abusive situation, then you should seek help and get out immediately. Find someone in your triathlon group, tell them you are being abused and move in with them. Then you can bike and train to your heart's content. In all seriousness, seek help.)

Finally, do not bother to tell your good triathlon stories to your partner if they will do nothing but rain on your parade. Find something else to talk about with him (like why he's such a butthead…okay, not that).

The best you can hope is that your butthead partner will begin to see the changes in your life and warm up to the new you. Maybe he'll even come along for the ride. We can hope for that. If he *does* join you—then you must implement a "no butthead" policy going forward and require that he be nice and supportive if he wants to come along and play with the cool people.

THE TWO ATHLETE COMPROMISE

When you have two people training for triathlon, you must compromise often, and negotiate like in a constant hostage situation. A two triathlete household is tough. Is it tougher than being married to someone who is *not* into triathlon? Who knows. But if you are asking your spouse or significant other to watch kids for hours on end or spend time alone much of the weekend, or take on the responsibilities of the house while you are out on your bike, you are either: 1) married to a saint (see the first scenario, above); or 2) cooking a recipe for disaster (see, the second scenario).

For me, I would have been just fine doing triathlon alone, without the Expert. But I am also no fool in my house. I knew that the man would *never* agree to let me vanish for five-hour bike rides and two-hour runs on a week-end saying, *Have fun with the kids, sucker!* He's (admittedly) just not that kind of character.

The *only* way to live in harmony in my house with triathlon *and* the Expert…was to pull him into the sport with me. So I signed *him* up for races. He trained, we found babysitters, and he's a triathlete now, too. It's not that the Expert would have been unsupportive of my triathlon dreams…it's just he doesn't want to be stuck solo with the kids for seven hours while I'm out having a good ole time. And I can't say that I blame him.

Now for a word about husbands and men, in general. *Sigh.*

The Expert came along without much convincing. Again, he didn't want to be stuck as the babysitter. Some men may require more convincing (not nagging). However, other men may come along just because *they* have something to prove. Ladies, don't think for a second that your sitting-on-the-couch man will like getting "chicked." If you are out there kicking triathlon butt, and he's sitting on *his* butt—eventually, his ego might not be able to take it—and he'll come running just to *prove* that he can beat you (whether he can or not).

That may be one way to get him involved—pure and simple peer pressure. If he *does* come along and he's having a coronary the first time he runs with you—go easy, let him "enjoy" the sport and focus on a team effort to bring him into triathlon. The long-run benefits for your family will be magical.

As far as scheduling in the two triathlete house, the Expert and I have found that making a simple training compromise calendar and sticking it on the refrigerator alleviates *some* of the arguments surrounding workout times. On my early morning workouts, the Expert is home with the kids or we have a sitter come in early so we can both go workout. On his early morning workouts, then I am home with the kids.

Our workout calendar looks something like this:

Day of Week	Swim Bike Mom	The Expert
*Sunday	Long Ride / Run	AM workout (gym with kids)
Monday	Recovery	AM Workout
Tuesday	AM Workout (Babysitter in early so both can train early)	AM Workout
Wednesday	AM workout	PM workout
Thursday	PM workout	AM workout
Friday	AM workout	Recovery
*Saturday	AM workout (gym with kids)	Long Ride / Run

*Sometimes on the weekend, we'll have a sitter come in so we can have a triathlon date together—long bike ride and lunch.

THE MARRIAGE THAT PLAYS TOGETHER...

A few days before the end of 2010, the Expert and I were in the living room, riding side by side on our respective Spin bike and trainer. He dusted off his road bike and hooked it up, and I tried out the discount stationary bike that Santa brought me. I jammed some Eminem and he watched *Star Wars II* on Netflix, but we were doing something productive together.

I had just registered us for our first Olympic distance race—which started the training for *his* first ever triathlon. We had not worked out together in a *very* long time. Finding time to workout with full time jobs and children is difficult to manage *alone*. To carve out time for a "real" workout *together* felt absolutely impossible. But when the kids went to bed, we were sometimes able to squeeze it in together.

A few times, we tried to jog at the park with the kidlets (ages two and three at the time) in jogging strollers. While the Expert did not mind doing this, I loathed it. *Loathed*! I hated it. To me, this kind of workout felt like Pay-Per-View wrestling combined with triathlon. I did not reach workout nirvana with the munchkins within one hundred yards of me. Sippy cups were thrown, large, messy poopy diapers were laid and I never seemed to bring along enough wipes.

Later, I realized that this frustration had nothing to do with the kids and was simply more about me *needing* the triathlon quiet time. I enjoy triathlon because it is time to myself. Ladies, it's not too much to ask. Truly, it's not. You deserve quiet time. Repeat after me.

> *Quiet time for yourself*
> *is not too much to ask.*

I had started triathlon by myself, but having a genuine "Expert" along for the ride was a fortunate turn of events. The Expert got his nickname for a reason. I love him dearly, but he is absolutely the biggest know-it-all in the entire world. So when he officially decided to join me in the triathlon journey, he was seriously on *board*—logging calories, stretching, planning workouts, getting the gear. He even had a sweatband that he would wear around the house, in case he spontaneously dropped down to do some pushups. Most would say that his cooperative/supportive spirit is just plain awesome ("you're so lucky to have a husband who wants to spend time with you").

However. I was dealing with a *beast*.

A mere week after joining me, the Expert became an expert in: calorie counting & dieting, injury prevention, sports medicine, running shoes, swimming caps, perfect cycling form, stretching, heart rate analysis, race day preparation, wetsuits, all the rules of USAT, Ironman, Hawaii (yes, the entire state) and triathlon (the entire sport).

For the record, at this time the Expert had absolutely no triathlon or swim experience under his belt. He could be called a former recreational cyclist, definitely a former weightlifter, but he had lost three pounds in the first four days, and was morphed into a svelte expert of a triathlete.

Also for the record, as we were lying in bed a few nights after he got "on board," he started yammering about how he thinks cyclists should be allowed to "draft" in triathlon. I told him what a bloody know-it-all he was. Then he started listing everything he knew—out loud. I mean everything. Everything that had ever come *near* his Expert brain. He was kidding, of course, as the list included things like neurosurgery and book publishing.

The amazing thing about the Expert though, is that he believes in himself. Sometimes, he believes in himself to the point where everyone around him wants to stab him or poke out his eyes. His know-it-all makes me crazy. At the same time, his confidence is a tad infectious which has turned out to be a good thing for us. I could take a few mental confidence lessons from him.

Long before the Expert and I started dating, we were on the Team Savannah Olympic-style weightlifting team together. I was sixteen years old. He was nineteen and a budding know-it-all, a mini-Expert if you will. I was cutting weight for a competition, and he was up in my grill with all of his vast cutting weight knowledge. Telling me what I was doing wrong. Argumentative. I thought to myself, "Ugh, I can't *stand* this guy. Who does he think he is?"

Three years later, I started dating him.

Three years after that, I married him.

Six years later, we welcomed our first child.

And now, almost four more years later, we are racing triathlons together. Shows you what I know. (I'm sure the Expert knew it was coming.)

ANNIVERSARY

When I registered us for our first half Ironman for our ten year anniversary, I was not certain how the Expert would react.

"So I signed *myself* up for a half Ironman," I told the Expert over the phone.

"How far is that?" he asked.

"Half of an Ironman. Get it?" I asked.

"Oh. I knew that," he said. (Of course he did.)

"It's 70.3 Miami," I said.

"What is 70.3?" he asked.

"The half Iron," I said.

"What?"

"For the love," I huffed. "70.3 is the number of miles—"

"—you are going to run seventy miles?!" he screeched.

"Holy cow," I said, rolling my eyes.

I paused.

"What?" he asked.

I slowed down.

"No. It's a triathlon. Okay," I went on, "So you know like the Ironman is 140.6 miles? Swim, bike and run? Total mileage?" I asked.

"Oh." He paused. "Right, right, right." (Of course he knew).

"This is half of that. 70.3," I said.

"Okay."

"So what do you think? About me doing the race? Will you go with me?" I asked.

"Sounds hard," he said. "When is it?"

"October. Anniversary time."

"Okay," he replied.

I paused, and said, "I registered you too."

"Okay."

I expected a little more than that for a reaction.

"Did you hear me?" I asked.

"Oh yes," he said, "I would expect nothing less from you, signing us up for something like that."

"Alrighty then. Bring it," I said.

"Bring it, bitches," he said.

Ten years of wedded bliss? Maybe not complete *bliss*. But when his response to my 70.3 lunacy was "bring it, bitches," I knew without a doubt that I had married the right man.

The Expert and I celebrated ten years of marriage crossing the Ironman Miami 70.3 finish line. We rang in eleven years of marriage at the finish of Ironman Augusta 70.3. It's kind of scary to think about what's coming for year twelve at the rate we're going…

MARRIAGE AIN'T EASY

To say that marriage was delightful over the past few years would be a dirty rotten lie. We had a solid marriage for quite a few years, but throwing kids into the mix was insane for us. Thus, we have struggled, even to the point of discussing the big "D" word.

Several times. *Divorce. Divorce. Ugh.*

We always decide against it, which is sometimes because of love, sometimes because of history, sometimes because of the kids. And sometimes because of sheer laziness and not wanting to divide up our things.

Marriage is difficult, period.

I think triathlon initially brought us farther apart, but then closer back together. It was hard to get rolling together with the training because we had been so lazy, so stressed for many years. The Expert resented me for holding him back from his cycling and running back in the early days of our marriage.

"What *now* you want to ride your bike? After the *years* of hard time you gave me for riding mine! Give me a break!" he rambled when I began.

I felt terrible for the way I had acted back then, but I had profusely apologized and was trying to move forward. He, understandably, wanted to punish me for it. So, training *almost* felt like another hurdle to overcome.

But overcome it, we did.

Even now, sometimes the Expert will see me come in from a long run and say, disbelieving, "Who *are* you and what have you done with my wife?" Only now, he means it in a good way.

Still, on a bad day in the world of marriage, sometimes the grudges and the general nastiness can creep back in.

And I can usually say, "Seriously, dude? We've done two half Ironmans. Let it go."

Or he'll say, "Mere, for the love. Get over yourself. Stop it. Stop. It."

We usually smile a little, and move on a little more quickly with each triathlon or grudge-holding fight. *Ahhhhh, marriage.* But the truth is that we have tirelessly worked and fought for the schedule and the triathlon rhythm that's part of our life. In triathlon, we found the *fight* within ourselves, and that has translated into a *fight* for our family. I am thankful because triathlon helps us set goals together, experience races together, and basically have things to talk about.

We are lucky to be a triathlon couple.

Leave Your Ego at the Door

The Expert was big into cycling back in the Day. "The Day" was about twelve years ago. Because he was already a bicycle "expert," triathlon was not a big leap. He kicked and screamed for about three weeks after I registered him for our first Olympic race. Then, he became hell bent and determined not to have *his woman* beat him in *any* athletic endeavor.

On a Sunday about six weeks before the Olympic distance race at St. Anthony's, I took off for a twenty-three mile bike and two-mile run. When I returned, it was the Expert's turn to head out for his ride.

He left around 2:45 in the afternoon. My loop had taken me about an hour and forty-five minutes, so I was expecting him back around 4:15 or so. Now, in addition to a know-it-all, the Expert is also bit of a show-off, so I assumed that he would go further than I did. So I waited until 4:45 before I started to worry. I began to call his cell phone, but he did not answer. 5:30 rolled around, and still nothing. Around 5:45, the phone rang.

"I'm lost," he said on the other end.

"Okay?" I said.

He mumbled, "I mean, I *was* lost. Now, I know where I am."

"Are you okay? Want me to come get you? How far have you gone?"

"I'm not sure," he said

"What does your bike computer say?" I asked him.

"Oh." (muffled noise) "Thirty-eight miles."

At this point, I realized that he was probably starting to crack up. The hills around these parts are mean and thirty-eight miles was a tall order for a baby triathlete, even one who easily managed half-centuries back in the Day.

"Holy cow. That's crazy. I'm coming to get you," I said.

"I'm okay. I'm okay. I got a drink at a gas station…and I've only got about ten miles left," he said, sounding very far away.

"Ten miles?!?! I'm coming to get you. Where are you?"

"No, no. I'm okay. Ten miles is okay," he paused. "Really, I'm okay. No need to drag the kids out. I will be fine."

I was *not* happy with him. I wanted to pick him up. But I am not certain *he* knew his location. I gave up. He was the Expert. A name well-earned.

"You be careful. Call me if you need me to come get you," I said.

"Yup."

"Do you hear me? Call me if—" He did not hear me, because he had hung up the phone.

At 6:45 p.m., exactly four hours from the start of his ride, the door opened. I heard a shuffle followed by some sort of *splat!* sound followed by the kids screaming, "Daddy!"

Then I heard a sad, muffled voice. "Please don't touch me, guys. I love you. But don't touch Daddy…"

I rounded the corner and the Expert was lying at the foot of the stairs in the foyer, looking like Oscar the Grouch goes bicycling. He was the funniest color I've ever seen on a live human. He was dirty. He was frozen like an animal carcass, his legs splayed in the air. I felt bad for him. Although I was also cursing in my head, *Dumbass man, always getting lost, why can't you pay attention, what about your GPS, for the love…*

But I remembered my vows "for better or for worse" (which should have said *for dumb or for dumber*), so I handed him Cytomax and food left over from the kids' dinner. I instructed him to roll on the foam roller and ice his legs.

After the kids went to bed, I lit into him. "I am so mad at you. I can't believe you got lost. You had me sick!"

He spoke in a scary, hoarse voice. "Careful there, Miss Know-it-All Triathlon Woman," he whispered. "Karma is a bitter pill to swallow."

I knew he was right about that, so I decided not to think bad thoughts about the Expert's four-hour tour. Instead, I put him to bed at 8:30 and kissed his Expert head full-o-brains goodnight.

MARRIAGE DNF (DID NOT FINISH)

In April, long after our big(gest) race was over, the Expert told me that he wanted a divorce. The D word.

I was not surprised.

We were riding in the car on the way to pick strawberries with the kids when he told me. The children were jabbering in the back of the car, and I was crying in the front. It started with a fight over money—a standard blame game—and turned south into a divorce. As we pulled up to the strawberry farm, he stared at me when I didn't leap out of the car.

"Are you coming?" he asked.

I looked at him like he was stupid. *I want a divorce. I want out. Are you coming to pick strawberries with me and my offspring?*

The kids were studying me, wondering why I was sitting motionless. I had my camera draped in my lap, and thought, *well, I guess I ought to get pictures from our last outing together as a family*.

So I got out of the car.

I walked twenty yards behind the three of them, because my boot was slowing me down. I had broken my foot just a month before and I was sporting one of those sexy walking boots. Strawberry field terrain was not exactly ideal for the boot. I tripped over everything in sight. I was wearing my Peachtree Road Race t-shirt and someone said, "Heh heh, guess you're not racing this year with that foot, eh?" That dude was so funny. I couldn't stand it. I almost killed him with my eyes.

I snapped pictures of the kids. I looked through the lens of the camera at the Expert, our little family. The last four years for us had been difficult, tougher than we had perhaps realized. Two kids, fourteen months apart, job changes, job stress, travel, other stressful things...

As I watched him pick strawberries with our kids, I knew there was more to our family than just stress. The Expert and I had eleven years of marriage, fifteen years of relationship history, and twenty years of friendship. Obviously, sometimes history sucks. Bad history is like a bad race. You may have prepared the best you thought you could, but the build-up of the pain, dehydration, cramps and a flat tube may end the day. But does it end triathlon forever? *No, not usually.*

At the same time, I had begun to find extreme peace in the raging agony of running, in the "purposeful suffering" of triathlon. I routinely found joy in the sweaty, crusty smell of old running shoes. I liked the zinging ouch of sweat in the eyes.

I'm stubborn and I did not want to DNF my marriage. At least not without some semblance of a fight. I slung my camera around my shoulders and hobbled over to him, boot and all.

"Whatever you decide is okay. I understand all this. This has felt impossible for a while. We will always be friends. We *are* good friends. It's okay," I said.

I saw it in his eyes in that moment: that our history was worth keeping, worth remembering and worth continuing to build. The Expert did not want a DNF marriage on his record either. We didn't talk much more the rest of the day, but I made the assumption that he was staying. After all, he was still there.

That night, before we went to sleep, he asked me, "You're planning to write about this…aren't you?"

I was quiet for a minute. I actually had not planned on blogging about it, because it felt *too* real.

But then I said, "I will write about it only if you say I can."

"You can. Plus, *only* you can figure out a way to tie in the events of today with triathlon."

I thought for all of six seconds.

"Well, marriage really *is* like a race…You have to make sure you have the proper fuel and energy and rest and recovery in order to keep going and…"

He smiled as I rambled on.

Over the next few months, the Expert and I focused on getting ourselves back in line with each other. While marriage will probably never be a walk in the park, it *is* an uphill run on a hot, humid day. And if I am willing to put up with those nasty conditions when I am simply *running*, I sure as hell better put up with it when it matters—with my family. And everyone knows that every uphill has a downhill—so we continue to push upward, praying for the glorious downhills.

PARENTHOOD

No one warns you how difficult parenthood will be. No one. Your friends are saying, "Have kids, they're wonderful"—when really they are thinking, "please come join me, I can't handle this craziness alone." I thought the movie, "Parenthood," was just a comedy. Actually certain parts of that movie were filmed at our house. (Who knew?!) Children are absolutely the greatest blessing—and children will make you absolutely insane—all at once.

Triathlon allows me a much-needed escape, and gives me *permission* to take care of myself. Triathlon has made me a better, more patient mother, and has brought my young children into the fold of swim, bike and run…which is incredibly exciting.

SETTING THE EXAMPLE

You may feel guilty taking time away from your kids for triathlon. But I urge you to put it in perspective. You are teaching the children wonderful lessons about health and perseverance. Stay the course.

Part of the reason I do triathlon, part of the reason I spend weekends running, and most importantly, the reason I am *capable* of telling my kids goodbye to go for a swim, is simple. I want my children to see the motion, to understand the weirdness (beauty) of waking up at unholy hours to run, bike and swim. Then, I want them to think it's no big deal to do so. (Oh, and I need some stinking time to myself!)

When I was in middle school, I was in class with an athletic girl who was always running and sweating. Not only that, she was always running with her *parents*. I thought that family was the weirdest group of people in the world back then. *Who runs on Saturdays? And with their parents? What a bunch of freaks.* Now? I look back and realize that their little unit was awesome. I want my kids to be healthy and to crave competition and movement. I hope they find a bike ride to be fun, not work. I hope they want to run with their nerdy parents.

The Expert and I love to watch videos of the past years' Ironman World Championships. Sometimes the kids will watch with us. One night, Stella saw Miranda Carfrae, the 2010 Ironman World Champion, and screamed "Ohhhh, there's Mommy!"

And then James said, "No, it's not. That's Daddy!"

Of course, neither I nor the Expert was in Kona in 2010 (vacation, racing or otherwise).

Then Stella hopped off my lap and took off running. She ran loops around the house, screaming, "I running! I like Mommy! I runnnnnning!"

James chimed in: "No, I am running like Mommy too!"

They continued running and arguing about who was running faster. Even though the Atwood House Rules disallow running inside the house, I let them go. In that moment, I felt it. I knew that I was doing right by my children, by my triathlon example, however small it was. In that space, I felt that my two babies would run and play and have their sweaty lives right out in front of them. They would be healthy and happy. And run. And sweat. And *love* it. Even if they choose not to race, then at least, the rugrats will know that it was a possibility.

Selfishly, I hope that my children will *never* know me as the mom who was too fat or too lazy. I don't want to embarrass them because I am huge—I want to embarrass them because I wear cycling shorts to Open House at their schools, along with my Ironman visor. *Mom, why can't you dress up? For once? Ughhhhh…*

Think about those things as you embark on your journey. Yes, it will be hard to leave and not see your kids sometimes in the mornings. You may miss them at night because you are running or swimming. But I promise you, they will benefit a million times more from a healthy, happy mother who misses some frosted cereal mornings—than a fat, sad mom who was just "around" all the time.

SINGLE MOMS

If you are a single mother, then you've got a whole other set of challenges in the world of triathlon. But hopefully, you can find ways to compromise with your saintly babysitters and find time to train. You *especially*—don't feel bad being away from your kids! You are playing the mom *and* the dad sometimes, too. So you *definitely* need a break. You are teaching them good things by your healthy example. Remember: it's not unfair to have time to yourself. You are bringing yourself back as a better mother and human being. A supermom.

Finding Your Quiet

I grew up an only child, so my surroundings were pretty quiet. I was a little lonely, although I do not think I ever really minded. I liked the quiet, the doing-whatever-I-wanted in my room. Even well into my teenage years, I would put on the black eyeliner, combat boots and a fake nose ring and go to poetry readings with friends. But really, I preferred to go alone.

Alone.

So I am wired to appreciate the solitary time, the quiet.

Well. Years and years later, I became a parent. I had no earthly idea how loud parenting would be. My parents did not warn me, because I was a pretty calm child. Parenting *me* was pretty quiet for them, also.

But the two kids that sprung forth from my—well, you know—they are *insanely* loud. To be frank and to the horror of helicopter parents everywhere, I love triathlon mostly because it gives me a break away from my loud house and the spastic munchkins. Sometimes the whiny kids, the horrible sounds of that blasted *Caillou* boy on the television and the breaking of my lamps and tables bothers me *so* much that I would rather suffer on a bike *for hours on end* than be at home with the circus monkeys.

Am I selfish? Maybe.

But really, I think I'm admitting that I am human. I am admitting that I have a breaking point. And that breaking point happens to be my lamps. Do I love my kids? Of course, more than anything. Do I *like* my kids? Yes, about 68% of the time. But when I have "mommy time" to swim and bike and run, I come back feeling like a real human again… and the *like* number goes up to around 93%. See, it's really simple math.

Mom x (Swim + Bike + Run) = Mommy is Nice

See? Very basic math.

Our little family spends a lot of time at our Mega Gym. The Expert and I squeeze in workouts and the kids play in the activity center. This is a big part of our training staple. After we finish our workouts and the kids have burned off some of their insane energy in the play center, then as a family we grab lunch, get frozen yogurt or hang by the pool.

On Mother's Day almost two years ago, I was halfway through a swim workout when I saw something out of the corner of my goggles. Someone had wandered to the pool deck carrying a small dry-erase board with my name written on it. *Crap.* The signal from the childcare center.

I pulled my goggles off and wiped my face with my hands. "Oh, no! What's wrong?"

The childcare person said, "Your daughter has taken off her clothes and we can't put them back on."

"Can't?" I asked, water dripping down my face.

"Well, because we are not a certified daycare, we *can't*. We can't touch the kids."

I blinked at her. *Seriously?*

She continued, "We tried to get her brother to put her clothes on her, but he refused."

I rolled my eyes at the last sentence. As if James, our three-year old, would have been any help.

I lugged myself out of the pool, cursing my half-completed workout. I dried off and headed to the childcare room. There, I saw the allegedly naked girl child—fully clothed. She, however, had removed her diaper (and placed it sweet baby Santa knows where) and then put her skirt back on.

James ran up to me, tattling on her: "Stella took her diaper off!"

Well, there went my swim. Once Stella saw me in the childcare center, there was no escaping her little teeny fingers to go back to the pool. *I go with you! I go with you, Mommmmmy.* Fine.

I let it go. It was Sunday and I had a lot to be thankful for. *Did someone say frozen yogurt?* Plus, it was Mother's Day. A perfect swim for a Mother's Day. *Just in case I had forgotten I had kids, I had a Mother's Day reminder.* (After that episode, we furiously began potty training, so we could finish a bloody workout).

THE *MOM*-CRUNCHED TRIATHLETE

I have a magnet on my fridge that says: "What Would You Do, If You Knew You Could Not Fail?" I love this question, because my answer never changes. If I could not fail, I would be a writer, a part-time triathlete and a good wife and mother. Three (four?) things I want more than anything in this world, and the things I strive for on a daily basis.

Chris Carmichael is making mint with his *Time-Crunched Triathlete* book.[xxiv] Time-crunched is an understatement for most women. But it begs the question: Are you *Mom*-Crunched (the nirvana state of time-crunched, haggard and exhausted)? Is your time *so* crunched that you can't see straight? And if so… how do you survive it, let alone take on triathlon? Perhaps a better question is: how do your children survive? (I guess we can worry about them later.)

Here's my best advice for when the motherhood plane is going down— put on *your* oxygen mask first, and then:

BE MOM AND BE AWESOME.

Yes, you can be *both* a mom and awesome. You can be a mom and a triathlete/runner/cyclist/chess champion (insert whatever you think is awesome here). You should go after what you think is awesome. Remember that *you* were *here* first. Take care of you. If you fail to take care of yourself, you are a useless pet rock to those around you. Stop wishing and start doing! Once you begin to *do*, do not feel guilty about the time you spend *doing* it.

Remind yourself that you are ingraining healthy ideals in your family: when they see you fall down on your bike and get back up, you are showing them a few lessons. The first lesson is to get back up when you fall. The second lesson is: never pay attention to Mommy when it comes to bike handling skills.

NOD AND SMILE

When the non-busy, non-important people of your world request stupid things of you that take you away from your family, work or training, remember to simply nod and smile, knowing that you have no intention of doing anything they ask.

By the nod and smile, the asker will find you polite. Then when you simply "forget" to bake that Sunshine Pie for the non-triathlon-related fundraiser, you can pretend to be horrifically embarrassed, wave your hands and blame it on your impossibly busy life. (Swim Bike Mom Note: From experience, I know that you can pull off the Nod and Smile *only twice per social function/group*. On the third time, you must say "yes" and deliver.)

Pee and Move.

This is an important lesson in triathlon and in life. You need to *go* where you can and get a move on. You think your bathroom time is your quiet time? Then you must have some seriously polite children. There's no time for potty in racing! Go, go, go! Either way, there is a time to learn to get it done and move on.

Take Care of Your Toes.

Triathletes and runners are prone to contract the dreaded black toenail, calluses and other nasty foot things. Just remember to paint your toenails every once in a while. The little splash of color will make you feel human. I promise. Even when you come in from a run and your toddler wipes a booger right on your big toe and screams, "So pretty, Mommy!"

You just smile and say, "You're darn right, kid. Those are manicured toes. Take notice!"

Sleep. Run. Do the Nasty. Repeat.

Just do *it*. Yes, *it*. You'll feel better. And whoever's on the receiving end might make you breakfast and say nice things about you to his cronies the next day.

Whatever.

So just do it because you'll feel better. Endorphins.

Ask for Help.

Find some good friends, neighbors or teenagers who will watch your offspring while you go on a long run or ride. If you are like the Expert and me, we are usually training for some race together, so it gives us a nice outing *without* the spawn.

However, if you are riding solo or if your other half is a non-triathlete, as discussed above, he might not like getting stuck babysitting every weekend while you are out flying high on your bike. He will need a break too. Get a sitter so the other half can see the latest sci-fi movie while you are out playing fancy Orca in your wetsuit. Who knows, this special consideration might lead to a little more of the "nasty" from the step above.

246

EAT WELL.

I am not one to talk about nutrition or diet or anything other than peanut butter and the deliciousness of all things Dairy Queen. But I have intuited that a healthy diet equals a happier momma. Again, kids are learning by watching you (me) stuff your (my) face. Alright, time to move on.

PUT YOURSELF IN TIMEOUT.

Overtraining, overworked, overstressed? Put yourself in timeout. If you don't, then God might put you in timeout, and you may not like what He decides. God recently broke my foot in order to make me slow down and appreciate my life. *I kid you not.*

When are you losing your mind from work, life and training, just take a rest day, haul out your crayons and coloring books and doodle. Whatever floats your sanity boat. It is a tough job being a hero. Sometimes you need to prop up your feet, be lazy with the kids and give those red, knee-high Wonder Woman boots a day off.

MAKE IT HAPPEN.

Time is short and life is busy. You must, somehow, make it all happen. Remember Coach Monster's wisdom: "You have a duty to *yourself* to find a way to get things done—rather than finding an excuse for why you didn't." Figure it out. Make time for your children, make time for training and handle your business at work/home/wherever you are beckoned. Something inevitably "gives" when a new project is added.

So. Somehow, you must pull it all together and make it look pretty, functional and awesome. (Hopefully, no one will pull back the curtain and see the She Wizard—with all the Scotch tape and stretch marks.)

WORK

Triathlon has made me more alert and thus, a better employee, even though most days, I still want to swim, bike, and run my way right out of the legal profession. Some people are born lawyers. I am not one of them.

I often have the same strange recurring dream: I am back in college and almost done with the end of the year. Suddenly, I break out in a cold sweat. In my dream, I realize that I forgot about a math class I needed to graduate. I had enrolled in it. I went to the first day, but then I forgot to go back to class. Literally, *forgot*. Then, I have four days before the end of the year and I am completely, utterly hosed. I seem to wake up at this point, so I never learn the solution. *Did I figure it out? Did I graduate?*

That dream bothers me for a few reasons. First, I think that maybe I really *did* forget about a class in college and my degree is really a fake. But really, I worry that it means I am forgetting something very important *now*.

Practicing law is like that dream. On a daily basis, I walk around panicking, just *knowing* that I am forgetting something important. The most disappointing part of lawyering? Hands down, when I found out that legal work was not like *The Practice*. Especially, when I ended up working with a chauvinistic boss instead of Dylan McDermott. I was really pissed and wanted my money back for my troubles.

The legal profession, like many (many) other jobs can be quite soul-sucking. During the beginning of my triathlon expedition, I was having trouble sleeping from all the work I had to do. Those whispering files sitting on my desk, the list of to-dos, the things I should be drafting, reading, reviewing. More endless lists of statutes, opinions and cases I would never find time to read. So, so many lists.

Triathlon was actually a big bonus to my endless lists. When I plopped my head on the pillow each night, I found myself worrying about my morning workout instead of the whispering files at the office. I was forced to barrel through the workout *before* I could get to the files. In a strange way, triathlon put up a manageable *barrier* to the law. I would deal with the law when I finished doing something for myself.

And while the files were still there, churning in my head, I could only see the files in abstract. I could not reach them or hear them or do anything while I was underwater or out on the bike. The sights and sounds of triathlon drowned out the law when I most needed it drowned out.

I liked that.

THE WORKING MOM DILEMMA.

Whether you work full-time, part-time, from home or as a stay-at-home wife and mother, your time is precious and tough to find. I swear (and I will swear this until kingdom come), that the best bet to make this triathlon thing work is to accomplish your training first thing in the morning.

But I'm not a morning person, you whine. Suck it up, buttercup! Races are in the morning. Babies cry and wake up in the morning. Matt Lauer is on the television in the morning. You can do it.

The bonus about the morning workouts? First, usually the house is quiet and the rest of the world is asleep. This is a good time to get your thoughts together, make your mental mom lists, and find some motivational quiet time.

Additionally, you are less likely to skip the workout if you knock it out first thing. I find it virtually impossible to accomplish a 6:30 p.m. workout after a hard day at work. Something always comes up and blows my nighttime workout. Or I am too tired. I just do not like it. For me, morning is rarely disturbed. Also, the morning workout makes me have a better day at work. I am more focused, energized and I feel better having done something for myself before working for the Dude.

As I mentioned earlier in this book, if you find a gym near where you work, the morning workouts may be even better. Or sometimes, you can squeeze in a lunchtime run. Of course, when and where you workout is going to depend on your life, your circumstances. I am simply trying to give you some good ideas to bounce around. Remember, it is up to *you* to make it happen.

FOURTEEN

Paratriathlon and Tri-ing with Disability

INTRODUCTION

When I began tri-ing, I would often complain about my feet hurting me. I would whine about my knees, my hips and my ankles giving me "trouble." Then I began to learn a little about paratriathlon, the heroic athletes and individuals who are training for triathlon in the midst of physical disabilities such as paralysis and limb loss. If you complain about your fatness or your aching knees, there is nothing like a visit with a paratriathlete to bring you back down to earth.

During my ramp-up to my first half Ironman, I gained some perspective on how fortunate I was, just in small areas of my life. One of the most important times in my life happened during a lunch with McBlessings. One of the Getting2Tri athletes, Kelly Casabere, joined us for lunch. Kelly is a single amputee, who lost her left leg above the knee after a boating accident in high school. She competed in her first triathlon only a year ago and she also plays soccer. Nothing could have wiped the smile off her face during lunch. She smiled and laughed, her joy was infectious. She immediately became "Giggles" to me.

I wanted to ask Giggles how she remained so positive. How she wasn't angry or sad about her limb loss. I really could not bear to ask such a negative question in such a positive presence. But selfishly, I had to know. So I asked her anyway.

She said, "There is no reason to be angry when I stared death in the face. And I won. Every day is a gift."

Many times during my training, my mind would go back to Giggles, to Janelle (below), and to others I met on my road to my half Iron—others who had *real* struggles, *real* battles and who had overcome the obstacles, and thrived.

In May 2012, I stood at the swim start of the Atlanta Iron Girl race with Mountain Goat. It was the Goat's first triathlon. She was shivering in the uncharacteristically cool morning and saying, "I can't do this. Why did you drag me to do this?"

"Because you can do this race, Mountain Goat!" I said.

"I hate you. What makes you think I can do this?" she wailed shaking her hands.

The swim wave ahead of us took off.

She looked at me, "Tell me something that will make me believe that I can do this race."

I thought for less than a split second. "You have all your limbs. You have two arms and two legs. You can do this."

Mountain Goat looked at me. "You are right. I got this."

Mountain Goat has been a long supporter of the Getting2Tri Foundation as well. When I said those words to her, I knew she recognized what I was saying. We both know of the amazing triathletes like Sarah Reinertsen, Jason Gunter and Scott Rigsby who have achieved amazing things with missing limbs (Hello, Iron People!). What was *our* excuse?

Your physical limitations, whether real or not, are largely in your own head. You can learn to swim, bike and run in the midst of severe physical limitations. And for those of us whose limitations are, for a lack of a better word, petty (like fatness and fear of water), then it's time for a lesson in perspective—one that I thankfully was taught early in my triathlon journey.

You can do this.

BLONDE AMBITION

On September 25, 2011, a group of five beautiful women crossed the finish line of the Ramblin' Rose Sprint Triathlon in Charlotte, North Carolina. The mini-team looked like a weekend girls' trip, a gaggle of good-looking ladies leaping into a 250 yard swim, 9 mile bike, and 2 mile run.

In the middle of the group was a svelte blonde woman with a prosthetic running leg. The woman is Janelle Hansberger. And Janelle is ridiculous. By ridiculous, I mean that Janelle is ridiculously smart, talented, and inspiring. The first time I met her, I wanted to pinch her and see if she was made of magic fairy dust. I have never met anyone like her.

Only a year ago, Janelle lost her leg below the knee. A deadly bacteria infection also known as the flesh-eating bacteria, which causes *necrotizing fasciitis*, had taken root in Janelle and she began to suffer extreme complications, including sepsis and organ failure. Within a few days, her left leg was amputated below the knee.

The limb loss was a tragedy. But the tragedy saved her life. If the bacteria had not been identified and stopped via the amputation, Janelle would have died. At the time of her illness, Janelle's marriage was on the rocks and divorce was inevitable. A month later, she found herself juggling single motherhood on one leg. Literally.

Janelle was a runner prior to her amputation, but decided that swimming and cycling might also be fun. After her recovery, an amputee friend introduced her to McBlessings. Janelle attended one the G2T camps only six months after her amputation. Only a year after losing her leg, Janelle crossed the finish of the Ramblin' Rose triathlon with her friends.

I asked Janelle when she began mourning her limb loss. When did she first get angry, yell and use the "F word" in inappropriate places like elevators and parking lots?

She had laughed, "I never had time to be angry. I have two young boys. They needed me. I had parents and a sister who scooped me up and supported me at every turn. I am alive. I am well. I am blessed." She paused and said again, "Alive. I am one of the few people I have known to survive this illness. Why would I be angry?"

PARATRIATHLON AND YOU

By Mike Lenhart, Getting2Tri Foundation
with Deanna Babcock

"[The] goal should not be defined by the distance traveled, but the athleticism, bravery and intelligence displayed along her abbreviated path."One of Deanna Babcock's favorite quotes shared with me in an email message (November 3, 2008)

I started The Getting2Tri Foundation ("G2T") in December 2006, with the focus of providing training, education and empowerment to non-elite athletes with disabilities who might consider the benefits that "we," as able-bodied triathletes, have appreciated over the years. I use the term "we" because many times I am asked why someone who has all his "parts and pieces" would become so passionate about creating an organization to help those with physical disabilities such as limb loss, paralysis and spinal cord injuries.

Triathlon has been an Olympic sport for *able*-bodied athletes since 2000. However, *paratriathlon* will enter the Summer Paralympics Games for the first time in 2016. *Paratriathlon* is essentially triathlon, but the athletes competing have some sort of physical disability ranging from loss of limbs to paralysis to visual impairment. The United States and many other nations are working tirelessly to prepare potential elite-level paratriathletes for the upcoming Games in Rio de Janeiro, Brazil.

I could write hundreds of stories about people G2T has helped since 2006. Instead, I'd like to share with you the story of one incredible woman's drive and determination.

I first met Deanna Babcock a little over five years ago, in 2007. She was a graduate student at North Carolina State University. Outside of her studies, Deanna was also training for the Ironman Florida triathlon, scheduled for November 2007.

On July 20, 2007 while swimming in the university pool, her heart suddenly stopped. This incident led to a series of life-threatening problems. Doctors were forced to medically induce a coma for four weeks. When she awoke from the coma, she learned that the doctors had removed her left leg above the knee as a necessary measure to save her life.

Fast forward to November 2008, when she and I were both competing in the Beach2Battleship triathlons in Wilmington, North Carolina. I was racing the full [140.6] distance and Deanna was racing the [70.3] distance.

I remember seeing her the day before the race. We chatted and her spirits were full of cautious optimism, as this was her first long distance race since her leg amputation. We shared high hopes for each other's races the next day.

I did not see Deanna during the race until the run. I came up on her on one of the bridges. I'll never forget seeing her and the look on her face. As we spoke, she told me that she was experiencing phantom pains on her residual limb-side of her body. We stopped on the bridge and adjusted her prosthetic running leg, liners, etc. That seemed to initially do the trick and she "soldiered on" for another six miles before finally having to drop out of the race.

Deanna, despite not finishing, displayed some of the greatest courage I've ever seen. She wrote in her race report, "I used to have two legs but now I only have one. I started the Beach2Battleship [70.3] triathlon and tapped out 9.75 hours later, five miles short of the finish line. It was fun."

She goes on to explain that *before* she lost her leg she had the goal of completing Ironman Florida in 2007. When her coach asked her why she wanted to do an Ironman, she responded, "Because it's hard." Excerpts from her 70.3 race report are below:

BEACH2BATTLESHIP RACE REPORT 2008

So, on I went to train for Ironman Florida. But on July 20th 2007, I missed my long ride and work because I decided to sleep in…for a *month*.

The day before, I suddenly cardiac arrested in the swimming pool at NC State. I'm no doctor, but suffice to say that crap goes downhill fast when your heart stops beating for extended periods of time. I got off pretty lucky, though…only one knee down. I didn't even need new kidneys…which, *hey dude, I'll take what I can get*. My friends are really crazy. Normal friends would have held my hand, rubbed my back, and brought me baked goods [while I was in the hospital]. Now don't get me wrong, some of these things did happen, but while I was still comatose, my friends had already taken the liberty of planning my comeback to triathlon. So instead of recalling quiet niceties spoken in tones fit for a hospital room, I only recall people saying "Don't worry, we'll have you a running leg in no time." They asked questions like, "So when are you getting back on the bike?"

Suffice to say that it was never an option to stop competing in triathlon. It took me a couple of months to learn how to walk without falling over, but after that I could move on to bigger and better things like swimming and biking and eventually running.

Additionally, I had a lot of help along the way. Wes Hall and Richard, whom I met at Ironman Florida, both helped me get going in the pool. Ossur Prosthetics and the Challenged Athletes Foundation teamed up to get a me a running leg, and Brian Frasure helped dial it in. Mike Lenhart, Sarah Reinertsen, and Scout Basset fielded tons of questions about the logistics of training and competing as a newly minted challenged athlete…

Sometime in early 2008, I decided things were coming together all right. Apparently I have a problem with dreaming big, because I decided somehow that it would be a great idea to sign up for the Beach2Battleship [70.3] distance race. My coach, Daren, must be crazy, too, because he didn't try to tell me otherwise…he just served up training plan after training plan to help me along.

Fast forward to October 30th…I knew the race coming on the 1st would be hard, but I didn't care. My race strategy was as follows: swim along merrily with the current, pedal 56 miles whilst snacking on PopTarts and crackers, and try not to die or give up on the run…

The race began, and I exited the water approximately 38 minutes later, and was considerably colder than when I had started. I popped on my running leg and trotted off to T1. The bike took about four hours, and I wasn't last…

I think I was a little foggy coming off the bike. My T2 time was really slow. It was very loud and people were so encouraging. …Daren came up and convinced me to move in the forward direction. We made it 0.5 miles very slowly and Mike Lenhart came up behind us. Without Daren and Mike (and the promise of cookies available at all aid stations), I wouldn't have made it to mile 1.

I didn't really have any running left in me. Maybe it was a combination of tired legs from biking, under-training for the run, and mental burnout. The run amounted to Daren and I walking along chatting it up…

At mile 3-ish, we were walking through downtown Wilmington and there were a lot of people. Everyone seemed very impressed that I was walking slowly with a prosthetic leg and they were encouraging, shouting things like "You're so inspiring," or "Keep it up. What an inspiration." I was grumpy, but Daren told me I should smile anyway. So I did…a little…sometimes. The racers that kept passing me said the same, but I was nicer to them because I figured they actually knew a little about what I was doing. One guy does stand out. He was racing, and blew past me with an enthusiastic, "Keep it up, you're #$%ing awesome!!!"

I liked that guy. Simple, elegant.

I told Daren that I'm a simple person, and profanity and jokes about flatulence will get me every time. Daren kept me laughing with stories about flatulence and the reason why boys feel the need to impress women by having loud tailpipes on their cars. His stories were the key to me making it to mile 8.

I made it to mile 8. By this time, it was 9.75 hours after I had begun swimming, and one hour after the official race cutoff time. I was pretty tired and pretty sore, so I decided to tap out. I stand by my decision."

— DEANNA BABCOCK

I hope this section gives you some perspective to your own efforts. You see, I believe we *all* have some form of disabilities, albeit many not visible to the naked eye.

If there's any parting advice I can pass along from my perspective of working with hundreds of disabled individuals over the past several years, it's that "sports" become one of the greatest vehicles for establishing goals, achieving goals, and presenting opportunities for self-confidence. What's holding you back from taking that first step to living a healthy, active lifestyle? What are your disabilities (both actual and perceived)? What can help you move forward? Without the gift of sports and getting back in the game, many of the individuals whom I've met through G2T's programs would have fallen into a downward spiral of obesity, depression or diabetes.

I'll conclude by putting a wonderful ribbon on Deanna's story. While she "tapped-out" in 2008, she returned to face her demons the next year. She finished the race and proved that with the proper amount of determination, just about anything is possible. As she did in 2008, Deanna provided a post-race report to share her experience. Her closing comments upon finishing the race:

"*I covered the last two miles in an impressively slow time. I eventually crossed the finish line though. I was very, very tired. Oh, and sore. And very happy.*"

FIFTEEN

Working Through Tough Times and Injury

INTRODUCTION: WHEN I WANTED TO QUIT

In January of 2012, I had a half Ironman under my belt. However, I was struggling to be grateful and proud of myself. I tried to remind myself how far I had come in just a little over a year. But something wasn't resonating.

The Expert and I headed out for a forty-five-mile bike ride, trying to get geared up for the *second* 70.3 race coming up in April. At Mile 32, I dismounted my bike and waited until the Expert rolled back to me. I was hurting and tired and angry. I looked at the Expert and said, "I'm not doing this anymore."

He stared at me. "You have to. You have like thirteen miles to get home."

"No. I mean. I don't want to do *this* anymore. This training. Triathlon. This this *this!*" I said, flailing my arms.

That bike ride was the first time I actually thought about hanging up all the triathlon insanity. Yes, I had been scared about races—thought that perhaps I should bow out of this race, or that race. But on that day, I was experiencing I-think-I-may-bow-out-of-this-entire-triathlon-thing.

I'm not sure what caused it. Yes, I was tired from a recent trip. Yes, the ride was the longest one in a while. Yes, my second 70.3 was creeping scary close.

But the quitting *feeling* was something bigger.

The temperature was forty degrees. My hands and feet were completely frozen from the ride. My kids were at home with a babysitter. I missed them. I worried about them. It was a Sunday afternoon. It was a perfectly good day, and I was *suffering* on a bike, when I could have been reading Elmo, shopping or watching a movie or organizing a closet. But instead, I was physically hurting myself, freezing my tail off, and doing it all *on purpose*. At Mile 32, I just couldn't take it anymore.

The Expert continued riding. He knows when I slip into crazy, to move along. He had his phone and said to call if I had a mechanical problem.

I told him to go on. I rode a few miles, stopped, and sat on a bench. I did this a few times. People on grocery-getter bikes were flying past me. I didn't care. I was hungry. I was tired, so tired of it all. *How did I go from motivated to falling flat out of space?*

I was sad. I was sad that I wasn't able to pep myself up, talk myself out of it, put my "yes you can" motivation tactic to work on myself. I just gave up for no real reason. Swim Bike Mom, the blog, was headed to a sad forum called simply, ~~Swim Bike~~ Mom.

The following day started out no better.

I woke up to complete chaos. Our daughter was sick. After taking her to the doctor, I dragged myself into the gym, missing the entire morning of work. I had also missed the scheduled indoor cycling class. So it was just me, sitting in the dark cycling studio on a Spin bike…by myself.

I sat on the front row under the dim lights and turned on Snow Patrol (instead of something peppier). I held on for the misery. I stared at myself in the mirror for the first fifteen minutes while I rode. Just bore a hole through my image with my beady, crabby little sad eyes. I stared and stared. Until, little by little, my legs picked up speed. Then, my heart rate climbed. The sweat started pouring off my visor. Thirty minutes later, I was pushing my heart rate into Zone 4.

An hour late, I was back on the triathlon high. In fact, I felt so good that I skipped on over to the treadmill and ran two miles for "fun." Then, I drove home.

The memory of the terrible ride from the day before was gone. And just like that, my head was back in the triathlon game. (Part of my new good mood *may* have been missing work that morning, but we'll leave that out of the equation for now).

The simple answer to all of these "I quit" emotions is simple: *just keep moving forward*. I will repeat this until I am blue in the face. If the day is bad, you must just close up shop and focus on the next day. Because the next day just might turn out fantastic. Don't give up.

> *"The hardest thing in life is knowing*
> *which bridge to cross,*
> *and which bridge to burn."*
>
> — DAVID RUSSELL

EVERYONE IS STRUGGLING

I am a big fan of the business magazine, *Inc*. In the November 2011 issue, I found an amazing one-page article titled: *Stop Feeling Like a Big Fat Loser*. Well, *that* got my attention. I read on:

> *"If nobody shares they are struggling, nobody will know anybody else is struggling. That results in a bunch of people feeling isolated and scared and like big, fat losers."*[xxv]

I find this so true in everyday life. Some people are intensely private and shuffle along in life preferring to have others glean nothing personal about them, see no faults, smell no farts, and only observe them flying high in their externally perfect world. I also understand that people may be introverts and sharing goes against their very nature. I am not criticizing being an introvert. Actually, on that Meyer-Briggs personality test, I am a partial introvert (figure that one out), so I'm not talking about intro-extro and verting.

People email me often: "OMG, I can't believe you wrote that!"

This was especially true after I shared all the food I ate after my half Ironman race, my wetsuit experiences and the millions of posts on my fatness. I have never lied about how hard it is to be a mother, especially a working mother. How sometimes marriage sucks. I figured that I was doing no good to anyone by candy-coating my journey. Most of all, I would be no good to myself.

Everyone struggles in life, in triathlon. The more I wrote over the years, the more I began to understand the importance of sharing struggles, adventures and advice with others.

In the triathlon context, I encourage advanced members of the sport to recall where they started and to always maintain a spirit of *encouragement* to baby triathletes—even slow or unfit babies. I remember people who said (say) encouraging things to me; I remember those who didn't (don't). Words matter big time to the "little" people wearing swim caps and Spandex for the first time. I find, for the most part, triathletes are some of the most amazing, encouraging and supporting group of athletes. But every bunch of bananas has their monkeys...so...

On your journey, remember to share your experiences more often. Even if you are an introvert—you can certainly find one person at your gym to encourage—and that makes a difference. One of my most encouraging triathlete friends, Karen (who I call "Yoda" because she is so wise), is a pretty quiet person—but she *quietly* offers me wise, balanced and genius advice. She shares her triathlon knowledge, freely, and has helped me more than she knows. Yoda pays it forward. *Share you must.*

If you can bravely stomach sharing your fears and struggles in an open forum like a blog or a seminar (or a book!?!), I encourage you to do it! Chances are, if you are feeling low or "like a big fat loser," someone else is feeling the same way. If we can all help each other become better people and stronger triathletes then we should do it. Really, what is the point of faking it? Everyone knows faking it is just for the bedroom and cocktail parties.

WORKING THROUGH INJURY - SWIM BIKE KLUTZ

I call myself Swim Bike *Klutz* probably more than Swim Bike *Mom*. Truthfully, I am a massive klutz. I often fall off my bike and crush my hands and knees. I fell off my bike during my first triathlon, which resulted in a seemingly permanent hip injury. I have scraped up my calves with chain bites. I do other stupid injury-prone things like wedging a sliver of laminate flooring under my thumbnail while cleaning up after the kids. I can get hurt anywhere: triathlon, cleaning or work.

I can get hurt on rest day, as I did before my first Olympic distance race— just walking to the bathroom. I was trucking to the bathroom and out of nowhere; my left hamstring started bothering me and got worse throughout the day. *Who gets hurt on rest day?* I grabbed ice and sat with my leg up at my desk so people could say: "Huh, what's wrong with your leg" and that sort of thing. I iced all night. The hamstring injury got better, then worse, and now that hamstring is always an issue.

Even in yoga class, I have managed to rip half of my big toenail off during my transition from plank to downward dog. This was almost as good as me stepping out of the car at a gas station and tripping over a chicken wing. I will not mention the stupid fact that there was a chicken wing in the parking lot (only in Georgia). But of course, I found it with my feet.

Then another time, leaving an awesome, sweat-busting cycling class, I was wearing flip-flops and managed to slip on a puddle of sweat. I landed flat on my ass, spewing water bottles, shoes and expletives right at the door. I had my hair colored and cut the day before *that* fall. The stylist had convinced me to change my part from one side to the other. I've parted my hair on the same side for my whole life. I joked with her, "If you change my part, I won't be able to walk. It'll throw me off balance." *Apparently, not far from truth.*

Oh, and I should not omit the time the Expert and I threw down a massive, yet injury-free, brick workout only for me to come home and injure myself doing laundry. I leaned over to pull clothes out of the dryer. I had rested my hand on the washer, and the washer lid came crashing down on my pinkie finger. The hand was instantly black and blue.

I continuously hurt my ankles. The Expert jokes that I should wear high-top sneakers for constant ankle support. Luckily, the ankle I destroy always seems to be the left one, which already contains hardware from a bone break back in 1993. Therefore, when I twist my ankle often, I am convinced that the hardware holds my entire foot together.

Before St. Anthony's triathlon, I was zooming out the front door for court (carrying ten bags, a file and a notebook), and I stepped on one of those little roly pinecones. *Twist! Left ankle!* I dropped bags, cursed the world. *I'm okay, okay, okay*, I thought, and really, nothing hurt. I guess I dodged that one. But, approximately *eight* hours later, I was zooming back into the house, returning from court and crunch, twist, ugh! *Again? The same roly pinecone! The same ankle? Seriously?*

Yes. But the second time, my pride and my ankle hurt a little. I dropped my bags for the second time that day, picked up that pinecone and threw it with a vengeance into the neighbor's yard, screaming something like, "I hate you tiny pinecone!" I limped into the house. By the end of the night, I was not feeling any real pain, so it was clear I avoided two ankle crises in one day.

Almost a year to the day later, I was not so lucky.

THE BIG INJURY

Eight weeks before my second 70.3, I encountered either my own two feet (entirely possible) or yet another roly pinecone.

Regardless of the cause, I took a spill in the driveway.

Only the day before, the Expert and I had put down a sizeable bike ride, then a little four-mile run. A bloody glorious brick where the sun was shining and I felt like a semi-real triathlete. I had a nice afternoon and a hefty dinner, and I was ready to begin the week. Monday morning rolled in with a bang, and the zoo that is our house was insane.

Consequently, in an attempt to escape to work, I ran out of the house a little too quickly towards the car.

I ended up on the ground. Again, not sure *how*. But all I do know is that I hit the ground, heard a snap, and glanced up to see the neighbor across the street staring at me. My work bag, my purse, my keys were splayed across the yard. I was so stinking humiliated that I popped up like a gimp Jack-in-the-box and limped to the house. *Bollocks! My house key is in the yard!*

Immediately, my foot was throbbing. I rang the doorbell sixteen times before the Expert open the door and screamed, "*What* do you want? Good grief, Mere!"

"Let me in," I wailed, "I fell!" I was sobbing. Messy tears, sweat and grass were spread across the side of my sweater and face.

"New Orleans," I muttered. "Oh, my Lord."

The Expert stared at me. The kids stared at me. I had fallen, then I had hobbled into the house crying like a maniac. And the only significant thing I had to say was, "New Orleans." Crying about my upcoming 70.3 race.

Later that day, I learned that I broke my 5th metatarsal bone in my right foot. Oh, I broke it good too. In two places. The doctor x-rayed me, walked in with her computer and said, "It's broken." I thought she was talking about her laptop. Nope, not the laptop. My foot.

Next, entered the man carrying the snazzy gray boot, smarting off something like, "Say hello to your little friend." I thought, *Say hello to my middle finger.* But I said nothing, I behaved, and I wore the boot outside the office, brandishing my crutches like a true champ. I was upset, but I was dealing. I called Coach Monster who proceeded to talk in a string of appropriately-timed expletives.

Broken foot! Argh! New Orleans 70.3 dreams dashed. The eight week countdown to the race had *just* begun, and *I fell in my flipping yard. I fell in my yard. My yard! My yard!!* And no training? I knew I would be seeing some depression and dark days.

Fast forward eight weeks.

I was up fifteen (!) pounds and had "lost" every ounce of my endurance. At least that was how I felt. I felt terrible. My food choices had been poor during the recovery period and the return to the gym and pool was less than pretty. I experienced four stages to my triathlon injury: grief, madness, coping and retrieval.

GRIEF

Much like a death, I mourned the death of my second 70.3 dream. I sobbed at the thought of my running legs melting down to super-fat stumpy things, much like they were two years ago. I was forced to look at my rear end and invite more of its fat cell friends to leap upon it. I had ingrained my upcoming race in my skin and now that life was gone. Of course, the life was not gone. It was only temporarily unavailable. But loss, no matter how small, is still a loss. I had to look my loss in the face, cry and grieve it.

MADNESS

After I cried for three straight days, I went mad. I entered crazy land. All I heard were crazy voices: *How are you ever going to run again? You are going to become mentally unstable! What about your bicycle? Won't your bicycle be lonely? Will the GU gels in the cabinet actually go bad?*

The voices started and I began to dream of nothing but running. I would run in my sleep and wake up whimpering from the pain. I would think about running at work. I would pack my cycling shoes for work, just in case I had time, forgetting that spin class was not on the list of acceptable behaviors for a newly broken metatarsal. The pure madness (insanity) then quickly turned to real madness (anger). I was mad, mad, and more mad.

COPING

After the grief and the madness, I began to cope. Notice I did not say that I began to "thrive." This stage was less insane, but it was merely manageable. I spent time coping with the fact that I could not run. I was dealing with my sadness for missing race day(s). I whined about missing my favorite cycling class. I learned new ways to get in some swimming (take off boot, limp to pool, get in carefully and hope no one kicked me and broke my foot in a third place).

RETRIEVAL

The last stage of a triathlon injury is retrieval. Retrieval? What? Yes. Trying to *retrieve* muscle memory and retrieve the drive to get moving again. This is a big mental stage. Putting weight on the foot and trying to move normally was strange, so my retrieval stage consisted of trying to get things back to normal.

Retrieval was harder than the actual injury phase, because I had to stop comparing myself to...myself. I could not dwell on how much farther along I was last year. I had to move on. Retrieve what I could, and get *back* to moving *forward*.

The biggest thing to remember about any injury is to follow your coach's, doctor's and therapist's orders. Whatever you do, do *not* read online about your prognosis. Create your own prognosis (within reason) and allow your mind to heal your body. Continue to stay mentally positive and it will serve you well in the dark times. Time really does pass quickly, and you'll be back in the game before you realize it.

TOUGH TIMES

AN UNEXPECTED ILLNESS

My fellow blogger pal, Christie O. from the blog, *Average Moms Wear Capes*, has had a roller coaster of a year. I asked her to share her story, and how triathlon has "saved" her and her family during a dark time.

TRIATHLON: A COMEBACK
by Christie O'Sullivan
AverageMomsWearCapes.com

I sat in the cold room in my beautiful white paper skirt, waiting for my oncologist to come in and deliver the news. *How bad was it?* I had spent the days since my cervical cancer diagnosis in a dark place in my mind, overwhelmed, crying, *wondering*.

I'm only thirty-six years old and I have two little boys. *They need me. There are proms and weddings and graduations ahead. The news has to be good. It has to.*

My head pounded. My hands were sweaty. My eyes were filled like they had been for days, and ready to burst.

My husband was there with me in the little room, waiting for the word. Together, we had run miles together, swam side by side (in our separate lanes) on our Friday night date nights, rode our bikes for miles and miles on the trails together. Barely runners before babies, we'd become triathletes together on my postpartum weight-loss journey. Sprint triathlons, Olympic distance, and then eventually a couple of half Ironman races, it was a journey that had brought us closer together as a couple and had really shown us what we were made of. (Until now, of course.) We had a race coming up, but it was the last thing on our minds that day.

Finally, the doctor came in. He examined me. I got dressed. He came back in and we sat down together. *This was it.*

"You have a tumor," he said. "And assuming you're ok with losing your fertility, you can have a hysterectomy and have it removed successfully," he said.

But I wasn't okay. I wasn't okay with losing my fertility at all. We were trying for more babies. I wasn't ready to be done. My eyes started to sting and he apologized profusely for assuming—and I'll forever love him for that—I haven't had too many doctors care about what they've said and *how* they've said it.

We decided that the hysterectomy was the best course of action as radiation would have ended the same way (in infertility) and it would have just dragged out the process. He said we caught it early and that he thought we could get it all. Given the circumstances, this was the best possible news he could have given me. Yes, I'd lose my fertility, but it meant I'd be here for the children I have.

We talked about scheduling the surgery and I laughingly mentioned our race coming up. To my surprise, he was all for it. He wanted me to do it! *Really? I can do this?* I was astonished! One last hurrah!

I'm so grateful that my doctor gave me the chance to race before the surgery. I did not race to go fast or to win that day. I woke up that morning not a bit nervous and I cherished every swim stroke, every drop of water on my face, the sun as it peeked up over the horizon as we stood on the shore, the wind on my face during the bike where I cried just a little and thanked God for my ability to do this. On the run, where my legs were starting to fail (I truly hadn't trained for this race as much as I should have), I continued to run. And then I walked. It didn't matter. I was *there.*

I chatted with runners around me. When the spectators were giving out beads (and beer) as we went by, I took both. I partied on the run. A butterfly flew with me as I ran for a while (I'm sure my grandma sent it to me).

On that day, racing took on a different meaning for me. The race took me *forever*, but I enjoyed every second of it; the pain, the heat, every excruciating, wonderful minute of it. I told the little tumor inside me to enjoy it too, because that was its last hurrah! By next week it would be a faint memory and headed to wherever tumors go!

Now, after the surgery, *things* are different. *I am different.*

But there's one thing that's always been here for me cheering me on and training me for future life events: triathlon. For me, triathlon has become a symbol for what's *possible.*

Triathlon has become a symbol of what these incredible bodies that we've been given can do. No matter what size, shape, age, or condition.

Triathlon has become a symbol of freedom for my body and all its parts and its uncanny ability to activate its super wonder powers while swimming and following it up with a bike and a run. *Something I'd never in a million years thought I'd ever do.*

Triathlon has become a symbol of pushing inconceivable limits.

And soon, triathlon will be *my* symbol for an *incredible comeback.*

======================================

CHOICES AND REGRETS

Triathlon has forced me to work through many regrets. A big issue in my life is my own self-loathing. A second issue was dealing with my regrets of the past. I had to move past the mistakes I had made in order to move forward. These mistakes were not just health mistakes either. I had to confront mistakes in my personal life and deal with those as well. Of course, the "how did I let this happen to me" part of my psychological fatness warfare was a big one.

After my first half Ironman, I took a trip to San Diego to spend time with some of my new Swim Bike Mom friends. I took a drive to Torrey Pines Beach with Coach Carrie from Tempo Life Coaching. She and I hiked the trail, and she solved many of my brain problems. Many. After Carrie took off for the day, I walked the beach alone.

For those of you who do not know Torrey Pines, there's a section of the beach covered in thousands and thousands of palm-sized, smooth, colorful stones. Incredibly beautiful. I looked at the stones, picked up and touched hundreds of them and thought (very dramatically) about my life.

I thought about choices. Our lives have *hundreds* of choices each day. To wake up, to brush teeth, to do or not to do. Thousands of choices over the course of our weeks, our months are presented. How many choices appear over a lifetime? Millions?

Life may be like a box of chocolates (hopefully, peanut butter ones), but I have begun to think of life as a beach full of magical stones. The stones represent choices. You can pick up the stones, one by one, and carry your choices with you. You can carry along the bad choices, the good choices, the regrets, the stupidity, the egotistical choices. You can pick them up and haul them with you, mile after mile after mile. Until eventually, the beach still has relentless miles of choices to walk, but you have nothing left in your soul or your legs to walk the rest of the way, hauling all those stones. Even though you are beaten and broken, you cling to your stones, the culmination of a life of good and bad choices.

I picked up two stones and put them in my pocket. I am sure I broke twelve California laws by taking the stones, but I took them anyway. I needed to remember that day.

I brought one stone for my past and one for my future. I will let my past be only a small memory, something I wouldn't notice if I carried it along in my pocket. I keep the future stone on my desk and I touch it every day I am at work. I think about what I *want* my future to be, I hold it tight and I carry that small weight with me also.

Two small stones, not *thousands* to weigh me down. I can *remember* the lessons of the past, but not be weighed down. I can *hope* for the future, but if the future doesn't turn out exactly like I've hoped, I can just throw that version out, and the regret won't weigh me down either.

That day on the beach, I made a promise to myself. I decided that going forward, I would strive to make the best choices I could. I also decided to release all of my past choices right there on the beach. Whether my choices were good or bad, smart or stupid, I let those waves crash over the choices and bury them deep in the sand. Going forward, I would not carry along the burdensome choices. I would not be weighed down. I repeated: *The bad things will not define me. The bad people will not discourage me.*

Choices should not *define* us. Yes, choices often make our paths. But paths and self-worth are two different things. Many times we cling to the regret, because we feel that we owe the guilt gods some sort of sacrifice. We don't. Let all those stones roll on. You are better than your mistakes.

TRIATHLON AS HEALING

I urge you to remember this phrase:

> *"The bad things will not define me.*
> *The bad people will not discourage me."*

Sometimes I use triathlon as a demon exorciser, a healthy power. Sometimes I run so far and swim so many laps, I forget how to even count.

One particular swim comes to mind after a hideous day in the legal profession. I started off the swim *mad as all hell* from work. I was absolutely fuming as I strapped on my goggles and took off for the first 300 meter warm-up. I had my fat swimsuit on, the one that I bought when I first started swimming for triathlon. I don't know why I packed that one, but as I swam wearing the I-have-come-so-far swimsuit, it made me feel better.

I swam and swam and swam. I got madder, then I got faster. Then I started to smolder instead of just fume. I swam more. 200s. 300s. 50s. 100s. 400s. I prayed. I cried a little, inside my goggles.

I swam for almost two straight hours. The longest swim I have logged to date. I swam until my shoulders and back ached more than my brain. I swam until my anger was washed away with the chlorine and nothing but a dull, throbbing memory of the day remained. I wandered to the shower exhausted, and as I rinsed off my suit and the chlorine, I began crying again. And I thanked God for triathlon.

That night, I walked in the door of our house with wet hair. I hugged the Expert. I cuddled my kids. I ate a giant bowl of spaghetti and two Reese's cups. I did not feel guilty. I felt healed. I knew that another day of worries would come (in approximately twelve hours). I understood that similar garbage would happen again, possibly the next day, in my miserable job with the other unhappy lawyers.

Triathlon has changed me. I will never be the same. During that one swim workout, I was able to remember to say: *The bad things will not define me. The bad people will not discourage me.* I can honestly say that I was shown the grace of God through a simple, yet very long, swim.

I wish the same for all of you.

Find the run. Find the swim. Find your quiet place. Hold onto those precious, quiet and difficult training moments. You will find that sometimes the most painful workouts, and the most hideous race photos, are often, the most healing.

> "In these bodies we will live
> In these bodies we will die
> Where you invest your love
> You invest your life."
>
> — MUMFORD & SONS

SIXTEEN

A Training Plan for your Triathlon

The purpose of this section is *not* to give you a fool-proof training plan. I cannot do that because I really have no idea what I am talking about in general. I still recommend a coach or a club to get you to your races… but I also understand what it's like to be a newbie triathlete, a woman (thus, needing *answers* and needing the answers *now*), on a budget, and searching for help, any help.

A beginner training plan is a good jumping-off point for you to gain an *idea* of the training, the reasonable time commitment, and to begin to search out your best training plans, coaching and motivation to get you to your race. *Do not tape this training plan to your mirror and hide it in your sports bra and call it gospel*. But *do* look at it, consider the steps and figure out how to make it work for you.

Here's your plan. Go to www.SwimBikeMom.com and download the free eBook: *The Swim Bike Mom Ultimate Sprint Triathlon Training Plan*. The eBook has three plans: one for the true beginner, one for a beginner with some athletic background, and another plan for someone a little more advanced. The plan is very general, but it should give you an idea of the types of workouts and distances you want to achieve before your first or next race.

If you cannot hire a coach or do not have access to a club, then I urge you to create your own calendar and do your homework to create your special plan. You can use Google Calendar, or even the free TrainingPeaks.com software. Keep records and hold yourself accountable.

Additionally, there are thousands of beginner triathlon training plans available for download online at BeginnerTriathlete.com. I urge you to use these plans as a *guide* to figure out what works for you and begin to formulate your own plan and schedule.

Starting out, you will want to aim to swim twice a week, bike/spin twice a week and walk/jog/run twice a week. Doing this methodically and religiously for three to six months will easily find you at the starting line of your first race. Work in 1-2 strength and core workouts each week as well. Every four weeks, take that week as a recovery to lower your intensity and distances.

But really, I do implore you to find a coach or a team that can help you—an online plan is no substitute for a person—and the motivation and accountability from *others* is a big part of triathlon. Remember, however, that the key is not a magic training plan or a coach, but a determination within yourself, a consistency to complete the workouts and moving forward the best you can! You will get there.

SEVENTEEN

Race Preparation and Race Day

INTRODUCTION

You can read about my crazy first triathlon experiences in Part II of this book, but for now, you can assume that most every triathlete, new or seasoned, has suffered through weird race experiences. I can promise you…you *will*, at some point, encounter some crazy triathlon things on race day. However, proper preparation for your race can certainly help alleviate some of the nuttiness that can come your way.

THE TAPER

One to two weeks before any longer distance race (Olympic and longer) comes the Taper. Also known as the sixth circle of triathlon hell. Well, that really depends on the athlete. Shorter distance races (sprint and Olympic distance) don't necessarily require a taper, and if they do, it will be a shorter amount of time, such as a week.

The idea behind the taper is that you have put in the miles and you are ready, but you must give the body time to recover and rest prior to the big day.

"The purpose of the taper is to allow your body to recover from the pounding and to restore the glycogen levels in your bloodstream and liver. Very common mistake is to show up for races tired. The point of the taper is to put *pop* back into your legs and your mind," says Coach Monster.

Again, for a shorter distance race like a sprint, you do not need to taper *per se*. But you can reduce the quantity of your workouts the week before and just stretch, swim and stay loosey-goosey. Practice your mental feats of strength during this time!

The Week Before: Pre-Race!

Pre-Race Rest

The amount of pre-race rest you require depends also on distance of race. Of course, you need a good night's sleep, but I'm talking about training "rest." As Coach Monster always says: "When in doubt, leave it out. If you doubt you can do it, just skip it and let it go. If life gets in the way… doesn't matter—you won't get any fitter, and chances are people aren't going to do it right."

Pre-Race Nutrition

In the days leading up to race day, you want to move to simple carbohydrates likes pastas and white rice—things that metabolize quickly. However, it is important to note that this is also more important for longer distances race than a sprint. Do not load up on pasta before your two-hour race. No need, and it will just make you feel icky.

Pre-Race Hydration

Hydration is extremely important during training and leading up to race day. You must, however, be careful that you are taking in the right amount of water, sodium and potassium. Drinking so much water that it dilutes the sodium in your blood can, in extreme cases, be fatal. Keeping the right electrolyte balance is important, but again, it is more important in the longer distance races.

Mental Preparation

Like everything else in triathlon, race day preparation is very much part of the mental game. Coach Monster told me, "I will go through the whole race in my mind in race week and through my training. I don't visualize the *perfect* race. Instead, I visualize things that could go wrong and I picture myself dealing with these issues calmly and confidently. I remind myself of the work I have done. I go back through my logs and think about the 'deposits' I have made. I bring my checkbook on race day, and I write the check."

[I laughed at him here.]

"You can laugh, but it works. When it starts to hurt, I look at pain as a family friend that I invite into my house. Pain is a technique that I have used and I keep adding detail to it and I go longer and longer before I give up. Everyone has a breaking point."

McBlessings says that it's important to remember control during a race. "Most swim coaches will advise 'Don't kick yourself out of a race' meaning to 'save' your legs on the swim portion. The most important thing in swimming is about using your legs to 'corkscrew' yourself through the water. The legs are not doing a lot of kicking *per se*, they are more helping us turn through the water. This will help save your legs for the bike and the run."

"As far as goal setting for a race," McBlessings continued, "I like to set time goals in order to keep me on track and focused. I look at my watch and set goals at the beginning of the race, which helps me pace. I have a plan before the race and that helps keep me on target. If I am looking at my watch and knowing my goals, if I am way ahead of that pace, then I am going too fast and I know to back off a little. I might need to step it up if I look at my watch and I am behind."

Coach Pete Farren, open-water swim coach extraordinaire who teaches Masters Swim at Concourse Athletic Club in Sandy Springs, Georgia, says, "You have *three separate races* in a triathlon. When you are swimming, don't think about anything but swimming. At the end of the swim, only then should you begin to think about getting to T1. But then once you are on the bike, think about the bike only until the end of the leg, when you begin to think about T2. The important thing is not to think about the whole big race, which is daunting. Break it down into small chunks. This will help you prepare mentally as well."

So get yourself into a good frame of mind. Visual success, and get ready!

Race Day Clothing

Listen up ladies. You want to get a triathlon suit or "kit" for your race. End of story. You have the option to go with a triathlon-like alternative, but you may *not* deviate far, as I have explained in Chapter Two. This is Newbie Rule 101. Trust me on this. And don't email me asking if you can change clothes in transition—I will tell you no!

The Day Before the Race

Packet Pick-up

Not all races will have athlete check-in or bike check the day prior to the race. However, many of the big races *do*. Read your registration and rules and know the schedule.

When you pick up your race packet, ensure that you have everything you need *in* the packet. Most races include a swim cap, race number, helmet and bike sticker and timing chip with a strap for your ankle. Do not leave the race venue until you have all the parts to your packet. I learned this lesson the hard way (the way I learn most of my lessons) at Iron Girl Atlanta 2012. I drove an hour to the race venue (with kids!) only to get home and realize that I had forgotten my timing chip. Back to the race venue (with kids!) I went.

Some packets will include number "tattoos" for you to apply to your arms and legs. Do not apply these until race morning. Read the instructions to the race tattoos carefully and do not apply your lotion or sunscreen until *after* you have affixed the numbers.

Bike Check-In

Confirm that your bike and components (spare tire tube, bike bag, lubed bike, pumped tires) are all in order *before* bike check-in. Do not place your water bottles or your bike "accessories" (helmet, shoes) in transition if you check your bike the day before the race. You want to wait until the morning of the race to *bring* all these items. The race officials will let you into transition on the morning of the race, so you will be able to reevaluate your bike and tires, bring all your gear and set up your transition area before the race start. You may be required to affix the bike number to your bike before checking it, but usually that's all that is required before checking the bike.

YOUR CHECKLISTS: SPRINT / OLYMPIC DISTANCE RACE

I highly recommend making a list of the things you need for the race and checking it twice, Santa-like. You need things before the race, during and after. Practice your transitions and take note of your list!

For your first race, pack your bag several days before. Unpack it and practice your transitions, then re-pack it. This will ensure that you have everything you need, and get you some extra transition practice.

The Swim Bike Mom You-Got-It-All Checklist

Pre-Race
Tri Kit / Tri Suit
Race Bag / Gym Bag
Pre-race snack
Helmet & Bike Numbers (affixed to helmet and bike)
Sunscreen (only after you have been marked with race number)

Swim
Goggles
Extra Pair of Goggles
Lubricant like Aquaphor or BodyGlide
Wetsuit (if needed)

T1 / Bike
Bike!
Towel or Transition Mat
Water bottle (to rinse feet after swim)
Small Towel (to wipe feet before putting on your shoes)
Water Bottles for Bike
Helmet

Cycling Shoes
Socks
Sunglasses
Race Number Belt with Race Number attached (Turn it backwards while you are on the bike leg)
Gel / Nutrition to consume on the bike
Heart rate monitor / GPS watch
Bike tools (tube, CO_2, tire levers)

T2 / Run
Running Shoes!
Ziploc Bag (in case it rains, you can put your running shoes in here to keep them semi-dry)
Hat / Visor
Sunglasses
Socks
Race Number Belt (Now, turned forward)
Fuel Belt (optional; usually for longer distances)
Gel / Nutrition

Post Race
Change of Clothes and Shoes
Camera
A Smile
A GPS to find the post-race beer

RACE DAY

THE MORNING OF YOUR RACE

Practice your positive race visualizations as you get ready for the race. Eat well in advance of the race (2-3 hours) and make sure you get your first poop in.

Coffee is good for this. You'll be glad you did. Trying to poop in a Porta-Potty with twenty people in line behind you is less than ideal.

Do not fret too much about your nutrition on a sprint distance race. Eat something substantial for breakfast, but low in grease and fiber. Think: bagel with peanut butter, oatmeal with nuts. Remember the rule: do not try anything new. This includes food. I would suggest eating what you did on days before you went on your longer bike rides. You know that agrees with you. Plus, your stomach may be nervous.

If you anticipate being on the race course for more than two hours, then consider packing a gel or a snack to eat on the bicycle leg. Typically, you will not need nutrition on a short race. However, if you are a big girl and are moving slower than others, pack some nutrition. Trust me. I eat *something* on *all* distance races. I may have a gel on the bike and another one at the start of the run. Triathlon is tough enough without the dreaded bonk. This is your race, so do what is best for *you*.

Setting Up Your Transition Area

You will likely have either an assigned spot in transition or an assigned area based on your race number. Once you have your race packet, numbers, bike and timing chip, you are ready to head into transition to set up.

Timing Chip

Your timing chip will be on an ankle strap. You can put this on immediately or wait until after you put on your wetsuit (if needed). I recommend putting it on as soon as possible, so it is not lost in the transition set-up. You can always remove it to pull on your wetsuit.

Find your spot

Usually races will have racks set up by groups of race numbers—large metal racks designate your place in transition. You will "rack" your bike usually by lifting the rear of your bike and hooking the front of your saddle on the rack.

If this is confusing now, it won't be on race morning. Just look around you and you will see how the bikes are resting by their saddles.

Of course, it varies by race but usually, there will be rows and rows of metal racks in transition. Depending on the size of the rack in each row, you may have 15-100 bikes on "your" row. As you rack your bike, remember to stagger it with your neighbor's bike. For example, if your transition neighbor's front wheel is facing one way, you should rack your bike the *opposite* way—with your *rear* wheel next to her *front* wheel. This prevents handlebars from getting tangled up when removing the bikes from the rack in T1, and also when you are re-racking your bike in T2.

SET UP YOUR AREA

Remember to be courteous with your transition area. Coach Monster says, "One of my biggest pet peeves is someone setting up a transition area the size of small town. A small town! They have a mayor and a small trolley that goes around their transition area!" he says, laughing. "It is important to be respectful. Your transition area should be no larger than a small towel. The key to transition—both setting up the area and executing T1 and T2—is practicing the ritual and finding a sequence. Once you find this sequence, then you should do it the same way every time. In order to have the consistency, you must practice so it's second nature."

The general consensus in triathlon transition area set-up is to place your gear to the *left* of your front bike wheel (when racked). No wait—the back wheel. No wait—to the side of the wheel that is down on the ground—which means the front wheel. *No wait…* The USAT rule says, "All participants shall place equipment only in the properly designated and individually assigned bicycle corral and shall at all times keep their equipment confined to such properly designated areas."[xxvi]

Helpful.

Okay, so there are a zillion options about where to place your transition area *stuff*. But the space to the left of the front wheel makes the most practical sense, after all. In T1 you will stand at your bike, put on your shoes, helmet, etc., and then unhook your bike and roll it towards the "bike out" banner. If your stuff is at your *rear* wheel—you'd theoretically have to either squeeze your bike *under* the rack (which is impossible if you are tall and have a large bike), or walk around the transition rack to the other side. So, go with the left of your front wheel.

- No matter the location of your transition area, keep it in line with your neighbors' set-up. Roll with the punches. If you are the first one there setting up, go with the left of your front wheel, because that makes the most sense, and that's how it's done in the big races.
- Keep your transition area small. Be courteous of others! A beach towel (folded in half!) or mat sold specifically for transitions is a perfect size for your area. Stay on your towel area, and your neighbors will be grateful.
- If you have a backpack in transition with you, find a friend or family member (who is not racing) to hold it during the race. If you are racing alone, squeeze your bag under your bike or against the transition area fence (if allowed).
- Don't be nosy. Mind your own business and don't tell others what to do or what *not* to do in transition. Unless they're infringing on your transition area real estate, just take a deep breath and let it go.

When you arrive at the race on race morning, you will have a certain period of time before transition closes. During this time, you should set up your area. First, lay down your transition mat or folded towel on the ground which will be your designated area. The next step is to place the items you need for the bike and the run on the towel *in the same manner that you practiced beforehand* during your training. Remember: you should not try anything new on race day and this includes your transition area set-up.

I like to place my cycling shoes on the front left of the mat or towel. Next to the shoes, I have my water bottle (to spray my feet), a small washcloth or towel, my helmet, which is upside down and precisely turned around so I can put it directly on my head. Inside my helmet, I have my sunglasses and race number belt. Some people like to put their helmet on their handlebars of the bike—this is a good reminder to put your helmet on—because you can't roll your bike without touching the helmet. My order for T1 is: sunglasses, helmet, race number belt (number to the rear), spray feet, wipe feet, shoes and go. It does not matter what order you choose; just find your order and keep it consistent.

If you wear a wetsuit in the swim, you will want to roll it up or fold it as you run into T1 and place it neatly under your bike, or behind your towel.

To the rear of my cycling gear on the mat, I have my T2 gear: my running shoes on the rear left of the mat, with one sock inside of each shoe. To the right, I have my visor and my hand-held water bottle or Fuel Belt (if I choose to race with either, and/or have gels or nutrition to carry).

As I come into T2, I rack my bike, unstrap my helmet and put my helmet on the seat of my bike. Then I slip off my cycling shoes and place them on the front of the mat. I slip *on* my socks, my running shoes and my visor, and a Fuel Belt or handheld bottle (if needed), and I run out.

HAVE YOUR BIKE IN GEAR

Your bike should be in the gear easiest for you to mount when coming out of transition. Don't forget to check this on race morning.

Additionally, ensure that you have bar caps on the ends of your handlebars before you check your bike into transition. Sometimes these plugs may fall out—if you don't have your handlebar ends plugged, you can't race. After all, you don't want to fall during a race and gore your cycling neighbor.

WETSUIT

Only after your transition area is set-up need you worry about your wetsuit. I recommend putting it on, only waist high, twenty minutes before the race start and pulling it up over your arms and zipping up only about 5-10 minutes before your wave takes off. Do not forget your timing chip! You will need to take it off or wait to put on the timing chip until after you are wearing the suit.

THE HOUR BEFORE

Transition will close about an hour before your race start, leaving you with an hour to panic and wander around aimlessly, muttering things like, *Why did I sign up for this?*

Don't Forget!

Make sure you have your swim cap and goggles when you leave transition. Once transition is "closed," it's really closed! I tuck my goggles and cap into my sports bra so I don't leave them behind.

Depending on your personality, you should find the best way for *you* to cope with this extra time before the race. Whatever you do, do *not* look at the other athletes and start comparing yourself to them. There will be athletes like Frank McHotBod and Sally O'FastLegs. Ignore them and concentrate on the hard work that you have done to prepare.

The Expert likes to get in the water and warm-up before a race. I like to find a place away from the crowd and separate myself from the hoopla. Depending on the race course set-up (and outside temperatures), it may be a good idea to get in the water if you can. Personally, I get in the water to pee. I'm sorry, but that's what 99% of everyone is doing in the water during "warm up." Just embrace the pee water and you'll be okay.

If you are wearing a wetsuit for the swim portion, do *not* put the suit on an *hour* beforehand. Wait until about twenty minutes before your wave. Even then, pull the suit up to your waist only, leaving your upper body exposed. Pull the suit onto your arms and zip up only about five or ten minutes before your swim wave. Otherwise, you can run the risk of overheating. Of course, if it's freezing outside, ignore everything I just wrote and do whatever you need to do to stay warm.

The Final Few Minutes

As you stand at the swim wave start with your new race swim cap on your head and your goggles pulled down over your eyes, take a look around you.

Then take a deep breath.

Remember: while you are taking part in a competition, *competing* is not the main goal here. Remember that this race is the start of something wonderful in your life. Look at the others around you, but do *not* compare yourself to them. Look at your fellow racers with the realization that they, too, are nervous and anxious about *their race*. Remember that this is *your* race. Be thankful.

Take another deep breath.

Look to the sky. Say "thank you" to your God for letting you stand on that beach, dock, boat, deck or grass. Embrace a feeling of gratitude and thankfulness as the national anthem is played (or if it's not your country's anthem, hum your own and be thankful anyway). Be humbled by your working body, your strong body that is going to get you across the finish line. Be thankful that you had the opportunity to train for the race. Realize that you have worked hard and you are ready for it. Thank your body for the hard work it is about to take on. Thank your mind for believing in *you*. Thank your soul for carrying the dream through.

Take another deep breath.

Carry the feeling of gratefulness during your entire race. Be strong between your ears, and that will keep your body strong. When you feel that you can't go on, then tell yourself, *Just keep moving forward* or use a mantra that you have used in training. Tell yourself, *I got this. I am ready.*

Take another deep breath. Because this is your day. You're here. Now, have fun!

PART TWO

THE MEMOIR

From Couch Potato Mom To Half-Iron Mother

Introduction

Now that smart people have told you all about triathlon and I have shared my little tidbits, I will tell you about *my* journey to a big finish line. I hope you find my story funny and honest. But I also hope that you see the take-home message: *Just keep moving forward and you can achieve more than you ever thought possible.*

The simple Decision to become a triathlete literally changed my entire life. Since my first half Ironman, I have finished a second half Ironman (Ironman Augusta 70.3, September 30, 2012), and I have registered for a full Ironman for June 2013. Talk about a 180 degree change from the Fat Stranger, eh?

And I believe your Decision will do the same for you. Perhaps you will see a little of yourself in my experiences and my journey will speak loud and clear that you *too* can accomplish big things—with just a little forward motion, consistency and very strong sense of humor.

My First Triathlon and Beyond

My First Triathlon – October 2010

My first triathlon was a mere month after my big Decision. It was, luckily, a sprint distance *reverse* triathlon: run, bike, and then finished with a swim. The trail was flat and the swim was in a pool, so it seemed like a good idea at the time. But I had decided to become a triathlete for like, *oh*, five minutes. So my first triathlon was a crazy idea.

On race morning, I woke up with sore knees and a gimpy feeling left hip, but I ignored the twinges completely and did some affirmations about "you can do this" and by the time I arrived at the race venue, nothing hurt. I set out with two goals only: 1) finish; and 2) run, bike and swim the whole thing—no stops, no walking, no getting off the bike, no walking up hills. Actually, that was more like five goals.

I arrived about an hour before race start. It was October and cold. I had completely forgotten a jacket. That stupid oversight made me wonder what else I forgot. I had a checklist, but this was my first time at the show. I wandered to the registration desk, picked up my number and someone wrote all over me with a permanent marker.

I checked the tube pressure in my old yellow bike and it seemed low. So I pulled out the Joe Blow and tried to pump the back tube. Nothing. *@#$%!* My tube stem was bent. *Holy cow, I am going to change a tube before the race even starts?* I was also (semi) prepared for a tire change, so I tried not to get all bothered. Even still, I had a minor freak out. The frustration helped warm me up, though. Eventually, I figured it out and the crisis was averted.

I hauled my stuff over to transition and found a place to park the bike. Unlike some races, there were no assigned spaces for the bikes. I laid out my gear. I put my bike on the rack. *Nope, wrong way.* I flipped it around. *Okay.*

The race announcer gave us the rules and a summary of the course. Before I knew it, the race started, and I was jogging. Remember this was a reverse triathlon, so the runners took off and they were zooooooming. I was wearing my brand new sneakers. [Rookie Mistake: *Do not do anything new on race day. Do not, especially, wear new shoes.*] I had purchased a triathlon top and shorts for the race. During the whole car trip to the venue, I was thinking, *this tri get-up is heinous. I can't wear this, I can't wear this.* [Rookie Mistake: *Do not do anything new on race day. Do not, especially, wear a new tri suit that hasn't been tested.*] At the last minute before the race, I threw a bike jersey over the tri top. Boy, am I glad. About twenty steps into the run, my jiggling caused the top to ride up. After a half mile, the tri top had settled underneath my boobs. The *horror* if I had *not* been wearing the bike jersey. I cannot imagine.

At the Mile 1 sign, I looked behind me and there were only fifteen people back. Which meant about two hundred were in front of me. And at that moment, I tripped on a root and nearly lost my footing.

Somewhere along Mile 2, I heard a crack-pop and felt a sharp pain in my left hip. I kept going and the pain switched to a low, slow throbbing. As I was jogging through the woods, I was more or less alone. I finished the trail run, passing about six walkers, with my 5k time around 38 minutes.

The transition from run to bike was pretty fast and smooth and flawless for the big klutz. I even clipped into my pedals without incident. I gulped down a strawberry GU during the first mile on the bike. My first gel ever. Wow. Just as horrible as imagined. [Rookie mistake: *Do not do anything new on race day, ever, in a million years. Never. Especially nutrition.*]

My bike handling skills were terrible. I was terrified the entire time on the bike. Corners, manholes, and cracks in the road completely unraveled me. At Mile 2.5, a massive hill appeared out of nowhere. I was heaving and puffing like a four-hundred pound male smoker. This was really my first ride in the hills. Ever. [Rookie mistake: *Do not do anything new on race day, ever, in a million years. Never.*] I was sucking wind hard enough that people in *front* of me heard me coming, looked *behind* at me and glared, perhaps thinking a train was on their heels. *Choo Choo! I'm suffocating here, people! Choo Choo! Better Watch out! Slow Fat Know-Nothing Triathlete on the way up the hill!* I watched as other riders acknowledged the horribleness of the hill and one-by-one, dismounted their bikes and began walking up the hill.

I was suffering in the smallest gear, squeaking like rusty wheels, but I was *not* getting off that bike. My body was screaming, *WTF Stooooop!*

But I refused.

Around Mile 4, that evil hill was done. However, the course consisted of one hill after another. Still, I found myself finishing the twelve miles with very little drama, but with a very sore rear end. In fact, my rear end and the Queen were so sore, I didn't even remember the hip pain. Plus, I seriously was terrified the entire time. I realized that I had not ridden my bike nearly enough to be out on a race course. [Rookie mistake: *Do not do anything new on race day, ever, in a million years. Never. Learn to ride your bike. And well.*] I could not wait to get off the bike.

As I biked into the crowded transition area, I noticed a large spectator crowd. I saw one of the race volunteers pointing at me and waving his arms. He was screaming, "Dismount your bike! Dismount here! Dismount! *Dismount!*"

I panicked. [Rookie mistake: *Do not do anything new on race day, ever, in a million years. Learn to dismount your bike in a graceful and on-demand manner.*] I clipped my right foot out of the pedal, but my left foot was stuck. I braked hard and tried to avoid hitting the volunteer. I did not hit him. But I hit the pavement and hit hard, landing on the same left hip that throbbed during the run.

Those few seconds happened in slow motion. Me hitting the pavement. My jiggling body reverberating for ten seconds after the hit. The crowd screeched, "Gasp!" followed by "Ooooooh!" When I stood up, they let out a big "Ahhhhhh" of relief and clapped.

The same volunteer who scared me with his "dismount! dismount!" shenanigans had rushed over after the fall and tried to pick me up under my armpits like I was a toddler. He was about 120 pounds.

"No, no, no no no no no no, I've got it," I said, when I really wanted to scream, *If you try and pick me up, small fry, I am SO going to bring you down to the ground with me.*

I felt like a clown. The sports photographer continued to take pictures of me. *Really, dude? Really?* I ignored him, because I still had a swim to do. I unbuckled and unlatched everything and ran to the pool.

Another volunteer was screaming, "No diving! No diving!"

No diving? *Uh, I have that under control.* I forgot my swim cap in transition, so my hair was flopping in my face, but the pool swim was a piece of cake. Before I knew it, a pre-teen helped wrench me out of the pool (I tried not to unintentionally take *him* down with me), and I was finished. I didn't even finish last (although it was close).

The book *Slow Fat Triathlete* by Jayne Williams, has the following very valuable information: *a slow, fat triathlete must not care about what she looks like during a race.* That stuck with me during the race (and continues to stick). Between my super sexy tri top riding up to my boobs and the bike fall, I could have been devastated by the way I looked. But for once in my life, I did not care.

The next day, I realized I ~~probably~~ definitely overdid myself with my first tri. I rushed into it and I was hurting. My post-tri joints and muscles were blown to pieces. The pop-crack during the run, followed by the spill on the bike, was the beginning of my still-lingering hip problem. But I was elated.

ONE FOOT IN FRONT OF THE OTHER

I pondered whether that race made me an actual triathlete. However, I seriously hesitated to use the word "athlete" . . . let alone tri-athlete.

Was I triathlete? I doubted it.

First, because I did a reverse-format tri and managed to crash in transition in front of a ton of people. Second, because I had no self-confidence and I could not, in good faith, consider myself any sort of athlete. But regardless of the pain and the crashes, I still knew that I had been bitten by the triathlon bug.

I began looking at races for the next season and figuring out what I might consider for my Main Goal. The triathlon world as my oyster was exciting, but the amount of information available was mind-boggling. A mere search on Active.com was endurance overload.

So instead of picking my Main Goal right away, I scheduled another Quick Goal 5k for the next month. I finished *that* 5k with a first place win (okay, so what if I was the only one in my group?). On the drive home from that race, I felt amazing, confident and completely worn out. I wished I could run a race every weekend! I felt so amazing! At that point, I had only four 5ks and one sprint tri under my lifetime belt. Still on that day, I thought to myself: *this is something I want to do forever.*

So I began to seriously think about my Main Goal.

Slowly, the idea of an Olympic distance triathlon crept in my head. St. Anthony's triathlon in St. Petersburg, Florida was a huge Olympic distance, came highly recommended, and was only six months away.

I wondered . . .

WHAT A BOOB

A few days later, I went to the pool for a short swim and run. After I swam, I began the process of squeezing my *wet* self into *dry* clothing for the run. I stretched and pulled and grunted my sports bra over my head.

I thought I had succeeded with a successful operation of getting dressed, but as I looked in the mirror, I was horrified. I had one boob sticking out the top of the bra. Nice and supportive. After squeezing the Queen into the leggings with a whole bunch of squealing and squatting, I headed out to run.

To this day, I declare the training exercise of putting tight, *dry* clothing onto a *wet* body to be the most difficult part of triathlon.

HURTING

I was in denial about the left hip discomfort resulting from my run and fall-a-palooza at my first triathlon. I tried to grit through the pain, but slowly, the pain became unbearable. After my second 5k, I decided I must give myself a break and slow down the training a little. Up until this point, I was swimming twice a week, running twice a week, and usually attending indoor cycling classes twice a week. The weather had turned cold and I hated my old bike, so I stayed indoors mostly. So I left off a workout or two, here and there.

One morning, after a pitiful and painful two-mile run, I was angry and frustrated. Then, the following day I suited up and braved the chilly weather on the bike, only to return home after only two miles. A few days before Thanksgiving, I had attended cycling class, made it through five minutes and dismounted the bike and quit.

A friend cornered me after class, demanding to know why I bailed. I explained to her my hip was killing me, to the point of suffering the horrific embarrassment of leaving class. She worked for an orthopedic surgeon and worked me in that same day for an appointment. A dozen x-rays later, the doc scheduled me for an MRI.

So, that was the Monday before Thanksgiving. When I got home that afternoon, I was wringing my hands and crying, shouting to the Expert, "You might as well tie me to a giant bed, force feed me cheeseburgers, and pre-pay the wrecker to tear down a wall to haul my 1,000 pound butt out of the house when I die."

"Why?" he asked.

"Because that's what's going to happen!" I screamed.

He stared at me like he was married to a crazy woman. (He was/is.) I spent Thanksgiving weekend lying like a slug and eating a steady diet of crap and doughnuts. Just as quickly as I was on a triathlon high, I found myself in a funk again. I felt like absolute garbage heading back into the work week. I had a terrible attitude. I was not having a bad attitude *on purpose*. I just had one.

But even in the middle of the negativity, I was still thinking about St. Anthony's.

Paying the Registration Fee

I thought about it for a few days. I thought some more. I was not ready to give up, gimp hip or not. Poor attitude or not. I consulted the wise Mountain Goat who told me to go forth and register for the race.

So I did. I registered for St. Anthony's Triathlon, which would take place on May 1, 2011. The distances were: 0.9 mile swim, 24 mile bike, and 10k (6.2 mile) run.

I had five months to get ready.

St. Anthony's was my first experience with a big-time race registration. Apparently, you had a choice of categories to enter in a large race. *Am I an age-grouper, novice or Athena? Athena? What is Athena?* I wondered. A quick read revealed that an Athena racer was a category reserved for women over 150 pounds. *Yep, that's me.*

But wait. I was also an age grouper.

Ugh, I was *also* a novice racer. Did I want to be a "big" girl or a "new" (also big) girl or just an age grouper? The category was hard to pick for me. I needed help. I needed an expert.

I called the Expert.

"Which category do I choose?" I asked him.

He thought for a minute, and said, "Go with your people. Be with the large ladies."

Some might be offended by this statement. But it did not hurt my feelings in the slightest. He was right. The novice group could be "first time" triathletes who have been running marathons straight out of the womb. I would certainly feel better in my wetsuit looking around at fellow larger ladies in neoprene. Although, as I would learn later, sometimes the 150+ ladies are about 150.2 pounds, true to the name Athena with their goddess-like looks, muscular building and towering height.

"Yes, I should be with the large ladies," I said.

"Good," he replied.

"Well, hold your horses," I said before he hung up.

"What?"

"I am registering you too."

He was silent. I heard a sound (a gulp? a sigh?).

"Sounds like fun," he said quietly.

I registered the Expert for the category of Clydesdales—these are the big boys of triathlon—weighing 200 pounds and over.

As I clicked the "submit order" on our registrations, I was glad the site did not ask *how* much over 150 pounds I was. When the order confirmation page appeared, I wondered if I had just thrown good money after fat.

Later that same day, I lay in a coffin-like tube for the MRI on my hip. Forty-five minutes of minor panic attacks and freak outs later, I was out of the MRI coffin. I don't like small spaces. I prayed that I was just making up the hip pain and that it was nothing serious because any real injury was going to be so disappointing.

I hoped that all would be well, because Athena needed a win.

THE FIRST OFFICIAL INJURY

The MRI showed a contusion/hematoma/edema in two places in the hip (e.g., a bruised bone with fluid and swelling), but no stress fracture. Going over the MRI results, the doctor repeatedly asked me, "Have you fallen recently? Are you sure?"

I said, "No, no, no."

What an idiot I was. I had totally forgotten about the several wipeouts on the bike, including a hefty fall at that triathlon. The doctor prescribed rest and therapy for the bone injury. A few weeks later, I learned that I was also dealing with a mildly torn labrum in my hip, which would explain the pop and pain in my hip during that first triathlon run. [*See? Super Quick Goals are dangerous. Do as I say, not as I did.*] To say the least, neither diagnosis was great news, but I was determined to work through it. I was allowed to spin and swim, but ordered to stay off the run.

But only a week later, I was doing absolutely nothing. Nothing. No walking, no running, no cycling. I was wallowing. *What in the hell?* I had a *huge* race coming up!

List of things I *was* doing: eating and laying. I was stretching, too. Stretching my big fat arm out reaching for snacks in the pantry. I tried to give myself a break. But really, there was no justification or jingle bells for the amount of garbage I was eating and drinking. Eating junk and sitting like a slug for the better part of December was doing me no good physically or mentally. Not to mention, hello, I had registered for that race.

On Christmas Eve, I was ready to get moving again. Instead of waiting for the New Year, I made my 2011 resolutions early:

1. Run, bike, or swim five days a week;
2. Complete St. Anthony's in May; and
3. Run a half marathon for my 32nd birthday (November 2011).

I was going to get serious. *I was. I was.*

As far as the Expert? Well, he had not thought about triathlon much up until this point. I always have some new project, idea or bandwagon to join, so he chalked triathlon up to the same impulse that once led me to buy and re-sell over three hundred pairs of 2XL panties on eBay.

However, I think the Expert was feeling a tad Fat Stranger-ish himself. He was ready to get moving too. When I registered him for the race, he realized I was serious. He made some resolutions too.

RUNNING OUTSIDE

A few days later, I took to the outdoors for a three-mile run. I had not run *outside* yet.

What?

Oh yes, it's true. Well, I had run a few races, but I had never *trained* outside. Never.

This one small step was a big move for me. I was historically embarrassed to be seen exercising in public. Fat jiggling phobia. The treadmill at the gym, the side of the road—the precise location of public exercise did not matter. To me, the public jiggle was death.

But one day, I was driving down the road and saw a man and a woman running together. I continued driving, without giving them much thought. Suddenly, it occurred to me that if I went outside to run, chances were that no one would give me a second thought either. Maybe some people would notice, but mostly people were probably too concerned about their own troubles to worry about my jiggles. *Yes!*

So I went outside, and I ran. And it was wonderful.

THE BRICK

In February, the month after Coach Monster started training me, I had one of my first official brick workouts. That particular day was sixteen miles on the bike followed by a one-mile run. I took Antonia out and we had a great ride. Antonia was new at the time, and because she was fitted properly—unlike my previous bike—for the first time, riding the bike was not torture on my entire body. Purchasing Antonia was a good move. Having a bike I did not want to throw into a ditch and give the middle finger helped with my desire to cycle. So the bike ride was good, and I felt strong.

But, just having a new bike did not take away the fact that I was a real live cartoon character. It was chilly outside during the ride. As I was riding, I could feel a place on the back of my right thigh stinging. *Maybe numbness from the cold? Something pinched from the new saddle? Just general weirdness from my big buns riding on a bicycle, perhaps?*

I continued riding, but the stinging began to seriously irritate me. I stopped and hopped off the bike. I craned my neck, twisted my body, lifted my leg and looked at the back of my thigh. *Ripped pants and bleeding flesh! Ew!*

My bike bag had come loose and the sharp Velcro strap rubbed against my leg each time I pedaled, tearing a hole straight through my bike tights. The stinging I felt was not cold weather, but rather the scratchy Velcro tearing a hole in my skin. As I was craning my head around, lifting my leg and looking at my rear end like a move from *Naughty Cirque du Solei*, a redneck guy driving a truck pulled up alongside me. (And yes, I can say *redneck*, because being from the South, I can identify a redneck as clearly as I can identify a large pizza... and most rednecks consider the nickname a badge of honor.)

"Hey hey hey, do you need some help?" He leaned out the truck window and looked me up and down six times, country music blaring from the radio. Then he winked at me.

I mumbled, "No thanks, I've got it." I was thinking, *Not the kind of help you are offering, Jimmy Bobby Redneck, Jr.*

After Jimmy Bobby Jr. drove away, I mended the Velcro crisis and finished up the ride. I zoomed into my driveway, rolled the bike into the house, stripped off my bike shoes and laced up my sneakers, ready for part two of my brick.

I took off running. *Only one mile to run! Here I go!*

About ten steps past the driveway and down the road, my hands flew to my head and I screamed, "Oh crap!"

I was still wearing my helmet. *My helmet!* I was wearing my helmet, running down the street. I realized at that moment that I was a special breed of triathlon nightmare.

Once I deposited my helmet on the front porch and properly took off running, I could not believe how crazy my legs felt. Just like bricks. Ah-ha! *That's why they call it...* The brick feeling subsided right about the time I finished my one mile.

10 Week Countdown

The list of competitors for St. Anthony's was released via the website. I skimmed it. My name was really on the list, along with the Expert's. At that point, I had swam a mile, biked seventeen, and run five miles. Not all in a row, but separately in single workouts. Putting these distances all together on race day would be the big kicker.

The workouts were gaining momentum and intensity. Coach Monster was really taking the guess work out of the triathlon confusion and craziness. I would read what he assigned and feel like he was absolutely insane, but then I would do the workout and that would be the story. No guesswork was necessary.

I knew the race would be exhausting, probably one of the most difficult things I would ever do. I also knew that I would be unable to walk for a week. Still, I believed in my heart that the race was doable. I went back to my favorite gun-to-the-head analogy.

At ten weeks out, I believed that if someone put a gun to my head, I could do the race.

6 Week Countdown

About six weeks before the race, I had a confidence-boosting brick workout, which consisted of twenty-three miles on the bike and a two-mile run. I remembered to take off my helmet before running, so that was a plus.

The bad news was that I got smashed in the face by a wood bee while heading downhill. That seriously hurt. Also, my cycling shorts rode down in the back and at one point around Mile 18, I could not bear to think about my butt crack anymore and sang *Brick House* out loud, "letting it all hang out."

The two mile run was misery, but accomplished.

The next day was something of a 2000 meter swim and yet another run. My shoulders were screaming by the time that swim was over. My legs were crying after the run. Coach Monster had been telling me that he was going to keep piling it on. His theory is to suffer in training so that race day feels easy. At six weeks out, I had to laugh at the thought of race day being "easy."

A few days later, I ran six miles. The run distance of the race. *Oh my goodness...this is actually going to happen*, I thought.

5 Week Countdown

I was starting to get the itch for the race. I felt weird, sort of ready, but mostly scared. But I also wanted to do a fun race, a new Quick Goal. I wanted the boost.

Coach Monster said that a 5k was not on the training plan at this juncture.

But I begged, so he said yes. I hit the 2011 Atlanta Women's 5k race, a massive event of 2,000 racers. All women. All running in the same direction. A man's complete and utter nightmare.

I learned quite a bit from running a race of this size. First and foremost, it is vitally important to get to the Porta-Potties early. While there may be plenty of johns for capacity, there is much less chance of landing in one with a giant stink bomb if you manage to pre-race potty early. For that matter, I think it's a smashing idea to get to the race early. My best pal, Mountain Goat, likes to show up to the race about three minutes before the start, leap out of her car and run. But she's crazy and cannot be trusted.

The Atlanta Women's 5k taught me to pay attention. Seriously. When you run—pay attention! I had no idea. I learned, though. I needed to watch where I was going the entire race. Potholes. Roots. Caution cones. Especially in a race of that size, where other runners were literally, everywhere. The race started off like a 5k sandwich.

Another thing to remember is where you park. This race finished in a different place than the start (which I tend to think is a dumb way to do things, but no one asked me). I did a little wandering around post-race before I figured out where I was and where I had parked. I wandered in front of a golfer during his shot on the adjacent golf course. He loved that.

I learned to check my mile markers. The other alternative is to purchase a reasonable GPS watch. My base-model Garmin and Foot Pod, which allegedly tracks distance and pace, was just plain wrong, wrong, wrong. After completing this race, Garmin stated that I completed 3.63 miles at a 10:00 pace. I realized that she was a dirty little liar. The race ended (3.1 miles), and my time was 34:15, an 11:00- minute mile pace. Those numbers did not work. Therefore, Garmin appeared to be off by about 0.2 of a mile (for every mile that I ran). After this race, I learned to be more careful with blind dependence on gadgets. During my training, I had believed I was running farther and faster than I was. But it was a good lesson to learn.

Regardless, the good news was that I was faster on that day than the race before. A prior 5k time ended at 36:11. This race was 34:15, which was just plain improvement.

4 WEEK COUNTDOWN

A seven-mile run popped up on the training schedule. I sent Coach Monster an email, "What? Are you crazy? Who is going to pick me up from the hospital after that?"

Seconds after sending the email, my phone rang. It was him.

"Are you serious?" he asked.

"About dying from seven miles? Yes, I'm serious," I said.

"Let me ask you a question."

"Shoot," I said.

Coach Monster asks, "Did you land in the hospital after 6 miles last week?"

I sat quietly, and did not respond.

"Hello???" he said loudly.

"No, master Ironman, sir," I shouted.

"So you mean to tell me that you can't run *one* more mile than last week?" he asked.

I thought for a minute. "Do you mean run outside?"

"What!!?" He paused, clearly frustrated. "Hey Missy! Does triathlon take place indoors?"

"Well, not usually, but I have seen those ones that Lifetime Fitne—"

"—The answer is: no. *No*, triathlon does not take place indoors. So yes, you should run outside," he huffed at me.

"Okay. I understand," I said. Then I whispered, "What about all those hills?"

"Hills?? Hills? You are worried about hills?"

"No. Not really. I mean, it's just—"

"—Yes, you run *outside* with the other people. On the hills. Got it?"

"Yes, I've got it."

I hung up and stuck my tongue out at the phone thinking, *I hate that Smarty Pants Ironman. Seven miles? Seven miles?!?*

I fretted for the entire day. I had never run seven miles (in my life). I had not even imagined running seven miles (in my life).

In the morning, I trudged out to a park just a few short miles from the house. I looked at the map near the parking lot. Five laps around the large trail equalled seven miles. I had new music on the iPod. *I am ready*, I thought.

Then the rain came. *Okay, I am still ready.*

During the run, I passed a guy (running the opposite direction on the trail) who was as slow and fluffy as I was. We smiled a little mutual encouragement. By the second time I saw him, I stuck up my hand and high-fived him. He played along a few more times, but by the end of the run, he tried to avoid eye contact with me. I still held out my hand. He high-fived me. *What a trooper! Yes!* An hour and twenty-one minutes later, I had completed the entire seven miles. I ran the full seven without stopping or being taken to the hospital.

I almost whispered to myself, *Good job.* For the first time, I believed that I was a runner. I ran. I was slow, but I was steady. Yes, that made me a runner.

Breakfast on the Go

After a Friday morning cycling class, I went to a fast food joint for a quick breakfast. I knew it was a bad idea, but I was in a hurry, had failed to prepare, so I was about to experience a big fail.

I pulled up to the drive-thru, rolled down my window and ordered something very reasonable: a plain breakfast wrap with egg and coffee. I asked if they had salsa (they did not). I reminded them that I did not want cheese or anything else (they understood).

"A plain egg wrap, no cheese. A large coffee," I said into the speaker.

"Do you want bacon?"

"No," I said, "Please no bacon. Just plain egg and wrap. Actually, do you have egg whites?"

"Who?"

"What?" I asked.

"Egg who?" the speaker asked.

"Egg whites, do you—"

"—no, we only got egg yellows."

"Egg yellows?"

"Yeah."

I stared at the speaker in disbelief. *Egg yellows?*

"Alright. Just yellow eggs and a wrap. Thanks."

"Drive around."

As I drove down the road with my decently healthy food sitting in brown bag in the seat beside me, I felt proud of myself. Proud that I did not give in to the Fat Stranger screaming: *Get the bacon, cheese biscuit! Oh, and a cinnamon roll! Two cinnamon rolls!*

So, I was on a bit of a high from spin class, feeling proud from ordering healthy and I thought I was ready to tackle my day. As I opened my little healthy breakfast on the highway, I gasped.

I was clutching a steaming hot wrap filed with egg alright.

But it was *also* boiling over with sausage, cheese and (wait for it…wait for it…) hash browns. Hash brown potatoes, snuggled up to the sausage and cheese. I cursed out loud and hit my steering wheel.

Dammit! I tried to do the right thing! I tried! I tried to be healthy! And this! *This!?* I was so mad. So mad.

So I ate it.

8 Mile

Next, as you might predict, an eight-mile run appeared on the Monster Schedule. Eight miles. After surmounting the seven-mile run of the week before, I was summoned to do eight? Coach Monster was certifiable.

I hit the same park where I ran the ominous seven miler. The good thing about the park and the loop course was the bathroom. I do not mean that anything special was happening with this bathroom, but rather the good thing was the mere *presence* of the bathroom.

On Mile 4.5, I thought I would be forced to dodge into the bushes. The stomach cramping. The rumblings. *Oh no oh no oh no.* I stumbled the half mile back around to the bathroom at the park. I was prairie-dogging, puckering and limping—all the moves I could muster to hold it all in. As I crashed into the bathroom, I thought, *I guess I'm done with this run.*

Then I thought, *Well, if I was in a race, I'd have to keep going or get picked up by the quit-mobile.*

I started some serious self-talk babble. Self-talk babble always begins with the word "well." *Well, I can surely run 2.5 miles and finish this up! Yes, I can!* This self-talk was happening while I was hovering over the toilet and playing peek-a-boo with a toddler who was sticking his head under the stall door.

Yes, you can. Yes, you can.

Sigh.

I looked at the toddler and squealed "Ooooh, peek-a-boo!"

Then I thought, *Well, what if I pass out? What if I fall down? What if I actually poop my pants this time?* But really, there was no time for negative talk. I needed to get home. I needed to make my 10:00 conference call. I needed to get a move on, one way or the other. After three or so more minutes in the john, the toddler was gone, the cramping had slowed and I felt semi-normal.

I grinded out the final 2.5 miles while gritting my teeth and singing explicit "8 Mile" Eminem lyrics out loud. The children on the playground and their mothers stared at me distastefully. Okay, so I was not really singing out loud. But I *was* struggling so hard that I received a heap of weird stares.

The last quarter mile, my knee and hip said, "We are done." I was having back spasms and my stomach said, "Hello, here's your breakfast, looking at you." I limped the last bit and brought it home.

Eight miles.

This run went down as the one of my five most difficult runs ever. But hours later and even now, I am thankful that I did not walk off the loop that day. Even though, I really, really wanted to hang that one up. Even though my body had given up on me. Even though I almost pooped my pants.

Those eight miles took me an hour and forty-five minutes to complete. Knowing that many people run half marathons in that time did not matter a hill of Jim Beam. Because on that day on that run, I gave it everything I had. Everything…but what I left in the bathroom.

THE BONK

Just as quickly as I felt good about myself, I experienced my first official bonk. And not the good kind. Something about a true "bonk" will rip a person apart. A bonk is also known as "hitting the wall" and pretty much feels like absolute crap murder poop face pain. As Ilana mentioned in Part I, Chapter Eleven, the triathlon bonk is caused by a depletion of glycogen storage in the body. Usually, you bonk because you are under-fueled.

I started out a brick workout at Harbins Park, a precious park about seven miles from my house. The goal was a twenty-eight mile ride plus a run of four miles. I mapped my cycling route on a Post-It note, zipped the tiny square up in a plastic bag and stuffed it in my sports bra. As I set out, the weather was fine and I was zooming down a hill.

Then…radio nowhere!

I apparently missed my turn and ended up somewhere wrong. But I actually knew where I was: it was the seventh circle of cycling hell. I looped and looped, ended up crawling up hill after hill. I was going up one hill at four miles an hour. I was not ready for this kind of mileage and hills, and I started to feel shaky around Mile 20. I used every ounce of love and willpower I had to ride back to the park. I hit the park at Mile 26, and knowing I still had two more miles on the schedule, I went one mile past the park and doubled-back. 28 miles done. I felt like death when I strapped on my sneakers for the run.

For the second time in my triathlon life, I forgot to take off my helmet when I began to run. *Crap!* Back to the car, I went. I took off running at the pace of what could have only been a fifteen-minute mile pace. I managed 1.5 miles and sat down on a bench. I do remember stopping. I do not remember sitting down. I just knew I was sitting. Then I got cold, and I knew that could not be a good sign. I stood up and walked/jogged back to the car, ending up with only 2.6 miles on my so-called run.

A sorry, crappy 2.6 miles at that.

Maybe I could have finished, but I was completely out of it, out of body. B-b-b-b-bonked. I had no other choice but to throw in the towel.

Later, it clicked: an English muffin with peanut butter, eaten three hours prior and nothing else during the entire workout is *not* enough fuel for a twenty-eight-mile ride plus four-mile brick run. *Duh.*

OPERATION WETSUIT

Coach Monster told me that if I didn't have a wetsuit for my training, I had better get one. I knew that day would come. I had been dreading it. I was not sure if I would need a wetsuit for the race itself. But I needed to get to the lake for a swim in the open water, because that's where triathlon swims usually happen. In open water. *Scary open water.*

Google said that the water in the nearby Lake Lanier was a lovely sixty-one degrees, which in case you were wondering, feels like ice. I noticed that

Coach Monster had scheduled an open water swim for me just a few weeks down the road. Time to get on board with the wetsuit.

The Expert and the kids were watching *Jumanji*, while I browsed wetsuits online. Out of the blue, I piped up.

"You know, I think I'm going to have to get a men's wetsuit," I said.

The Expert looked at me.

I continued, "Because the women's wetsuits are going to be too small."

He looked at me and laughed. "You know," he said, "that's something I never thought I'd hear come out of your mouth. 'I think I'm going to need a wetsuit.'" He continued, "I mean, we get married and I could never anticipate some things you say. But that statement takes the cake."

I started giggling too.

"I imagine it won't be the last weird thing I say doing this triathlon thing," I said.

I thought to myself: *my legs are going to fall off* and *are there sharks in this water?* were probably also things I would say in my triathlon future.

I realized that I could not shop for a wetsuit online. I had no clue what to get. I emailed Coach Monster who told me: take your triathlon clothing to All3Sports and get *fitted* for the wetsuit. *Oh, the horror. Someone to fit me? Into a wetsuit? What did that mean? Would I have to get naked??* Regardless, I was not getting out of the wetsuit ordeal. If I wanted to do an open water swim, then I needed a wetsuit to practice swimming in the frigid open water at the nearby lake.

The day before my scheduled wetsuit fitting, Coach Monster asked me again if I had a wetsuit. I wanted to yell at him, *No! And stop pestering me, man!* But instead, I told him that I had read the horrors of wetsuits for fat-bottomed girls in my *Slow Fat Triathlete* book and I was absolutely terrified.

He told me, "Suck it up and stop with the negative self-talk!"

"Easy for zero-fat-bottomed Ironman to say," I muttered under my breath.

I was feeling helpless and ridiculous. The wetsuit was the part of triathlon that felt most cruel. Me in neoprene? Ugh.

On The Day, my worst fear was realized.

If a wetsuit fits properly, then it will be tight as all hell and require mad skills to properly put it on. Truer words have never been uttered. Wetsuits are like the most evil type of Spanx® imaginable.

I walked into All3Sports very scared. A super fit saleswoman looked at me suspiciously when I asked her about trying on a wetsuit. She eyed my pants.

"Did you bring anything to change into?" she asked me.

"Yep, yep yep, got it right here in my purse." She did not look convinced.

The sizing chart for the women's suit said to add ten pounds to your *normal* weight and find *that* weight on the chart. Wherever you fell, there was your wetsuit size. Well, it wasn't *adding ten* pounds that sent me into the men's sizing chart. Perhaps if the chart said: add fifty pounds.

"Height? Weight?" she asked. *Now is not the time to pull the twenty pound lie. I need this suit to actually fit*, I told myself. So I took a deep breath and mumbled the numbers. She disappeared for the span of a lifetime and returned with a suit. The suit was shiny and pretty. And had O-R-C-A spelled across the chest.

"Super. ORCA?" I whined.

"ORCA is a great suit," she said.

"Yeah, for someone like you, Miss Teeny," I said, huffing. Secretly, I was glad to be helped by a female (albeit one with zero body fat). I could just imagine Mr. Male Triathlete wrestling my body into a suit, not knowing what to do with all my extra…stuff.

So Miss Teeny walked me through the ins and outs of wetsuit handling, from turning it inside-out and pulling from the inside of the suit only to avoid tearing the neoprene. The whole thing was amazingly difficult. I stopped and had a bit of an out-of-body experience, hovering over myself, as I tend to do quite often. I watched myself struggling into this suit and the whole thing was ridiculous. *I could be at the Olive Garden having all you can eat salad and breadsticks right now! What am I doing here?*

My fingers started cramping before I had the suit over my hips. Miss Teeny helped me pull it up on the arms. This is why it's a good idea to have a buddy help with the wetsuit (you shouldn't be swimming alone anyway!).

A grand total of forty-five minutes later, I was zipped up and ORCA proud. I shook my head as I looked in the mirror, thankful that triathlon is not a beauty pageant.

After the initial shock of the wetsuit applying process, Miss Teeny told me the secret: L-U-B-E. A can of spray lube safe for the wetsuit (I like TriSlide now). We were not allowed to use it because, obviously, I had not purchased the suit. But she told me to lather that stuff all over my body (ankles, wrist, arms, legs, everywhere), the suit would slide on a million times easier. I was glad to hear it, because if the wetsuit process was that bad all the time, I would be forced to give up my triathlon dreams.

I walked out of All3Sports with the men's version of the ORCA brand suit. Orca. A whale suit. A freaking Free Willy freak show. But the mission was accomplished and something about the wetsuit made the Main Goal feel very *real*. Carrying the wetsuit out to the car. Texting Coach Monster to tell him that the original Free Willy had been found. It all felt legit. Too legit to quit (obviously).

THE FIRST OPEN WATER SWIM: PANIC. BIKE. WALK.

PANIC.

Two weeks before the race and on the morning of my first open water swim, it was forty-three degrees. The lake was a chilly sixty-two degrees. The babysitter arrived, and the Expert and I headed out to the lake while it was still dark. We drove for thirty minutes and stopped at the gate to Lake Lanier's Mary Alice Park.

I could not get a read on the Expert about his thoughts on the open water swim. We had secured *his* wetsuit earlier that week, with a little less freakiness than mine, but he had not said much about swimming in the lake. Swimming was definitely his weakness out of the triad, whereas I felt swimming was my strength. Maybe he was quiet because he was scared to death too.

The older gentleman guarding the park entrance asked, "You swimming today?"

I looked across at the Expert and said, "Yep. Where's the beach?"

The guard whistled and shook his head, "Oh, *you're* the one *he* was talking about."

He? He? He who? Ooooooh. I sucked in my breath. *Coach Monster.*

Coach Monster had apparently beaten us to the park and warned the guard (and perhaps, the Coast Guard) about me.

The guard waved us through. "This will be the hardest thing you've ever done. If you can survive this water, this cold, you can survive anything," he said.

Duly noted, I thought.

Coach Monster had talked to *me* just the day before. "I will go with you to the Lake. I'll be there anyway for a swim," Coach Monster had said.

"No," I said, "Really, I'm sure I'll be fine. No need."

"I'm going. See you there."

That was the end of the conversation. He had spoken. And he was there.

I was geared up, all fidgety and hyper. As we pulled through the gates, I saw Coach Monster and other people milling about. *Oh no,* I thought. *Others. Real triathletes. And me. And the Expert. No. No no no no.* My heart raced. The Expert parked the car. We fumbled with our gear and wetsuits at the back of the car. The Expert and I had matching wetsuits. (Stupid ORCA sale. Two little love whales.)

Coach Monster spotted us. We all made introductions. I think that was the first time my Expert met my Monster. We chit-chatted while putting on our wetsuits. Coach M helped the Expert wiggle into his suit by pulling up the suit from the back to get the suit up as high as possible.

The Expert looks pretty cute in that wetsuit, I winked at him. *We could have some fun in our suits later…Oh, never mind.*

WETSUIT TIP

A goal with the wetsuit, much like pantyhose, is to have the thing as high in the crotch as possible. Not for looks, obviously, but rather this practice reduces the pressure on the shoulders and chest, making for better, less-claustrophobic fit. Just use extreme caution when pulling…

As I pulled on my suit, the Expert decided to be a Super Expert. Attempting to mimic Coach Monster's helpful yank on *his* suit, the Expert turned me around and gave my suit a good pull from the rear.

Yank! Rip! I gasped. "Did you just rip my wetsuit?!" I wailed.

"No. No, uh, no," he mumbled.

"Oh my gawd! Did you just rip my wetsuit?!" I screamed louder.

"Yes," he stuttered, "Oh no. I'm sorry!" He was pleading with his puppy dog eyes, looking as shocked as I was.

"Oh, for the love," I mumbled, shooting him dead with open water daggers from my eyes.

I was not mad, if you can believe it. Rather, I was absolutely horror-stricken. I had heard of wetsuits being filled with water, followed by sinking and inevitable death. Okay, that's not completely true. But I have heard that a wetsuit can fill up with water. Regardless, I was freaked. The good thing was that my suit fit like a neoprene spray-on tan, so I did not completely fear the sinking issue. No water was getting inside that whale versioned Spanx®. *Panic Number One.*

As I walked towards the beach in my holey wetsuit with the Expert and Coach Monster, I was so freaking nervous. But my subconscious told me that I would be okay. I fastened my swim cap, my goggles. I walked into the lake, up to the ankles. A thin film of yellow pollen covered the surface of the water. The water was cold. Really cold. *It's okay,* I told myself, *you have been in cold water before.*

I waded up to my thighs, then my belly. I had a flashback to my weightlifting days and the notorious ice baths. The chill took my breath away. The water crept up to my elbows and finally my shoulders. My heart was pounding. *This $^!# is cold. This $^!# is also bananas.*

Then I put my face in the water. The instant my face hit the water, I gasped and inhaled what could only have been the entire lake. The shock of sixty-something degree water on my face floored me and I immediately panicked and snapped my head out of the water, sputtering.

Beginner's bad luck. I got this. I stuck my face into the water for a second time. I gasped yet again and inhaled more pollen-filled water into my lungs. My body was fighting me. Each time I placed my face in the water, I tried my best not to inhale, but the reaction was automatic: I sucked in water. *Crap crap crap. $^!#. Bananas. $^!#. Bananas. Crap.*

Coach Monster gestured out to the lake. "We're going to swim out to that first buoy and then take a left and swim to each of those four buoys and circle back."

I could not breathe.

The pressure on my shoulders and chest from the wetsuit was mind-boggling. I had been warned that the wetsuit would make my chest feel heavy. But I was not prepared for the coffin-like feeling on my chest, my back, my shoulders and my entire upper body. The pressure felt like an elephant. *Was I having a heart attack? Panic Number Two.*

I am severely claustrophobic. With my face in the dark water, I was certain that I was burying myself alive. *Panic Number Three.* I tried to swim forward, but I could not freestyle. I could not manage to breaststroke, sidestroke or even float. I was completely paralyzed. I swam three strokes, but then I would shoot up gasping all again. I saw Coach Monster 100 meters away, gesturing and shouting, "Just come to the buoy."

If only it were that simple, Iron dude, I thought.

But three strokes at a time, I made it to the buoy. I looked back and saw the Expert. I don't think he was *behind* me, *per se. He* seemed fine. More like he was waiting for me and guarding the closest-to-shore position in case I needed to be dragged there. I clawed at the slick sides of the buoy, searching and begging for a place to grab on. *There's nowhere to grab on this damn buoy!* I finally understood why drowning people take down others in the process of their drowning. When I couldn't get a grip on the buoy, it took everything I had inside *not* to wrap my arms around Coach Monster and use him as a life preserver. (I would have chosen the Expert to grab, but I needed him to be alive to raise the children if I drowned. I couldn't be taking the father of my kids down with me. Coach Monster, while very beloved and dear to my heart, would have been necessarily sacrificed.)

I continued to claw at the buoy, whispering to Coach Monster, "I. Can. Not. Breathe. I. Need. To. Go. Back." I could not estimate how much surface pollen I had swallowed. *Panic Number Four. Anaphylactic semi-shock.*

My mind flashed to that scene from the HBO comedy "Sex and the City" where the lead character, Carrie, tries on a wedding gown and immediately breaks out into hives and rips the wedding gown from her body, deciding that she could not possibly get married. I felt exactly that way: *I could not possibly do triathlon.* I needed the freaking wetsuit off my Orca body. *Panic Number Five. The pressure on my chest. The panic. I was overwhelmed.*

Coach Monster was talking to me. I could see his lips moving, but I could not hear him. He was attempting to lock eyes with me, but I was having trouble maintaining eye contact. The Expert was doing okay. I could see him and Coach Monster exchanging glances. *Stop talking about me with your eyes,* I wanted to shout at them. *But just get me out of here, boys. Please. Please.*

I swam out a little farther. I listened to Coach Monster's calm Barry White voice, but the panic would not subside. I looked at the Expert, who seemed just fine, but his eyes were wide as saucers as he watched me. Coach Monster looked calm, but he was starting to have trouble hiding his concern. He urged me to stop flailing my arms.

"Lay on your back," he said, "Just float. Relax."

I barrel-rolled over and floated on my back. But the pressure was worse and being on my back more closely resembled burying death by wetsuit. *Panic Number Six.* I felt the tears coming. I just floated upright and bobbed around while my goggles filled with tears. Coach Monster was still talking. I heard the Charlie Brown teacher in his Barry White voice. *Wah wah wah wah, I can't get enough of your love, wah wah wah, I don't know why, I can't get enough of your love, babe, wah wah wah. . .* I looked at the Expert, beseeching him with my eyes and wanting him to stop this somehow.

Screw it, I finally thought. *The longer I bob here, the longer I'm going to be stuck out here.* I looked at the boys, the buoys and said, "I'm ready. Let's go." I had to swim, so I could get out of that water. Seeing as how Coach M was apparently *not* letting me make a beeline for shore, I figured I better get to the next buoy and the next and the next, so I could *then* get to shore.

The three of us swam to the next buoy. And the next. And the next. I would start off okay, but then five strokes in to each set, I sat up, sputtering and gasping and melting down from the fear. I was wheezing profusely. Face back in the water, swim a few strokes, feel like I was being buried alive, then pop up again, panic and cry. *Panics Number Seven Through Eleven.*

At the end of thirty minutes, the Expert, Coach Monster and I had made complete circle of the buoys, about 800 meters. At the last buoy, I turned towards shore. I doggie paddled back to the beach, the whole time praying that I would make it back to the sand before my heart exploded.

Once on land, I was dizzy.

I was deflated.

I was scared.

But I was mostly sad.

I had believed that the swim would be my thing—the best part of triathlon for me. But thanks to the blasted wetsuit, the cold water, the compression coupled with some sort of crazy allergic reaction and a 100% panic attack, I felt as if I would be forced to give up triathlon.

My workout for the day was a scheduled mini-triathlon. The swim was behind me, so I decided to move on, keep my head up and conquer the bike.

Bike.

I was still wheezing after a fifteen minute T1. Coach Monster, the Expert and I mounted our bikes. Three's Company slowly pedaled away from the parking lot. I still could not breathe. My heart rate was in low Zone 2, but I was sucking wind like I was running hill repeats. A few minutes later, I saw spots across my eyes and I could not keep up with Coach Monster and the Expert, who were already going slow for my sake.

I slurped down a gel, thinking the eye spots needed some fuel, but I choked on it twice. We went out five miles and I had to stop. I told the boys, "I just can't. I j-j-j-ust can't."

They agreed. My plans for a twenty-mile bike ride were crushed.

Walk.

I spent ten minutes in faux T2, still trying to catch my breath. I thought I was feeling a little better when the three of us took off for the run. I took a few steps. Coach Monster asked, "Do you think you can handle running? Are you still breathing through a straw? We need to be careful here."

I nodded twice, answering affirmatively to both questions. "I can do it," I said.

I ran 100 yards. *Nope.* I could not do it. I was wheezing. I looked at my Garmin. My heart rate was in Zone 1, but I could not breathe. I was done. I told the Expert to finish his run. I would not be joining him.

Coach Monster looked at me nonchalantly and said, "We'll walk." So we did.

Truth be told? I was absolutely humiliated. Forget the humiliation of wearing a wetsuit, because the failure was so much worse. We walked out for some time, until we could no longer see the Expert running. Coach M talked to me, calmly. I was able to get my breathing under control. He was so compassionate, so kind to me that day. Yes, I was embarrassed, but somehow he would not let me accept the embarrassment as a final exclamation point on my triathlon dream.

He veered me in other directions. He talked through facts and details. He told me stories of his bad training and racing moments. He made me feel better. We walked back to the car, and I hugged him, apologizing.

"No need to apologize," he said, matter of factly. "This happens to everyone at some point during triathlon. You just got yours out of the way early. We'll get you there. You can do this."

A few moments later, the Expert came into view, successfully finishing his four-mile run. I felt about six inches tall. And six feet wide. And all of this happened *two weeks* before the race. *Two weeks!*

Later, I wondered what Coach Monster told his friends and his wife about my day. Did he say, "You should have seen this freak show. This girl will never do a triathlon"?

Knowing him as I do now, I think he said, "This girl just took ten years off my life, but we'll get her there." To this day, I do not know what he said to *others* after that day, but I know what he *never* said *to* me. He never once told me that I would fail. He never once blinked and said, *Maybe you should take up cross-stitching.* He never gave up on me. Not once, not for a single second.

And because of him, I kept going.

REFLECT.

As the Expert drove me home, I was emotionally and physically broken. "It's okay, baby," the Expert said to me. "You just had a bad day. It's okay."

"Were you scared out there?" I asked him.

"Yes, I was. But I was too worried about you."

The day had been beautiful. I had been prepared. I had put in the effort, the training. Everything had been set up for a great day. But I completely crashed. That swim was the first time I had ever experienced a pure panic attack. I had birthed two babies. During labor, I was 90% certain that entire bottom half would be ripped open like a scene from a horror movie, but I was never even close to scared like that first open water day. The panic attack was so terrible, that I landed in the doctor's office the next day with a round of steroids and a shot.

Coach Monster sent me home with the task of figuring out what I learned from the horrible experience.

Not at first, but after a few days, I began to turn the fear I had experienced into something positive. Even though the swim experience was a slice to my heart, something in me changed that day. Five years ago, if I had encountered that kind of difficulty, I would have undoubtedly said, *F it!* I would have walked away. I would have said, *Guess I'll never be able to do an open water triathlon. Guess I'm a loser. Guess that's it. Poor me. I suck. Waaa.*

While I was panicking in the water, I battled these exact thoughts. But as the hours passed, the distance from the fear increased. I was able to turn the fear around into something positive. All that ran through my head: *I can't wait to get back out to that lake and figure this out.*

Later that night, I sat on the back porch with the Expert and drove him crazy with my plans, my open water swim fixes for the next time. I talked and talked and talked through the fear. I told him, "Two weeks from today, I will finish the swim at St. Anthony's. And that's that. I may be wearing my wetsuit to the pool every night for the next two weeks, but I'm going to make it."

He listened.

"But," I repeated over and over again, "I can do this." I told the Expert over and over, "I think I can. I really think I just need another chance." I talked to myself, *You can. It was just a fear. You know you can conquer it. You can.*

He listened some more.

"You can," he said, smiling.

Just Keep Swimming

Triathletes rely on the animated Pixar movie "Finding Nemo" more than adults probably should. But the fish Dory's advice is priceless, especially in the wake of scary swims, open water panic attacks and general ickiness.

> *"When life gets you down...*
> *You know what you gotta do?*
> *Just keep swimming, just keep swimming..."*
>
> — Finding Nemo

With only eight days left until St. Anthony's, I knew I had to grab the Orca by the flippers, get back to the open water and somehow just keep swimming. I told Coach Monster that I did not want him to bother coming to my second swim (panic attack?), but he insisted. I think he needed a clear coach conscience with me going into the race—that way, if I drowned he would know he did what he could do—twice. I could not bear the humiliation, but the Coach named Monster was relentless.

"I'll be there," he said.

In my fretting about Coach M showing up, it suddenly occurred to me that *my* swim experience was all about *me*—the new relationship with myself and finding the courage to make it happen. I was desperately trying. And despite the fear, I tried to enjoy the pre-race process. I tried to relax, but I was not sure that I was following my own advice.

The Expert called me on his way to work. I was at my desk already.

"I didn't hear you get up this morning. What time did you leave?" the Expert asked over the phone.

"Oh, about 4:50," I said.

He asked, "How was Spinning class?"

"Just great. Good class."

He paused for a minute. "Did I imagine this, or did you get up at 2:00 this morning, leave the bedroom and come back to tell me that you tried on *my* wetsuit?"

"No. You didn't imagine that. Yeah, I wanted to see if yours fit me better than mine fit me," I replied. "With the hole and all," I added.

He ignored the last comment. "At 2:00am? You were trying on wetsuits? In the middle of the night?" he asked.

"No. Just wetsuit. One. Yours."

"In the living room? In the dark?" he questioned.

I paused. "No, I was in the kids' playroom."

"You are insane."

I said, "Am not. I couldn't sleep."

"Then you got back in the bed and woke up at 4:30 for Spinning?" he asked.

"Yes."

He paused, "So, how did it fit?"

"It's too big," I said. "I think I need the size in between yours and mine."

"Well, glad you found that out," he replied. "At two o'clock in the morning. In the playroom."

Because of the hole in my current suit and with no time for repair I went to All3Sports again to get a new (larger) wetsuit. Miss Teeny helped me again. She assured me that I would be fine with a looser suit, because the peace of mind from not feeling completely buried alive would go a long way towards my confidence.

Miss Teeny then gave me that excellent advice that bears repeating:

> "During an open water swim, do not let a single negative thought creep in your head. If you feel a negative thought coming, push it away. Sing a song, breaststroke, but do not let negativity in."

These were some of the most powerful words I have received in triathlon. True, the prior week's swim had been a complete and utter disaster. But I would not let that one incident define *me*. I would not focus on the panic. In fact, I would not even think about panic.

To this day, I am blown away at the vast differences between a pool swim and an open water swim. Yes, I had read about it, but until I experienced the swim firsthand, I had no idea. I had read everything I could find about open water. But people who *write* about open water swims do not use enough exclamation points (!!!!!!!!).

Regardless, I began working on swimming visualizations and repeating "just keep swimming." Coach Monster told me that someday I would laugh about the whole experience. I hoped he was right, because the whole thing was not really that funny to me.

And a few days passed. The time had come to "tri" the open water again.

OPEN WATER: PART DEUX

I was back. The older gentleman at the park gate paid me no mind this time and I was thankful.

Coach Monster probably told him, "Say *nothing* to her! Do you hear me?! Be quiet! Don't even make eye contact with her!"

The water was equally icy as before, but my head was on straight. I did not panic. In fact, I did not even think about panic.

Coach Monster was there as promised. I swam about 800 meters without thinking, dying or freaking. I swam crooked, but I straightened out. I swallowed water, but I did not choke. My wetsuit was awful, but tolerable. After that, I hit a fifteen-mile bike in the rain with the Expert. And then a run. Quickly, it was over, and I felt like I could have done a half marathon. (Okay, maybe a 10k).

What changed? A few things, actually. I spent the week telling myself that I could do it. I removed the negative thoughts from my head. I purged the negative words from my vocabulary. When I entered the cold water, I did so slowly. Up to the knees, and then I waited. Up to the hips, and then I waited some more. I took time to lower my face into the water. Then I waited some more. I was cautious but deliberate. I had worked on my mind—and my body had worked *for* me.

Upon leaving the park, I felt ready for my race. I felt thankful. Being a wife, a mother, a working professional had made for a difficult three years. But I felt like I was doing something amazing, that I was ready for the change. Something about triathlon made things feel less insane—even though triathlon *is* insane.

I had hope again—hope that I had not felt in a very long time.

6 Days

I was excited about the race, but mostly I was excited about a trip with the Expert for the first time in what seemed like forever. Eight hours of driving in a car with my super cute husband and our bikes felt like a sort of impending heaven.

I had set out with the Main Goal for an Olympic distance race only six months before. I told the Expert that he was coming along too. At first, he fussed a little, ignored me. Then he gave up and succumbed to the pain. He and I have accomplished all sorts of crazy things in our many years together, but never a true health and fitness goal. St. Anthony's was a big deal for us, for our relationship, and for our little family of four.

After training, I had huge hopes that our family would someday be the weird running family. The weird people who were always training for something. Throughout the training, I watched myself get stronger, faster and better, each week. I am not, nor have I ever been what someone would call fast, but six days before the race, I could acknowledge that I was faster than I had been the year before. And the year before that.

Two Days Left: Friday

Before we left for St. Petersburg, Florida, the packing and race list was carefully made and checked seventeen times. The Expert and I packed and packed and packed. We began packing at around 7:30 on Thursday night and did not finish for almost three hours. Not that we had tons of stuff to pack (we did), but the fear of forgetting something required careful attention. And of course, the Expert had to practice his transitions in the bedroom like twelve times.

We left Atlanta around 8:30 am on Friday and arrived in St. Petersburg around rush hour. We headed to athlete check-in and picked up our packets. A volunteer weighed us at check-in. Yes, *weighed* us. Apparently, when you race in the Athena or Clyde class, the race check-in people *may* weigh you to make sure you are really in the super groups. I suppose some people could weigh 145 and cheat, and race Athena for a win. Either way, if you are racing Athena and Clyde, someone *may* put you on a scale to decide if you are *fit* to race big. Don't worry, they don't tell anyone. And not every race weighs you.

We wandered down to the pier to see where the swim started and finished. Then we had an amazing dinner and drove through the run course while sipping some decaf coffee. After a stop by the grocery, we hit the hotel for some serious shut-eye in our Cleaver (separate) beds. After this race, we've made it a habit to *always* sleep in separate beds on race trips. It just plain rocks.

The Day Before

The Expert and I slept in reasonably late and headed out to do the scheduled quick swim, bike and run before checking our bikes. The water, unlike the prior day's calm surface, was ugly and angry. The temperature was warm, so the race was not slated as wetsuit-legal. I was secretly happy about this, but the Expert was a little nervous. He was looking forward to the flotation advantage the wetsuit brings.

But for me, I was glad to avoid the swim coffin.

After procrastinating for a while, the Expert and I stepped into the water and proceeded to be beat around by the waves. We proceeded slowly forward in the water and swam in a washing machine for fifteen minutes. I had never imagined swimming in water like that. The swells were huge. We rode the waves up and down, swallowing large quantities of salt water. The Expert looked like he was having a similar experience to my first open water swim. His eyes were a little wild and I could see the fear on his face.

I shouted out to him, "It's okay, we can do this!"

He gargled, "Shut up! Leave me alone!"

Yep, he was scared alright. I left him alone, but not out of eyesight.

This was only my third open water swim, but the difference from the first open water swim was night and day. When I first stepped into the water, I felt a familiar little panic rising up in my throat. But I channelled Miss Teeny. I refused to let the fear creep in. I swallowed it and chose to attack the waves like they were a jar of peanut butter. After a few minutes, I was able to feel the rhythm of the breakers and swim a little. The experience became less frightening and more fun. The Expert spent some more time fighting the breakers, but slowly he seemed to become more comfortable. We exited the water and walked across the sand to the car. Time to bike a little.

The bike was fine. Until I stopped at a red light and experienced one of my famous low-speed tipovers. After some serious expletives, I was up and back on the bike. I was bleeding full-force from a hideous chain bite on the back of my right leg. To this day, I still have the scars.

One final, slow, ten-minute jog, and the Expert and I headed to check our bikes. I was ready to rest, but then the Expert declared that he needed a haircut before the race.

The wild goose chase for the nearest Great Clips was insane. He said the haircut would make him faster, so there was no stopping him. The lady cutting the Expert's hair asked if we were in town for the "Triampalon." I giggled a little—visions of trampolines and wetsuits came to mind.

After stopping at the store for hydrogen peroxide and liquid bandage for my chain bite, we began the pre-race veg-a-thon. The Expert and I watched CNN as we wound down for the night and saw reports from the violent storms that had ripped across the South. Ironically, swimming through some rough water and a stinging chain bite was my biggest problem at the moment. Perspective.

Closing the Book

I knew that once I finished the race, I would never be the same. Consequently, even the night before the race I was at peace for the first time in a long time. Some of the peace could be attributed to the preparation and training. But much of the peace came from hope, my family and the promise of just becoming a better person through triathlon.

As Coach Monster tells his Spinning class each Friday morning: *You did not wake up at 4:30 in the morning to pose. Close your eyes and think about what you are going to accomplish today. Aim to walk out of this place a better person. Today, you will be a better person.*

I knew that I would wake up at 4:30 for a race and hours later, I would run across a finish line a better person. I was forever closing the book on my past, and getting rid of that person I did not like.

My First Olympic Distance Race
St. Anthony's Triathlon

May 1, 2011
1.5k (0.9 mile) swim
40k (24.8 mile) bike
10k (6.2 mile) run

The Expert and I woke up at 4:15 a.m. The night before, we had rested our legs and eaten lobster pasta from the hotel room service. I did not sleep well, but with the nerves, I had not really expected to. We arrived at the race venue and set up our transition area.

SWIM

I was in the sixth wave start. My fellow green swim-capped Athenas and I were all together. It was a beach start, meaning we were all corralled in a place on the beach, and when the buzzer went off, we would run towards the water and begin the swim. The Expert was on the beach, his wave leaving much later. He waved at me and I waved back. So many waves.

The buzzer went off, and the other ladies took off running at the speed of light. *Zoom!* into the water. I jogged a little slower and was one of the last ones into the water. I thought it best not to have a coronary before getting to the waves. The swim was fabulous. No panic, no freak outs, and I even passed a few people. I was out of the water in 20:25. The race officials did cut the usual 1600 meter swim to 1000 meters because of the water conditions. Fine by me.

When the swim course was shortened, it was also moved, causing the distance from the swim exit to the bike transition to be lengthened by a half mile. So out we came from the water only to be greeted with a half-mile barefoot run before reaching transition. Barefoot running may be all the rage, but I do not care for it, especially before a twenty-four- mile bike ride. Therefore, I took my sweet time in T1. I had a 10:23 transition time from the swim to the bike. By all stretches of the imagination, that is hideous. I went to the bathroom. I wandered around my bike a little. I was slow. I was okay with that.

BIKE

I was most concerned with two things about the bike portion of the race: mount and dismount. A small miracle happened for me: both were non-issues.

The bike course was amazing—flat, fast and humbling. I passed only twenty or so riders during the entire twenty-four miles. I was passed by hundreds and hundreds. I was riding a good clip, but I might as well have been moving backwards. I was passed by several amputee riders, one who saw my shirt and cheered, "Go Getting2Tri!"

We all wore our ages on our left calf, written with Sharpie. My bike buddy was eighty years old. She and I rode most of the race together, switching back and forth. Later, as we racked our bikes for the run, I found out that this amazing woman was eighty-year-old Sister Madonna Buder, a multiple finisher at the world's biggest Ironman race, the World Championships in Kona.

She had a finish time of 3:20:50 at St. Anthony's, beating me by a solid three minutes.

Run

T2 was a little faster than T1. I dashed out of the transition area with fury (without my helmet, I'm proud to add). Okay, so that statement is not accurate. I trotted out slowly and carefully, knowing full well that 6.2 miles is no joke, especially after a swim and a bike. I didn't want to lose any of my precious steam.

The run course was an "out and back" format. The Expert had started his race about forty-five minutes after me, so I knew I would see him at some point on the course. As I had 1.2 miles left on the run, the Expert and I passed each other. I was so happy to see him, and I would later learn that seeing a friend on the course always makes the pain stop, even if only for a few seconds.

I was incredibly slow. My right calf was still a mess from my low-speed tipover from the day before. Most people must have thought I had fallen on the course, because I received many, many "way to go" comments and "just keep going" shouts. I may have been moving ridiculously slow, but really, I had never felt so good in a run—well, until I reached Mile 5.5. My calves started cramping, the sun was beating down and I was praying for the end of the race. I could hear drums in the distance. *The finish line!* I brought the run home in 1:18:59 (12:44 pace), and as I turned into the final stretch, the street was lined with cheering people, happy faces, and I felt blessed to the point of tears.

The goal was accomplished…and felt amazing! But as I crossed the finish, I gained much more than just a personal pat on the back. I gained a true sense of thankfulness and humility, and I stand in absolute awe of all the amazing athletes who compete in this sport.

Never once during the race did I have a single negative thought like "I can't" or "this is impossible." Not once. That in itself is a miracle. Every time I began to hurt or feel some negative clouds rolling in, I closed my eyes and remembered to be thankful, to consider the able body I had, and think of the countless heroic paratriathletes I saw on the course.

The Expert finished about forty minutes later (only two minutes after me on his official time). We celebrated with a fabulous Italian meal, wine and an early bedtime. My official race time was 3:22:34, with the longest T1 time in the history of man.

First Main Goal. Accomplished.

My Road to the Semi-Crazy Goal

What Next?

After finishing St. Anthony's (and not finishing last), I thought I would be feeling d-o-n-e and completely satisfied. Don't get me wrong, I was stoked to have finished that race.

However.

I had not told anyone at this point, but two months *before* St. Anthony's, I had already registered for the next big thing. Two months before being certain that I could even *finish* an *Olympic* distance, I registered for a semi-crazy goal race.

A half Ironman.

Ironman 70.3 Miami would take place six months after St. Anthony's, on October 30, 2011.

The 70.3 is a race distance consisting of a 1.2 mile swim, 56 mile bike, and a half marathon. Pretty close to *double* the distance I had just completed. I was certain that Coach Monster would faint with exhaustion and shred his clothes in horror to train me to 70.3.

A week after St. Anthony's, the registration had been paid and the hotel booked. Not only *one* registration though. (Did you really think I'd leave the Expert out of the fun?)

Goat-Like Encouragement

I remembered having a conversation with Mountain Goat about the Olympic distance race registration. Mountain Goat is certifiably insane in the fitness department. She ran the Great Wall of China Marathon in 2010 and loves to run trails more than anything. It's literally NBD (no big deal) for her to run 13 miles in the mountains on any given weekend. She's crazy. And that is part of the reason we bond. I like her especially because I can run all my crazy fitness ideas past her first.

For example, the conversation before I registered for St. Anthony's went something like this:

"So, I am thinking I should sign up for this Olympic distance triathlon," I said, standing in the doorway to her office.

"You should do it," Mountain Goat said.

"It's really far. For me," I whined.

"Do it," she said.

I went on, "Like a one mile swim, twenty-four miles on the bike, followed by a 10k."

"Do it," Mountain Goat said.

I said, "But I was thinking—"

"—Do it," she said.

A few months later, I was once again standing in the doorway to her office. I told her that I wanted to do a half Ironman. The conversation went like this:

"I think I want to sign up for Miami 70.3. It's a half Ironman distance race. It's eight months away and I think—"

"—Do it," she interjected.

"Did you hear me? A half Iron," I said.

"Yes, do it."

"What are you? A freaking Nike commercial?" I giggled.

"No. Nike is 'just do it.' I said 'do it.'"

She had a point, and I had a Mountain Goat in my corner. A friend and a person who would give me the "do it" factor when I needed it most.

The Post-Race Slug (And New Kids on the Block)

So, I had started a new job, but I was off kilter with routine and schedule. My workouts were off kilter as well. Plus, I knew we had a vacation happening two weeks later. The Expert and I were going on our first cruise.

Two things were completely awesome about the cruise: 1) the vacation was completely kid-free; and 2) it was the New Kids on the Block cruise. Yes, the boy band. A boat full of 1500 screaming washed up middle-aged ladies and the New Kids on the Block. I could not hold my glee. The idea of the cruise started out as a joke between me and a girlfriend, but then, as the time drew near, I bought the tickets. The girlfriend then bailed, which meant that I roped in my best girlfriend to go with me—the Expert.

(That took some arm twisting).

I had to explain to him that it was still a cruise ship, and we were still porting in the Bahamas. I told him there would be cruise things for him to do while I was finding one of the boys in the band, Danny Wood, to marry me on board.

So we were excited about the trip, but I was worried about my training trajectory. I had emailed Coach Monster a few times with the subject line "Bad Athlete" and then explained my sorrow for missing my workouts. Seeing as how I would have access to limitless buffets of buttery things on the boat, I was feeling a tad Operation Miami derailed.

I had questions about what to do. Should I really try and stay on hard-nosed track with my workouts and eat carrots on the ship? Would that really be possible? I had never (ever) worked out on a vacation (ever). To do a workout, even just one, would be a milestone.

Having a good balance was never my best angle. If I had a mantra it would be: moderation-schmoderation. I figured it was hopeless. I knew that after a day of cruise life, I would be found somewhere on Half Moon Cay, passed out in the sand, extremely sunburned, wearing an inappropriate bikini along with my bike shoes, clutching a Corona and babbling about big triathlon dreams.

STILL SLUGGING

Well, I didn't exactly end up washed up on a beach, but the vacation *was* officially over. During the trip, we actually worked out twice—and I had the joy of running right next to one of the New Kids, Danny Wood, on a treadmill in the ship gym. *Holy cow.*

Once we returned, I sent Coach Monster an email asking for a few days to get my 70.3 bearings and prepare for the beating that was undoubtedly headed my way. Truth be told, when we returned from the cruise, I clicked on my email and saw the schedule for the next morning's workout and I completely chickened out. My brain was still floating in the Bahamas somewhere, and I was beginning to feel the fear of the semi-crazy race creeping in.

Not only that, but the last month was literally chock full of big, emotional changes: a new job, new people (some nice, some not), missing my former co-workers, finishing a big race, dealing with some family issues, and finally a whopping vacation. All in one month. Of course, that is an insane amount of dealings to handle, but the vast majority were good dealings, so I needed to focus.

Sometimes when I am hurting, whether physically or emotionally, I forget to be grateful. I needed a giant whip to crack over my head to get me moving on the 70.3 training. After a few more lagging days up to Memorial Day, I packed my gym bag for a swim and a run, and I set out to make the 70.3 something possible. The motivation to that point was fairly external, meaning that folks through the blog and emails were rooting for me: "yay go you, Swim Bike Mom."

The problem was that I had not quite tapped into the inner "go me" yet.

LEARNING TO SQUEEZE IT IN

During my 70.3 training, I was forced to do the workout squeeze. That is, fitting in workouts whenever and wherever humanly possible. The squeeze often included lunchtime. Up until the 70.3 training, I found many reasons to avoid and frown upon the lunchtime workouts, such as sweaty head, sweaty face, sweaty feet, and sweaty pits. The plain fact that I had already gotten up, showered and dressed *one* time in a day seemed sufficient. I hesitated to do it again, only a few hours later. I am and have always been, a sweat box. I am not the type of kid who can run to the gym for a quick workout and skip the shower. I am disgustingly sweaty within ten minutes of lacing up my shoes.

However, my new office was directly across the street from the Mega Gym. I decided because I would not be wasting time driving very far, that I could take a lunch break sometimes, and swim, bike or run. Perhaps, I could do yoga or Zumba. Oh, I was getting carried away. I doubted that Zumba would benefit my tri training.

So in late May 2011, I had my first lunchtime three miler on the treadmill. I felt much better after a little mid-day Eminem. I was fast. Fast for me, anyway. I was fast getting to the gym, fast running, fast showering, and fast running back to my desk with my lunch. The mid-day run is quite refreshing, and my afternoon was crazy productive. My sweaty pits were another story. But really, no one seemed to stare too long, and I stopped sweating by about three o'clock.

8 MILE, PART DEUX

Only a few weeks after vacation, Coach Monster put eight miles on my run schedule. He had finally lost his mind. I was not ready for eight miles again.

Interestingly, I woke up and ran 8 miles.

It was only the second time in my life that I had run that far. Luckily, I had no gastro-intestinal distress like the first run at the park. However, instead of gastro distress, I had knee, hip and hamstring distress.

At Mile 2, my IT band was hurting so badly, that I stopped, took off my shoes, and jogged a little in my socks. Once the pain subsided a little, I put my shoes back on and Forrest Gumped my way through the remaining 5.5 miles. The run took absolutely forever, but almost an hour and forty minutes later, I had done the deal. As I was leaving the gym, I checked my iPhone and saw a comment on the Swim Bike Mom Facebook page that said "Today is National Running Day."

I am in line with the times. For once, I thought.

Ten hours later, I was hurting. However, somehow, being flung into the running fire helped fling me back into movement forward. But I became concerned about the knee and the IT band pain.

Was it my shoes? Was it my running form? I was fairly certain that runner error was probably a huge factor. Along with the bumbling fat girl factor. I had trudged along in heavy supportive shoes since I started this crazy journey, but I realized very quickly that a mid-foot strike, which I was/am desperately trying to obtain, was impossible with clunky running shoes.

I tried a lighter, less restrictive pair of shoes. I was able to run a little more midfoot, but then I hurt. And I mean, everywhere. At this point, I knew that I had to really get fitted for shoes, once and for all.

I went to a local running store. I ended up with a pair of Brooks Adrenaline GTS 12. To date, I have been through three pairs of this shoe— love. I had dismissed Brooks as a shoe that was entirely too narrow for me (based on Google readings), but it turned out to be a darn good fit. To date, I have run both half Irons in the Brooks, in addition to many, many 9+ mile runs, and a half-marathon. Of course, I am not endorsing Brooks (unless they would like to start sponsoring me. *Wink Wink*), but I am simply making the point that a solid time commitment and investment to finding the right shoe *for you* is worth making. Just do it (no endorsement here, either), but do it early in your journey.

SUNDAY RIDES

Sunday rides became a thing for the Expert and me leading up to Miami. We easily rode forty or fifty miles on a given weekend morning. Most of the days were beautiful and sometimes muddy after a Saturday night Georgia thunderstorm. The Expert and I had a babysitter come in for the weekend rides and while we arguably spent a small fortune on early morning childcare during this time, we considered it money we would have otherwise spent going out to dinner and drinks in our former, non-triathlon-addicted life. We simply shifted the finances elsewhere.

Our summer bike routine was easy:

* Early rise around 5:30 a.m.;
* Get in some sort of fight because we were tired or because the Expert was not moving quickly enough for the Schedule Tyrant (me);
* After fussing at him and him telling me to jump off a bridge, the angry Expert would load up the car; and
* I'd stomp around the house equally mad, but trying not to wake the children.

The night before the ride, we'd warn the children as to which babysitter they would wake up to. The kids were resilient. After we had been training for Miami for a few months, James would ask me, "Who is coming tomorrow to play with us?"

"Oh, nobody, baby. Daddy and I rode yesterday. It's Mommy and Daddy today," I would say.

"Aw, man," James said. "I don't want to play with you, Mommy."

"Well, you got Mom today," I said.

Stella would then chime in against me, "You ride your bike, Mommy."

"Yes," James said. "Go ride your bike."

Needless to say, the kids enjoyed having some young person to run them ragged for a few hours while the Expert and I killed ourselves on the bikes. After fighting a little, packing up the car, and squeaking out of the house in the dark by 6:20, we'd drive to a gas station for coffee and some sort of sugar snack to get the blood pumping. By the time we reached the trail (about a 40 mile drive), we'd be caffeinated and cordial with each other again.

After a butt-busting ride, we would share a greasy lunch together (because we deserved it). Hence, our triathlon weekend dating began: wake up, fight, ride, make up, and eat.

BRICK IN MY HEAD

Four months before Miami, I had my first brick workout since St. Anthony's. The Expert and I did not start the day out in the best of conditions. The night before, we had a couple of people over (i.e., a little too much to drink) and I woke up feeling the drums in my head. Not big huge drums, but little ones. Think: snare drums, not tympanis.

I *knew* better than to squeeze life and fun into the hours outside of triathlon training. I had ignored my better instincts. And the ride was a living, breathing testament to the prior night's fun. The Expert and I knocked down thirty-four miles in about two hours and fifteen minutes. The bad news is that only two weeks before, we had done six more miles, in almost the same time.

In the car on the way home, the Expert said, "I like to look at the ground when I run."

I glanced at him, "Why?"

"Because," he said, "if I look ahead of me, at how far I have to go, I just get sad. So if I stare at the ground, then I am fine."

"You know that's terrible form, right?" I asked.

"What's worse? Looking at the ground ...or laying on the ground?"

"Good point," I said.

OPEN WATER = NOT SO SCARY

The following weekend was the July 4th holiday weekend. The Expert and I got a late start out to the lake, meaning the beach was sprinkled with "normal" beach goers—people with umbrellas, but without spandex and goggles. So we had a few funny stares. But I no longer panicked in the open water. The water was finally warm enough to leave off the wetsuit. Even still, I forced myself to *ignore* the fact that the open water has no walls to grab onto, no bottom of the pool to touch, and no black lines to follow. I had to concentrate, forcing myself not to focus on the fact that I could not see six inches in front of my face in the water.

Instead, I chose to focus on sighting, the efficiency of my stroke, and keeping an eye out for boats, waves and sticks pretending to be water snakes that floated past me.

The (Massive 10k) Peachtree Road Race

On July 4th, 2011, I took on the epic Peachtree Road Race, a 10k Atlanta tradition. I was nervous because of the horrendous crowd factor (hundreds 'o thousands of runners) and the Porta-Potty lines. I do not care for serious mob situations. Consequently, I do not care for mob potty situations. Regardless, I knew that the Peachtree Road Race was an event that any person who claims to be a runner and an Atlantian was required to do, at least once.

Mountain Goat was my partner in running grime. I knew she would be finished with her run a million years before I was and probably sipping booze across the street, but she was the tour guide for the day. I had absolutely no goals for the race other than to have a good time and try not to die from heat stroke.

I met Mountain Goat at her condo in Midtown Atlanta around 7:00 in the morning with my Fuel Belt, my race number and a whole lot of questions. I was so thrilled when she hopped in front of my car wearing her Swim Bike Mom shirt. What a trooper, especially because she has no baby goats. (Kids. Ha ha.)

We hopped the MARTA train with about one thousand of our closest pre-race friends. After a half mile walk, we ended up at the Porta-Potty depot, where we waited for another twenty minutes to pee. I was in line behind a grandfather and his two evil grandchildren (a boy and a girl, about ages 8 and 9) who did nothing but hit each other and kick at shins: "*You stop touching me, stop it, quit it, Grandpa, she hit me!*" When Grandpa went in the Porta-Potty, the boy pulled the girl's braid so hard, I thought her head was about to pop off her neck and roll down Peachtree Street. She turned and kicked him in the thigh so hard, I thought she broke his femur.

"Hey!" I screamed, "You are both going to go to timeout if you don't stop that!" It came out of my mouth before I could stop it. Mom habit. The kids looked at me like I had slapped them across their faces (which was probably coming next for them if they kept it up). But they stopped, so that was good.

Oh, it was so hot (I can't emphasize this enough) and I was pouring sweat waiting for the start. About ten minutes after potty, our corral was released and we were running. Mountain Goat was g-o-n-e before I could say "have a good race." I settled in and felt pretty snappy. I must have missed the one mile mark, because I hit mile two before I knew what happened. I glanced down at my Garmin: 22:23. *Hey, that's not terrible*, I thought

What a circus of a race! I watched as the Statue of Liberty ran past me, ladies in sequined running skirts, and women wearing (fake) moustaches and (real) moustaches. I zoomed past some runners. Many zoomed past me. I paced with one girl most of the run. The spectators were encouraging and funny. I slowed down to watch one of the runners pull off to do a keg stand with a bunch of his frat brothers. Mmmmm…beer.

At mile three (or so), I was still feeling great, despite internally combusting from the heat. I ran through the Holy Water sprinkler at the Episcopal Church, and that's when things started going downhill. Er, uphill. Pretty soon after I was anointed with the Spirit, I witnessed and then experienced first-hand the Cardiac Hill that I was warned about. I pushed upward and onward on Cardiac Hill for as long I could take it. I was so hot (in case you were wondering).

My jogging came to a screeching halt, until I was at a ridiculous pace that could neither be called running nor jogging, but was some sort of hybrid walk. I don't remember much about Mile 4 or Mile 5. It's entirely possible that I stopped off and did a keg stand myself. Before I knew it, Mile 6 was approaching. I managed to knock one of my Fuel Belt bottles to the ground and backtracked to find it.

"Hey, you're going the wrong way," someone yelled.

Really, I thought. *Know-it-all runners.*

I crossed the finish line at 1:15:15, regardless of the fact that the Peachtree official results said 1:26:45 (dirty whore liars). I pressed "start" at the beginning of the race on my Garmin. I pressed "stop" when I crossed the finish line. I'm not sure where I lost eleven minutes, sayeth the Peachtree timers. I was okay with a 1:15:15 time. I was not okay with the other time, so I refuse to claim it. After all, I completed the run portion of St. Anthony's in 1:14:59. I could not conceivably be eleven minutes behind that. But what did it really matter?

I was glad to see the finish line, pick up my t-shirt, Popsicle and banana. Mountain Goat and I finally found each other. She finished in forty-something minutes (fast, hello). She had bought new shoes the night before at the expo and wore them to run. [Note: do not try anything new on race day!] Her heels were bloody and ripped open from the run, but the Goat has some tough hooves.

10 Mile Milestone

A few days after the Peachtree, Coach Monster wanted me to run ten miles. On a *Thursday*. Ten miles during the work week is tricky with a full-time job and all. Especially because it takes me days to run that far. I told my boss I would be in late that morning. He didn't ask why. I didn't elaborate.

I left the house in the dark and drove the forty minutes to the flat Silver Comet trail. I am a massive wastrel of gasoline, I get it. But Atlanta is very hilly and sometimes when I have a big run, I need the confidence to run the distance, so I often opt for flat land. Ten miles of hills is not the way to boost the confidence.

The trail was quiet at six in the morning. I loaded up my Camelbak because ten miles needed a whole lot more hydration than my Fuel Belt could carry. I started off running pretty easily. The first four miles turned out fairly uneventful. It was eighty-one degrees and about 1000000% humidity. At Mile 4.3, I started to feel a little rough. I chewed a few Shot Bloks® and I pepped up near the Mile 5 turnaround.

However, something happened when I turned the corner to head back home. I was hit with a sick reality: *Oh. Crap. I have to do what I just did. Again.*

I had about 4.6 miles remaining when I entered into some sort of runner's coma. I was floating above my body. I was the Floating Me. The Floating Me recognized that the whole exercise was insane. Floating Me noticed that the woman running below appeared to be suffering. Floating Me could not do anything to speed this woman up or slow her down (or make her stop, for that matter). Floating Me just continued floating and watching the insane runner below. At some point, Floating Me went away because I was back on the ground and the real me was running.

I looked up to see a sign that read: 1.6 miles.

1.6 miles? 1.6 miles remaining? I had daydreamed away three entire miles while I was floating? Holy…

Okay. 1.6 miles. *I can do that in my sleep*, I thought. But the next 0.6 of a mile was the hardest run of my life. I had a side stitch. My hip throbbed. My left calf cramped. Also, during my visit as the Floating Me, the runner below had sucked down every last drop in the Camelbak and eaten two GU packs. *So thirsty*, I thought.

My feet were heavy. I never thought about quitting, though because I *had* to get home. What good would quitting have served? I passed the sign that read 0.9 miles left. Less than a mile! Thirsty, cramping or not, I knew I could finish intact.

When 0.3 mile of suffering remained, one of my favorite songs started on the iPod. I morphed into a sissy pants. Not a giving-up type of sissy pants, but rather a boohooing, hysterically crying type of sissy pants. I actually tend to cry a lot during workouts. I can cry from pain, from passion, from boredom, whatever. I cry most during training. On that day, I cried and continued to cry before I realized what happened. Runners stared at me. I was sure they were thinking, *Awwww, that poor chunky girl is just plain suffering.*

If they only knew.

In that moment, I felt the enormity of what it meant to be outside running on two healthy (yet, weary) legs, and finishing something that I had never in a zillion years believed I would *ever* do. Ten miles.

After ten miles, I could not comprehend what it must feel like to finish a full Ironman. I could not understand how I would feel after finishing the half Ironman. But I wanted to remember what it felt like to run ten miles in *that* body, on *that* day. So I cried, I ran and I slowed to a heaving walk as I neared the car. I soaked it up and I was proud.

I may have looked like ten *dollars* when I finished. But I felt like ten million bucks.

Fifty Mile Milestone

I rode fifty miles on my bike in a training ride and couldn't believe it. A few observations about the half-century distance: ouch. I felt pretty darn good at Mile 30. But by Mile 38, my legs were hating me. And the Queen? We cannot even talk about how badly the Queen was hurting. Pain persisted even in the presence of the great ISM Adamo Road saddle.

As usual, I encountered interesting things on my ride. First, I saw a group of cyclists rounding a huge snake out of the path with a small stick (like the size of a chopstick). Then, I saw a little old lady yelling to a passing cyclist: "Watch where you're going, you big *GOON!*" Finally, I saw a thirty-something couple wearing matching vinyl solar suits and walking no less than thirty ankle biter dogs.

I mean really. Who doesn't love to ride a bike?

Eleven Miles & Gratitude

During training, I often have grateful moments. Sometimes unexpected. Sometimes I am forced to *make* the gratitude happen. Regardless of how or when, I have found gratitude to be a key component to triathlon.

One of my favorite gratitude moments happened on a day I was scheduled to run eleven miles, which would be a new milestone. I was scared. I had barely run ten miles the week before.

The morning was hot and quiet. I ran out 5.5 miles without issue. Then I made the turnaround and a little while later, I saw two big guys running towards me. I was alarmed for a minute, but then I realized they were jogging. Two men who appeared to be a father and son, running directly towards me. I'll call them Fred and Ben. Fred is the dad in this story.

The most remarkable thing about Fred and Ben was their size: both were very heavy, big dudes. Fred had to be pushing three hundred and fifty pounds, where Ben was probably hovering in the high two-hundred range.

Fred and Ben were shuffling along, just like me.

"Good morning," I shouted as they approached.

Both smiled and as we passed each other Fred shouted, "What are you training for?"

I turned and screamed, "A half Iron! What about you?"

Fred craned his neck back towards me and shouted, "A marathon, with my boy, here! December!"

And just like that, we lumbered past each other, going on our own paths. I found myself back in sissy land, crying and running. Two things about that little exchange brought me to welled-up scrunchy cry face.

First, Fred and Ben were two large people and I am no stranger to big people. They were out there *together* making it happen, hobbling along, just like I was doing. My tears flowed from being an eyewitness to their mission and ultimate goal. To see and hear people vocalizing their crazy dreams is wonderful and affirming. People who are big, move slowly, and dream even bigger make me so happy!

The second remarkable thing was the moment when I shouted that I was training for my half-Iron. I had said it few times out loud to anyone who cared to listen. But to literally scream it across a trail to complete strangers felt amazing. "Half Iron!"

I was crying for those reasons. I was crying because I was still fat according to all standards in this country. I was crying because on that day, I may have been fat, but I was a fat girl who continued going and finished the morning with eleven miles in her shoes.

LISTENING

During a workout following the big eleven, I learned a big lesson about putting everything into training. When I give training my all (of course, with the exception of energy for kids, family and work) the reward is usually pretty good. Of course, this is the standard "get what you give" idea—the reciprocity principle, also known as the Golden Rule. Regardless of these adages, an important ideal to remember is: *listen to your body*. On a particular workout in which my face sported massive under-eye bags and my body made absolutely no response to an espresso shot, it was clear that my insides were screaming: *rest rest rest*.

Sometimes during the year, I felt that I had nothing to give myself or my training, which left virtually zero *me* for the others around me. After a great forward trajectory, a ten and eleven-mile run and a big fifty-mile bike, I found myself worn out. My body was talking to me.

I was not listening.

I ran four miles and found myself sick, dizzy, and cramping the entire run. The next day, in cycling class, my legs would not move. I closed my eyes, pedalled slowly, and *listened*. I could hear the old worn-down body talking.

So I listened some more. I pedalled even more slowly. Then afterwards, I stretched carefully. For the rest of the day, I was nicer to my body, even though I ate some garbage at work and had to "ingest" some jerks around me. But regardless, my body had spoken and I had listened. That night, I iced the parts that hurt. I stretched some more and I went to bed early.

WATERLOGGED & TRAIL RUN DREAD

After some solid recovery days, I had a super long 3500 meter swim (yep, that's over 2 miles). Even after I was showered, wearing jammies and staring longingly at the night-night room, I swore someone could pick me up and wring water out of me. That is, if someone could actually *pick me up*. I was waterlogged. The pool was hot as the devil. The July Atlanta weather was well over one hundred degrees.

Sometimes, I do not mind being in the pool forever. Sometimes, I do. That 3500 meter swim was a case of "get me out of this pool." I think part of it was swimming late in the day. I like early morning and early afternoon workouts. When workouts start cutting into my lay on the couch and Facebook time, I tend to get grouchy.

The day after the long swim was a recovery day, but then I had a crazy race on the schedule for the weekend: a 9.3 mile trail run at Red Top Mountain in Cartersville, Georgia. Insanity. 9.3 miles in the mountains?

Okay, so why was I doing a 9.3 mile trail run? Well, I blame the Mountain Goat. I had signed up for that race sometime last year when Mountain Goat talked me into it. At that time, I was not running more than three miles at a time and thought, *I'll sign up for that craziness but there's no way I will do it.* There was some special and the registration fee was actually five dollars, so what did I care?

Well, I cared the night before the race when I was packing my bag for the darn event. I thought about bringing the small video recorder, because I was sure to have several *Blair Witch Project* jokes by Mile 8. Mountain Goat would be on her second piña colada at the finish line when I rolled in, sticks wedged in between my ribs and leaves tangled in my hair.

I emailed Coach Monster a few days before the trail race.

I wrote: *Saturday's run is a 9.3 trail run at Red Top Mountain in Cartersville. Do you think I am going to die? They have a 3.1 version...I could do that. That might be better. What say you?*

He wrote back: *Nope, 9.3 is a good number.*

I typed: *How did I know that would be your response?*

His response: *Because you are learning, Grasshopper.*

I wrote back: *Mountain Goat said that 9.3 on trails feels like 15. And the cutoff for the race is 2.5 hours. I better scurry.*

Four words followed in an email: *Scurry if you must.*

So that's what I learned: 9.3 is a good number. And I must scurry. I was very nervous about trail running and anything that involved scurrying. But scurry seemed like an appropriate word for the woods.

THE FINAL NINETY DAYS TO CRAZY

THE MONTH OF RACES

I had four intense, insane weekends of races scheduled. After those races were complete, I would begin the final four-week countdown to Miami. The first race was the trail run from hell, the second race was a sprint triathlon, the third an Olympic distance tri in the boonies, and finally, a 5k.

RACE 1: TRAIL RUN FROM HELL, JULY 30, 2011

The Expert agreed to watch the kids and let me go about the trail run on my own. I woke up at 5:45 and headed to Cartersville, Georgia, for the 1st Annual Red Top Roaster Trail Run. I will refrain from wisecracks like this was the "1st Annual and Last Ever" race.

My first clue into trouble should have been the race venue alone: Red Top *Mountain*. A normal person would say, "Mountain? Yeah, that's probably going to be steep. And hurt." But me? The little detail like "mountain" flew right past me.

Secondly, I knew I was in trouble when I saw the array of runners. Usually, at any given race I will see a few runners who make me think, *okay, I can beat that dude; I won't be last.* The problem with the mountain race, I did *not* see *those* people milling around. Everyone looked serious. And seriously fit.

Mountain Goat was running the 10k. My good friend Carol (who I call "W" for undisclosed reasons) was taking a stab at her first ever 5k. We met at the park and wandered to the start line together.

Three minutes into the race I found the third troublesome clue: the first hill. To my credit, the legs were less than fresh, working off the week's workouts and Coach Monster's cycling class the day before. But in all reality, the freshness of the legs was less of a problem then the fatness of the body.

The suffering had commenced. And commenced with a vengeance. Up, up, up the trail went. My heart rate was in high Zone 4, and my legs were burning with the fire of the woods.

I passed a sign: *Mile 1.* Oh. Dear. Lord.

More of the same pain happened for the next mile, but I popped a chocolate gel and that helped pick me up a bit. The hills flattened out a tad and I settled into a rhythm for a bit. I walked up the super-terrible hills, steadily ran up the manageable hills and tried not to fly down the others like I had morphed into a human wheelbarrow. In hindsight, the so-called rhythm was because Miles 1-2 were relatively friendly.

Then came somewhere near Mile 3. I was trucking along for another half mile. Oh! There was a water station. Mmmmm. Not that I needed water with my seventy-two ounce Camelbak, but I stopped anyway, along with a dude. After a quick sip, the two of us moved forward. About ten minutes later, we realized that we were moving forward in the wrong direction. We somehow missed the turn. We found a race volunteer who had no idea where to tell us to go, and offered the helpful advice of: "Go back where you came from."

Oh really? Thank you. Great. I was going to be hard-pressed to make the 2.5 hour cutoff and now I was supposed to backtrack a half mile? Not seeing any other options, the two of us backtracked.

That little deviation from the plan got in my head.

The suffering really started to set in about Mile 5-6. The fast runners were on their last leg of the race, passing me. No matter what race I am in, no matter my level of fitness, seeing people on their way to the finish (when I have an eternity left) never ceases to completely demoralize me.

I wanted to quit.

I remember distinctly having a mind-versation with myself around this time. *I wonder if this is harder than childbirth? I mean, I pushed Stella out pretty quickly—this doesn't really seem to end.* To compare a trail run to childbirth is insane. Of course childbirth is worse.

But really, quitting would not get me home any quicker. The funny thing about running: if you go out, you must come back. Plus, the "sweeper" dude who sweeps up the rear telling everyone the race is over was actually on a mountain bike, so he could not even give me a ride home.

I had a rock or a stick in my shoe which had been tormenting me for a while. I slowed down several times, dug around a little, but I could not get rid of it. Finally, I stopped and slipped off my shoe. But I did not see anything in the shoe. I thought that it must be in my sock. I pulled my sock down and found the "rock." I had been digging at a blister the size of a quarter. No rock there, just bleeding flesh. Moving along, nothing to see there.

Only three or four miles to go, I whispered. I saw a water station. Whew! *Two or three miles remaining,* I thought. I could have given up at this water station. I was near the parking lot. I could see my car. I could have snapped my keys right out of the Camelbak, sent Mountain Goat and W a text message ["sorry guys, I left"] and got the hell out, called it a day. But approaching the aide station, I made a decision that I was going to finish. Even though my timetable was closing in and my time would not be counted.

"How much further and where do I go?" I asked the volunteer at the station.

"You are almost done! Just another half mile or so!" I look down at my Garmin.

"What? No. I have more. Where do I go?" I asked her, pleading. *Didn't she know I had a time limit? What's with all this chitchat?* I thought.

"No, you are almost done!"

"But I got lost awhile back," I protested. "I have more to do. Am I supposed to loop again or something? Am I supposed to run this loop again?"

"No. Did you go around here, up the trail around here, then back down there and back up......then...." she goes on and on.

I was nodding, because I had been everywhere she mentioned except the part where I detoured (got lost).

The volunteer smiled and smiled and shooed me along, saying, "Go! Go! Go!"

So I went. And maybe a half mile or so later, I was rolling into the finish, with a time just under two hours.

After I crossed the finish and Mountain Goat gave me her electrolyte drink, I realized that I missed about 2 miles due to the little lost excursion. I was watching fast looking people, people *I* had never passed, finish after me. *Crap*, I thought. At a time around 2 hours, if I had run 2 more, then I could have probably finished around 2:30:00, which with the detour, would have been about right.

I still have no idea what happened. Regardless, I was very glad to only do about 7.3 miles (or whatever I did). I do not know how I get into these situations.

Coach Monster wanted the standard report about what I had learned. I could genuinely say that I learned a lot from my 7.3 mile trail run.

First, on trail races in the *mountains*, it might be a good idea for me to walk up the hills, especially at the start. Thou shalt not blow up at the start of the race. Next, it is vitally important to stay on the course, pay attention and ask questions of race volunteers who might know the answer. I learned to always pack way more fuel than needed. I sucked down three GU gels and had only one left. I was conserving it. If I had run the final-however-many miles, I could have been in a mess. If a mountain lion had found me, I would have had no offering of GU to make to him.

I received some good advice about good trial running form—picking up my knees on the uphills and leaning slightly forward on the downhills. I tried to do this, but I felt like a bat out of hell on the downhills. I simply wasn't strong enough to pick up my knees well on the hills.

I learned that mental strength was everything in that race. The pain was present and very real. Letting that pain seep into the brain cells would have meant total disaster. I fell apart a little during the race, but was able to regroup as quickly as I fell apart.

I learned the importance of running my own race. No matter how many people pepper the course, a race is very personal. A race is all about me, my legs and my run. To compare myself to others gets me absolutely nowhere. I also learned to have realistic expectations. I should have just started out walking this one. I got a little caught up in the "race" aspect, when I knew this wasn't a "race for me." The next important lessons: get foot powder (stat) and pace, pace, pace. Oh, and pace some more.

RACE 2: SPRINT TRIATHLON, AUGUST 7, 2011

The following weekend was my second ever sprint triathlon, the Acworth Women's Sprint Triathlon, which consisted of a 400 yard swim, 13 mile bike, and 5k (3.1 mile) run. The Expert obviously was not competing in the women's race, but he agreed to crew for me.

The Expert and I loaded up the car and headed out of the house around 4:50 a.m., and arrived in Acworth around 6:00. We got lost, which made me a complete basketcase. We found our way to the race site at about 6:45, but I had a half-mile walk to the transition area, I had no race packet or timing chip, and I had to pee. After a potty break (one in the woods, and one in the Porta-Potty), I had my transition area set up, my race numbers marked on my arm and leg, and finally, I was wandering into the lake to warm-up.

© Bird's Eye View, Inc. | Tricycle Studios

341

I was in the next-to-last wave start. I was also racing Athena. It came as quite a shock to me in the beginning of my triathlon journey that there was a class for women over 150 pounds. But after racing Athena during St. Anthony's, I realized that I loved that group. I watched the other waves run into the water and take off on the 400 yard course. I was not really nervous, but more like ready to get a move on. Watching wave after wave is draining in itself. I think the first wave took off about 7:30, and my wave reached the start line about 7:50.

"*10-9-8-7...*" The countdown...

And the splash-fest commenced. I started off way too far to the left and probably flopped down into the water a little too soon, so I got a little clogged up in some of the other swimmers. However, I managed a pretty fast swim. I was suffering a little, so I knew it was as good as I could have done. The run from the sand to the bikes is always fun.

T1 was efficient and before I knew it, I was out on the bike, feeling surprisingly great. The sky was overcast, perfect weather for a typically hot Georgia day. The course was 13 miles of rolling hills. After the prior weekend on the mountainous trail run, I did not think the hills were massive, and the downhills were fun and fast. I did a lot of passing on the bike and was not passed much, which was a testament to Coach Monster's Spinning classes and coaching. I averaged a speed of 18.1 MPH on the road bike. The fast bike did blow my legs to pieces. But I figured at a sprint distance, I could survive.

As I rolled out of T2 and into the run, I heard the Expert yell: "Run and done, baby! Run and done!!" Ugh, I thought. I am done... don't want to run. Tough uphill right out the gate. I was in the hurt locker on the first mile. I did not impress anyone with my run pace. *Lawd, I am so slow.* I had put the hammer down on the bike, and I could feel the death of *my* hammers by Mile 2.

Overall, the race was awesome, fun and encouraging. My back tire went flat on the ride to the car. Whew, just dodged that bullet—only a few minutes was the difference between a great race and a rotten one. I guess that's the way it goes.

My time was 1:32:32, and I placed 211 out of 503, and 7th out of 22 in my Athena division. My swim time was under nine minutes, my bike just over forty-three minutes, and I had a slow 5k with 37:05.

RACE 3: THE OLYMPIC DISTANCE RACE

The following weekend consisted of an Intermediate/Olympic distance race: 1500 meter swim (0.9 mile), 22 mile bike, and 6.2 mile run.

Pre-Race Deliverance

The Expert and I were racing this one together. The race venue was eighty miles away, which we figured to be a solid 1.5 hour drive. We planned to leave at 4:30 a.m., which would put us there by 6:00, about one hour before transition closed and way before the start of the race. We woke up, packed up and got in the car. I looked at the clock in the car: 5:00am. *Crap! Thirty minutes late getting on the road? What happened?* Automatically, we were behind the eight ball. We pressed on and at 6:25 a.m., we thought we would make it on time. Timing was a little close, but we thought we'd be okay.

However. The wrong turn.

"Where are we???" I screeched. I started to wait and wring my hands.

The Expert says, "I don't know. You have the directions!"

"Well, this isn't right!" I said flapping papers in my hand and wailing.

"What does the paper say?" he asked.

"I don't know!" I screeched (more screeching).

"You don't know? You don't know?" he screamed.

He pulled the car over to a gas station. I was supposed to turn on my navigation, but I did not have a cell signal on my wireless service. The Expert, who had another cell provider, conveniently announced that he left his cell at home.

"Well, that is just *super! Super!*" I yelled.

"Oh nevermind," he said, "I have it." He found his phone. Luckily (really the only *lucky* thing), the navigation worked.

Go two miles and turn left on, said Nancy Navigator. We had 9.9 miles to go.

It was 6:40am. Transition closed at 7:00. We had 9.9 miles to cover in 20 minutes, in a rural county, and we did not have our race packets or timing chips yet.

Turn right on Jack Rucker Road, said Nancy Navigator. The Expert turned on Jack Rucker, bringing a word that rhymed with Rucker to mind. Jack Rucker Road was a dirt road, with some gravel. And dirt. Mostly dirt. I heard music from *Deliverance* leaking in through the car windows. I swear I did.

The clock said: 6:42 and the Expert had *had* it. I mean "had it" like something about the dirt road flipped his ever-loving lid. It was 6:43, we both had to pee, we were on a dirt road in the middle of nowhere with bicycles.

I started crying.

"Why are you crying? Why do you cry before every race?" he asked me.

"Because…this is a deeeeesaaaaaaaaaster…I-I-I just want—" I blubbered.

"—you have to stop crying."

"I can't stop crying! We aren't going to make it," I wailed.

"You got that right," he spat out. I looked at the clock: 6:45am. Fifteen minutes and transition would be closed. We were still on the effing dirt road.

Finally, the dirt road ended, and Nancy Navigation declared that we had two miles to our destination.

"We can make it," I said, "If we can go fast."

The Expert snorted. He was completely furious.

"By the way," he said, "I am never doing a triathlon again. Not with you! This is a *ridiculous* way to spend a Saturday. And you are ridiculous!"

"Fine," I screamed. "*You* are ridiculous! And it's not like we are doing a triathlon *today* anyway!"

6:48am. Park Entrance.

There was a long line at the gate and after standing up in my seat and looking out the window, I saw that we were five cars back. The 4,000-year-old Gatekeeper lady was apparently telling everyone the history of the park.

6:51am

"That'll be five dollars," she said, as we pulled up to the window.

I threw $20 at the Expert. "Tell her to keep the change. Let's *goooooooo!*" The Expert waited for the change. Of course.

6:52am

We parked.

6:54am.

We scrambled and rushed and were riding the bikes down the hill towards transition, backpacks in tow when the Expert said, "Crap!"

"What?" I asked.

He said, "I forgot my water bottles."

I threw up a little in my mouth, "What???"

"The water bottles are in the car. Go on. I've gotta go back."

"No, I'll wait," I said. I mutter expletives against him under my breath.

"GO!!!!" he screamed.

I wasn't waiting on him when he gave me permission to go.

6:55am

So I went. I pulled up to the registration table, panting for breath.

6:56am

The Expert arrived at the table.

6:59am

We got our race numbers. Our bodies were marked and our timing chips were installed.

7:05am

We made it. Transition was still open. We made it.

The Swim

After setting up everything, the race was ten minutes from start. Ten minutes. I forgot to put on my helmet number and my bike number (I did not realize this small fact until *after* I got home and saw the numbers in my race bag). I scurried to the potties, and down to the beach.

By the time the race started, I felt like I had already *done* a race. I was sweating, I was emotionally drained. I had seven minutes to compose myself once we were on the beach. The Expert was in the second swim wave (the green caps) and I was in the third wave (the pink caps).

"*GO!*" I watched the Expert start swimming. Three minutes until my wave.

The course was a 750 meter triangle shape, which we had to swim twice. Swim the triangle once. Get out of the water, walk about 20 feet, and swim it again.

"*GO!*" And the pink caps were off. About 100 meters into the swim, my left goggle was completely flooded. *Crap.* I floated up for a minute, released the water, and started off again. Instantly, it filled up again. I decide to swim one-eyed. Approaching the beach, I realized I forgot to start Constance (my new Garmin 310xt fancy pants GPS watch). All that money and I could not remember to *start* the watch.

Out of the water. I ran twenty feet, emptied my goggle, and dove back in. The swim to the first buoy (for the second time) was annoying as all hell. This green cap dude insisted on swimming as if we were long-lost Siamese twins. Now, I understand that swim starts get bottled up, you crawl, kick and jump across people. But this was Loop Two. The whole lake was our triathlon playground. There was plenty of space. And this dude wanted to kick, punch and snuggle up to me like a warm blanket. I took a few kicks. I made a concerted effort to pull to the side, pull forward. But he was pacing me, Chuck Norris-ing me. I took about sixteen more kicks to the legs, to the feet, to the ribs. I tried to move away again. He moved towards me and kicked me some more. Then I got mad. [Insert whatever you imagine I might do under these circumstances.]

He moved.

I was swimming like I was in la-la land. I definitely wasn't *there.* I felt slow, foggy-brained. I headed back towards the beach and I could see the Expert swimming near me.

Then, another green cap dude swam in front of me. I was swimming *towards the beach,* and here he comes swimming *parallel* to the beach. He swam across me and scared the life out of me. I thought he was a sea creature (yes, in the *lake*). A guy with an oar tried to get his attention, but green cap dude was going fast and furious *across* the course.

Finally, I was out of the water and sighed when I saw the uphill run to transition. I opted for an uphill *walk* instead.

The Bike

I decided to also opt out of socks on the bike. I was soaking wet and I *hate* having wet socks. So I chose no socks, and this was the first time I had done this.

Right out of the transition gate, there was a climb. Not a horrible one, but a climb nonetheless (nothing like the climb at Mile 2). The Mile 2 climb was from hell. I had left the Expert in transition, hoping to get a bit of a lead on him. But on that Mile 2 Hill from Hell, here comes the Expert.

Nicknamed "Quadzilla" by Coach Monster for his massive legs, the Expert has powerful, giant man legs and he loves the bike discipline of triathlon best.

The funny thing was, however, that I was also beginning to enjoy riding my bike. As he pedalled past me, he gave me some motivational words, and continued past me. Somehow, I decided that I was not letting him drop me.

The bike course was fun, but challenging. Three or four hills brought some serious pain and the rest were just moderately painful. The Expert stayed ahead of me, consistently attempting to drop me. I saw him look back every so often, trying to get rid of me. I gritted my teeth and thought, *You aren't losing me, Quadzilla.* And he didn't. (However, he *did* stop to help a guy with a flat, but I am not counting that). My official story is that he could not drop me.

As I pulled into T2, shortly behind him, the Expert laughed and screamed across the bike racks, "I can't get rid of you!"

I said, "That's right! I'm like lightning!"

The Run

The Expert took off ahead of me on the run. I was forty yards behind him. Catching him, obviously, was my only concern. The run, a two loop course, started with a half mile trail run. *For the love,* I muttered, *please no more trail runs.*

An Olympic distance triathlon has a 10k run tacked on at the end, so the two-loop course meant: run two 3.1 miles, do *not* cross the finish line (but instead, observe the fast racers finishing as you slug past), then do 3.1 miles *again.* I like "out and back" courses much better. You run half the distance, turn around, and run home. Loops are demoralizing. *I just did that loop. Now I have to do it again?* Repeating territory should not be allowed. Plus, that is contrary to my *move forward* mantra.

I caught up to the Expert. He said, "And here she is!"

We ran together for a little bit, people flying past us. I said, "Hey, we're like Macca and Raelert!" Macca is Chris McCormack, the 2010 Ironman World Champion. Raelert is Andreas Raelert, the runner-up in that same race. The race that year was decided in the last mile, with Macca and Raelert running side by side, and Macca pulling ahead for the win.

Of course, the Expert and I were more like Mutt and Jeff compared to Macca and Raelert.

The Expert asked, "Who am I?"

"I think you're Raelert, because I'm about to lay down the hammer!" I said. We both laughed, knowing full well that no hammers were being laid down, anywhere. We pounded fists, and I pulled ahead. We ran our own races from this point forward. I felt awesome on the run. Really awesome. Best I had ever felt running. That is, until I saw a sign: *Mile 1*

I believed I was at least 2 miles in. Something about that observation deflated me. I was not sure I had another 5.2 miles inside of me. Plus, the entire run was uphill. Both ways. All loops. Uphill. Uphill. The irony was that the race description had the freaking nerve to call the run course "flat and fast." If that course was flat and fast, then I was *also* flat bottomed and fast.

Still, I plodded along, my feet hitting the concrete with a *plop plop plop*. I felt a rock in my shoe, and I stopped to pull it out. I shuffled along. I walked sometimes, but I was hanging in there.

I saw the Mile 4 sign and I started to get *cold*. Of course, there is something completely ridiculous about running in the middle of August, in the Georgia humidity and feeling cold. I was under-fueled and stressed out from the ride into the race with Deliverance, and maybe I pushed too hard trying to avoid getting dropped by the Expert on the bike. Either way, I was suffering. The Expert and I pounded fists as we passed each other going opposite ways on the homestretch, saying "run and done."

About 3:25:00, I rolled through the finish feeling terrible, but I gave the thumbs-up for the camera, and was thankful to be done.[xxvii] The Expert was not too far behind, and I cheered him in. Only then did I realize that he was wearing his race number upside down. Fail.

I learned some valuable lessons from that race. I learned once again that some people are fast and I was not one of those people. The biggest lesson came from the pre-race shenanigans: always leave for the race early. I will forever leave one hour before I believe necessary or stay overnight in a hotel next to the lake. Otherwise, the issues resulting from the lateness may ultimately lead to quitting triathlon or divorce.

At the next race, I need to fuel, fuel and fuel some more. I was weak and tired at the end of the race, and I felt clammy. I would later learn from my wise nutritionist that weak and clammy means dehydration and glycogen depletion.

Another big lesson from that race was an appreciation for my improvements. I was clearly improving. My St. Anthony's time was only a few minutes shorter, but St. Anthony's was (really) fast and flat, the swim was cut in half, and the bike course was flat. It was an improvement, which was enough to keep me moving forward.

On the drive home, the Expert was not quitting triathlon after all. He looked at me and said, "If I had a million dollars two years ago, I would have bet against you ever doing something like this. This is awesome, and you are amazing."

It was a nice thing to hear. But I thought about what he said for a minute, and then I got irritated.

"So. You would have bet against *me* doing this?" I smirked, "What about you?"

He laughed, "Oh, *I* would have bet a million bucks that I *would* do it."

I laughed too, "Of course you would. And that's why we call you—"

"—I love you," he says.

"I love you, too."

RACE 4: FAST 5K RACING AN EXPERT

The final race of the four in a row was a 5k with the Expert. I was not expecting much from myself, as it had been a tough couple of weeks.

The day before the race, the Expert asked me: "Are you going to run this race balls out?"

I had shrugged, "Oh, I don't know. I'll have to see. Coach Monster said that it was a Zone 2 training run."

On race morning, the Expert and I warmed up together. At the last second before the starting buzzer went off, I decided that I would, in fact, run the race "balls out." Forget Zone 2.

So, I took off running hard right away. About a half mile in, I was regretting my choice. I was suffering. But I had made my bed and decided to continue to lay in it. I dug in and crawled completely into the hurt locker.

Then, I saw a flash of green shirt fly by. *Zoooooom.*

There went the Expert! I looked down at my watch and I was *flying* at a 6.5 pace. By Mile 1, I was still pushing a sub-ten-minute mile pace. I caught up to the Expert again. He cut his eyes at me, giving me the hairy eyeball and then rolled his eyes, which completely flabbergasted and annoyed me.

He ran clear past the first water station.

Who runs past water in this heat, I thought. I slowed down, grabbed a cup and fell about ten yards behind him. He ran like a cartoon character, all fast and crazy and giving me hateful glances the entire time.

Dude, what is his problem? I thought.

At the halfway turn-around, my GPS watch told me that I had been running for 14:28. *Wait? What? If I had been running for 14:28, that meant I could have a possible sub-twenty-nine minute race? What? What? Fast! Zoom!* I had a chance to obliterate my previous 5k times, which were all over thirty minutes.

After the turn around, the Expert and I traded places constantly, back and forth, back and forth. I was huffing and puffing. My dreams of my prior 5k race obliterations were crushed. My *out* pace was not the *back* pace.

With about 200 yards to go, the Expert looked at me and ran past me. *Fine,* I thought, *go ahead.* He took off for about 100 yards and I hit a sprint coming up the last hill and caught him at the rotten hilltop finish.

His time: 32:17. I finished two seconds behind him to take home the third place slot in Female 30-34 (might have only been three people…not sure).

The Expert was still glaring at me after the race. I had enough. "What is your problem, man?" I asked him.

He scrunched his face at me, "Were you even *hurting* out there?"

"Uhhhhh, *yeah,*" I said, "Like death."

"Really?" he looked stunned.

"Yes," I said. "I saw a bright light at the finish."

"Oh." His face relaxed a little.

"What is going on?" I asked.

He said "I just thought this was a Zone 2 training run or something. But then you took off, and I was dying to keep up. And I was getting madder and madder."

"Why were you *mad?*" I asked.

"Because I thought you were pulling that pace in a Zone 2 heart rate."

I laughed at him. First, I laughed because of the ridiculousness of our competitive natures, then, I cracked up because he thought I was *breezily* running that entire race.

It was a good day, and a great way to finish up the four weekends of races before the final four week countdown to 70.3. I beat my best 5k pace by two minutes on a pretty difficult little course. The pace broke down to 10:25-minute mile, the fastest run pace to date.

Silent Sunday

The next day at lunch, the Expert and I stared at each other over ~~grilled chicken salads~~ a giant plate of nachos. No talking. On the twenty-minute ride to lunch we did not speak. All during lunch: *silencio*. And on the drive home? Dead quiet.

We weren't fighting.

Rather, we were living a silence born out of complete triathlon exhaustion. Four weekends of races, followed by fifty-two miles on the bike and a three-mile run. I was tired. The Expert was tired.

In eight weeks, we would embark on 70.3, and I don't think either of us were too sure how that would actually *feel*.

13.1 and Done

On the one-year anniversary of my big Decision, I went a little crazier. I ran 13.1 miles. The big half marathon distance *and* the distance I would allegedly cover on the last third of the half Ironman that was sixty-three days away.

I was only supposed to run 11 miles on that day. But I wanted to get the 13.1 over with.

I cannot lie and say that 13.1 miles felt great. My pace was 12:24 minutes per mile which was not horrendous considering that a year before 12:40 was my 5k pace. Of course, I had a big fat sissy cry moment around Mile 5. I felt awesome at Mile 6. Mile 7 was okay, and I continued to feel pretty grateful for about two more miles.

But when Mile 9 arrived, I began to wonder why in the world I put myself through the torture of triathlon. I was starving and thirsty and could not shove enough gels or water in me to feel well. I felt as if I was wearing some-body else's legs. Somebody who had legs made of jelly and whose joints were attached together with tape.

Then came Mile 11: the place where I was supposed to stop running according to Coach Monster's schedule. I wished I could stop. But if I wanted to get home, I had to run there. I was cramping. At Mile 12, I was so lost and had no idea where I was really. I did know, however, that my legs were moving a little and I could see signs that I was moving in the right direction. I finished the run shuffling, wincing and mildly bent over from leg cramps.

When I stopped running, the real *goodness* set in. As I eased myself into the car, my hamstrings and buns were knotted and screaming profanity at me. Tears were pouring down my face from the pain.

I thought, *This is almost as bad as childbirth* (it was not). *Oh*, I thought, *I'd rather have birthed a baby than do what I just did* (I would not). [It's weird how often I compare running to childbirth. Yet, I continue to run, but have no plans for any more children.] Three hours later, I was walking funny, but I felt alright.

Most importantly, the 13.1 Race Monkey was officially off my back! I was worried that I could not run 13.1 miles (ever). But I made the distance and the Race Monkey's free piggyback ride was over. I had completed the 70.3 swim distance in my training (1.2 miles). I had come within 4 miles of the bike dis-tance (56 miles). So with the new 13.1 accomplishment, I felt complete. Each prong of the race had virtually been met.

THE RACE MONKEY

I attended Coach Monster's indoor cycling class a few days later. As I skipped into the room, he gave me the Monster Evil Eyes.

Oh no, I thought.

I walked over to him. "So you did 13.1 on Saturday?" he asked me.

"Yep," I said, grinning all full of triathlon pride.

"What did your schedule tell you to do?" he asked.

The grin slid off my face.

"Ummmmm," I mumbled.

He said, "Okay, maybe I can remind you. How about e-lev-en miles?"

I nodded, "I know, but I was so close and I thought I could go ahead and—"

"—How did it feel?" he asked.

"Well, the first eleven miles were good."

"The distance your schedule said to do?" he asked.

"Yes."

He looked at me.

"And the last two miles?" he asked.

"Welllllll…Not so—"

"—uh huh!" He interrupted.

I protested, "B-b-but I wanted the race monkey off my back!"

Coach M looked at me harder. "The race monkey? The race monkey? He's been gone! He's not anywhere!"

"Yes," I protested, "Yes, yes he is. He was. The race monkey, he was—"

"—Then on Sunday, your schedule said 'forty-mile bike ride'?"

"Yes," I said.

"And you rode twenty-five miles and said, '*waaaa, there's a lot of hills*' and somehow you think that equals forty miles on flat road?" he asked.

"Doesn't it?" I asked.

"You wacko," he said, smiling.

"Yes," I said.

Okay, so I saw his point. Why did I have a coach if I was not doing the workouts he wrote? Race monkey or not, I would have physically felt better doing the eleven miles as he wanted. But sometimes, doing what I *want* is liberating, even if it results in a verbal lashing, followed by an equally evil physical lashing during his cycling class. Coach Monster then gave me a wicked quotation. Wicked. I put this one in my pipe and smoke it often:

> *"You either will pay in your training,*
> *or you will pay on race day.*
> *Either way, you will pay.*
> *But payday is your choice."*
>
> — Coach Monster

Of course, he then went on to qualify his statement, "Well, sometimes, you'll pay in training *and* a race. But anyway."

Regardless, I received his point, loud and clear. I still go back to that statement during training. If I train and suffer and bleed and cry and whine in the weeks prior, then maybe race day will not hurt quite so bad.

And maybe, just maybe, the Race Monkey will stay home for good.

6 WEEK COUNTDOWN

I had a great 10k (6.2 miles) training run. I ran lots of hills around my house and managed a 10:50-minute mile pace. For over six miles. With hills. In other words, I experienced a pretty little Swim Bike Mom Christmas-in-September miracle. I felt strong and grateful, and I was suddenly pretty excited about the prospect of my half Ironman.

I was all excited in my report to Coach Monster, who reminded me to calm down.

"Stay neutral in your emotions," he said. "Do not let the big days elate you too much, because the bad days can make you crash," he explained. In other words, avoid the manic depressive nature of triathlon.

Coach Monster further explained that "cumulative fatigue" becomes a big issue during a final ramp up to a race. He said, "All of the training and stress on the body builds and builds, causing a feeling of overwhelming fatigue. You do not want to also emotionally crash during this time." He also said that once taper started, my fatigue would wane and the magic would happen at the race. I prayed he was right.

GRATEFULNESS ON THE GREENWAY

On the morning of an eleven-mile run, our daughter Stella, age three, woke up at 4:00 and decided it was time to play. We have a "no kids in the bed" policy but I was so tired and pulled her into bed. The Expert retreated to the couch around 5:30, where he was greeted with rounds of *Twinkle, Twinkle* from upstairs. James, age four, was singing at the top of his lungs.

Ah, parenthood and triathlon. Magic.

Needless to say, we were not heading out the door feeling particularly spunky. We were slow to get started. We walked for about a half mile before starting to run. Even before that, I crawled into the woods and practiced my natural potty skills. I am never very good at peeing in the woods, but at least this time I avoided my shoes (not always the case).

The Suwanee Greenway, the locale of our run, is one of my favorite places to run. The trail has awesome scenery, wooden walkways and bridges. The weather on that particular morning was fabulously cool and I could feel the change in the seasons coming. Knowing that October was just around the corner and that the 70.3 was looming made the eleven-mile run complete and meaningful. Before we knew it, another day of tri training was on the books. The Expert finished and applauded himself for his PR distance.

As if you needed to ask: yes, I approached Mile 10 in the usual crying way. I was running in tears, wearing my ugly cry face and a few heaving sobs. I still have no idea why I cry on every long run. Something about suffering and sweating in nature, pushing through all the "can nots" and regrets makes me weep.

I am always grateful to be *finished* with a hard workout. But during the ramp up to Miami I concentrated on being *grateful* for the workouts, no matter how hard. I firmly believe that gratefulness means more than almost anything else in this sport.

FORTY DAYS, FORTY NIGHTS

With forty-days left until race day, the movie *Evan Almighty* appeared on the tube. In that movie Steve Carell is a modern day, successful senator who is called by God to build an ark. He spontaneously grows a beard, animals start following him, and he proceeds to build a massive ark. A modern day Noah.

I drew the comparison. I was beginning to feel like a modern day Noah. I knew that the next forty days would be some sort of flood. Not a rain type of flood, but rather a flood of emotions, flood of pain, flood of *I can'ts* followed by *Yes, I can!* I would probably throw in a little, *I don't wanna anymore* and *Somebody please make this stop* and *I can't take it anymore* and *Please Coach Monster, stop whipping me* and *Yessir, may I have another.*

I knew that I must focus, must remember that I had come a long way in just a year. From walking into the bike shop almost thirty pounds heavier and picking out Antonia. From riding her only ten miles on the first outing, to falling off Antonia several times and tripping on my own two feet over and over again, to completing several fifty-mile rides. From running only two miles at a 14:25-minute mile pace, to running 11 miles or more, multiple times and at an 11:00-12:00-minute mile pace. From swimming my first lap in the pool, sputtering and being scared to death, to putting down a 1.2 mile swim and several open water swims.

A year can work miracles.

Forty days and forty nights.

Life *really* is about the journey. Triathlon is *seriously* a journey, but I like to think about the race destination being super amazing.

WHAT'S THE POINT?

I sat on a bike on a Wednesday morning, pedalling to nowhere in a local indoor cycling class, looking around, thinking about how much I hated that class and all the people in it. This was not my usual cycling class and I hated it. I watched the clock slowly tick from 5:30 all the way to 6:30.

Thank God, I thought. *6:30. Stupid class.* I plodded to the nearby aerobics studio to stretch when I got a call from my mom on my cell. *6:30am phone call from my mom? Not a good sign.*

"Our house is on fire," she said, crying.

"What?" I whispered.

"Our house. It's burning, Meredith. Oh my gosh…" she faded away.

She was standing outside their home in Savannah with my father watching their home, my childhood home, burn. After a few moments, I hung up, ran down the stairs and out of the gym, carrying my cycling shoes and my phone. Then I ran *back* into the gym, because I forgot my car keys and really, I needed to shower somewhere. I showered. I left my gym card in the locker. I got in the car and I started to drive home from Atlanta to Savannah, but I realized it was rush hour and there was no point. Then I started to drive to *my* house, but that didn't make any sense, because no one was home.

So instead, I went to work.

I tried to find all the loose ends to tie before I left. But then I remembered the Expert was leaving for Australia. I could not take the kids with me to Savannah, to a house that was burned. The kids. Deadlines. The complicated things. I could not connect the dots to make any sense. Over the course of the morning, I talked to my parents.

"The fire is out. We don't know the damage. We don't know what we are going to do. Yes, we called the insurance company. No need for you to come home. There's nowhere for you to---" my dad trailed off.

So I did not go home to Savannah.

I should have, but I listened to them. Plus, I could not figure out how to handle the kids and where we would stay. Instead I booked my parents a hotel in which to take up residence and I waited for updates from them. A family friend texted me a picture of the damage of the house, and I was dumb-struck. The major living area was salvaged and saved from fire, but the smoke damage would be irreparable.

Later that day, my mom told me, "We smell like smoke. Even my deodor-ant smells like smoke. I don't know when we can go home. The wiring is shot. So much has to be replaced. I don't know if the smoke smell will ever go away."

I told her I should be there, I should have come home.

"No," she said, "It's too sad. There's nothing for you to do. And I want you home with my grandbabies. They need you more than this mess needs you."

The next day, I headed to the Greenway for a run, hoping that somehow I could run all the sadness away. I figured that my last long run before Miami would help me figure things out.

Thirteen miles.

My plan did not work. Instead, the thirteen mile planned run came to a sad halt. At four miles, I stopped and started sobbing. I did not cry my usual gratefulness cry, but rather just a helpless cry.

From the Greenway, I was not helping my parents. I was not helping my children. I was not at work. I was not curing cancer. *For God's sake*, I thought to myself. *I am running. In the woods. For what? For w-h-a-t?*

I called the Expert, but it went straight to voicemail. I called my dad, but he didn't answer. Then I sat down on a bench and dialed Coach Monster. I needed him to talk me off the triathlon ledge. But he didn't answer either. So I continued to sit on the bench, listen to the birds and stare into the woods. The trail was quiet. I cried, I questioned all of my life, my motives, my intentions. I ate a Shot Blok® or two. I cried some more. I sobbed and inhaled a Blok. Literally, during a sob I snorted Blok.

But then, I stood up and I ran.

Everything hurt. My feet hurt from the cracked-up shoes I wore to work the day before. My hip hurt. My head hurt. My brain hurt. My back, the muscles and the place where the heart rate monitor strap continues to tear into my skin, run after run, well, that hurt too. My heart hurt for my parents. Everything ached. The so-called "cumulative fatigue" was above my tolerance. I did not want this pain invited into my house anymore. I tried to run it all away, because this often worked. The angry run. The sad run. The purposeful run. One of my favorite quotes (unknown attribu-tion) is:

Swim happy, bike smart, and run angry —
and you will never be disappointed.

But everything just hurt. At 8.5 miles, I stopped running. I walked to my car and I left. *What's the point*, I snorted, slamming the car door.

That afternoon, I found out from my parents that the house was in worse condition than they thought and they were bracing for the tough times ahead.

The next day, I put on my big girl padded pants and went to a lunchtime Spinning class in an attempt to wrap my head back around my goal. I arrived twenty minutes before class, hoping to get in some extra time.

On the screen in the class, the cycling instructor was playing the 2006 Ironman World Championships. I watched. The story about Dick Hoyt and his son, Rick, flashed across the screen.

Rick, as a baby, was diagnosed as a spastic quadriplegic with cerebral palsy. His parents were told to institutionalize Rick because there was no chance of him recovering and living a normal life. Rick's parents did not accept this fate. While Rick could not speak, he was smart.

> "Rick told his father that he wanted to participate in a 5-mile benefit run for a Lacrosse player who had been paralyzed in an accident. Far from being a long-distance runner, Dick agreed to push Rick in his wheelchair and they finished all 5 miles, coming in next to last. That night, Rick told his father, 'Dad, when I'm running, it feels like I'm not handicapped.' This realization was just the beginning of what would become over 1,000 races completed, including marathons, duathlons and triathlons (six of them being Ironman competitions)."[xxviii]

It was almost as if God reached down with giant marker and wrote on the wall in the cycling studio: *That's the point, missy. That is the point of all of this.*

And as I watched the flashbacks to the race where Team Hoyt crossed the finish line at Kona, I got the point.

Triathlon is about so many things: fitness, health, drive, and all the good things that sports bring to a life. But triathlon, perhaps more than any sport, is about the human condition. Triathlon embodies a fight for life, going against the easy way out. It fires up the desire for freedom, for love and for the love of freedom. Any triathlete can tell you that there is something about triathlon, something that makes you feel during those long periods of quiet suffering on a bike or on a run that you can find yourself, seek your purpose in life, help others in ways that would have, at one time, seemed impossible. In those moments, I find that I am immeasurably blessed.

And that is the point.

5 Week Countdown

The final long training days were drawing to a close with a mini-triathlon workout. I could not find anywhere to do an open-water swim, bike, run by myself (safety reasons), so the plan was to go to the pool, then drive to the trail for ride and run.

I approached the swim like a race start and pushed as I believe I would in the race. I finished one mile in thirty-five minutes. Then I dried off, put on my tri top and bottoms, drove thru Starbucks for a coffee and headed to the Silver Comet Trail. If only race day worked like that! Swim, Starbucks and then bike: triathlon would be booming with more members than ever.

Earlier that week I bought Antonia a new rear-mount water bottle cage. Along with the other two holders, I could hold *four* water bottles at one time. Some people made fun of me for doing so—saying that I did not need a rear mount bottle holder for the 70.3 distance race. I still do not know what they are talking about. A 70.3 is seven hours of racing for me, three and a half of which is on the bike. Four bottles is completely reasonable. Yes, I understood completely that water bottle exchanges exist at races. But I also understood that a water bottle exchange could be potentially lethal for someone like me.

In order to use the bottle exchange at a race, I had two options:

1. Exhibit extraordinary feats of non-Swim Bike Klutz and grab a water bottle on the fly (while navigating the other riders doing the same… assuming they haven't all passed me); or
2. Lose "valuable" time and get off the bike to exchange the bottles. I abso- lutely mean "valuable" time, because when I am racing against the DNF (did not finish) clock, time is going to be more precious than ever.

I opted for my four water bottles.

The bike ride was great. I wore tri bottoms (very thin pad in the tri shorts), because I was getting the Queen in race shape. I piled on the Aquaphor and finished thirty-six miles in 2:13:00. I transitioned to the run in about four minutes, which was not bad considering I had to load the bike in the car.

The first two miles of the run felt ridiculously good. So I knew what was coming: the ridiculously bad. But really, the *bad* never came. The *hard?* Yes. But not the *bad?* No.

I ran five miles in fifty-five minutes which was close to a PR for just a run workout. However, that day, I had run fifty-five minutes *with* a swim and bike in front of it.

A triathlon friend asked me that night, "So are you feeling fit, confident and ready (for Miami)?"

I had to think about that question. My answer was: no, no and no. Even still, I knew I would finish the race barring any tragedies or "mechanicals."

I often try to use workout successes to gain confidence. I also try to listen to my inner cheerleader. (In case you were wondering, my inner cheerleader has bright red hair, nice legs and perky boobs.) Unfortunately, days where I *truly* believe in my capabilities are few and far between. So when I do feel capable, I try hard to enjoy the feeling of capability.

FALLING APART

I was scheduled for another eleven-mile run with four weeks left. Time for the vital workouts. But at Mile 3, I fell apart just like the last long run. The *bad* kind of falling apart too. Crying on the trail, and not from being in awe and in a spirit of Oprah-infused gratefulness. But rather we're talking an all-out bawl fest for no apparent reason. No reason other than *I can't do this. Why am I always crying? I can't do this race. I can't. I can't. I'm crying again, geez. This is the second long run I've "blown" in a row. I can't.*

On the way home, I called Coach Monster. I left a blubbering message on his voicemail (he loves me, he *really* does). He called me back a few hours later. We talked. I climbed down from the roof of the building.

The four-weeks-to-70.3 Coach Monster wisdom:

> *"You are not dying. This is not a big deal - it's not cancer, it's not homelessness, it's not job loss. It's triathlon, for God's sake. Enjoy your journey. Stop trying to be what you're not. Listen to your body. Be who you are, right in this second. Be that person. Be grateful. And give yourself a break."*
>
> — COACH MONSTER

Oh, the recurring theme: *Give. Yourself. A. Break.*

The next day, my countdown ticker for 70.3 clicked down to twenty-nine days. I went to the gym before the sun came up. I was beat up a little at work by clients and by a tyrant of a partner at my job. I got a haircut. The Expert was returning from Australia with all his stinky travel laundry. I mean really, life was good.

Why was I having such a hard time remembering the important things?

A TAD INSANE

Triathletes are, without question, a tad insane. Over a year ago, I thought Mountain Goat was crazy for all her self-made Fitness Weekends. Fitness Weekends meant she would run twelve miles then do a bootcamp class. I thought she was crazy then, but now I *know* she's crazy. But now, I am just like her. (Well, I am just like her plus 100 pounds, but equally crazy.)

For example, at the beginning of October I planned to participate in a twenty-four hour bike ride as a part of the 24 Hours of Booty charity event. I planned to ride for "only" two or three or five hours, though. I would ride that *after* I did a 10k race in the morning followed by a swim. Coach Monster was also planning to be at the 24 Hours of Booty ride, but he was "only" going to ride for four of five hours. Said his legs were still sore from his half Ironman (a week ago).

See? Insane.

The Georgia Race for Autism was my first official 10k race. The year before, I had run my first 5k as a wannabe triathlete. My time for the 5k was 38:48, a 12:30-mile pace. That morning, I tackled the 10k and I finished a little over 1:06:00 with a 10:37-minute mile pace. I knocked *two minutes* off my 5k pace from the prior year in a *10k* event. To say I was stoked would be an understatement. The "hills" that were impossible on the 5k course last year were absolutely non-issues. I felt good. It proved to be a much needed boost rolling into Miami.

After a little swim, I headed to Stone Mountain for the cycling event benefitting cancer research with Coach Monster and a few pals.

Run, swim and bike in one day. Yes, insane. And so much fun.

LISTENING

I love Jillian Michaels, trainer and insane motivator from the "The Biggest Loser" television show. I was flipping through the October 2011 edition of a *Redbook* magazine at a hair appointment and I read a great one-on-one interview with her. The interview was so good that I tore out the last part of the article. From a magazine. At a salon. It was very tacky of me, but I was scared I would forget it. After I tore it out, I realized I could have just snapped a picture of the relevant portion on my iPhone. Terrible of me, really.

The interviewer asked Jillian how someone knows when she is ready for a change.

Jillian said, "You feel it. You wake up one morning and you're miserable. Or you're numb. If you feel nothing, obviously you're shutting down the parts of you that are unhappy. We've evolved to have emotions for a reason. They *guide* us."

I found that so interesting. Parts of me had been feeling quite numb lately, and for reasons completely unrelated to the half Iron quest. I acknowledged that my job was absolutely numbing me.

I wanted to call Jillian and ask: "Okay, so when you are numb, how do you become less numb? How do you really change (or change what's eating at you)?"

The article continued. First, Jillian explained that you must trust yourself. She said that the vast majority of people are fear-based and have a "monkey-bar approach to life," meaning that they are paralyzed, unable to leave one bar/place until the next bar is in their grasp. She noted that the monkey-bar approach means that "you never get time to reflect or to create space for what's right," because you're grabbing on to the next thing before the other *thing* is complete. Finally, she said, "you *cannot* listen to the advice of other people. You've got to listen—to the universe, to life, to God…because it's going to speak to you." ^xxix

As I walked out of the salon that day, I wondered if I had been *really listening.* I wondered if the reason I cried all the time when I was running was because I was missing something.

Then, I wondered if I had been listening so intently, that I could not hear anything at all.

Coming Apart at the Seams

With only three weeks until race day, I thought of giving up on Miami. My training in the home stretch (24 days to go) was a complete disaster. The streak of bad workouts rolled into some superstitious streak of bad life luck, an ominous crabby aura that spread around me and my family.

The only funny things that were happening involved me and nakedness at the gym. As I was walking from the shower during a lunchtime swim, wearing nothing but a bitty towel, I slipped. I did not fall. But during the slip, I showed all my goodies to a host of Korean women in the sauna. Who, *God bless them*, did not even flinch.

Then I came home from work to find my baby girl looking like Sloth from *Goonies* with her left eye completely swollen shut. *Some weird, freak bug bite*, said the Doctor. *It should be better pretty quickly with Benedryl.*

Four hours later, she looked as if she had been in the ring with Tyson, and the doc was calling in antibiotics and talking about CT scans, fretting about potential eye damage or worse. *What? From a bug bite?*

Then my parent's received the bad news that their house would be completely gutted as a result of the house fire. They would be displaced for up to a year.

Finally, job-related crap began flying around my life like the scene in *Gremlins II* when the Gremlins took over that office building and started singing "New York, New York."

I took a deep breath and I decided that this was all too much bad luck and I would be turning the frown upside down. I made a conscious effort to find the good and turn the bad streak around. No matter what.

THE MISFITS

But then more bad news.

Steve Jobs, the co-founder of Apple Inc., died on October 5, 2011. I must include him in this book because I owe a lot to him. Many miles of my runs would not have survived without Apple. My iPod. My Eminem. I am thankful for God, my family, triathlon and Steve Jobs.

> *"Here's to the crazy ones. The misfits. The rebels. The troublemakers. The round pegs in the square holes. The ones who see things differently. They're not fond of rules, and they have no respect for the status quo. You can quote them, disagree with them, glorify or vilify them, but the only thing you can't do is ignore them - because they change things. They push the human race forward. And while some may see them as the crazy ones, we see genius. Because the people who are crazy enough to think they can change the world are the ones who do."*
>
> — STEVE JOBS, 1955-2011

THE LAST LONG WORKOUT

The last long workout before the big race was upon me before I could believe it: one-mile swim, forty miles on the bike, followed up by a six-mile run.

Twenty days until the race.

After a good solid hangover and less than five hours of sleep, the Expert and I were ready to roll. A hangover??? Yes. I attended a work event the night before. Hanging out with lawyers means an absolute impossibility not to drink.

Unfortunately, this work event was taking place at the same time the 2011 Ironman World Championships was streaming live online, so I was crabby. The event turned out to be reasonably fun, but it resulted in a late bedtime and early wake-up call.

Well, I thought, *if I can do this crazy workout feeling like dog poop, then I think I will feel ready for the race.* Dog poop is precisely how I felt and smelled. The swim was fine. The bike was torture. Gosh, the Queen was so very unhappy in the saddle for forty straight miles with no break. Finally, the six-mile run was soaring somewhere in the seventh circle of hell.

The Expert and I decided to split up for the bike ride and ride our own ride for the day. He has always been fast on the bike. After thirteen miles, I could no longer see him up ahead of me. We passed each other near the twenty-mile turnaround, and I knew he was gone. He easily had five or six minutes on me by the time I got to the car. He had packed up his bike and headed out for the run. I put Antonia in the car, waited in line at the bathroom for a few minutes, so I was fairly sure I would not catch him. My legs were throbbing. I had been experiencing cramping issues lately (without the hangover), so *with* the hangover, I was cramping pretty badly during the run. Kids on trikes were passing me on the trail.

Near the Mile 3 turnaround, I saw the Expert heading towards me. We bumped fists and passed each other. After I made the turn back home, I could see him up ahead. Little by little, I was getting closer. Finally, about Mile 3.5, I caught him.

He screamed, "What's up, Craig Alexander?"

Gotcha, Lieto.

Chris Lieto is a professional triathlete who creams everyone on the bike leg. Craig Alexander is a master professional triathlete who creams everyone on the run and is remembered well for catching and demoralizing poor Lieto in the World Championships. Much like the Macca and Raelert analogy from our triathlon the month before, the Lieto/Alexander reference was equally as ridiculous.

As soon as I passed the Expert, I got a side stitch that caused me to run crooked and bent to the side for a half mile or so. But, eventually, the darn run was over, and Lieto was only about a minute back.

The Expert said that I was going to smoke him in Miami, but he was absolutely insane. Well, insane people do pretty remarkable things. For example, he had run approximately three total miles before St. Anthony's. He *might* have trained for ten workouts. I followed an intense training program and stuck to it like glue. Which allowed me to beat him by two minutes. Two minutes for my 400 extra hours of training. See? Insane.

The scary part was looming in the distance: the taper. The psychological warfare. The checklists. I could not believe the time had almost come for 70.3.

WETSUIT PART TRES

I had been in a wetsuit three times leading up to Miami. Why? Because Georgia has some pretty warm water (sometimes), I had not encountered a wetsuit race (yet), and because I *@#$!^& hate my wetsuit and would rather grow icicles from my eyeballs and enter the starting stages of hypothermia than wear it. I hate the way it feels, smells, and looks. I feel like a giant, slow moving ORCA in the thing. I do not care about the floatation advantage. I swear the darn thing slows me down. My stroke is restricted. It chokes me no matter how high I pull it up.

The Expert and I went to the lake for a final open water swim. The minute I hit the cool water, I mumbled, "Oh, Lord." I felt panicky, like my first wetsuit encounter, which was not good at all.

The Expert was ahead of me already taking some strokes. He turned back to see me wearing the Freak Out Face.

He screamed, "Oh come on! You've got a Coach. You've done five races. Get a grip! Don't be a sissy!"

"A sissy!? A sissy!?!" I shouted back at him. "You are horrific. And…and…mean!"

"Whatever! Get swimming!" he screamed.

He was right. I did okay. We swam for twenty-five minutes, managed a twenty-mile bike (with about 900 feet of elevation gain) and a one-mile run. I should have run four miles, but I felt a knee pain, and decided nineteen days out was not the time to push it.

During the bike, there were some good climbs. I repeatedly shouted to the Expert, "I can't make it up the hill!"

The Expert called me names again. "You go to cycling class like a madwoman! Get moving! Turn your legs! Coach Monster would be embarrassed *for* you today!"

He was right. I was a complete sissy and Coach M *would* have been so embarrassed. After the turnaround on the bike, I put on my big girl chamois and eventually finished the ride, feeling strong with the final two week countdown to 70.3 bouncing around inside my head.

THE HALF IRONMAN DREAM

TAPER

With nine days until Miami, the word taper sounded like "tapeworm," leaving me to wish I had a tapeworm. A tapeworm would have been more bearable than the taper. Plus, the benefit of tapeworm is skinniness.

The benefits of the race taper are pure insanity, mild depression and serious doubt. And rested legs, hydration and whatever else. At the beginning of the taper, I believed I had a 95% chance of surviving the race. Those odds were way better than I could have predicted a few months earlier.

5 DAYS LEFT

My left hamstring started bothering me with five days left. I believed I would be fine by the race on Sunday. I had five days to rest, ice, rub, and repeat. Admittedly, I was a tad overwhelmed with the magnitude of the 70.3 miles, but only when I thought about it in terms of miles, not hours.

But really, I was overwhelmed with gratitude that I had a body that was even contemplating 70.3 miles. One of my favorite Swim Bike Mom friends, Charlie, sent me a snail mail card prior to the race saying, "You can do this! You *get to do this!*" I put it on the fridge, and I looked at it every day.

On the days when I felt unable to fill my cup with coffee and make it out the door in a forward motion, I realized how blessed I was to have so many people rooting for me.

A 70.3 PRAYER

I wrote a little prayer on my blog with three days remaining.

Dear God,

You may know by now that I am doing something very crazy on Sunday. Travelling by car about 650 miles, so that I can travel by sea, bike and legs another 70.3 miles. It's quite insane really.

Please forgive me for this stupidity.

That being said, please help me remember to be in the moment during the race. To say "thank you", to be thankful, to be appreciative, to enjoy the sun and the sweat, the tears and the aches.

I pray that I will stay upright on my own two feet.

Please guide me through the aid stations, so that I do not harm the volunteers with my flailing arms or wandering bicycle.

I pray that you will place your guiding hand across me as I swim, keeping me going towards the buoys, and not back to the shore where my instincts will try to take me. Please keep the sharks away.

Please please please do not let me have a flat. And if I do have a flat, please cause my feeble girl arms to become super Go-Go Gadget arms with massive tube-changing powers. Help me keep my greasy hands away from my face. Race pictures are perilous enough.

Let the 1.2 mile swim feel like 100 yards, the bike as if I am giggling away on a tricycle, and the run like a skip in the park. (Okay, that's alot to ask). I amend: please help the cramping, delirium and the desire to curse to remain at a minimum.

I am so thankful for the Expert, my family, and my Swim Bike Mom blog friends. I am able to do this race. I am able to start, and hopefully finish.

And for that small fact, I am thankful.

Amen.

PACKING: THE CHECKLIST: HALF IRONMAN

Goggles. Extra Goggles. Extra Goggles. Extra Goggles. Sunscreen. Gels. Shot Bloks. Aquaphor. Trisuit. Backup Trisuit. Salt Tablets. Gatorade G2. Bike. Helmet. Water Bottles. Bike Shoes. Socks (2 pairs). Running Shoes. Visor. Glasses. Race Number Belt. Fuel Belt. Nuun. Tire Tubes. Tire Levers. C02 Cartridges. Plastic Bag (in case of rain or for wet clothes). Post-Race Clothes. Flip-flops. Transition Area Mat. Deodorant. Hair Bands. Backpack. Money. ID. Phone. Camera. Lip Balm. Inhaler. Towel. Peanut Butter. Vodka. Valium. Barf Bag. Done.

As I packed my race bag, I was amazed that I did not have to think twice about the gear I needed for the race. I had put in so much time and work, sucked 1,000,000 gels into my belly so many times that I just packed my bag and it was done. I looked over my checklist and race plan from Coach Monster to confirm, but all the right stuff was there, by instinct.

My favorite part of the packing story, of course, involved the Expert, and went something like this.

"Do you think we can fit both wetsuits in this bag?" I asked him.

"Yes, we do it all the time," he said.

"All the time?"

"Yes."

"All the time? You mean, like the one time we took the wetsuits on a trip?" I asked.

"Yes," he said.

FRIDAY: TRAVEL DAY

The car was packed and ready, promising what appeared to be an eleven or twelve hour drive to Miami depending on traffic and my hydration levels. We were waiting for the sun to come up, the sitter to arrive and the vicious Atlanta traffic to die down. I sat on the couch, sandwiched in between my two baby monkeys and twiddling my thumbs watching Mickey Mouse Clubhouse ("come inside, it's fun inside!").

I remembered packing the car for St. Anthony's only six months before. I was so freaked out by the idea of travelling to a race. Plus, I was freaked out about actually racing, but that's beside the point. St. Anthony's was a huge deal for me and the Expert. Huge. Not to mention, we were huge-er, too. I tipped over and injured myself before the race. I was scared. But it was an amazing experience.

I found that when I create new, larger-than-life goals I also have a tendency to "forget" how far I've come during the journey. Really, that's a collective issue with triathletes in general. Something as simple as: *"I never could run a half-mile, and now I can, and pretty darn fast…and without death or destruction to others"* should be memorized, held close to heart and repeated daily.

Waiting for the road trip and holding my children, I was amazed at the sheer goodness of moving forward. Just moving forward, a little, every day. Plugging along steadily, honestly and with accountability. Some days required a whole lot more moving than others. But with that forward motion, the Expert and I had made it. We were traveling to a half Ironman. The two of us. Half Ironman. Insanity.

No matter what happened in Miami, I promised myself that I would remain proud of the craziness that I had created from just a simple Decision. I figured I would surely vomit a little when I picked up my race packet. But as long as my race number was not "666," I thought I would be okay.

RACE PACKET PICKUP

I was bib #806. I do not like round numbers. I like pointy numbers, because I think they make me look leaner.

As far as the weather forecast for Miami, a tropical storm was brewing and causing some disgusting weather. The forecast predicted massive thunderstorms for race day. I was freaking out because the last thing in the world I wanted was a cancelled swim. So I just remained hopeful that Miami 70.3 would just turn into some big Xterra® type adventure (mud, wind, and crazy) versus just a duathlon or half marathon. I know the concern is safety when the weather booms in, but I had worked so hard for a shot at my 70.3 sticker for my car. [If they cancelled the swim, where would I find the 69.1 bumper sticker? And even if I found one, could I really put that on my car?]

I had orders from Coach Monster to do nothing but lay because I was having a terrible time with my left hip and hamstring. On Friday morning, I woke up with a screaming head cold. I was coughing up small children and sneezing like crazy. The cold was most likely from being cooped up with so much knowledge in the car with an Expert for 11 hours. My head was so clogged! So much knowledge I had to hear!

The clouds were rolling in and hovering over Miami during athlete check-in. By then, my head was completely clogged up and pounding. I could not believe the crazy last-minute factors that entered an already nutty situation (the race itself): the evil weather, a hamstring injury, a head cold, an Expert and a two *loop* run course (boo). Plus, I had not moved in a week, trying to stay off the hamstring, so I felt downright strange.

The race packet was in my possession, which made the race countdown clock terrifying. Truly, I was fine until I saw my swim cap. And my race numbers. And pretty much all the super lean-mean people wandering around the race venue.

I spent a fortune in the merchandise tent, sweating in the heat, the Expert aggravated at me. I knew I had to finish. Otherwise, I would be stuck with a 70.3 race kit, sweatshirt, coffee cup, visor, wicking tee.... *Well*, I thought, *I'll just open up an eBay store if the wheels fly off this race.*

At bedtime, I still felt bizarre. I had big hopes: hoping that all the training was enough. Hoping that the head cold would stop pounding. I looked over at the Expert in his bed. (Cleaver beds, remember = a race secret).

The Expert was very quiet. The next day we would check the bikes and begin the twenty-four-hour long prayer vigil.

21 Hours

The head cold was in full force. I looked and felt like the spawn of Satan. I chose to ignore it. The weather seemed to be smiling a little after raining all night. I had ants in my pants. Antonia was racked at the race venue, along with the Expert's nameless bike. Everything was ready. I sat around in my compression socks, icing miscellaneous body parts and snuggling up to ice packs and listening to the rain.

During the thunderstorms the night before, I received a "fan" email that changed this race for me. A woman told me that her life (and her racing) was forever changed when she decided to stop believing the lies about her efforts not being good enough. She chose to stop believing the lies about her body not being good enough. She wrote that once she made *that* simple choice she gained a newfound confidence, crushed her race, and it changed her forever.

That email was a valuable thing for me to read: *choose to ignore the lies.* The lies from others, yes. But most importantly, the lies in my own head.

The Expert and I watched the odometer on our Honda Pilot turn to "77777" as we traveled down to Miami. I thought it a stroke of luck, but also something about our journey together. We had purchased the Pilot in 2007, with just a few miles on it. I was pregnant with James, our first. Of course, life changed forever once the kids started showing up. Life continues to change, by the day, by the moment. If the 2007 Me could have looked in the future to see the 2011 Me, the 2007 Me would have laughed out loud and declared the future downright wrong.

No matter what happened in the race, I knew that I had learned a huge lesson:

> *Don't count yourself out.*
> *Ever.*
> *Anything is possible.*

Just Give it a Year

August 26, 2010:

- I could not run two miles without dying, bike eight miles without falling, or swim two laps without drowning

- My heart rate was off the charts from the second I laced up my shoes
- I was 25 pounds heavier
- I was worn out, run down, and on the verge of giving up on *ever* being an athlete again
- I had no idea what I wanted out of my life
- A triathlon seemed like a pipe dream, although I dreamed it anyway
- An Olympic distance tri seemed unreachable
- A half Ironman would be impossible
- An Ironman…unthinkable

One Year Later: October 29, 2011:

- I had run 13.1 miles; I had biked fifty-two miles; I swam two miles. I was still alive.
- My heart rate was steady, consistent, and improving
- I was two jeans sizes smaller
- Yes, I was still tired. But I was a tired *athlete*, not a tired couch potato.
- I was not giving up. Period.
- I was learning *what* my life should be
- Not just one…but I had completed four triathlons …Including two Olympic distance triathlons
- My first half Ironman was just hours away
- An Ironman? Well…

I looked over this list right before I went to bed, less than twelve hours away from the race start. I closed my eyes and I appreciated how far I had come. I fell asleep. I actually slept well.

And just like that…the day had arrived.

THE IRONMAN 70.3 MIAMI RACE REPORT

PRE-RACE

Our alarm went off at 4:15. I looked over to the other bed, housing the Expert.
I said, "Oh no."
He opened one eye and said, "I know."

I was so tired. He was tired. I was so sniffly. I was so flipping puffy from the salt intake. Oh, the salt. Even better, I had not completed a single workout in almost ten days, due to my hamstring issues.

At 4:20 on race morning, I found myself just plain dumbstruck. ~~I knew what was about to happen. I suspected what was about to happen.~~

I had no idea what was coming.

SET-UP AND WATERLOGGED

We arrived at the race venue about 5:15 am. The rain was pouring. Pouring. Pouring. We parked about 12,000 miles from transition.

"Five-dollar parking! Goody!" said the Expert.

The dichotomy in the parking garage was amazing. The race was Halloween weekend. On one hand, the triathletes were rolling in, ready to race. On the other hand, a nightclub was closing and releasing the drunken Halloweeners out into the early morning. Crazy drunk kitty cats and witches. Crazy drunk nurses and ghosts. Crazy sober tired people with helmets (oh wait, that was us). The Expert and I sat in the car and watched the circus for a bit. We cheered from inside the car as a Chippendale tried to go home with a Naughty Devil. He succeeded.

We walked to transition in the pouring rain. Coach Monster called me. I knew who was calling without even looking at the phone. Only two crazy people could be calling me at that hour. And I had already talked to my dad for the early morning pep talk. I answered. As Coach M was in process of giving me the awesome pep talk, I slid on the wet pavement and cracked my toe on the curb. Flip-flops may be the name of the game on race morning, but I am way too clumsy for flops. Lesson learned. I cursed a little and listened intently to Coach M.

At 5:25, we were standing in transition, near soaking wet Antonia. The Expert hugged me, said he'd be back in a bit, and went off to prepare his transition spot.

I stood near Antonia for a long while, letting the rain pound the top of my head, my shoulders. The water dripped down my face and I did not bother to wipe it away. I stared at all the bikes. I looked at Antonia. I could not figure out where exactly my transition space was. I thought transition space was always under the back wheel. But all the fit people were using the front wheel as the guide. I was paralyzed with this tiny decision.

I stood, holding my bag and staring into the rain for fifteen minutes. In fact, I stood there flabbergasted for so long, the Expert had time to pump his tires and set up his entire transition area.

He came over to me. "You ready?" he asked. I blinked and stared at him. He looked at me, standing there all doe-eyed, with my race bag completely packed.

"Do I look like I am ready?" I wailed. "Oh mah gawdddddd."

Swim Start

I do not remember doing so, but I must have unpacked my stuff and set up my transition area. I remember the Expert pumped my tires. I was thankful for that. No way my hands could have worked. My transition area was ready, probably from no help of my own.

The Expert and I wandered to the swim start about 5:50 a.m. The rain continued to mercilessly come down, and we began to get cold. In Miami? Cold? Ridiculous. We found a place under a tree to sit, but the mean tree just poured fat, sloppy rain on us. There was nowhere to hide from the rain. Finally, I slapped on my swim cap just to keep my head warm. That worked a little.

"What have you gotten us into?" the Expert asked me.

"I don't want to talk about it," I said.

The Sun appeared to come up, but only because the sky brightened. There was no actual sighting of said Sun. About 7:30ish, the first starting gun went off, and the Pro Men took off swimming. The swim was set up like an evil triangle. A triangle that started with a jump off a dock, a swim out and tread water until the gun started.

I was in Wave 9. The Expert was in Wave 15, I think. I kissed the Expert and waddled off in the rain to find my people. I did not go far, however, before I slipped one more time on the pavement. I did not fall, but as I was cursing, I had to dodge a falling age grouper as he hit the pavement.

This race is already sheer carnage, I thought.

I was pretty impressed with the wave organization. I followed a person waving a sign that said "Female 30-34" and had a silver swim cap attached to it. That was my wave! My wave! I looked around at my fellow silver caps. Unlike local races, there were no Average Janes. In local races, where I can race Athena, I felt a little more in place. Here? There were no Athenas in sight. In fact, there were no women who were within 15 pounds of Athena.

Where are the other fat girls? I thought to myself. *Where are ANY fat people, for that matter?*

In that moment, I felt a little sick. Not nervous. But sick. Had I had bit off more than I could chew? Was I overconfident? Was I clinically insane? The silver caps inched our way down to the dock. I pulled my goggles down over my eyes. I could see the Expert from the shore. At most races, we have a hard time distinguishing each other from the other swim capped people. I waved. He immediately waved. Oh. He could easily distinguish me. I was a sore thumb in my group. Like the one who had just attacked Krispy Kreme a few moments before. I felt sick again.

Another starting gun and the wave ahead, the pink caps, took off. The silver caps all walked to the edge of the dock and we jumped in the water. I swam out.

Swim

One minute to start, the announcer said. I felt strangely calm. I repeated to myself: *This is just a workout. Just a workout. This is just a long workout.*

The announcer boomed, *Thirty seconds to start.* I counted down the seconds in my head. I said a quick prayer. As I said, *Amen,* the starting gun went off and I pushed forward. Once my face hit the water, I was calm. I felt in control. I felt so strong. *Yes,* I thought, *this is going to be awesome!*

Then I realized that I was experiencing the longest, saltiest swim in the history of the world. I had never seen so many buoys in my life. Yellow, red, orange. Hundreds of them. (Okay, maybe ten). I pushed on, spitting sea grass out of my mouth. Ahead, I saw some pink swim caps, meaning that I had caught up to the previous wave. Forward progress!

More sea grass attacked me. And so did the men in the green cap and purple cap waves behind me. One guy swam over me. Literally. I felt a hand on my butt, then I felt an entire body go over me. Out of the corner of my eye, I saw a furry belly pass right over my face – and not in a sexy way. In an *OMG, I'm being killed* kind of way. Repeatedly, I was knocked around and kicked in the head. I was elbowed.

No matter how far to the side I attempted to be, to stay out of the way of the fast people, I was constantly in someone's way. At the same time, people were in *my* way, too. Maybe that's just open water swimming. We are fish without the ability to swim like fish and know our territory.

I rounded the last turn buoy and swam the last 500 meters to safety.

Swim Time, 1.2 Miles: 46:08

I walked my jelly legs up the stairs, and went through the fresh water rinse. As I "ran" to transition, I swore the crowd of people was judging me. I might as well have been naked. I felt huge and seriously out of place.

In that moment, I had a decision to make. Was I going to spend the entire race looking down? Thinking I did not belong? And why? Because (to quote Bridget Jones): "I can't ski, I can't ride, I can't speak Latin, my legs only come up to here and yes...I will always be just a little bit fat"?

No. I was not going to do that. I had worked too hard. I held my salty head up, and made it alive into transition.

I had a good, rather uneventful T1, considering the distance to travel from the swim finish to the transition area. Coach Monster had mentioned how imprecise the fine motor skills can be in transition, which is part of the reason to practice transitions. This swim was the longest race swim I had done, and I noticed how correct he was. My fingers seemed to go in opposite directions.

I could not bear the thought of putting on socks or gloves. I was so soggy, and with the rain, plus the swim – well, I had been soggy for almost four hours. I did not want wet socks or wet gloves, because that's what happens. No matter how much you try to prevent it, wet socks happen from coming out of the water. Water squeezes out of your suit as you pedal, runs down the legs, and wets the socks. I was not up for it. I slapped on my wet helmet. I slipped on my dry shoes (which had been in a plastic bag), and I tucked my wet sunglasses into my trisuit.

I exited T1 with a time of about six minutes.

Bike

The bike leg was ridiculous. Ri-dic-ulous. Headwinds, side winds, rain, bumpy pavement, traffic, railroad crossings. The ride was on a major roadway, and although the entire left lane was blocked off with orange cones for the race, the traffic was sketchy and scary. Coupled with horrendous winds, it was a nasty bike leg. I could not believe the amount of sheer cyclist carnage on the road. I saw a pile-up of six super-fit athletes on the side of the road heading out on the course and I was shaken to my core. Apparently, there were several crashes at the railroad crossings.

The bike was mostly this: "On your left" "On your left" "On your left" "On your left" "On your left" "On your left" "On your left" "On your left" "On your left" "On your left" "On your left" "On your left" "On your left" "On your left!!!!"

Despite the headwind, I had a good time on the bike, averaging about 16.5 MPH. The first half of the bike was much better, as the wind caught me hardcore after the turn-around. I found plenty of time to be grateful during the bike portion, despite the evil winds and tough conditions. I spent moments thanking God for the day, and I really took the time to appreciate that I was half-way through the race—and still alive.

I saw two aide stations on the bike course. I avoided them like the plague. I had four bottles on my bike, which was a good idea (despite some of the criticisms I received about the extra weight). When people would say, "Why would you want the extra weight of bottles on your bike?" I would look at them and stare blankly. *Really? When I am carrying around 60 POUNDS of extra weight, do you think 2 pounds of necessary water is going to be the straw that breaks the camel's back?* Anyway, I was thrilled to have my water on my bike, because apparently no one can operate a bike and grab food/water simultaneously. I stayed far away from the hand-offs, and I still almost fell victim to other cyclists clambering for water.

On the "left," experienced cyclists blew by. On the right, eighteen wheeler trucks flew past me. Sometimes it was scary. Of course, an argument can be made to get rid of the sissies like me, and the course would have been roomy.

I hit the bike wall about Mile 44. I wanted off that bike. The Queen was an angry, bitter Queen at this point. I stood up in the saddle to give her some relief, but she yelled louder when I sat back down. I decided she would have to tough it out. So the Queen was angry, and I was also hungry, but sort of shaky and not feeling like swallowing anything. I did take a few salt tabs, because the sun had come out, promising a hot run.

My total nutrition taken in during the bike consisted of:

4 bottles of Gatorade G2
1 pack of Clif Shot Bloks
4 GU gels
3 salt tabs

In hindsight and knowing now what I know about sports "drinks" versus "beverages," the Gatorade G2 was not enough of anything. This nutrition was not enough nutrition. For my next 70.3, I'm packing a peanut butter and jelly sandwich, and scarfing it down right out of the gate. All jokes aside.

Bike Time, 56 miles: 3:23:38

I had never been so glad to see a sign in my life: Bike In. After an uneventful dismount (thank you sweet Lord), I ~~trotted~~ ~~walked~~ limped to my transition spot. I had to pee so badly. But I could not, for the life of me, see the Porta-Potties. Even though I swore I had scoped them out the day before.

Where is the potty? Where? I searched and mumbled.

Finally, I knew it was hopeless. I sat on the grass, put on my socks, shoes, Fuel Belt, and just peed in the grass, sitting there right under Antonia. Yes, through my trisuit. And no, not near anyone else's transition stuff. Plus, my transition neighbors were long gone, off on the run. My potty break was not sexy, but it was the best idea ever. And it was still drizzling a little, so it felt sanitary. You gotta do what you gotta do.

Run

I ran out of transition, feeling pretty good. *Run and done, run and done,* I repeated to myself, over and over. I had a two-loop course ahead of me. As I've mentioned, I like two-loop courses almost as much as I like childbirth. I started off pacing at about a 12:00-minute mile, which according to my training, would have been reasonable. Strategically, I was thinking, I could finish with about a 12:30 pace.

At the Mile 1 sign, I almost cursed out loud. Mile 1? Mile 1!? *That means I have 12.1 to go. 12.1! 12.1!*

My legs stopped working shortly thereafter. The legs were moving forward, but my hamstrings were not *firing*. I could not get the legs to *turn over*. Instead, I was dragging them behind me like tree trunks. By Mile 2, I knew I was in for a 70.3 special treat.

The run went over the McArthur Causeway, which on fresh legs would have been tough, although arguably fun. But after four hours of swimming and biking, the trek over the causeways did not bring "fun" to mind. I was thinking more along the lines of alien autopsy, or anal probe.

I jogged the first 3 miles of the run. I looked at my Garmin at one point, and I was chugging along at a 4.4 mph pace. *I can walk faster than this*, I thought. At the top of the bridge, I had to walk. I walked because I knew I had 9.5 miles to go. I trotted downhill, thinking that the turn-around was close, thinking that I could say I was one-quarter complete. But I was wrong.

On the way back up the causeway, I started to feel a tad better. I had a few GU gels. Plus, the aide stations were awesome. With ice, water, coke, bananas, oranges, there was something for me at every turn. I never thought I would want fruit during a race, but I devoured oranges at every turn. The texture was divine. After five solid hours of baby food (gels), real fruit was delicious.

However, I only felt good for a little while. I was beginning to cramp up a little, and my legs refused to turn over.

The first loop was bad. The second loop was hell.

As I headed down the home chute (but to start my second loop), the crowd was cheering. They clearly thought I was about to finish. As I made the turn around, I was deflated. Another 6.2 virtually felt impossible. I walked for a solid five minutes, slowly moving right past the crowd that cheered me in.

The sun was out and the rain had stopped completely. The heat began to take over, wear me down. Somewhere on the way out on the second loop, I saw the Expert. I began to cry. I saw him coming for about 100 yards. The closer he got, the more I cried. We crossed, slapped hands and he asked, "Are you okay?"

I sobbed, "Yes. I am just glad to see you. How do you feel?"

"Great!" he said.

Going up the causeway for the second time, I was wrecked. The left lane was blocked off for the runners, but traffic continued to flow in the right lane. Frankly, I was pretty disoriented. At one point, I lost my whereabouts, and I stumbled. A Mazda honked at me. I was over the cones, and I had no clue.

On and on I ran. I walked. I had ZERO grateful moments. Not because I wasn't grateful, but because I was lost. I was wandering. I do not remember much from Mile 7 to Mile 10. I just remember constantly talking to myself, with every footstep, I thought, *Just. Move. Forward. Just. Move. Forward. Just. Move. Forward.*

Bridge up, bridge down, bridge up, bridge down.

I had snagged a small washcloth from the hotel room before the race. I am not sure how I ended up with it during the run. Maybe because it was raining, and I thought I might want to wipe my face? Regardless, I had a washcloth with me. Several times during the run I took some ice from the aide station, placed it in my washcloth and held it in my fist. Every so often, I would wipe my face, my arms, and my chest. The ice was amazing and it truly helped keep me cool. I always thought it extremely dorky that the professional triathlete wore a glove filled with ice. Boy, he is on to something. Next half, I will be wearing latex gloves. Maybe the kitchen variety, just for fun.

At Mile 8.5, I stopped to pee in a Porta-Potty. I opened the door, shut the door, locked the door. I turned around, and as my eyes adjusted to the darkness, I saw something on the seat. *What IS that?* I wondered. I squinted. *Oh. That's poop. Poop. Poop. Poop.* I repeated it in my mind. "Crap," I said out loud.

Indeed.

I was in a Porta Potty. I had been moving for going on six hours. I was tired. I was thirsty. I was hungry. And now, I was talking with a poo pile. A real, live steamy poo. On the seat. On. The. Seat. I closed my eyes. And I hovered over it. *This is it*, I thought. *I am in this to finish, and finish strong. Because otherwise I truly cannot justify this moment. Poop. I cannot tell my kids one day that I peed, hovering over a stranger's poop, and then say,* yeah, well I didn't finish that race. *Oh, hell no. I am going to finish.*

I kept moving. *Just. Move. Forward. Just. Move. Forward.* It was then I saw the Mile 9 sign. Four more miles. Four More. Miles. No. No. No.

My Nutrition taken in during the run:

2 bananas
2 oranges
2 GUs
2 packs of Shot Bloks
6 Nuun tablets
1 Gatorade G2
7 cups of water
2 handfuls of ice
1 cup of cola

In hindsight, that was not enough nutrition. I wish I could have had cola. I have a corn allergy, so I believed it best not to gulp down corn syrup based liquid. But man, I wanted cola. So I had a small cup. It did give me a boost, but it also impacted my respiratory system. I felt it immediately, so the cola was both a good and bad idea.

With 1.5 miles to go, I saw a race volunteer. He was a long-haired, teenager—a kid, really. As I shuffled by him, only a short distance remaining to completing my ultimate quest, he snickered, snorted and then laughed at me. I thought I was mistaken. But then he looked at me, nudged his buddy standing next to him, and snorted again.

I stopped.

For just a second. I stood still. I looked at him, and I said, "Did you @#%*ing just laugh at me?"

His little baby eyes grew big, and he turned away, embarrassed. I knew I had not imagined the scoffing when a crowd member said, "YEAH! What she said! Go girl!!" Oh boy. A mean teenager laughed at me. What was I? A five-year old? At this stage of the race? Yes. Yes, I was.

After all, I was eating gels and peeing on myself, wearing the chamois diaper, drinking out of bottles. My article, "Triathletes are Babies" was born on the Miami course, after that mean kid laughed at me. So I guess I can thank him for that.

So I snorted, and I kept going. *Just. Move. Forward. Just. Move. Forward.* Mile 12.5.

Before I knew it, I could hear the finish line. Hear the finish line? Yes. Anyone who races knows exactly what I mean. Sometimes you can hear music, an announcer, and maybe some cheers. But somehow, I swear my ears ingest sounds of finish, applause and satisfaction a few seconds before the ears could possibly physically, actually *hear* these sounds. Maybe it's the sheer *hope* for the finish that makes me hear things.

As I was running down the chute, I looked at my watch. I had hoped for a 6:50:00 time. I looked at my watch 7:14:00 and I was thrilled. I had made it. I took a few minutes to enjoy the run home. People clapped and cheered. I saw surprised faces, encouragement, laughter, smiles and heard lots of "go girl" and "way to go!" I heard it all. When I saw the Ironman 70.3 Miami Finish Line banner, I put my hand on my heart, then my head, and I said, "Thank you, God. Thank you." And I meant it with every fiber of my being.

Run Time: 13.1 miles, 2:54:40

As I crossed the finish line, I threw out my thumbs-up, I did a fist pump, and I jumped. I was foolish.

It. Was. Done. I was half an Ironman.

70.3 Miles
Total Race Time: 7:15:24

The Expert finished a little while later and I cried. Yes, again. I smelled like the dirtiest, smelliest billy goat in the entire world. Salt was crystallized on every surface of my skin. I was sunburned. I looked beaten. We had planned for a big night out. I had brought a fancy dress to wear. But we couldn't walk. We didn't want to walk. I could not hold my arms up to dry my hair.

We decided the hotel restaurant was perfect. We devoured everything they had on the menu: chicken wings, spring rolls, pizza, hamburger, and cake. Between the two of us: 3 glasses of wine, 3 beers, and a mojito. In an hour.

As I was stuffing cake into my mouth, Coach Monster called me.

"How is my half Ironman?" he asked.

"Hungry!" I said.

"What happened on your swim?" he asked.

"What do you mean?"

"Well, it was slow," he said, teasing me.

I said, "No, my run was slow!"

He laughed and turned on his serious voice, "Congratulations. I am so proud of you. You did the work. You earned your finish. Congratulations."

I got a little teary. "Thank you."

"Now," he said, "Tell me about the race...."

As I finished telling him about the race, Coach M told me to put together a race report as quickly as I could remember, to consider the good and the bad about the race, and the lessons learned. I promised I would. As I hung up the phone, finished my cake, I felt as proud as I had ever been in my life.

But I was still hungry.

The Expert and I headed up to the hotel room, exhausted and crashed out, dead asleep. But not before I realized that I only had one bike shoe and no flip-flops. Oh, and no helmet. I abandoned an entire bag in the transition area as we left the race venue, including the Expert's race shirt. Then, the next day driving home, the Expert and I realized we left all of our Ironman 70.3 goodies and shirts and magnets in the hotel. I called the manager, frantic. He shipped the goods to me, and I was grateful.

What I Learned from 70.3

I finished 67 out of 75 in my division, number 340 out of 367 women. I finished 51 in the swim, 57 on the bike. The run obliterated me, obviously. But what did I learn?

I needed to run more. I needed to perfect my run. My run suffered. I suffered. I cursed the running gods. I knew I needed to run more.

I learned that while I may be fat, sometimes people are often fat buttheads. I was so thankful for the hordes of supportive crowd-goers. That one kid was really the only bad apple I encountered. As I had rounded the finish, one lady yelled, "Hey you!" and I looked to her. She was about my size, about my age, and she said, "You are awesome!" The best part about that comment? I could tell that she meant it. So the crowd was incredible.

Still. To have someone *laugh* at me, to have someone scoff at my seven-hour effort? It was bizarre. I wanted to scream, cry and curse. But I didn't. Because to focus on that kind of poisonous negativity, with only 1.5 miles to go, would have made *my* hard work, *my* race...about *that kid,* about *negativity.* And there was no way *that kid* deserved my day. So instead, I repeated, *Just. Move. Forward.*

Interestingly, I learned that I was worthy of the finish. I had worked for it, and I deserved the happy finish. Truly there are few things in life that are "deserved". Think about it. In our entitled society, what is truly earned, and truly deserved? I am *blessed* with a good family, a job, a healthy body—I do not *deserve* these things. But a race finish? That is something that can be *deserved.*

Finally, I learned that really, no one cares. I had completed an epic thing in my mind, my soul and in my heart. But guess what? No one cared. People outside of triathlon thought I was incredibly weird. People at work wondered why I would come to work smelling like a pool. The lesson to this?

When *you* do something epic, then *you* better care. Because *you* are *all* that *you* have. Remember to tuck away your victories and hold them close. You better know. You better believe. In quiet moments when you doubt your abilities, you can go back to these victories and your strengths, your capabilities. You can find more fight inside yourself. Remember the feelings, the sounds and the smells. Because no one else will. Even if they do remember, chances are, they really do not care.

Most importantly, I learned the importance of believing in myself. The importance of *Just. Keeping. Moving. Forward.* As I crossed the Miami finish line, I was exhausted. But I remember thinking, *Everyone should have the chance to do this. Everyone.*

When the Expert and I returned to Atlanta, our daughter, Stella, ran to me screaming, "Mommy! Mommy!"

"Hi baby!" I said.

"Oh," Stella said, "You run? You ride your *tricycle*? You swim, Mommy?"

"Yes, baby," I smiled, "Yes, Mommy did."

I didn't have the heart to tell her that…indeed, Mommy at times felt like she was riding a *tricycle*.

BrightRoom.com

384

In Closing

> *"The question isn't who is going to let me;*
> *it's who is going to stop me."*
>
> — AYN RAND

Whether you are embarking on your triathlon journey or continuing it, embrace this attitude. This frame of mind is deliciously obnoxious, and will carry you far in your training and on race day.

People who are content to sit, to watch their lives roll on past, will not understand this kind of attitude. I was previously one of these people, but triathlon changed that. When you find yourself on the right side of the motivational fence, be aware that others may not feel the love.

Others may (will) start to resent you for your new outlook on life. The resentment will start small and harmless, like in the break room at work, "OMG, how can you get up at 4:30 a.m. to go to the *gym?*" Then the more determined you become, the more you will actually see the resentment, the eye-rolling, the snickers.

Even people close to you, people who love you may try to derail you. Say you will accomplish something big. Say it out loud, blog about it, scream it from the rooftops, and watch the negativity and resentment unfold right before your eyes. I watched it happen from the time St. Anthony's was a glimmer in my eyes until I crossed the finish line at Miami 70.3. Actually, I still see it. When I say, "I am training for an Ironman."

Outside negativity does one of two things *to* you when you are seeking to accomplish a new, scary goal:

1. The negativity either thrusts you into "I'll show you" mode and acts as a facilitator for your training, or

2. The negativity knocks you down completely, deflating your confidence and ending the goal.

Choose the first one. Stay focused. Let the bad days "go," and just do better the next day.

© BrightRoom.com

I hope you know how much *I* believe in you. I may have never met you, but here's what I accept as true: You can do a triathlon. You can do a sprint distance. You can do a half Ironman. You can do an Ironman. Just pick your poison—and go for it. You can do it. I believe in *you*, because I believed in myself—I could not swim, bike or run worth a hill of beans two years ago— but with some hard work, I finished a half Ironman. Then I finished another.

You can do this.

Repeat After Me

Whatever your goal, show those negative people who you are.
Better yet, prove yourself to <u>*yourself*</u>*.*
Let the only person who can stop you…be you.
Believe in yourself.
You are stronger than you imagine.
Importantly, tell yourself:
"Yes. I. Can. And. I.Will."
Take one step at a time.

But always…

Just keep moving forward, my friend.

From Swim Bike Mom Friends

Swim Bike Mom blog friends are the best. The SBM Blog community is a huge source of inspiration, and I am forever grateful. When I asked the question: "Who Are You?" I was flooded with amazing answers. I thank all of you for your willingness to share, to keep moving and to be exactly who you are.

WHO ARE YOU?

- **JT:** My life fell apart when my husband told me he was done with our marriage. I have found healing through triathlon training. It all allows me to reflect on my past, in order to make a better future.
- **Maryann:** I am a working mother of three children (ages 9, 6, 4). I have always been active, but began participating in triathlons last year at the age of forty-one. I was diagnosed with early stage breast cancer in 2010. I started my training while in the middle of radiation treatment. I firmly believe that triathlon has saved my sanity and in some regards, my life.
- **Trish:** I see triathlon as a way to learn to love the body I live in now. If that body lets me swim, bike and run, then it's harder to beat myself up about the number on the scale!
- **Leslie**: I secretly want to complete a full [140.6]; I am thinking Ironman Cozumel November 2012. I will be forty-years old.
- **Jennifer**: I am a lawyer. Contrary to popular belief, most lawyers are okay people. I turned down Harvard law because, well, they didn't have Duke basketball. I won first place in the Athena division of last year's Tri Rock Sprint in Rockwall, TX, much to my surprise. Clearly, the 150 pound Athenas had somewhere else to be that day. But the slab of rock I got for a trophy is pretty sweet.

- **Marison:** I'm stronger, fitter and healthier today (at age forty-five) that I was in my twenties. I love that I'm an example for my nieces who have embraced an active and healthy lifestyle even at such young ages.
- **Lauri:** I lost my mother and grandmother within six months of each another to ovarian cancer. I figured the best way that I could fight against a disease that is a hereditary threat to me, my sister, my nieces and most of all, my own daughter, is through my love of endurance sports. Plus, I've always wanted to hear the words "You are an Ironman!" [Note: per Lauri's website, she finished Ironman Texas in May 2012 in a little over fifteen hours!]
- **Kandi:** I competed in my first triathlon when I was fifty-years old. Triathlon is a good way to have fun and be fit. Nothing gets overworked, but everything gets worked! I love to cycle, I enjoy swimming and I am learning to tolerate running. Put all three activities together, throw in a stopwatch to see how fast you can transition from one sport to the next... well, it's so wacky, it makes me smile!
- **Kathy**: I have been married to a wonderful guy for twenty-eight years. We have a twenty-year old son who has a disability and two dogs. I fell in *love* with triathlon. I always feel at peace during a tri, more than I do at any other race.
- **Holly**: I found [SwimBikeMom.com] earlier in the year right after I started writing my own blog. Her goals inspire me to believe in myself (so basically she's free therapy). (www.mamagetsmoving.com)
- **Bonnie**: Currently, I am a stay-at-home wife (with three kids). I say "wife" instead of "mother" because I want my marriage to always be the primary family relationship...I am passionate about positive birth experiences for women and had a wonderful homebirth in November 2011 with my third child. Someday, I would love to hear "Bonnie-you are an Ironman!" (even if my time is 16:59:59).
- **Amanda**: Three years ago my son was born with a congenital heart defect and cystic fibrosis. For the first eighteen months, everything I did was about him. Then after losing two later pregnancies, a friend dragged me back into triathlon to gain my life and confidence back. I haven't looked back since.

- **Jenee:** I'm a tri-ing mom of two (a special-needs teen and a healthy toddler) and wife to an infinitely patient man. And I do mean *infinitely* patient. It's like he's not human.
- **Elizabeth:** I'm part of the Ironheart Racing Team. We race to raise awareness for congenital heart disease and defects and to encourage healthy heart living. I race in honor of my niece who was born with a congenital heart defect.
- **Myrna:** I am a happily married forty-year-old professional who's been lucky enough to work at a great company for most of my career. I am young at heart, but very much an introvert and happy to have finally found my soul mate. I am childless by choice...and I discovered I was a triathlete when I suffered a knee injury from running that forced me to master swimming. Triathlon is my hope to keep on doing what I love most, being active, competitive, and staying fit...it's my inner extrovert.
- **Robyn:** I am more blessed that almost anyone I know. I am thankful every single day for that...and know that it's through the grace of God that I am where I am. I have also finished two half Ironman races.
- **Cheryl**: I'm forty-one-years old, mom of two boys, business owner, vegetarian and now I guess triathlete.
- **Joan**: My running goal is to complete a half marathon. My personal record is 34:26 for the 5k, and I refer to myself as "Le Tortue Enflamme'" because I'm a very slow runner. (But I *always* finish...even if I end up at the medical tent, which happened after the Peachtree Road Race in Atlanta.)
- **Traci**: I lost eighty pounds over eight years ago, have three young children and now am a group exercise instructor at a local health club. Almost three years ago, a member invited me to do a sprint triathlon with her...I trained, competed and got hooked. Since then I have completed several sprint triathlons, a handful of Olympic distance tris, and two 70.3 races. Don't ever tell me what I can't do...I'll just show you that I can!
- **Cortney:** Growing up, my dad's nickname for me was Cort the Sport, but it never quite fit. I became an out-of-shape working mom and decided to make a lifestyle change. I started running, then learned to bike and swim, and so began my triathlon journey. Four

years later, I am a sponsored athlete, part of a racing team, and will represent Team USA at ITU Age Group World Championships in New Zealand. I strive to encourage other women to pursue activities that bring them the energy, joy, and satisfaction I have discovered through personal challenge. Finally, at age forty-five, I really feel like Cort the Sport! (www.cortthesport.com).

- **Katherine:** My motivation to train and complete a tri was due to a challenge from my boss at the time. After he beat me, I trained for an entire year to come back and defeat him. My boss is long forgotten— now I do triathlons for *me*. To prove that I'm stronger than I think I am and that I can do anything I set my mind to!

- **Doug:** I tri because no matter how my day went, a mile is always the same and it will never lie to me. It will punish ego and reward effort. And because I'm exactly as vain as I say I am. (www.dirtbagfitness. blogspot.com)

- **Amy:** It took me ten years of infertility treatments to finally get pregnant with the most amazing boy/girl twins. My husband and I went through four years of active treatments and stopped after our first unsuccessful round. I am ready to get back into shape to really keep up with them.

- **Stephanie:** I'm a thirty-nine-year-old single mom of three. I work in theater which means 60-90 hour weeks at work during the season. I'm almost done with my master's degree and needed a new challenge; I will be competing in my first tri and marathon this year.

- **Matt:** I'm a Pastor with a passion for the Lord; the loves of my life, Jennifer, and my dog; and living a healthy life. I believe that life is a gift, and I want to use every minute of it to the best of my ability. Triathlon is a goal, a gift, and a swift kick in the pants!

- **Julie:** I never ran a day in my life before I was forty-years old. After watching Kona for years, and crying my eyes out watching the seventy and eighty-year olds cross the finish line, I tried a local sprint tri. I beat one seventy-year- old woman and not by much, mind you! Now I'm almost forty-three, completed four triathlons and a half marathon last year. I'm doing my first half Ironman and full marathon next summer. My training and my training buddies are my sanity with three boys under eight years old in my house! I also work as a nurse (RN), but finding time to swim, bike and run is a huge priority.

- **Mary:** Being able to participate in triathlon was a wish of mine for over ten years. After beating cancer at the age of forty, I made it my mission. Finishing is great, but the friends I have made and the health I achieved is for a lifetime!
- **Diane:** I challenged myself to do my first triathlon at the age of fifty-eight. I was overweight and had never in my life had any type of exercise in my life. It took me a little over four hours to finish my first tri—but I finished. I have now completed three more, each time bettering my previous time. And I have two more races this spring just in time to celebrate my sixty-ninth birthday. Triathlon has changed my life—I only wish I had found it sooner. But then maybe I wasn't ready for it way back then. I am proof positive that you can be older, completely out of shape and still train and finish what you set your mind to do. I may be slow, still a bit overweight—but I am a triathlete!
- **Jennifer:** Mom of five...tri that! And yes, I am an Ironman. (Live, laugh, love and tri often!)
- **Colleen:** I'm a forty-five-year-old lawyer, single mom and triathlete...I put them in that order because law was one of the first things I ever felt really successful at. Then it became unfulfilling. So I became a mom. And while that has yet to become unfulfilling, there are days when I feel unwanted ("Mom drop me off around the corner!") or unsuccessful...so I started triathlon. My bike always wants to see me. My goggles wait for my attention. And while I'm not always successful at triathlon, it can be 70.3 miles of peace, quiet with no sibling rivalry.
- **Sara:** Triathlon gives me something to strive for as my kids grow up and leave home. I miss them a little less because of triathlon. And it gives me an out for my competitive nature.
- **Tara:** I'm thirty-eight-years old, a mom, a wife, an educator, and a triathlete. Triathlon is my place to knock down the barriers between what I think I can and can't do. I can *always* do more—whether it is one more lap, one more mile...triathlon shows me that power, and reminds me how truly good life is.
- **Teresa:** Four years ago, I needed motivation to get back in shape after having my two babies and I finished my first (sprint) triathlon next to last. Last summer, I finished that same triathlon third in my age group and completed an Olympic distance tri. I now work at a gym, am getting my Spinning instructor certification and eyeing some

half-distance triathlons. I hope to inspire others to get in shape and live a quality life too.

- **Carrie C.**: I'm a new stepmom to two tween girls. Training for triathlon helps me set a healthy, active example for them and gives me some much-needed time and space to breathe and process.

- **Darris**: 2012 will be my fortieth year and I'm competing in my second Ironman in Ironman Canada. I planned on doing my first Ironman a little later, but got a little excited with how my training was going and decided to give it a go a year early with Ironman Arizona. It was an amazing journey but hope to have learned a lot & give it one more shot before putting this baby to rest.

- **Sarah**: Who am I? In the past twenty-four hours, this has changed. Now I can say, I am a triathlete. I just completed my first triathlon—it was a sprint—I thought it was just a warm-up for an Olympic distance race in two months, but the feeling of accomplishment was overwhelming. I am a mom, a wife, a runner, a friend, and an endurance athlete.

- **Blake:** I fell into the world of triathlon when two friends approached me to do a sprint with them. At the time I had only run one 5k. I did not know how to ride a bike at all. And I couldn't swim more than one length of the pool! That's where my journey began...discovering just how far I could push myself. I am currently training for my first half Ironman, Ironman Florida 70.3. I will be forty-one-years young!!

- **Jennifer:** I'm a married mother of two girls. My oldest is a triathlete and total motivator. At eight-years old she has completed three triathlons—and asked that I try to complete a triathlon by the end of 2012. I've lost eighty pounds and signed up for my first tri!

- **Wendy:** I *tri* to be a better wife, a better sister, a better daughter. I am a better person because I *tri*. (www.never2old2tri.com)

- **Kerri:** Who am I? A mom, science geek and a friend. This triathlon business? Well, I can barely swim, really. I battle the negative thoughts in my mind every time I get ready to run. And yet, I have this crazy idea...Vineman 70.3 in July 2013. Once I start I never want to stop, and I guess that's why I keep moving forward!

- **Charlie:** I am a full time working mom who has struggled for years with my weight & always led myself to believe that is why I run (now bike and swim too). However, when my brother (who also is a runner) was diagnosed with Stage Three Melanoma, running took on a whole new meaning. Since he could no longer run after surgery, I was running for the two of us. Now when I feel like I can't go on I am inspired to run for those who can't! (www.yRun.org)

- **Sandi:** I'm a fifty-three-year-old mother of two, grandmother of one, and this year I've signed up for my first 70.3 distance race…I've finally garnered the confidence to think I can do this distance. It took six years of racing sprint and Olympic distance races to get here but my brain and my body are finally ready…You are never too old to hit your peak. Up until last year, I was just a middle of the pack racer. I would start training and then back off when it started to get tough… It's funny how your thoughts have such power over your physical body. I came back home and raced in a local sprint tri with a small field of participants and won it…Last year I kept saying to my training buddies, "This is my year." This year I'm saying it again but with a stronger voice: "This year is definitely going to be my year." [Note: According to the race results, Sandi met her goal!]

- **Monica:** I'm a mom of twin boys and an OR nurse. I told myself I wanted to do a triathlon before I turned forty. A few months before, I did my first sprint tri. I finished it and was hooked. One year later, I did the same tri and took first in the Athena division with a personal record that was twenty-nine minutes faster than the year before. Triathlons have turned me into a new woman, feeling better than ever and helping my family feel the same! My training partner lost her husband to colon cancer in the fall of 2011, and this season I'm doing my first Olympic distance tri, the Rev3 Half Full, while raising money for the Ulman Cancer Foundation in memory of her husband. My goal is to finish, and to give back to those young adults with cancer!

- **Stefanie:** I am a strong, bold, gifted writer and businesswoman. Triathlon helped me find the courage to start a real business after leaving my conventional lawyer job behind. Never have I needed my record of perseverance more than in business. It all started with a goal that at the time seemed impossible—the 70.3 distance at a race called Silverman. Crossing that finish line changed my life. Without Silverman (and the two years it took to get to the start line) I would not have a business. I'd also have never had the courage to apply for (and win) a lottery slot into the 2012 Ironman 70.3 World Championships. But I do. And I did! Whatever it takes to believe in yourself—do it.

- **Cherie:** I am wife, mother, daughter, and I go to work away from home so I have three full time jobs. Triathlons are social alone time. I get to do what I want race hard or just enjoy it with my amazing family cheering me along the whole time.

The Big Fat Thank Yous...

...FOR ALL OF YOU WHO MADE THIS DREAM A REALITY

My parents, Ray and Carla Nesbitt:

Papa. The one day I watched you set an entire tile floor with your hands (and on your knees), I realized the sacrifices and back-breaking work you endured to raise me and spoil me stinking rotten. You taught me to push through pain and doubts—not through your words—but by your example. You have helped me with *every* sport out there, always ready to help me be the best "me" possible. I have learned a lot from you, but most importantly, I have learned how to carry *all* the groceries from the car in one single trip. I love you.

Mom. We had a rough year when I was thirteen. And fourteen. And fift— okay, so until I moved out of the house for good. Unfortunately, I did not understand your grace, strength and beauty until I became a wife and birthed two children of my own. I have come to love and respect and admire you a hundred-fold over the years. Your enthusiasm is infectious, and your laughter contagious. I am thankful for your love of books, which you passed on to me. And you give the best hugs. Thank you for the mom and friend that you *are* to me...and the Mia you are to my children. I love you.

My grandparents, Carl and Alberta Schlogl. Thank you both for supporting me and loving me. You always showed up and cheered, no matter what I was doing—and I am so thankful for that. Thank you for loving "Poor Jason" too. You mean so much to us. I love you, Mombow & Papooh.

Gerry Halphen. Coach Monster. You are the anchoring force behind this book, and the annoying voice in my head when I want to quit running. *Do not stop, Grasshopper. Be strong of mind. Focus. It's a great day to suffer on a bike.* "Thank you" seems inadequate—because with just one cycling class you changed the trajectory of my entire life. You've made me believe in myself. You're a swell friend and coach, too, so thank you. But I'll be sending you a lifetime supply of peanut butter to say thanks like I really mean it.

Carrie Hanson. I am so proud to call you my friend. Thank you for helping me believe in myself enough to get this book off the ground. And thank you for your contribution. And your editing. And editing. And editing…

Mike "McBlessings" Lenhart. You are truly one of the great blessings in this world. When I think I can't go on, I hear your lessons in perspective, and I see the heroic athletes at the Getting2Tri Foundation. Thank you for your contribution to this book, your example and your friendship.

Ilana Katz. I thank you for your involvement with this book. You are an amazing nutritionist and friend. I had been completely hopeless with food—now I see the light. Although sometimes I *ignore* the light…at least I know it's there. Thank you from the bottom of my non-fat Greek yogurt.

Sylvia Marino and Cheryl Kellond. I cannot wait to watch Bia annihilate Garmin. Sylvia, I thank you for your great influence and section in this book. I love that you hate wetsuits too. And someday, I hope to see you at Alcatraz.

Elizabeth George. Mountain Goat. Thank you for the Mountain Goatly section of this book. It's a riot. I look forward to you, me and W all working together again. Someday. Soon. But I'm still not doing Red Top again. Ever.

Tanya Maslach. I thank you for your support, always. You are a shining star, a bright positive force in this world, and I am honored to be a part of the Tribe.

Thanks for the artistic and literary awesomeness: Becca Paro with Jumping Jax Designs, Meg Davidson Photography, Christie O'Sullivan, and Heather Tomlinson.

Jennifer Nesbitt. You are uber-talented. Love ya.

Dr. Hamid Sadri. Dr. Miracle Man Hands. Thank you for "fixing" me more times than I can count. You rock.

Robyn Weller, Mickey Forrest and Susan Wintersteen My trip to San Diego renewed my soul and my hope for the SBM future. But Robyn, you're just so *dangerous*…

Karen Whitlock. Yoda. You are so tri-wise. Thank you for never dropping me.

Ansley Sebring. Sweet Red. My dear new friend (not from the blog, of course), but I feel like I have known you forever. #isthatforsale #eggplant

Elizabeth Gaylor. You have been such a great encouragement since the "beginning."

Linda Hanson. Thank you for your amazing example.

Beth Morris. *Me Too Iguana* means you must start triathlon. Thank you for being my friend. Go Team Us.

Carol ("W") Bailey. Oh, the Wet and Boggy *giant* trail races in our future. Thank you for making me look like a competent lawyer—even when I couldn't find Browns Forms.

Roger Smith and Mary Sprague. Thank you for such a wonderful writing foundation. You both changed my life.

Mary Hartman. Thank you for letting me see that this book was not only a possibility, but too close to ignore.

Chrissie Wellington. I thank you for your inspiration and support of this book. I stand in awe of you.

Bree Wee. Thank you for writing the Foreward and proving that you can be a mom, a triathlete…and awesome.

Jayne Williams. *Slow Fat Triathlete* is amazing.

The Concourse Athletic Club and friends—where it all began. Thank you all for keeping me moving.

All3Sports. Thank you for our triathlon partnership. I love Andy Potts (the bike).

The Swim Bike Mom blog friends. There are so many of you now, but some of you are actually real, live *friends* now. How bizarre. It's like online dating for triathlon. Your encouragement and support—amazing. Love to you all.

My wonderful Nesbitt and Schlogl families. My family through marriage to the dear Expert—thank you for your support. Love you.

And finally…

James and Stella. The Swim Bike Kids. I love you with all of my heart. You inspire me to keep moving forward, always. I hope someday you will love triathlon as much as I do. And if not, I hope you find something you *do* love. Go for what makes you happy. Be smart, but be full of heart. And eat beans, because they are good for your heart, too.

Dr. James A. Atwood, III. The Expert. I'm sure it wasn't easy reading about our lives online, but "you take a good ribbing, Swim Bike Dad." Thank you for being a part of this dream. And though sometimes I did not appear to appreciate your tough love—("No, you can't quit your job to write a book! The President wrote his book at night, in his spare time. Do that! Don't be a sissy!")—I must say that I can now thank you for it. Most of all, thank you for being a great friend and life partner—and an amazing father. I feel lucky to ride bikes with the one and only Quadzilla (except when you speed ahead and sacrifice me to vicious dogs chasing us). I love you. (Do you love me like *The Notebook?*)

God. My Lord and Savior. I am far from perfect and I have a dirty mouth sometimes, but fathers often lovingly put up with renegade children. By your Grace I am saved and forgiven. I could not handle life (or triathlon) without that hope.

Thank you *all* for reading. See you at the finish line!

Just Keep Moving Forward,
Meredith

Appendix 1: How to Speak Triathlon

25 meter pool – 64 lengths equal one mile.

25 yard pool – 70 lengths equal one mile.

400 meter track – A track that is regulation will be 400 meters for one lap; four times around will equal 1 mile.

Aerobic – "Used to refer to running or other exercise at an intensity that's sufficiently easy for your respiratory and cardiovascular systems to deliver all or most of the oxygen required by your muscles, and slow enough that lactic acid doesn't appreciably build up in your muscles. Generally, you can sustain a slow aerobic pace for long periods of time, provided you have the endurance to go long distances."[xxx]

Aero Position – This is the position that triathletes are often seen riding on their bikes. The use of aero bars (installed on a road bike, or included on a triathlon bike) allows the rider to rest her forearms on pads on the handlebars, to assume a more aerodynamic position, which helps with drag, but also conserving energy.

Age Group / Age Grouper – Divisions in triathlon races. Usually, the divisions are divided into gender and age. For example, Female 35-40. There are other optional divisions such as "**Athena**" and "**Clydesdales.**"

Anaerobic – "Used to refer to running or other exercise at an intensity that makes it impossible for your respiratory and cardiovascular systems to deliver all or most of the oxygen required by your muscles, and fast enough that lactic acid begins to build up in your muscles, thus producing a tired, heavy feeling. The pace associated with anaerobic running cannot be sustained very long."[xxxi]

Anaerobic threshold (AT) – Also known as "lactate threshold"; the transition phase between aerobic and anaerobic running. Good training will increase AT by teaching the muscles to use oxygen more efficiently, so that less lactic acid is produced. Also known as "lactate threshold."[xxxii]

AquaBike – A race that leaves out the run. You swim and bike only.

Athena Division – An *optional* female division to enter in *some* races. Instead of entering into the Age Group, a female can choose "Athena," which is women who are 150 pounds or higher. This is changing in 2013 to 165 pounds, according to the USAT.

Body Marking – In a race, you will be required to wear your race number on your body, often on the upper arm, lower leg and sometimes the thigh. Before a race, there will be designated "Body Markers," volunteers who write your race number on your body with either a permanent marker, or applying a temporary tattoo peel-off number.

Bonk – Also, known as "hitting the wall." The dreaded point (and awful feeling similar to what your body would feel like if you ran into a wall) during a race when your muscle glycogen stores become depleted and a feeling of fatigue engulfs you.[xxxiii]

BOSU® Ball – This is a half ball and half platform training tool. Originally the name "BOSU" was an acronym for "Both Sides Up." It meant that the BOSU® Balance Trainer could be used on either side, the dome or the platform. This little jewel will rock your strength and core training. [www.Bosu.com]

Bottle Cage – The rack installed on your bike to hold your water bottle.

Cadence – Also, known as **RPM,** or revolutions per minute, cadence means the rhythm of your swim stroke, bike pedal stroke, or run turnover of the feet (as they hit the ground), which is usually measured in "revolutions" per minute.[xxxiv] According to *Train Like a Mother*, the book, experts recommend about 180 steps per minute. I hope. Someday.[xxxv]

Check-in – Before a larger sized race, the race may require you to check-in yourself and/or your bike. Read the rules of each race carefully so you will know.

Cleat – The part on the bottom of the cycling shoe where your shoe attaches to your **clipless pedals.**

Clipless Pedals – Pedals installed on your bike that allow you to "clip in" your shoes. These help your feet remain attached to the bike so you can use a full revolution in your pedaling.

Clydesdale – The boy version of the **Athenas -** male racers weighing over 200 pounds.

CO_2 Cartridge – Sold at bike stores, these are essentials for your bike bag for inflating a tube with a touch of a button.

Derailleur – A system on a **mountain bike**, **road bike** or **triathlon bike** made of up sprockets and a chain with a method to move the chain from one to the other – this causes the shifting of **gears.**

DNF – Acronym for "Did Not Finish" (the race).

DNS – Acronym for "Did Not Start" (the race).

Drafting – Most commonly a term used in cycling, drafting entails riding close behind the rider ahead of you in order to avoid wind drag and assist in decreasing your effort. Drafting, for the most part, is legal in the sport of cycling, but illegal in triathlon.

Duathlon – A race consisting of run and bike and run again.

Fartlek – Another name for interval training which creates a mixture of slow running, running at a moderate pace, and short, fast bursts. Fartlek training is a "creative way" to increase speed and endurance.[xxxvi]

Foam Roller – A training tool made out of cylindrical foam that helps release "trigger points" in the muscles.

Foot Strike – How your foot makes contact with the ground when walking or running; two types of strikes include midfoot and heel. With the midfoot strike, your foot makes contact in the middle portion of the foot, whereas a heel strike makes contact with the heel first. The jury is still out on the benefits of each, though the midfoot strike appears to be winning in the race to proper running form.

Fred – Someone who has all the newest and fanciest triathlon gear, but has no idea how to use it. "Look at the Fred, falling off his $4,000 bike." Get good gear, but be wary of looking like Fred.

Gears – You may not know what these are now, but you will.

Gels – A form of sports nutrition typically used by triathletes in races due to the ease of digestibility, quick energy and convenience. Makers of gels include GU, Clif® and Hammer Nutrition®.

Gloves – Gloves are used in cycling to protect the hands in the event of crash. They also provide padding and comfort on the bike.

Goggles – Protective eyewear for the swim, not to be confused with "Googles."

Half-Ironman® – A triathlon event consisting of a 1.2 mile swim, a 56 mile bike and a 13.1mile half-marathon run (total of 70.3 miles). Note: that "Ironman®"[xxxvii] is a registered trademark of the World Triathlon Corporation and while some races may consist of the "half Ironman®" distance of 70.3 miles, there is only one official Ironman® brand, and as such only races sanctioned and hosted by Ironman® are "half Ironmans®."

Half-marathon – A race consisting of a 13.1 run.

Hill Repeats – Just as it sounds. Running or riding up hills and down hills, and then turning around and doing it again.

Holding the Line – Imagine when you are pedaling on your bike that you are following a solid line. Holding your line is necessary for group rides and general bike safety.

Indoor Trainer – A contraption that allows you to ride your bike indoors, essentially transforming it into a stationary bike.

Intervals – Training using short, fast "repeats" or "repetitions"…interval training builds speed and endurance. [xxxviii] Another term for "pure misery."

Ironman® – A triathlon event consisting of a 2.4 mile swim, a 112 mile bike, and a 26.2 mile marathon run (total of 140.6 miles). [xxxix] See, **Half Ironman**® for disclaimers.

IT Band – The IT band stands for the iliotibial band, which is a tissue ("band" of tissue) that runs along the outside of the thigh, over the hip, down the knee and below the knee. The IT band keeps the knee stable during walking and running. The only thing to *help* the IT band when it starts to act up is to exert pain *on* the IT band: to roll on a foam roller, to get a deep tissue massage, to embark on ART (Active Release Therapy), to roll on a lacrosse, tennis, baseball, Trigger Point Ball, or do whatever you can to punish and work that IT band loose.

Kickboard – A flat rectangular piece of Styrofoam used to isolate leg muscles in kick sets. [xl]

Lactate Threshold – See, **Anaerobic Threshold**.

Lane – Place in the pool where a swimmer swims; if you pick a lane, by all means, stay in it. Learn how to share.

Lap - Distance from one end of the pool to the other end…and back.

Length – Distance from one end of the pool to the other.

Long Course Triathlon – See, **Half-Ironman**®.

Lube – Can be used to keep your chain on your bike greased; other types of lube include Aquaphor®, BodyGlide®, and Hoo Ha Ride Glide™, and those lubes can be used under your arms, under the bra strap(s), between the knees and anywhere else you might experience chafing. On the bike, make sure you lube your chain…and the **Queen**.

Marathon – A running race consisting of 26.2 miles.

Mash – To push a higher gear while riding on a bike. [xli]

MOP – An acronym used to designate someone who tends to swim, bike, run and finish in the "middle of the pack" during a race.

Mountain Bike – A bike designed to be used "off-road" on surfaces like trails and in the woods. Typically, these bikes are heavier than **road bikes**

and made to withstand the rough terrain of an off-road trail. While a sprint triathlon may be finished using a mountain bike, a road bike or triathlon bike should be considered on Santa's list ASAP.

Off Road Triathlon – Usually a swim, mountain bike and trail run race, as opposed to a swim, road bike and road run race.

Olympic Distance – May also be known as an "Intermediate Distance" or a "Short Course Triathlon" and usually a race of a 0.9 mile swim, 26 mile bike, and 10k (6.2 mile run).

"On Your Left" – The safety phrase to alert someone *on your right* that you are coming up *on the left* and passing them...*on the left*.

Overpronation – Is an excessive inward rolling of the feet.[xlii]

Paddles – These paddles make you look like a frog in the water and are worn on your hands to help build your stroke strength.

Plank – An abdominal move for strengthening the core, looks like the start of a push-up position, only resting on forearms and elbows, and holding the position for periods of time; builds endurance in the abdominals and back, as well as the core stabilizer muscles.[xliii]

PR – Acronym for "personal record."

Pull Float – A floatation device used between the knees while swimming, which aids in keeping the bottom half of your body up in the water and allowing you to concentrate on your stroke.

Puncture – A flat tube.

Queen – Swim Bike Mom lingo for your bottom-half lady parts.

Race Number Belt – A belt where you can attach your race number. This is helpful for putting on your number after the swim. You clip the belt around your waist with your number to the back (on the bike), and then when you run, you rotate your number to the front. You do *not* swim in your race number.

Refueling – The term used for your first food, meal or sustenance after a workout. This is a valuable time and important time for good nutrition. See, Nutrition, Part I, Chapter 11.

Rim – On a bike, the rim is the outside of the bike wheel that holds the tire in place.

Road Bike – A bike made for travelling on paved roads; they are lighter than cruising or mountain bikes and have many gears with which to confuse you. Typically the road bike will have the skinny, high-pressurized tires for a smoother ride.

Road Rash — Road Rash is slang term for the scrapes and abrasions resulting from your sweet lady skin hitting the hard, evil pavement.

RPM — See, **Cadence.**

Saddle Sores — Ride too far, too early and without lube and your rear end will learn about these.

Spinning and Spinning® — To pedal at a relatively easy, but high cadence; also, short for indoor cycling classes, but SPIN®, Spinner®, Spinning® and the Spinning® logo are all registered trademarks owned by Mad Dogg Athletics, Inc.

Split — Typically used to describe the time it takes you to do a sport in the race. For example, the "bike split" would be your time from the start of the bike portion of the race, to the time you enter **T2.**

Sprint Triathlon — A short distance triathlon usually consisting of approximately a ¼ mile swim, 15 mile bike ride, and 5k (3.1 mile) run.

Strike — see, **Foot Strike.**

Swim Sets — The way a swim workout is written.

Swim Wave — Most races divide the start of the event into "waves." That means that groups start at different times, thus keeping the crowding on the swim down, but also on the entire course. In larger longer-distances races, such as Ironman® races, sometimes there is only one swim wave.

T1 — see, **Transition.**

T2 — see, **Transition.**

T3 — Fooled you. There is no such thing. Well, not really. I consider T3 the time after the race when I can finally have a beer and take a shower.

Taper — The period of time before a race where you slow down the frequency and intensity of the workouts in order to give your body time to recover and rest before the event. The taper will make you crazy.

Timing Chip — Usually handed out in race packets, these may be worn on your shoes (running race) or on an ankle strap (triathlon). When you pass over certain points during a race, the timing chip registers your time for the official race results.

Tire Lever — Small, plastic tool for your bike bag. The tire lever helps you remove the flat tire tube from the rim of the wheel.

Toe Clips — The in-between regular bike pedals and clipless pedals. You can ride your bike with sneakers and clip your toes into these plastic clips installed on your pedals to give you the benefit of a full revolution on the bike without the beginner scariness of the **Clipless Pedals.**

Trainer – See, **Indoor Trainer.**

Transition – Two time periods within a triathlon. **T1** is the period of time between the swim and bike; **T2** is the period of time between the bike and the run. Frequently, in triathlon you will feel "lost" in transition, wandering about, clueless. Transition is also the physical place in the race where you will transition from one sport to another, usually marked by bike racks and Porta-Potties. Race directors will label the area where the bikes are racked as "transition."

Triathlete – One who competes in a triathlon, also known as YOU.

Triathlon Bike – A type of road bike that is specifically and ergonomically designed to keep the rider in a more streamlined and aerodynamic position. A tri bike is not usually the first stop in a bike purchase. Often triathletes will start with a road bike and purchase a tri bike as a second bike.

Triathlon Widow – A term coined by the *Wall Street Journal*, meaning the spouse of the non-triathlete, who often finds himself/herself abandoned in the early morning by the spouse who is swimming, biking or running.

Tri Kit – A matching top and bottom often worn during a race. The material is meant to wear from start to finish, during the swim, bike and run, and if necessary, under the wetsuit. The tri bottoms will have a small chamois pad, which should be tried ahead of time, especially if you are accustomed to wearing a thick chamois pad for cycling.

Tube – On a bike, the tube is the inflatable part *inside* of the tire. You remove the tube, not the tire, when you have a flat.

Wave – See, **Swim Wave.**

USAT – USA Triathlon (USAT) is "the sanctioning authority for more than 3,500 diverse events, ranging from grassroots to high-profile races nationwide. The organization works to create interest and participation in a variety of programs, including camps, clinics, races and educational opportunities. USA Triathlon's 140,000-strong membership is comprised of athletes of all ages, coaches, officials, parents and fans striving to strengthen multisport." For most larger/national races, you will need either a temporary USAT membership pass for the day ($10-20), or a yearly membership. (www.usatriathlon.org)

Wetsuit – Neoprene suit worn during open-water swim training and races. The neoprene suit is to protect against cold water, but also to provide buoyancy. You either love or hate your wetsuit.

Wicking Material – Usually a material made of a poly blend fabric that does not absorb sweat (like cotton), but rather shifts it away from the skin.

Appendix 2: Resources

Reader tested and Swim Bike Mom approved. Check out this list of great resources.

Swim

Go Swim Freestyle (DVD) Karlyn Pipes-Neilsen.
Lane Lines to Shore Lines (DVD) by Gary Emich
(http://www.lanelinestoshorelines.com/)
Swim Smooth (http://www.swimsmooth.com/)

Bike

The Noncyclist's Guide to the Century and Other Road Races, Dawn Dais
The Time-Crunched Cyclist, Chris Carmichael

Run

The Non Runners Marathon Guide, Dawn Dais
Run Like a Mother, Dimity McDowell & Sarah Bowen Shea

Triathlon

Slow Fat Triathlete, Jayne Williams
Transformed by Triathlon, Jane Booth
Triathlons for Women, Sally Edwards
Your First Triathlon, Joe Friel
Holistic Strength Training for Triathlon, Andrew Johnston

Inspiration

A Life without Limits, Chrissie Wellington

i   http://www.urbandictionary.com/define.php?term=triathlon

ii   http://www.usatriathlon.org/about-multisport/demographics. aspx

iii   "Angels on the Moon" by Thriving Ivory

iv   *Slow Fat Triathlete: Live Your Athletic Dreams in the Body You Have Now*, Jayne Williams, Da Capo Press, (2004)

v   http://plusrunner.com/dont-run-naked/

vi   Miriam Webster Online

vii   www.Spinning.com

viii Solutions for Numb Toes While Cycling, Gale Bernhardt, Active. com, http://www.active.com/cycling/Articles/Solutions-for-Numb-Toes-While-Cycling.htm

ix   http://www.jeffgalloway.com/training/walk_breaks.html

x   http://video.nytimes.com/video/2011/11/02/ magazine/100000001149415/the-lost-secret-of-running.html

xi   Swim Bike Mom note: Dr. Hamid Sadri, Atlanta, First Choice Healthcare, www.1stchoiceonline.com.

xii   *Your First Triathlon*, Joe Friel, VeloPress, 2006.

xiii http://www.cnn.com/2012/02/21/health/chrissie-wellington-triathlete-champion/index.html?hpt=hp_c2

xiv http://www.cnn.com/2012/02/21/health/chrissie-wellington-triathlete-champion/index.html?hpt=hp_c2

xv   http://www.butterfliesandmoths.org/species/Junonia-coenia

xvi http://en.wikipedia.org/wiki/Scaphella_junonia

xvii http://en.wikipedia.org/wiki/Colonia_Junonia

xviii Louis Burke and Vicki Deakin. Clinical Sports Nutrition (Book, 2nd edition 2011).

xix Louis Burke and Vicki Deakin. Clinical Sports Nutrition (Book, 2nd edition 2011).

xx   Overcoming Athletic GI Distress, ILANA KATZ MS, RD, CSSD. www.onforlife.com and www.poweringmuscles.com.

xxi   http://www.merckmanuals.com/professional/endocrine_and_metabolic_disorders/electrolyte_disorders/hypernatremia.html?qt=&sc=&alt=

xxii   http://www.trifuel.com/training/health-nutrition/hyponatremia-salt-water-intake-mistakes

xxiii   http://www.trifuel.com/training/health-nutrition/hyponatremia-salt-water-intake-mistakes

xxiv   *The Time-Crunched Triathlete: Race-Winning Fitness in 8 Hours a Week,* Chris Carmichael and Jim Rutberg, Velo Press (2010).

xxv   http://www.inc.com/magazine/201111/stop-feeling-like-a-big-fat-loser.html

xxvi   Rule 7.2. Placement of Equipment; http://www.usatriathlon.org/about-multisport/multisport-zone/rules-education/articles/transition-area-conduct-placement-of-equipment.aspx

xxvii   The cover photo to this book was taken from this race. One of my all-time favorite race photos because I remember exactly where I was when it was taken, I remember the feeling, and pretty much I look the skinniest I have in my life.

xxviii   http://www.teamhoyt.com/about/index.html

xxix   October 2011, Redbook magazine; http://www.celebrity-gossip.net/jillian-michaels/jillian-michaels-covers-redbook-october-2011-540670

xxx   http://www.runnersworld.com/article/0,7120,s6-238-267--439-0,00.html

xxxi   http://www.runnersworld.com/article/0,7120,s6-238-267--439-0,00.html

xxxii   http://www.runnersworld.com/article/0,7120,s6-238-267--439-0,00.html

xxxiii   http://www.runnersworld.com/article/0,7120,s6-238-267--439-0,00.html

xxxiv   Your First Triathlon, Joe Friel, p. 179

xxxv   *Train like a Mother*, Dimity McDowell and Sarah Bowen Shea

xxxvi   http://www.runnersworld.com/article/0,7120,s6-238-267--439-0,00.html

xxxvii   http://www.ironman.com

xxxviii   http://www.runnersworld.com/article/0,7120,s6-238-267--439-0,00.html

xxxix	http://www.thefreedictionary.com/triathlon
xl	http://www.staps.uhp-nancy.fr/foad_natation/swimterms.htm
xli	Your First Triathlon, Joe Friel, p. 180
xlii	http://www.runnersworld.com/article/0,7120,s6-240-319-327-425-0,00.html
xliii	http://exercise.about.com/od/abs/ss/abexercises_10.htm

13776871R00248

Made in the USA
San Bernardino, CA
04 August 2014